The Continuity of Legal Systems in Theory and Practice

Benjamin Spagnolo

•HART•
PUBLISHING
OXFORD AND PORTLAND, OREGON
2018

Hart Publishing
An imprint of Bloomsbury Publishing Plc

Hart Publishing Ltd
Kemp House
Chawley Park
Cumnor Hill
Oxford OX2 9PH
UK

Bloomsbury Publishing Plc
50 Bedford Square
London
WC1B 3DP
UK

www.hartpub.co.uk
www.bloomsbury.com

Published in North America (US and Canada) by
Hart Publishing
c/o International Specialized Book Services
920 NE 58th Avenue, Suite 300
Portland, OR 97213-3786
USA

www.isbs.com

First published in hardback, 2015
Paperback edition, 2018

British Library Cataloguing-in-Publication Data
A catalogue record for this book is available from the British Library.

ISBN: PB: 978-1-50992-006-8
HB: 978-1-84946-883-1

Typeset by Compuscript Ltd, Shannon

Acknowledgements

This book is the product of research carried out in the course of doctoral studies at the University of Oxford under the supervision of Professor John Finnis FBA. For their generous financial support of my studies in Oxford, I record my sincere appreciation to the Menzies Foundation, the Sir Robert Menzies Memorial Trust and the Clarendon Fund.

Contents

Table of Abbreviations

ACT	Australian Capital Territory
ANZAC	Australian and New Zealand Army Corps
C	Command Papers (1870–1899)
CA	Court of Appeal of England and Wales
CAB	Cabinet Papers (United Kingdom National Archives)
Cd	Command Papers (1900–1918)
Ch	Court of Chancery
CKI	Cocos (Keeling) Islands
Cmd	Command Papers (1919–1956)
CP	Court of Common Pleas
Cth	Commonwealth of Australia
CUP	Cambridge University Press
EEZ	Exclusive Economic Zone
Eng	England (Parliament)
Exch Ch	Court of Exchequer Chamber
Exch	Court of Exchequer
HC	House of Commons
HCA	High Court of Australia
HL	House of Lords
HL(E)	House of Lords (England)
HMSO	Her Majesty's Stationery Office
Imp	Imperial (Parliament)
KB	Court of King's Bench
LBC	Law Book Company
LNTS	League of Nations Treaty Series
NG	Territory of New Guinea
NI	Norfolk Island
NSW Ct Civ Jrn	New South Wales Court of Civil Jurisdiction
NSW	New South Wales
NSWCA	Court of Appeal of New South Wales
NSWSC	Supreme Court of New South Wales
NT	Northern Territory
NTSC	Supreme Court of the Northern Territory
NZ	New Zealand
OUP	Oxford University Press
PC	Privy Council
Qld	Queensland

SA	South Australia
SCC	Supreme Court of Canada
SR&O	Statutory Rules and Orders (United Kingdom)
Tas	Tasmania
UK	United Kingdom (of Great Britain and Ireland 1801–1922 and of Great Britain and Northern Ireland from 1922)
UN	United Nations
UNGA	United Nations General Assembly
UNTS	United Nations Treaty Series
US	United States (of America)
VDL	Van Diemen's Land[1]
Vic	Victoria
VSC	Supreme Court of Victoria
WA	Western Australia

[1] The Colony of Van Diemen's Land changed its name to Tasmania with effect from 1 January 1856: Order in Council (21.07.1855) (Imp), available at <http://foundingdocs.gov.au/item-sdid-35.html>.

Table of Cases

Australia

England (pre-1707), Great Britain (1707–1801) and United Kingdom (post-1801)

Other

Table of Statutes

Note: The titles of Acts that do not have short titles are given as cited in the Chronological Table of the Statutes for the relevant jurisdiction.

Commonwealth—Constitution and Acts

Commonwealth—Legislative Instruments

New South Wales—Legislative Instruments

Norfolk Island—Acts and Legislative Instruments

Queensland—Acts and Legislative Instruments

South Australia—Acts and Legislative Instruments

Tasmania (Van Diemen's Land)—Acts

Victoria—Acts

Western Australia—Acts and Legislative Instruments

Imperial Legislative Instruments

England—Acts

United Kingdom—Acts and Legislative Instruments

Other

Table of Treaties and International Instruments

1

Introduction

THIS BOOK EXAMINES the theoretical accounts offered by Hans Kelsen and Joseph Raz to explain the temporal continuity and discontinuity of legal systems: accounts, that is, of how to determine whether a legal system existing in a given place at a given time is the same legal system as one existing in that place at a different time. In particular, the book tests the explanatory power of those accounts by applying them to one specific instance or historical context: the legal system (or systems) of British derivation in Australia between 1788 and 2001. The book's primary objective is to establish whether a sustained analysis vindicates Kelsen's and Raz's accounts, or highlights aspects that are flawed or in need of refinement.[1] Exposition and reconstruction of Kelsen's and Raz's accounts in light of their application to a complex body of legal materials reveals where development and enrichment is required, and permits evaluation of the accounts, individually and in comparison.

In this book, 'continuity' and 'discontinuity' are used in relation to propositions about whether a legal system existing at one time is, or is not, the same legal system as one that existed, or may exist, at another time. Propositions about continuity and discontinuity are thus propositions about the identity of a legal system—or the non-identity of legal systems—over time. Because of its sense of non-identity, discontinuity is also implicated in propositions that a *discrete* legal system can be identified—a legal system separate from, and not hierarchically related to, any other legal system, whether existing in the past, the present or the future. Continuity and discontinuity in the sense of the diachronic identity of legal systems is a jurisprudential phenomenon. Depending on the criterion operative in a given account, there may be significant continuities or discontinuities in other senses (for example, social, political or economic senses)—connections or disconnections over time, despite, or as a result of, change. Save to the extent implicated in the theoretical accounts of Kelsen and Raz, those other senses of continuity and discontinuity are not the subject of enquiry here. While continuity and discontinuity is analysed in this book as an independent jurisprudential phenomenon, it provides conceptual

[1] Language is here borrowed from MD Adler and KE Himma, 'Introduction' in MD Adler and KE Himma (eds), *The Rule of Recognition and the US Constitution* (Oxford, OUP, 2009) xiv.

context for other purposes involving propositions about the identity of legal systems over time. Such propositions may, for example, be put to use in solving practical legal problems connected with allegiance, political and legal independence or authority in the wake of a successful revolution.[2] A clearer, more plausible understanding of the leading accounts of continuity and discontinuity of legal systems helps make sense of such debates, be they in history or in prospect.

I. 'APPLYING' THEORETICAL ACCOUNTS

In this book, the notion of 'applying' an account to a particular context denotes a critical enquiry into, and evaluation of, the *explanatory power* of an account or model (these terms are used interchangeably). Application is thus one mode of testing or evaluating an account's *factual fit*: how adequately the account corresponds to, accords with and persuasively makes sense of, the facts—including complex social facts, attitudes and normative standards—for which it purports to account.[3] Fit is a matter of degree: an account may connect to the facts more or less consistently; it may represent or characterise the facts in all their complexity more or less accurately (and more or less efficiently); and it may accord more or less closely with intuitive judgements about the facts made by contemporary and subsequent participants, observers and commentators. An account might achieve so poor a fit as, in whole or in part, to be unserviceable, or it might articulate some new insight into, or understanding of, the facts.[4] In addition to this central function of testing fit, application—as a mode of testing theoretical accounts—can reveal gaps, inconsistencies and unexpressed assumptions in the models themselves, deficiencies that may not necessarily appear in the abstract.[5] Further, application to a concrete instance affords a common point of reference for evaluating the relative success of competing theoretical accounts.

Of course, despite encompassing the dimensions just mentioned—consistency, accuracy, efficiency, concordance with intuitive judgements

[2] Some theorists deny that an account of continuity and discontinuity is necessary or even relevant background to solving practical legal problems of this kind: see C Arnold, 'Institutional Aspects of Law' (1979) 42 *MLR* 667, 678–79.

[3] The language of 'fit' is borrowed from Dworkin: see, eg, RM Dworkin, *Justice in Robes* (Cambridge, Mass, Harvard University Press, 2006) 15.

[4] FP Hubbard, '"One Man's Theory…": A Metatheoretical Analysis of HLA Hart's Model of Law' (1976) 36 *Maryland Law Review* 39, 47–48.

[5] See, eg, Greenawalt's application of Hart's account of the rule of recognition to the constitutional law of the United States of America, which identifies 'at least ten possibilities that are omitted or underdeveloped': K Greenawalt, 'The Rule of Recognition and the Constitution' (1987) in MD Adler and KE Himma (eds), *The Rule of Recognition and the US Constitution* (Oxford, OUP, 2009) 1, 37–38.

and articulation of new insight—factual fit is not the sole criterion by which the explanatory power of a theoretical account may be evaluated. A comprehensive evaluation may implicate wider issues in legal philosophy and in social science more generally. However, there is consensus that a sufficient working sense of the explanatory power of an account of the continuity and discontinuity of legal systems may be obtained by reference to fit, even though corroboration according to some further measure(s) may be desirable. Theorists such as Finnis, whose philosophical approach holds that even the descriptive parts of jurisprudence require a richly normative perspective, as well as theorists such as Kelsen, who maintains that legal phenomena may rationally and usefully be described without reliance on normative considerations about desirable forms of social life, find considerable scope for analysis and evaluation by reference to factual fit. This book focuses on that area of common ground, and nothing in the analysis conducted suggests that a meaningful evaluation is impossible without reference to a set of deeper normative criteria.[6]

II. KELSEN AND RAZ

Theoretical accounts of the continuity and discontinuity of legal systems vary. Some theorists deny that it is possible to discern anything more than the continuing existence (or not) of particular laws or institutions that make up a legal system: continuity of the system or set of laws and institutions taken as a whole is thus treated as a matter of degree, and to point to any diachronic feature as indicating continuity beyond the continuing existence of any of those particular elements is, in view of the vagueness of law, held to be arbitrary.[7] Other theorists—arguably moving away from the notion of a legal system—treat propositions of continuity or identity over time in the context of a broader notion of tradition,[8] or as a normative matter, grounded in a continuity of legal practice and common life that '*has to be determined* practically, deliberatively within a judicial and social frame of thinking that is mindful of time in the manner modeled by melody'.[9]

Notwithstanding this range of views, the dominant type of account understands a legal system as a sequence of sets of laws that form a

[6] Accordingly, in this book, 'evaluate' and its cognates are used in the general sense of testing, and not in the sense in which 'evaluative' sometimes refers to normative judgements concerning, eg, conceptions of justice or desirable forms of social life.

[7] Arnold (n 2), 679–82.

[8] HP Glenn, 'Doin' the Transsystemic: Legal Systems and Legal Traditions' (2005) 50 *McGill Law Journal* 863.

[9] GJ Postema, 'Melody and Law's Mindfulness of Time' (2004) 17 *Ratio Juris* 203, 225. Others have also been attracted to musical metaphors of symphony, harmony and cacophony: see, eg, J Stone, *Legal System and Lawyers' Reasonings* (London, Stevens & Sons, 1964) 27–28.

system—both at each given point in time and across time—in view of some unifying criterion or feature (other than the fact that they comprise laws).[10] This book considers Kelsen's and Raz's accounts because they are, within that dominant type of account, amongst the most developed (and, especially in Kelsen's case, the most critiqued) theories of legal systems, and because their accounts are usually understood to differ in their approach to the unifying criterion. Kelsen's account focuses on an internal or formal criterion: authorised constitutional change. In contrast, Raz's account ultimately locates the unifying criterion in the continuity of the society in which the legal system exists. This extra-systemic criterion is generally perceived to entail a wider and more substantive range of considerations, drawing on politics and history in addition to legal authorisation, which is the focus of Kelsen's account.

III. AUSTRALIA 1788–2001

The diversity, subtlety and complexity of the circumstances presented by the historical instance of Australia between settlement and the centenary of Federation (a convenient end-point because it captures the principal phases of evolution in Australian law and society to date) make it a concrete case that is particularly apt for evaluating the explanatory success of accounts of continuity and discontinuity of legal systems. The advantage lies both in the relative lack of existing scholarship considering the evolution of Australian law in light of jurisprudential theories of legal systems,[11] and in the variety of challenges to accounts of continuity that the Australian context affords. While Australia has not endured the kinds of revolution, often violent, experienced elsewhere,[12] it presents interesting and difficult phenomena for which a model of continuity and

[10] J Raz, *The Concept of a Legal System: An Introduction to the Theory of Legal System*, 2nd edn (Oxford, Clarendon Press, 1980) 35, 187; J Raz, *Practical Reason and Norms*, 2nd edn (Oxford, OUP, 1990) 9; JM Finnis, 'Revolutions and Continuity of Law' (1971) in *Philosophy of Law—Collected Essays: Volume IV* (Oxford, OUP, 2011) 407, 426 (but cp 428); G MacCormack, '"Law" and "Legal System"' (1979) 42 *MLR* 285, 285.

[11] To date, the most substantive discussion that considers Kelsen and Raz in the Australian context appears in PC Oliver, *The Constitution of Independence: the Development of Constitutional Theory in Australia, Canada, and New Zealand* (Oxford, OUP, 2005) chs 12–13. Oliver, however, focuses on the Commonwealth of Australia, and his enquiry concerns not the abstract notion of the continuity of legal systems but the related, though distinct, question of 'constitutional independence': the 'ability in formal legal terms to determine with finality the rules, constitutional and other, in their respective legal systems': ibid, 1–2.

[12] It was the spate of revolutions and coups d'état such as those summarised in M Tayyab, 'Jurisprudence of Successful Treason: Coup d'Etat & Common Law' (1994) 27 *Cornell International Law Journal* 49 that stimulated academic interest in the topic, a sample of which is noted in MS Green, 'Legal Revolutions: Six Mistakes about Discontinuity in the Legal Order' (2005) 83 *North Carolina Law Review* 331, 334, fn 10.

discontinuity must account. These phenomena include: settlement and colonisation by an imperial power; a sustained period of government that may well have been unconstitutional in important respects; merger of formerly discrete political units; divided sovereignty—in terms of twentieth-century federalism, but also imperially imposed colonial-era limitations on political and legal change, control over natural resources and defence; the co-existence of multiple but coordinate courts of final appeal; derivative and original acquisition, and cession, of territory; attempted (or at least actively initiated) legal secession; maturation of an independent international legal personality; an emergent economic, cultural and social national identity; and—fundamentally—growth, over a relatively confined period of time, from a small autocratic British penal colony at Botany Bay to a federal, multicultural Western liberal democracy spanning a continent. The principal candidate legal systems for analysing continuity and discontinuity in this historical context are the Imperial, Australian (national), Commonwealth (central, federal), Colonial, State and Territory legal systems. The intricacies of potential subsystems or partial systems within these candidate legal systems fall to be characterised according to the tenets of each theoretical model; accounting for these complexities coherently and persuasively is an important factor in evaluating the models' success.

There is an additional advantage to the methodology adopted in this book: systematically applying theoretical accounts to a concrete instance not only tests the accounts, but simultaneously tests our understanding of the concrete case in issue—the light of theory reveals fresh questions and prompts us to re-evaluate historical and doctrinal orthodoxies. Examining the explanatory success of an account and understanding the instance to which it is applied cannot reasonably be dissociated: the relationship between these activities is captured by something approximating the Rawlsian notion of 'reflective equilibrium'.[13] In asking whether the depiction of Australian legal systems presented by a given theory achieves an adequate fit, it proves necessary to reconsider our intuitive judgements—say, in relation to the role of the Westminster Parliament at a given point in time. In some cases, the detail of the Australian materials to which a fine-grained application of the accounts requires the legal theorist to have regard has previously passed unnoticed, and accepted characterisations have passed unchallenged. This book contributes to better understanding both the evolution of Australian legal systems between 1788 and 2001 taken as a whole, and also particular discrete developments and controversies within that period.

[13] J Rawls, *A Theory of Justice*, revised edn (Oxford, OUP, 1999) 18–19, 42–45.

IV. A NOTE ON METHODOLOGY

While the distinctive methodology of this book involves significant recourse to constitutional law and theory and to legal history, as well as passing reference to questions of political philosophy, the book is not a historical, social, political or economic study of legal systems in Australia. Rather, it is concerned with the *interactions* between legal systems and the features that are the concern of those disciplines more or less cognate to general jurisprudence. Whether driving or being driven by legal changes, the features with which those other disciplines are concerned interact with legal systems in ways that are captured in legal materials of standard kinds. This book is therefore concerned with describing the *legal* materials connected with—those that instantiate or reflect—the non-legal features that are implicated in the application or evaluation of the accounts of continuity and discontinuity. For example, applying Raz's model entails analysing membership of a political community, while evaluating Kelsen's and Raz's accounts involves measuring how successfully they accord with realities of Australian economic and political independence. This book (and, in particular, chapter two) accordingly looks to the legal manifestations of these factors: community membership is instantiated in nationality and citizenship laws, and in oaths of allegiance and office; economic independence finds reflections in constitutional and legal principles governing control over natural resources, responsibility for public debts and control of borrowing power, while political independence is reflected in measures such as the Statute of Westminster 1931 (Imp).

V. OUTLINE

This book is structured so as to present the relevant legal materials first, in a neutral, predominantly factual framework, deliberately eschewing the categories of Kelsen's and Raz's models to avoid characterising the legal materials in the terms of a particular theoretical account. Chapter two reviews developments bearing on the continuity and discontinuity of legal systems in Australia between 1788 and 2001, dividing the material into strands corresponding to the nature and material scope, the spatial scope and the personal scope of Australian law over the period. The arguments of constitutional law and theory, and the original legal historical research presented in this chapter, expose the complex detail against which Kelsen's and Raz's accounts are later tested.

Chapter three critically reconstructs Kelsen's model of authorised constitutional change and identifies three exceptions or qualifications provided for in his analysis. Controversial features that appear in abstract criticisms of the account are explicated, and possible corrections to the distortions those features introduce are suggested and interrogated, again at the theoretical level. Particular difficulties connected with the core notion of 'historically first constitutions' are recognised and flagged for further consideration in the context of the model's application. That application is undertaken in chapter four, which tackles at an early stage problems connected with inferring multiple sufficient basic norms for a given set of legal materials. A possible modification of Kelsen's account is suggested to accommodate a degree of temporary unconstitutional action, to avoid the counter-intuitive judgements that the unmodified model would produce in the context of early colonial New South Wales. A central argument developed in chapter four highlights the interrelationship of Kelsen's theory of total and partial legal systems and his accounts of national legal systems and of historically first constitutions. On the basis of this argument, it is contended that the model implies a fourth exception to the criterion of constitutionally authorised change, one that has not been noticed in the academic commentary. Ultimately, chapters three and four argue that Kelsen's account of continuity and discontinuity is more subtle than has often been supposed, and that, while still flawed in important respects, it provides, when applied in its own terms, a reasonably satisfactory fit in explaining the historical context of Australia between 1788 and 2001.

Chapter five critically reconstructs Raz's account of legal systems and embarks on the delicate task of teasing out the implications of (consciously) relatively underdeveloped aspects of its treatment of continuity and discontinuity. The chapter synthesises elements of Raz's consideration of the subject at different points in time and amplifies that consideration in light of related work, elaborating the model in greater detail than has been undertaken in the existing literature. Application of the model in chapter six reveals significant gaps in Raz's theory in relation to subsystems or partial legal systems, but also demonstrates the potential sophistication that is possible within the account as reconstructed. A central function is shown to be performed by the test of 'exclusion', integrating Raz's analysis of the existence of legal systems in the face of competing institutionalised normative orders into his model of their existence over time. Taken together, chapters five and six argue that Raz's model, though underdeveloped in important respects compared to Kelsen's, offers a more flexible and comprehensive framework for establishing continuity or discontinuity, and achieves a sound fit with the facts in issue in Australia between 1788 and 2001.

Chapter seven concludes the book with a comparative evaluation of Kelsen's and Raz's accounts, highlighting the convergence of the two models' conclusions when tested against the instance of Australia, despite significant differences in their structure, composition and operation. Notwithstanding that convergence, and despite the fact that both models are revealed to exhibit important flaws and limitations, it is argued that Raz's account offers a better fit in terms of accuracy and concordance with intuitive judgements about the diachronic identity of legal systems in Australia. Chapter seven also offers a brief reflection on the insights into doctrine and history revealed by the book's application of jurisprudential theory—in particular, in terms of reconceptualising the role of certain Imperial laws and institutions during the late nineteenth and early twentieth centuries, and clarifying the relationship between Colonial, State, Commonwealth and Imperial legal systems both before and after Federation.

2

Australia 1788–2001

THE DISTINCTIVE METHODOLOGY of this book is to test Kelsen's and Raz's accounts of continuity by applying them to the concrete instance of Australia. Accordingly, this chapter sets out the changing features of Australian law between 1788 and 2001, against which the accounts will be tested in chapters three to six. Needless to say, this chapter does not detail every aspect of, or every change in, Australian law during this period. Because of the similarities in their foundation and evolution, it will in many instances be sufficient to deal only with representative examples of the Colonies, States and Territories. It will standardly be convenient to take New South Wales as a representative example: both for reasons of consistency and because, as the 'constitutional pioneer of the [British] crown colonies of European population',[1] the first European settlement in Australia and the template for those that followed, it existed throughout the period. When the Commonwealth comes into existence, it is obviously the other principal example to be considered. Nonetheless, reference is also made to the Federal Council of Australasia (a precursor to Federation), and to other States and Territories, where they present relevant phenomena in a unique or different fashion—for example, Western Australia in relation to secession, or Norfolk Island in relation to citizenship.

Kelsen's and Raz's accounts invoke different features of legal systems in explaining continuity. Both accounts draw on—and Kelsen's account largely focuses on—intra-systemic or autonomous considerations of constitutional and legal change. Accordingly, section I of this chapter surveys features connected with the nature and material scope of Australian law. It presents material relevant to the enquiry, 'What were the principal constitutional and legal changes in Australia between 1788 and 2001, and how were they effected?' Kelsen's model of continuity by international law also makes important reference to considerations of territory and

[1] M Wight, *The Development of the Legislative Council 1606–1945* (London, Faber & Faber, 1946) 74. NSW was the constitutional pioneer of the *second* British empire; the term 'crown colony' here identifies a colony in which direct control of public officers was retained by the Imperial Government, in contrast to the charter colonies and proprietary colonies of the first British Empire (when first established) in North America: see, eg, W Blackstone, *Commentaries on the Laws of England*, 16th edn (London, Butterworths, 1825) [109].

geographical administrative control. Section II therefore outlines the spatial scope of legal systems in Australia over time. It provides a basis for addressing the enquiry, 'What spaces were subject to or connected with the application of law in Australia between 1788 and 2001, and how did they change?' Finally, Raz's account invokes features that are not 'purely' legal: features connected with identity and community in constitutional and political theory or legal and social history. The approach of section III is to survey the personal scope of legal systems in Australia, looking to legal reflections of society and community over time through notions such as allegiance, nationality and electoral franchise. It establishes a corpus of material directed to the enquiry, 'What social communities of people were subject to or connected with law in Australia between 1788 and 2001, and how did they change?' Certain features of the material presented in this chapter are obvious or standardly noticed, but others are more obscure and some are highlighted for the first time. Though large questions of continuity and discontinuity are in issue, it is submitted that the insight very often lies in the detail.

The different strands of material presented in this chapter—the nature and material scope, the spatial scope and the personal scope of the law applicable in Australia over the period—exhibit relevant changes at different points in time, and so defy a single over-arching periodisation.[2] The material is nonetheless presented in an essentially chronological fashion within each section, as befits the subsequent analysis of the continuity or discontinuity over time. The application chapters themselves, chapters four and six, recombine so much of the material presented in the three strands of this chapter as is relevant to the consideration of their respective accounts, according to a periodisation that is tailored to the application of those accounts.

In organising the material around laws, law-areas and law-subjects, this chapter is structured in an essentially pre-theoretical way, despite the particular relevance, as just noted, of section II to Kelsen's model and of section III to Raz's account. No effort is made in this chapter to associate the relevance of particular features with either or both of the accounts: the purpose of this chapter is to describe changes in Australian law otherwise than through the prism of any particular theory, and so to provide a corpus of material prima facie connected with continuity, against which the accounts can, in due course, be tested. While the aim of this chapter is thus to survey the salient facts without reference to the theories subsequently to be applied to them, the selection of material necessarily anticipates, or at least has broadly in contemplation, the material to be invoked by

[2] A seven-stage periodisation is adopted in relation to the States in G Carney, *The Constitutional Systems of the Australian States and Territories* (Cambridge, CUP, 2006) 36–37. However, this periodisation is germane only to constitutional developments; the chapter canvasses a wider range of material.

the theoretical accounts. This approach is designed to approximate the Rawlsian device of 'reflective equilibrium';[3] refinement of the relevant materials will be undertaken in the course of applying the accounts in chapters four and six.

I. NATURE AND MATERIAL SCOPE

Inherent in both Kelsen's and Raz's accounts is the insight that the set of laws comprised in a legal system differs at different points in time. Changes in some laws, and the method of those changes, feature in accounts of continuity, either directly, as indicia of continuity or discontinuity, or indirectly, reflecting shifts in the governing political framework. Of most direct relevance are constitutional laws, consideration of which comprises the greater part of this section. The survey of constitutional laws canvasses, in particular, the structures and powers of Australian legislative, executive and judicial institutions, and their relationship to Imperial institutions, including the shifting allocations of responsibility between Imperial and local institutions and officials over time. The balance of the section is devoted to legal materials connected with particular instantiations or reflections of constitutional and legal control and identity, including the form of legislation, symbols of governmental authority and control of armed force.

A. Constitutional History: New South Wales

i. Gubernatorial Autocracy 1788–1823

British law distinguished between settled and conquered or ceded colonies.[4] In settled colonies, 'desart and uncultivated'[5] and settled by British subjects, English law prevailed, subject to important exceptions, and imported with it English constitutional doctrines such as the limitation of the royal prerogative and the supremacy of Parliament. In conquered and ceded colonies, existing law continued until changed by the King, in the exercise of his prerogative, or by Parliament.[6] The classification of New South Wales as a settled colony[7] thus had important consequences for the laws and institutions that governed it.

[3] J Rawls, *A Theory of Justice*, revised edn (Oxford, OUP, 1999) 18–19, 42–45.

[4] The classification was established before 1788: *Anonymous* (1722) 2 P Wms 75 (Ch), 24 ER 646; *Campbell v Hall* (1774) Lofft 655 (KB), 98 ER 848.

[5] Blackstone (n 1), vol 1, [108].

[6] ibid, [108]–[109].

[7] By the Imperial Law Officers (S Shepherd and R Gifford, 'Opinion re illegality of taxes imposed by governors in NSW' (1819) in F Watson (ed), *Historical Records of Australia*, vol 1, series IV (Sydney, Library Committee of the Commonwealth Parliament, 1922) 330;

New South Wales was initially conceived as a penal settlement, policed by a marine corps, entirely under the control of an officer of the Crown.[8] By Commission dated 2 April 1787, the King appointed a naval officer, Arthur Phillip, 'Captain-General and Governor-in-Chief in and over our territory called New South Wales', and commanded him to 'do and execute all things in due manner that shall belong to [his] said command' according to instructions and authorities given or to be given.[9] All inhabitants of the territory were commanded 'to be obedient aiding and assisting … Phillip in the execution of [the] commission and of the powers and authorities [t]herein contained'.[10]

With his Commission, Phillip received detailed Instructions.[11] Instructions, approved in draft by the Privy Council, and issued under the Royal Sign Manual and Signet,[12] were private commands addressing matters of administrative detail (albeit with a continuing operation and legislative in effect), as opposed to matters of principle, which were addressed in the public Commission.[13] Phillip's Instructions, for example, ordered him to secure the settlement, begin cultivating the land, enforce observance of religion and conciliate the affections of the indigenous population.[14]

Phillip's Commission and Instructions granted him ample executive power but were silent as to general legislative authority. Specific legislative authority was encompassed in, for example, the power to make regulations relating to convicts, but general legislative power was absent.[15]

J Stephen, 'Opinion re validity of statute 20 George II c xix' (1822) in Watson (ed), ibid, 412, 414), the NSW courts (*Macdonald v Levy* (1833) 1 Legge 39 (NSWSC), 51–54 (Forbes CJ), 60–61 (Dowling J)) and eventually the Privy Council (*Cooper v Stuart* (1889) LR 14 App Cas 286 (PC), 291).

[8] See the extracts from Lord Sydney's speech: HV Evatt, 'The Legal Foundations of New South Wales' (1938) 11 *Australian Law Journal* 409, 409. NSW was nominated as a place for the transportation of convicts by Orders in Council dated 06.12.1786 made under the Transportation, etc Act 1784 (Imp), s 1: see ibid, 411; WJV Windeyer, *Lectures on Legal History* (Sydney, LBC, 1938) 252–53.

[9] Commission (02.04.1787) in FM Bladen (ed), *Historical Records of New South Wales*, vol I, pt 2 (Sydney, Government Printer, 1892), 62. Phillip's immediate successors—Governors Hunter, King, Bligh, Macquarie and Brisbane—all received commissions in similar terms: F Watson, 'Introduction' in F Watson (ed), *Historical Records of Australia*, vol 1, series IV (Sydney, Library Committee of the Commonwealth Parliament, 1922) viii. An earlier commission issued to Phillip simply commanded him to perform the duties of Governor and to follow instructions from the King, his military superiors, the Privy Council or the Secretary of State: Commission (12.10.1786) in Bladen (ed), above, 24–25.

[10] Commission (02.04.1787) (n 9), 67.

[11] Instructions (25.04.1787) in Bladen (ed) (n 9). Again, the Instructions issued to Phillip's five immediate successors were in similar terms, save for the omission of clauses relating to the establishment of the settlement: Watson, 'Introduction' (n 9), x.

[12] K Roberts-Wray, *Commonwealth and Colonial Law* (London, Stevens & Sons, 1966) 149.

[13] DB Swinfen, 'The Legal Status of Royal Instructions to Colonial Governors' [1968] *Juridical Review* 21, 22–23. For a description of typical Instructions, see BH McPherson, *The Reception of English Law Abroad* (Brisbane, Supreme Court of Queensland Library, 2007) 133–34.

[14] Instructions (n 11).

[15] ibid, 87.

Without statutory authority, the Crown's prerogative power of legislation in a settled colony like New South Wales was limited to establishing a constitution.[16] Nevertheless, the early Governors 'claimed to exercise almost unlimited power of legislation by orders and proclamations',[17] and did so from settlement until 1824,[18] albeit largely in relation to matters where the law of England was insufficient for the administration of the Colony.[19] This assumption of legislative power was criticised,[20] but it was defended by the Governors,[21] and their proclamations were recognised as valid laws by Colonial courts.[22] Nor did the Colonial Office raise any objection, until a series of disputes beginning in 1819 led to the Law Officers' opining that the Governors had no power to impose taxes,[23] regulate wage disputes[24] or make port regulations.[25] The Westminster Parliament then legislated to prevent suits against the Governor or any other person for advising, commanding or executing the impugned gubernatorial legislation and authorising, prospectively, similar legislation.[26] The fact that the Imperial authorities only began to consider these issues 30 years after settlement confirms the view that the 'legal foundation of the penal settlement, being the first dependency that was at once both a settled colony

[16] *Case of Proclamations* (1610) 12 Co Rep 74 (KB), 75–76; 77 ER 1352, 1353–54; *Kielley v Carson* (1842) 4 Moo PC 63, 84–85; 13 ER 225, 233; *Sammut v Strickland* [1938] AC 678 (PC), 701.

[17] Windeyer (n 8), 255.

[18] AC Castles, *An Introduction to Australian Legal History* (Sydney, LBC, 1971) 118–20. See, eg, Port Regulations and Orders (01.10.1810) (NSW) in FM Bladen (ed), *Historical Records of New South Wales*, vol VII (Sydney, Government Printer, 1901).

[19] PG King, 'Memorandum on the legality of government and general orders' (1806) in Watson (ed) (n 7), 43, 44–45.

[20] See, locally, E Bent, 'Deputy Judge-Advocate Bent to Earl Bathurst' (1814) in Watson (ed) (n 7), 100, 106; E Bent, 'Deputy Judge-Advocate Bent to Earl Bathurst' (1815) in Watson (ed) (n 7), 122, 124, and, in Britain, J Bentham, *A Plea for the Constitution* (London, Mawman, Poultry and Hatchard, 1803).

[21] See King (n 19), especially 44–45.

[22] See *Marsden v Lawson* (1823) in Watson, F (ed), *Historical Records of Australia*, vol 11, Series I (Sydney, Library Committee of the Commonwealth Parliament, 1917) 775 (NSWSC); Castles (n 18), 119; AC Castles, *An Australian Legal History* (Sydney, LBC, 1982) 378; 'Judicial Evidence taken by Mr Commissioner Bigge' (1819) in Watson (ed) (n 7), 755, 803–04 (evidence of Deputy Judge-Advocate Wylde); WJV Windeyer, '"A Birthright and Inheritance": The Establishment of the Rule of Law in Australia' (1962) 1 *Tasmanian University Law Review* 635, 649.

[23] B Field, 'Legal opinion on validity of duties imposed in the colony' (1818) in F Watson (ed), *Historical Records of Australia*, vol 9, series I (Sydney, Library Committee of the Commonwealth Parliament, 1917) 774; Shepherd and Gifford (n 7). See also McPherson (n 13), 115.

[24] Stephen (n 7).

[25] J Stephen, 'Opinion re prosecution under port regulations' (1823) in Watson (ed) (n 7), 486.

[26] Duties in New South Wales Act 1819 (Imp), continued by the Duties, New South Wales Act 1820 (Imp) and the New South Wales Duties Act 1821 (Imp), and then continued to 01.01.1824 and expanded by the authorisation to levy further duties by the Duties in New South Wales Act 1822 (Imp).

and a crown colony, was anomalous, and had never been properly examined by the home government'.[27]

In relation to judicial power, the King issued letters patent pursuant to the New South Wales Act 1787 (Imp), providing for the establishment of a Criminal Court and a Court of Civil Jurisdiction,[28] and for the Governor, Lieutenant Governor, Judge-Advocate and other members of each court to be Justices of the Peace with the same powers as Justices in England.[29] The Criminal Court was staffed by naval and military officers, and the Civil Court by the Judge-Advocate and two others appointed by the Governor (who were also usually servicemen), and procedures in both courts were essentially summary. Civil appeals lay to the Governor and, in certain matters, to the Privy Council. A Vice-Admiralty Court was also established under an Order in Council and Commissions issued by the Lords of the Admiralty.[30] A different structure of civil courts was established by letters patent in 1814, creating separate inferior courts for New South Wales and Van Diemen's Land (Tasmania), and a Supreme Court with jurisdiction in probate and equity.[31]

From the beginning, magistrates appointed by the Governors played the most significant role in the day-to-day administration of justice, particularly in remote areas and in Tasmania, where the criminal court did not sit until 1821.[32] With the exception of the magistrates' enforcement of the Governors' legislation,[33] these bodies all applied the law of England

[27] Wight (n 1), 67. Evatt and Windeyer argue that the Governors' power was lawful, on the basis that NSW was a 'penitentiary, situated, not in England, but at the other end of the world': Evatt (n 8), 420; Windeyer (n 8), 255. Some modern commentators suggest that the prerogative power was sufficient, save for the imposition of taxation: Carney (n 2), 38; R Else-Mitchell, 'The Foundation of New South Wales and the Inheritance of the Common Law' (1963) 49 *Royal Australian Historical Society Journal* 1, 5; E Campbell, 'Prerogative Rule in New South Wales, 1788–1823' (1964) 50 *Royal Australian Historical Society Journal* 161. Others conclude that the legislative power the Governors asserted had no legal basis: J Quick and RR Garran, *The Annotated Constitution of the Australian Commonwealth* (Sydney, Angus & Robertson, 1901) 36; Watson, 'Introduction' (n 9), vii; WB Campbell, 'A Note on Jeremy Bentham's "A Plea for the Constitution of New South Wales"' (1951) 25 *Australian Law Journal* 59.

[28] The validity of the civil court's establishment was questioned by Bentham and others on the basis that the Act only authorised the creation of a court to try offences against the *criminal law of England*: Bentham (n 20), 26–27. However, the view of other contemporary and later commentators has been that the establishment of a court to administer civil justice was supported either by the royal prerogative or, invoking notions of necessity, by the peculiar nature of NSW as a penal establishment subject to the absolute superintendence of the Governor: Evatt (n 8), 420–22; Windeyer (n 8), 254.

[29] Charter for Establishing Courts of Civil and Criminal Jurisdiction on the Eastern Coast of New South Wales (02.04.1787) in Watson (ed) (n 7), 11–12.

[30] See Letters Patent Constituting the Vice-Admiralty Court (05.05.1787) in Watson (ed) (n 7), 13; Windeyer (n 22), 650.

[31] Letters Patent to establish Courts of Civil Judicature in New South Wales (04.02.1814) in Watson (ed) (n 7), 77.

[32] Castles (n 22), 67–69.

[33] WC Wentworth, *A Statistical, Historical, and Political Description of The Colony of New South Wales, and its dependent Settlements in Van Diemen's Land*, 2nd edn (London, G and WB Whittaker, 1820) 42–43; Castles (n 22), 76.

as received in the Colony, in accordance with the settled doctrine of British courts:[34]

> That if there be a new and uninhabited country found out by English subjects, as the law is the birthright of every subject, so, wherever they go, they carry their laws with them, and therefore such new found country is to be governed by the laws of England; though, after such country is inhabited by the English, acts of parliament made in England, without naming the foreign plantations, will not bind them [...]

The qualification to this principle was expressed by Blackstone:[35]

> Such colonists carry with them only so much of the English law, as is applicable to their own situation and the condition of an infant colony; such, for instance, as the general rules of inheritance, and of protection from personal injuries ... What shall be admitted and what rejected, at what times, and under what restrictions, must, in case of dispute, be decided in the first instance by their own provincial judicature, subject to the revision and control of the king in council [...]

The New South Wales Supreme Court in 1833 observed that both of these sources were 'considered to be a sound exposition of the law by all the writers on Colonial law; and ... received as authority in our courts'.[36] Blackstone's qualification was also approved by the Privy Council.[37] By 1855, the common law rule had been confirmed in New South Wales by Imperial statute.[38]

ii. Governor and Council 1823–42

In view, in particular, of the arrogation of general legislative powers by the early Governors, it has been suggested that New South Wales was governed unconstitutionally, or at least without a constitution, until 1823.[39] In that year, Imperial legislation first provided for a (largely consultative) Legislative Council, whose members were to number between five and seven and to be appointed by the King (in substance, by the Imperial Government).[40] The powers of the Governor in Council were general: 'to make Laws and Ordinances for the Peace, Welfare and good Government' of the Colony, but limited to laws consistent with the laws of England.[41] Importantly, only for local purposes could taxation be levied.[42] Laws

[34] *Anonymous* (1722) 2 P Wms 75 (Ch), 75; 24 ER 646, 646 (emphasis omitted).
[35] Blackstone (n 1), vol 1, [108].
[36] *Macdonald v Levy* (1833) 1 Legge 39 (NSWSC), 52.
[37] *Cooper v Stuart* (1889) LR 14 App Cas 286 (PC), 291–92.
[38] Australian Courts Act 1828 (Imp), s 24; *Macdonald v Levy* (1833) 1 Legge 39 (NSWSC), 53–54.
[39] Watson, 'Introduction' (n 9), vii; F Watson, 'Editorial Note' in Watson (ed) (n 7), v. As to the latter point, much depends on what is meant by 'constitution'.
[40] Justice, New South Wales Act 1823 (Imp), s 24.
[41] ibid.
[42] ibid, s 27.

could not be passed until the Chief Justice certified that they were not repugnant to the laws of England.[43] Once passed, laws had to be transmitted to the Secretary of State—who could, on behalf of the King, disallow them within three years—and also laid before both Houses of the Imperial Parliament.[44]

The 1823 Act also authorised the creation of a Supreme Court and inferior Courts of Session and Requests.[45] The Supreme Court was granted the jurisdiction of the royal courts at Westminster, together with equity, admiralty and ecclesiastical jurisdiction. Provision was made for appeals to the Governor and to the Privy Council. Supreme Court trials were, initially, to be conducted before military juries, but His Majesty (again, in substance, the Imperial Government) was empowered to extend trial by ordinary jury when the time was ripe.

The 1823 Act was, however, limited by a sunset clause,[46] and minor amendments to the scheme were made in 1828,[47] just after New South Wales became economically self-supporting.[48] Under the 1828 Act, the Supreme Court was, in effect, continued as under the 1823 Act.[49] The King was empowered to permit appeals to the Privy Council and to appoint circuit courts, while the Governor and Council were authorised to convene inferior courts.[50] The 1828 Act made detailed provision with respect to the procedure and rules of the Supreme Court, in particular,[51] though the opportunity to appeal to the Privy Council rested on the prerogative rather than statute until an Order in Council under section 15 of the 1828 Act was made in 1850.[52] The Act also expressly directed the courts to apply English law so far as possible in the circumstances of the Colony.[53] The 1828 Act was continued several times, with only one significant amendment: in 1839, the Legislative Council was granted power to legislate 'for the better Administration of Justice, and for defining the Constitution of the Courts of Law and Equity, and of Juries'.[54] It exercised this power on several occasions.[55]

[43] ibid, s 29.

[44] ibid, ss 30–31.

[45] ibid, ss 1–17, 19–21. The creation was effected by letters patent under the Act: Charter establishing Courts of Judicature in New South Wales (13.10.1823) in Watson (ed) (n 7), 509.

[46] Justice, New South Wales Act 1823 (Imp), s 45.

[47] Australian Courts Act 1828 (Imp).

[48] E Jenks, *A History of the Australasian Colonies* (Cambridge, CUP, 1896) 56–57.

[49] Australian Courts Act 1828 (Imp), ss 1–6, 11–12.

[50] ibid, ss 13, 15, 17–18.

[51] ibid, ss 5–6, 8, 14, 16, 19.

[52] See A Twomey, *The Constitution of New South Wales* (Annandale, NSW, Federation Press, 2004) 154–55.

[53] Australian Courts Act 1828 (Imp), s 24.

[54] New South Wales and Van Diemen's Land Act 1839 (Imp), s 2. The continuing Acts were: New South Wales, etc Act 1836 (Imp); New South Wales, etc, Government Act 1837 (Imp); Administration of Justice, New South Wales, etc Act 1838 (Imp); New South Wales and Van Diemen's Land Act 1840 (Imp); New South Wales, etc Government Act 1841 (Imp).

[55] See, eg, *Administration of Justice Act 1840* (NSW).

The 1828 Act enlarged the appointed Legislative Council to between 10 and 15 members.[56] It operated in much the same way as under the 1823 Act, save that notice of proposed laws had to be published eight days in advance and submitted to the Supreme Court within seven days afterwards to be reviewed for consistency with the laws of England; though a law could come into force notwithstanding an adverse report of the judges if the Governor and Council so determined, they were obliged to send the report to the Secretary of State along with the law.[57] Again, power to tax was confined to local purposes.[58] The provisions for disallowance and tabling of New South Wales legislation before the Imperial Parliament were continued, while the period for disallowance was extended to four years.[59]

The full scheme, however, only appears in conjunction with the Instructions to the Governor, who alone was competent to propose legislation and who presided over meetings of the Council.[60] Governor Darling's Instructions closely controlled the course he was to take in respect of legislation: tacking of unrelated measures into the same Act was to be avoided; no law that had been disallowed was to be re-enacted without prior leave of the Secretary of State; repeal of local Acts was to be suspended until the King's pleasure be known; no laws were to be made to continue for less than two years (except in emergencies); no law was to be made that might impair the revenue; no law could be made with respect to naturalisation, divorce or the land rights of those who had acquired land before naturalisation; no law that might prejudice the prerogatives of the Crown or the property of British subjects, or that might affect British trade or shipping, could be made without prior leave or a suspension clause; private laws had to save the rights of all those not mentioned in them, and could not be passed without a suspension clause and certification of prior public notification; and all laws raising revenue had to reserve the moneys to the King for the government of the Colony.[61]

Changes to the laws governing executive authority were also made in this period. Like those of his predecessors, Darling's Commission required him to do and execute all things belonging to his command, subject to his Instructions and subsequent Instructions from the King, the Privy Council or the Secretary of State, but it differed in directing him to appoint an Executive Council.[62] The King's Instructions nominated and

[56] Australian Courts Act 1828 (Imp), s 20.
[57] ibid, ss 21–22.
[58] ibid, s 25.
[59] ibid, ss 28–29.
[60] ibid, ss 21, 23.
[61] Instructions (17.07.1825) in F Watson (ed), *Historical Records of Australia*, vol 12, Series I (Sydney, Library Committee of the Commonwealth Parliament, 1919) 111–13.
[62] Commission (06.07.1825), ibid, 100–01.

appointed the initial members of the Council and, except in emergencies, commanded Darling that he 'do in all things consult and advise with Our said Council, and that [he] do not exercise the powers and authorities aforesaid, or any of them, except by and with the concurrence and advice of Our said Council'.[63] Darling could, nevertheless, act against advice, on condition that he notify the measure to the Secretary of State, together with the minutes of the Council's objections.[64]

iii. Representative and Responsible Government

The Australian Constitutions Act 1842 (Imp) introduced representative government into New South Wales, constituting a Legislative Council of 36 members, 24 elected and 12 appointed by the Queen.[65] While authorising the existing Council to determine electoral boundaries, the Act included detailed provisions relating to elections and procedure.[66] The legislature was empowered to make laws for the Colony's 'Peace, Welfare, and good Government', provided they were not repugnant to the laws of England and did not 'interfere in any Manner with the Sale or other Appropriation of the Lands belonging to the Crown within the said Colony, or with the Revenue thence arising'.[67] The Governor could assent to laws in his discretion, subject to his Instructions and to the requirement that he reserve for Her Majesty's pleasure Bills concerning electoral divisions, the salaries of the principal government officials and customs duties.[68] Laws had to be sent to London and could be disallowed within two years, but they no longer had to be tabled before the Imperial Parliament.[69] The court system established under the 1828 Act, with the local power of amendment conferred in 1839, was left undisturbed.

Roughly contemporaneous with the constitutional reforms of 1842 was an important social change, the 'gradual disappearance of the penal element'.[70] Following comprehensive investigations and recommendations by a Select Committee of the Imperial Parliament,[71] transportation to New South Wales was abolished in 1840,[72] and the practice of assigning

[63] Instructions (n 61), 108–09.

[64] ibid, 110.

[65] Australian Constitutions Act 1842 (Imp), s 1. Certain provisions of this Act were clarified and amended by the Australian Constitutions Act 1844 (Imp). The composition of the Council was adjusted on the separation of Victoria in 1851: Australian Constitutions Act 1850 (Imp), ss 2–3.

[66] Australian Constitutions Act 1842 (Imp), ss 2–28.

[67] ibid, s 29.

[68] ibid, ss 31, 40. Power to impose customs duties (other than on military supplies) was later granted by the Australian Constitutions Act 1850 (Imp), ss 27, 31.

[69] Australian Constitutions Act 1842 (Imp), s 32.

[70] Jenks (n 48), 66.

[71] Select Committee on Transportation, *Report* (HC 669, 1838), xlvi.

[72] Order-in-Council (22.05.1840) (Imp) in F Watson (ed), *Historical Records of Australia*, vol 20, series I (Sydney, Library Committee of the Commonwealth Parliament, 1924).

convicts to settlers as workers or servants essentially ceased in 1841.[73] Jenks observes that '[t]he Constitution of 1842 by implication allowed equal political rights to freemen and emancipists; and this policy, combined with the cessation of convict immigration and distribution, did much to break down the old line of social cleavage'.[74]

A different consequence was economic: the Imperial Government had paid a significant subsidy while convicts were transported, and its cessation no doubt contributed to the depression of 1840–43 that was an important part of the background to the next wave of constitutional reforms. As Twomey explains:[75]

> The introduction of representative government, with the first elections in 1843, provided an outlet for grievances both against the government of New South Wales and the Colonial Office. At the time, New South Wales was in a financial depression. The burden of the civil list upon the resources of the colony, when combined with the denial to it of access to the revenue from the disposal of land in New South Wales, led to resentment amongst the elected Members of the Legislative Council. Attempts to reduce the salaries of government officials were thwarted by the Governor or disallowed in Britain. Select committees were appointed in 1844 to inquire into and report on grievances in relation to land matters, and general grievances.

The Imperial Government rejected the Council's petitions but the grievances remained, aggravated by the Colonial Office's moves in 1848 to impose constitutional reform without local consultation.[76] When the 1848 proposals were abandoned in the face of local hostility, a committee of the Privy Council produced a report, the result of which was the settlement provided in the Australian Constitutions Act 1850 (Imp).[77] The Act confirmed the Legislative Council's power to regulate the justice system, and empowered it to reconstitute the legislature and amend electoral laws, subject to such Bills' being reserved for Her Majesty's pleasure and laid before the Imperial Parliament.[78]

The changes effected by the Australian Constitutions Act 1850 (Imp) were not enough: the New South Wales Legislative Council 'had not succeeded in having any of its other grievances addressed, such as those concerning control of wastelands [Crown lands], revenue, patronage, and most importantly local legislative sovereignty', and it issued a 'declaration, protest and remonstrance' to the Imperial Government in May 1851.[79] As Twomey records, despite Governor FitzRoy's encouragement that they

[73] Government Notice (1841) (NSW) in F Watson (ed), *Historical Records of Australia*, vol 21, series I (Sydney, Library Committee of the Commonwealth Parliament, 1924).

[74] Jenks (n 48), 67.

[75] Twomey (n 52), 4.

[76] ibid, 4–5.

[77] ibid, 5–6.

[78] Australian Constitutions Act 1850 (Imp), ss 29, 32.

[79] Twomey (n 52), 7–8.

be taken seriously, the claims in the remonstrance were largely rejected by the Secretary of State, leading to another resolution in August 1852, reiterating the Council's resentment and frustration at interference in legislation by disallowance and amendment in London, and observing that the exercise of the veto power was one of the chief grievances leading to the revolt of the American Colonies.[80] Subsequent Secretaries of State responded in a conciliatory fashion, and a new constitution was drafted by the Council.[81] Because it exceeded the power granted by the 1850 Act, the Bill had to be passed by the Imperial Parliament, which made certain changes—in particular, removing the clause that would have abolished the power of disallowance (directly or by instruction to the Governor to withhold assent) altogether.[82]

The Imperial Act authorised the Queen to assent to the constitution Bill in its amended form and vested control of wastelands, Colonial revenues and mining royalties in the New South Wales Parliament, but it retained the provisions of the 1842 and 1850 Acts with respect to assent and disallowance.[83] As before, the Governors' Instructions enumerated categories of Bills to be reserved for the signification of Her Majesty's pleasure.[84] The New South Wales Parliament was empowered to amend the constitution, which was included as schedule 1 to the Imperial Act.[85] The constitution provided for a bicameral Parliament with power 'to make Laws for the Peace, Welfare, and good Government of the said Colony in all Cases whatsoever'.[86] The Legislative Council comprised at least 21 members appointed by the Governor on the advice of the Executive Council, and the Legislative Assembly 54 elected members.[87] The constitution provided for responsible government, with ministers obliquely termed 'Officers liable to retire from Office on political Grounds'.[88] Existing laws and courts

[80] ibid, 8–10. See also, with respect to the reform process, Quick and Garran (n 27), 41–44.

[81] Twomey (n 52), 10–16.

[82] ibid, 16–18.

[83] New South Wales Constitution Act 1855 (Imp), ss 1–3.

[84] As part of the reforms, new Instructions were issued in September 1855. When the Instructions were made permanent in 1879, the categories of laws to be reserved included, eg, Bills relating to divorce and currency, Bills inconsistent with treaty obligations and Bills interfering with the control of military or naval forces: Instructions to the Governor and Commander-in-Chief of the Colony of New South Wales (29.04.1879) in New South Wales Legislative Council (ed), *Journal of the Legislative Council of New South Wales*, vol 30, pt 1 (Sydney, Government Printer, 1880) cl X.

[85] New South Wales Constitution Act 1855 (Imp), s 4.

[86] ibid, sch 1, s 1.

[87] ibid, sch 1, ss 2, 10.

[88] ibid, sch 1, s 37. The principles of responsible government were (and, in most State constitutions, still are) not otherwise mentioned: Carney (n 2), 45. Their application in Australia took time to mature, with 19th-century Governors rather more at liberty to act independently of, or contrary to, local ministerial advice: ibid, 259–60.

were expressly preserved.[89] With minor amendments,[90] the constitutional structure implemented in 1855 remained in place until Federation.

The continuing role of Imperial institutions and Imperial law after 1855 requires closer examination, which may be conducted without anachronism by giving a synchronic panorama of examples from a long period of constitutional, legal and political development. New South Wales was not, in or after 1855, an independent realm sharing a monarch with Great Britain, as the Commonwealth of Australia became in the early twentieth century:[91] it was a Colony in the British Empire. However, by the time that it had come to include self-governing Colonies with representative and responsible local institutions, the Empire could be described as 'something in the nature of an imperial federation'.[92] The mechanisms of Imperial administration combined local self-government in some matters with central oversight and control in others. Certainly, the powers reserved to Imperial authorities to issue Instructions and to disallow legislation were exercised by reference to Imperial, and not merely New South Wales, interests. In fact, State Governors continued to act as agents of the Imperial Government as well as on the advice of responsible State ministries until the end of World War II.[93] However, New South Wales was a part of the Empire, and Imperial interests included New South Wales interests. Imperial authorities thus began to play multiple, overlapping roles. The Judicial Committee of the Privy Council provides a vivid illustration. The Privy Council came to regard itself as a court in, for example, the Canadian hierarchy, a court sitting as 'an Imperial, not merely a British, tribunal',[94] and it continued to be part of the judicial system of, for example, Sri Lanka, even after independence.[95] Viscount Haldane explained (in an advice of the Privy Council) that the Judicial Committee was 'not an English body in any exclusive sense. It [was] no more an English body than it [was] an Indian body, or a Canadian body, or a South African body'.[96] Accordingly, the Privy Council was, as a matter of course, regarded as an organ of Australian judicial systems when hearing Australian appeals.[97]

[89] New South Wales Constitution Act 1855 (Imp), sch 1, ss 41–42.

[90] Summarised in Quick and Garran (n 27), 47–48.

[91] See A Twomey, 'Responsible Government and the Divisibility of the Crown' [2008] *PL* 742.

[92] McPherson (n 13), 86. It was not a true federation because Colonial governments were legally subordinate to the British Government, rather than coordinate and independent: ie, they could be unilaterally abolished by the British Government. This feature of federations is discussed in KC Wheare, *Federal Government*, 4th edn (London, OUP, 1963), 10.

[93] Carney (n 2), 259–60.

[94] *British Coal Corporation v The King* [1935] AC 500 (PC), 522.

[95] See *Ibralebbe v The Queen* [1964] AC 900 (PC), especially 921–22.

[96] *Hull v M'Kenna* [1926] IR 402 (PC), 403–04.

[97] See JM Finnis, 'The Responsibilities of the United Kingdom Parliament and Government under the Australian Constitution' (1983) 9 *Adelaide Law Review* 91, 107 and the authorities there cited.

Imperial law, like Imperial institutions, was, and can still be, understood to have an overlapping or 'amphibious'[98] character. An Act of the Westminster Parliament granting independence can reasonably be considered part of the legal system of the newly independent entity, but the Act is nevertheless part of UK law.[99] Similarly, in enacting the New South Wales Constitution Act 1855 (Imp), the Westminster Parliament certainly created Imperial law, but the nature (and geographical scope) of the Imperial Act's provisions, the circumstances of its drafting and enactment, and the method for altering its provisions provide a firm basis for characterising it as distinctly New South Wales law, albeit enacted by Imperial means. In the context of the federal external affairs power, at least one member of the High Court expressly adopted the view that[100]

> [t]he exercise of Imperial legislative power was the exercise of a power forming part of the local legal system of the colony, State or Commonwealth of Australia, as the case may be. The resulting law applied and, to the extent it remains part of the law of the States, applies by paramount force. There is no element of externality about either the law or its source.

An extreme version of this view characterises the Imperial Parliament as a 'mere agent' and its power as 'derivative'.[101] That extreme view is to be contrasted with that of the Secretary of State in introducing the Bill for the Commonwealth of Australia Constitution Act 1900 (Imp), where, after relating the drafting of virtually the whole of the Bill in Australia, he denied 'altogether that the Australian people have ever considered, or shown that they consider, the Imperial Parliament as merely a Court for the registration of their decrees'.[102] Further, as Finnis, Selway and Twomey have observed, the Government in London formally acted as the Imperial Government and not as an agent of New South Wales—and was responsible to the Imperial Parliament—in advising Her Majesty in relation to New South Wales matters until the passage of the Australia Act 1986 (Imp).[103] The significant observation here is that, in applying an

[98] *R(Bancoult) v Foreign Secretary (No 2)* [2008] UKHL 61, [2009] 1 AC 453 (HL(E)), 484 [40] (Lord Hoffmann).

[99] On the contrary position adopted by Lord Hoffmann in *R(Quark Fishing Ltd) v Secretary of State for Foreign and Commonwealth Affairs* [2005] UKHL 57, [2006] 1 AC 529 (HL(E)), 552–53 [64], see Twomey (n 91), 762–63. His Lordship later indicated a reconsideration of some of his views in that case: *R(Bancoult) v Foreign Secretary (No 2)* [2008] UKHL 61, [2009] 1 AC 453 (HL(E)), 486 [48].

[100] *Kirmani v Captain Cook Cruises Pty Ltd [No 1]* (1985) 159 CLR 351 (HCA), 458–59 (Dawson J); see also at 371 (Gibbs CJ).

[101] RTE Latham, *The Law and the Commonwealth* (London, OUP, 1949), 526.

[102] United Kingdom, *Parliamentary Debates (Fourth Series)*, vol 83 (HC, 14.05.1900), col 55 (Mr Chamberlain).

[103] A Twomey, 'The States, the Commonwealth and the Crown—the Battle for Sovereignty' in K Walsh (ed), Papers on Parliament No 48: The Senate and Accountability (Canberra, Department of the Senate, 2008) 21, 23–27; BM Selway, 'The Constitutional Role of the Queen

account of continuity to the concrete instance of Australia, care must be taken to appreciate—but also not to overstate—the changing role of Imperial institutions and laws in the self-governing Colonies: the fact that the New South Wales Constitution Act 1855 (Imp) was enacted by the Imperial Parliament must be considered in context.

iv. Federation to the Australia Acts

At Federation, New South Wales became a State in the Commonwealth of Australia and thereby ceased, for many practical purposes—though not for all legal purposes—to be a Colony. The *Commonwealth Constitution* effected the changes necessary to establish the federal union and to create a central, national government with certain exclusive and certain concurrent powers, but otherwise 'saved' or 'continued' the constitutions, powers and laws of the States.[104] New letters patent were issued constituting the Governor of the State of New South Wales but, apart from omitting the title 'Commander-in-Chief' and the associated military command clause,[105] these effected little change—they preserved, for example, the Imperial Government's power to issue Instructions.[106] Apart from the High Court contemplated by Chapter III of the *Commonwealth Constitution*, few changes were made in relation to judicial power either: Privy Council appeals, for example, remained available, subject only to the requirement for a certificate in the case of an appeal from the High Court on a matter involving the constitutional powers of the integers in the Federation inter se.[107] Soon after Federation, however, the Commonwealth Parliament legislated to abolish Privy Council appeals from State courts exercising federal jurisdiction.[108]

of Australia' (2003) 32 *Commonwealth Law World Review* 248, 251–53; JM Finnis, 'Common Law Constraints: Whose Common Good Counts?' (2008) *University of Oxford Faculty of Law Legal Studies Research Paper Series Working Paper No 10/2008*, available at <http://papers.ssrn.com/sol3/papers.cfm?abstract_id=1100628>, [16]–[18]; Twomey (n 91), 752–55. See also Finnis, (n 97).

[104] *Commonwealth Constitution*, ss 106–108.

[105] Letters Patent Constituting the Office of Governor and Commander-in-Chief of the Colony of New South Wales (29.04.1879) in New South Wales Legislative Council (ed) (n 84), cl XIV.

[106] Letters Patent constituting the Office of the Governor of the State of New South Wales and its Dependencies, in the Commonwealth of Australia (29.10.1900, as amended to 16.11.1938) (Imp) in Statute Law Committee (ed), *The Statutory Rules & Orders and Statutory Instruments Revised to December 31, 1948*, vol II (London, HMSO, 1950), cl II.

[107] *Commonwealth Constitution*, s 74. A new order in council under the Australian Courts Act 1828 (Imp), s 15 was made in 1909 to regulate such appeals: Order in Council Regulating Appeals to His Majesty in Council from the Supreme Court of the State of New South Wales, SI 1909/1521 (Imp).

[108] *Judiciary Act 1903* (Cth), s 39(2)(a). The High Court did not regard itself as bound by, and declined to follow, the Privy Council's advice in *Webb v Outrim* [1907] AC 81 (PC), 91–92 that the provision was invalid: *Baxter v Commissioners of Taxation (NSW)* (1907) 4 CLR 1087 (HCA), 1118 (Griffith CJ, Barton and O'Connor JJ), 1152–54 (Isaacs J).

The *Commonwealth Constitution* was also a source of, and limit on, New South Wales legislative,[109] executive[110] and judicial[111] power. Views diverge on whether section 106's provision that State constitutions 'shall continue' entailed that the New South Wales constitution[112] now derived legal authority from the *Commonwealth Constitution* itself. Until the 1970s, the orthodox view was that, after Federation, the New South Wales constitution continued to derive its legal authority from the relevant pre-Federation sources.[113] Beginning in the 1970s, however, Barwick CJ and Murphy J, in particular, advanced the view that section 106 'conferred' constitutions on the States, which derived their existence as States from the *Commonwealth Constitution*.[114] This view appears to have become established by the centenary of Federation in 2001. Although members of the High Court often simply used the language of 'preservation', 'continuance' or 'saving' without explanation,[115] the express or implied endorsement of the 'conferral' view,[116] and the lack of any Justice supporting the original view,

[109] See, eg, *Commonwealth Constitution*, ss 7, 9, 29, 52, 90, 92, 107–108, 112, 114–116.

[110] See, eg, ibid, ss 7, 12, 15, 70, 84, 110.

[111] See, eg, ibid, ss 71, 77.

[112] Meaning not simply the *Constitution Act 1902* (NSW) but all 'those provisions or terms, wherever found, which really define and describe the framework and scheme of its government': *Stuart-Robinson v Lloyd* (1932) 47 CLR 482 (HCA), 491 (Evatt J).

[113] *Clayton v Heffron* (1960) 105 CLR 214 (HCA), 251 (Dixon CJ, McTiernan, Taylor and Windeyer JJ). In relation to other State constitutions, see, eg, *Cooper v Commissioner of Income Tax (Qld)* (1907) 4 CLR 1304 (HCA), 1314 (Griffith CJ); *McCawley v The King* (1918) 26 CLR 9 (HCA), 20, 22 (Griffith CJ).

[114] *Victoria v The Commonwealth* (1971) 122 CLR 353 (HCA), 371 (Barwick CJ), 386 (Menzies J); *Commonwealth v Queensland* (1975) 134 CLR 298 (HCA), 337 (Murphy J); *New South Wales v Commonwealth* (1975) 135 CLR 337 (HCA), 372 (Barwick CJ); *Bistricic v Rokov* (1976) 135 CLR 552 (HCA), 566 (Murphy J); *China Ocean Shipping Co v South Australia* (1979) 145 CLR 172 (HCA), 182 (Barwick CJ); *Western Australia v Wilsmore* (1982) 149 CLR 79 (HCA), 86 (Murphy J).

[115] *Kirmani v Captain Cook Cruises Pty Ltd [No 1]* (1985) 159 CLR 351 (HCA), 430 (Deane J); *Re Australian Education Union; Ex parte Victoria* (1995) 184 CLR 188 (HCA), 229 (Mason CJ, Brennan, Deane, Toohey, Gaudron and McHugh JJ); *Breavington v Godleman* (1988) 169 CLR 41 (HCA), 97 (Wilson and Gaudron JJ), 107 (Brennan J), 120–21 (Deane J); *Re Tracey; Ex parte Ryan* (1989) 166 CLR 518 (HCA), 575 (Brennan and Toohey JJ), 599 (Gaudron J); *Port MacDonnell Professional Fishermen's Association Inc v South Australia* (1989) 168 CLR 340 (HCA), 381 (Mason CJ, Brennan, Deane, Dawson, Toohey, Gaudron and McHugh JJ); *Nationwide News Pty Ltd v Wills* (1992) 177 CLR 1 (HCA), 76 (Deane and Toohey JJ); *Australian Capital Television Pty Ltd v Commonwealth* (1992) 177 CLR 106 (HCA), 163 (Brennan J), 202 (Dawson J), 241–42 (McHugh J); *Capital Duplicators Pty Ltd v Australian Capital Territory* (1992) 177 CLR 248 (HCA), 275 (Brennan, Deane and Toohey JJ); *Re Residential Tenancies Tribunal (NSW); Ex parte Defence Housing Authority* (1997) 190 CLR 410 (HCA), 504 (Kirby J); *Gould v Brown* (1998) 193 CLR 346 (HCA), 480 (Kirby J); *Re Wakim; Ex parte McNally* (1999) 198 CLR 511 (HCA), 559 [62] (McHugh J), 606 [201] (Kirby J); *Re Governor, Goulburn CC; Ex parte Eastman* (1999) 200 CLR 322 (HCA), 374 [135] (Kirby J).

[116] *Theophanous v Herald & Weekly Times Ltd* (1994) 182 CLR 104 (HCA), 164–65 (Deane J); *McGinty v Western Australia* (1996) 186 CLR 140 (HCA), 171–72 (Brennan CJ), 208 (Toohey J); *Muldowney v South Australia* (1996) 186 CLR 352 (HCA), 377 (Gaudron J); *Kable v Director of Public Prosecutions (NSW)* (1996) 189 CLR 51 (HCA), 65–66 (Brennan CJ); *Kruger v Commonwealth* (1997) 190 CLR 1 (HCA), 42 (Brennan CJ).

suggest that this facially neutral language—'preservation', 'continuance' and 'saving'—indicates acceptance of the conferral view, consistently with the Court's recent position that 'constitutional norms, whatever may be their historical origins, are now to be traced to Australian sources'.[117]

Shortly after Federation, the *Constitution Act 1902* (NSW) replaced the Constitution included in the schedule to the 1855 Imperial Act. The express purpose of the 1902 Act was consolidation rather than reform, but several amendments acknowledged the new status of the polity as a State in the Federation: all references to the 'Colony' were omitted,[118] and the legislative powers of the New South Wales Parliament, for example, were expressed to be 'subject to the provisions of the Commonwealth of Australia Constitution Act'.[119] While the general Imperial limitations with respect to reservation were repealed in 1907, leaving only those in relation to certain constitutional amendments,[120] the provisions preserved in the New South Wales Constitution Act 1855 (Imp) in relation to disallowance continued to apply, as did Imperial limitations in relation to repugnancy[121] and matters of Imperial concern such as merchant shipping.[122] The powers to disallow local Acts and to advise the Queen to withhold assent to reserved Bills were in practice rarely used, although their availability allowed the Imperial Government to insist on amendments to Colonial—and later State—legislation: the use of the disallowance power was seriously considered as late as 1930, and the power to advise the withholding of assent as late as the 1980s.[123]

Of the various amendments effected to the *Constitution Act 1902* (NSW) in the century following Federation, only a few are significant. In 1932, the Legislative Council became indirectly elected, with 60 members, chosen by both Houses of the Parliament for 12-year terms.[124] In 1978 (much later than in the other States), the Legislative Council became directly democratic, with (by its third election, when the reforms were fully implemented) 45 members elected, one third of the House at a time, by

[117] *Attorney-General (WA) v Marquet* [2003] HCA 67; (2003) 217 CLR 545 (HCA), 570 [66] (Gleeson CJ, Gummow, Hayne and Heydon JJ). See also *Pfeiffer v Stevens* [2001] HCA 71; (2001) 209 CLR 57 (HCA), 88 [113] (Kirby J); *Shaw v Minister for Immigration and Multicultural Affairs* [2003] HCA 72; (2003) 218 CLR 28 (HCA), 66 [108] (Kirby J).

[118] Nonetheless, a reference to the 'Colonial Treasurer' survived in *Constitution Act 1902* (NSW), s 44 until repealed by *Constitution (Consolidated Fund) Amendment Act 1982* (NSW), s 4, sch 1, item (6).

[119] *Constitution Act 1902* (NSW), s 5.

[120] Australian States Constitution Act 1907 (Imp), s 1. See also *Constitution Act 1902* (NSW), s 7.

[121] See, in particular, the Colonial Laws Validity Act 1865 (Imp).

[122] See, in particular, *Constitution Act 1902* (NSW), s 9; Colonial Courts of Admiralty Act 1890 (Imp), ss 4, 7; Merchant Shipping Act 1894 (Imp), ss 735–736. See *China Ocean Shipping Co v South Australia* (1979) 145 CLR 172 (HCA).

[123] Twomey (n 52), 239–40; A Twomey, *The Australia Acts 1986: Australia's Statutes of Independence* (Leichhardt, NSW, Federation Press, 2010), 11–17, 113, 123, 279–80, 283–84.

[124] *Constitution Amendment (Legislative Council) Act 1932* (NSW).

proportional representation for a period corresponding to three terms of the Legislative Assembly.[125] At the same time, the requirement that Bills concerning the Legislative Council be reserved for signification of His Majesty's pleasure was repealed.[126]

Although primarily concerned with the Commonwealth as a Dominion, the Statute of Westminster 1931 (Imp) had two effects on the States: the reservation provisions in the Colonial Courts of Admiralty Act 1890 (Imp) ceased to apply[127] and the States formally ceased to be 'Colonies' for the purposes of legislation at Westminster.[128] The Imperial Parliament could still enact legislation applying by paramount force by extending it to the States by name,[129] though, by convention, it came to do so only at the request and consent of the State.[130] As Twomey amply demonstrates, Her Majesty acted on the advice of responsible ministers in the UK in relation to a few residual State matters until 1986.[131] However, while Governors still served in a dual role,[132] the Imperial authorities had abandoned the power to issue Instructions as to the exercise of gubernatorial powers by 1926.[133] Otherwise, the changes in the status of Dominions that were given legislative form in the Statute of Westminster 1931 (Imp) and in the changes recognised at the Imperial Conferences that preceded it did not apply to the States.[134]

[125] *Constitution Act 1902* (NSW), pt 3, div 2, as amended by *Constitution and Parliamentary Electorates and Elections (Amendment) Act 1978* (NSW), s 3, sch 1, item (9). The Council was later reduced to 42 members elected, half the House at a time, for terms corresponding to two terms of the Assembly: *Constitution (Legislative Council) Amendment Act 1991* (NSW), s 3, sch 1.

[126] The requirement appears to have been repealed twice: *Constitution (Amendment) Act 1978* (NSW), s 2; *Constitution and Parliamentary Electorates and Elections (Amendment) Act 1978* (NSW), s 3, sch 1, item (4). As Twomey notes, repugnancy was avoided because reservation was dealt with in the Australian States Constitution Act 1907 (Imp), s 1: Twomey (n 52), 234.

[127] Statute of Westminster 1931 (Imp), s 6.

[128] ibid, s 11. The application to the States of legislation enacted at Westminster that was expressed to apply to the 'Colonies' would have been inconsistent with the autonomous self-governing status of the Dominion of which they were part.

[129] *Bistricic v Rokov* (1976) 135 CLR 552 (HCA), 557 (Mason J).

[130] *Ukley v Ukley* [1977] VR 121 (VSC), 127, 129–30 (Young CJ, Barber and Nelson JJ); Joint Committee appointed to consider the petition of the State of Western Australia, *Report* (HL 52 and 75; HC 88, 1935), viii [7].

[131] Twomey (n 52), 134–45. See also JL Goldring, 'The Australia Act 1986 and the Formal Independence of Australia' [1986] *PL* 192, 196 and the authorities cited above, n 103. Her Majesty's representative in the States acted, of course, on the initiative and advice of State ministers responsible to the State Parliament: *Theodore v Duncan* [1919] AC 696 (PC), 706; *Amalgamated Society of Engineers v Adelaide Steamship Co Ltd* (1920) 28 CLR 129 (HCA), 152 (Knox CJ, Isaacs, Rich and Starke JJ).

[132] Above, text to n 93.

[133] United Kingdom, *Parliamentary Debates (Fifth Series)*, vol 193 (HC, 15.03.1926), col 58 (Mr Amery).

[134] As the Secretary of State made clear to Cabinet and in oral answers to questions in Parliament at Westminster: JH Thomas, *The Constitutional Position in New South Wales* (CAB 24/222; former reference CP 177 (31), 1931), 2; United Kingdom, *Parliamentary Debates (Fifth Series)*, vol 246 (HC, 16.12.1930), col 1037 (Mr Thomas). Both sources are mentioned in Twomey (n 52), 133–34. The saving provisions were enacted as Statute of Westminster 1931 (Imp), ss 1, 8, 9.

Appeals to the Privy Council from the High Court were abolished by Commonwealth legislation in 1968 and 1975.[135] While this legislation could not remove the constitutional availability of appeals in respect of decisions as to the limits inter se of the powers of the Commonwealth and the States upon the grant of a certificate by the High Court, only one such certificate was ever granted,[136] and the jurisdiction, described as 'theoretical' by 1978,[137] was later expressly abandoned by the Court.[138] Accordingly, it was only possible to appeal to the Privy Council on a matter outside federal jurisdiction and directly from the Supreme Court. As Gibbs J observed:[139]

> The effect of these legislative changes is extraordinary and perhaps unprecedented. It is that from the Supreme Courts of the Australian States, when not exercising federal jurisdiction, there are two final courts of appeal, neither of which is subordinate to the other.

The possibility of divergent legal development was accentuated when, in consequence of the virtual abolition of appeals from the High Court, the High Court held in 1978 that it was no longer bound by decisions of the Privy Council, whenever given (though State courts might still be bound, absent High Court authority).[140] Faced with the potential chaos of conflicting authorities from alternative ultimate courts of appeal, the New South Wales Court of Appeal in 1978 decided that it should, at least in general, prefer decisions of the High Court to those of the Privy Council, and further that, where appeal to Her Majesty in Council lay by leave of the New South Wales Court, it would, in view of the potential for conflicting authorities to be produced, never be appropriate to grant leave.[141] Accordingly, only where an appeal lay by right—where a claim valued

[135] *Privy Council (Limitation of Appeals) Act 1968* (Cth), s 3; *Privy Council (Appeals from the High Court) Act 1975* (Cth), s 3.

[136] *Colonial Sugar Refining Co Ltd v Attorney-General for the Commonwealth* (1912) 15 CLR 182 (HCA), 234.

[137] *Viro v The Queen* (1978) 141 CLR 88 (HCA), 93 (Barwick CJ).

[138] *Kirmani v Captain Cook Cruises Pty Ltd [No 2]* (1985) 159 CLR 461 (HCA), 464–65 (Gibbs CJ, Mason, Wilson, Brennan, Deane and Dawson JJ). The constitutional power nonetheless remains: a proposal to repeal s 74 was included in Constitution Alteration (Establishment of Republic) Bill 1999 (Cth), sch 2, cl 34, but the electors rejected the Bill at the referendum.

[139] *Viro v The Queen* (1978) 141 CLR 88 (HCA), 120; see also 130–31 (Stephen J), 175–76 (Aickin J). The Court confirmed that the Commonwealth legislation abolishing appeals to the Privy Council from the High Court did not have the incidental effect of abolishing such appeals from State courts as well, in *Southern Centre of Theosophy Inc v South Australia* (1979) 145 CLR 246 (HCA), 260–61 (Gibbs J; Barwick CJ, Stephen, Mason, Aickin and Wilson JJ separately concurring).

[140] *Viro v The Queen* (1978) 141 CLR 88 (HCA), 93 (Barwick CJ), 120 (Gibbs J), 129–30 (Stephen J), 135 (Mason J), 150–51 (Jacobs J), 166 (Murphy J), 174 (Aickin J).

[141] *National Employers' Mutual General Association Ltd v Waind and Hill [No 2]* [1978] 1 NSWLR 466 (NSWCA), 476–77 (Moffitt P; Reynolds, Hutley, Glass and Samuels JJA separately agreeing).

at £500 or more was in issue[142]—was it possible to appeal to the Privy Council from New South Wales in 1978. A 1979 Bill to abolish such appeals was passed by the Legislative Council and the Legislative Assembly, but the Bill languished (until it was 'annulled' in 1986 in connection with the passage of the *Australia Acts*) due to concerns about repugnancy to Imperial law and advice that the Governor might have been obliged to reserve the Bill, in which case it was likely that the Imperial Government would, because of the potential repugnancy, advise Her Majesty to withhold assent.[143]

v. After the Australia Acts

The *Australia Acts* are arguably the most important post-Federation change so far as the States are concerned. Twomey helpfully and comprehensively canvasses the background to, and procedure for, their enactment.[144] For present purposes, it suffices to observe that, pursuant to the request and consent of the Commonwealth (under section 4 of the Statute of Westminster 1931 (Imp)) and of the States to legislation by the Imperial Parliament, and to the request of the States to legislation by the Commonwealth Parliament under section 51(xxxviii) of the *Commonwealth Constitution*,[145] the essentially identical Australia Act 1986 (Imp) and *Australia Act 1986* (Cth) were enacted, and came into force simultaneously on 3 March 1986.[146] The effects of the Acts were:

- to terminate the power of the Westminster Parliament to legislate for the Commonwealth, the States and the Territories;[147] and
- to confirm the States' extra-territorial legislative competence and expand that competence to include matters previously only within the competence of the Westminster Parliament (such as the sovereign),[148] subject to the *Commonwealth Constitution* and the Commonwealth of Australia Constitution Act 1900 (Imp) and without permitting the States to legislate contrary to those Acts, the Statute of Westminster 1931 (Imp) or the *Australia Acts* themselves,[149] or to legislate without

[142] Order in Council Regulating Appeals to His Majesty in Council from the Supreme Court of the State of New South Wales, SI 1909/1521 (Imp), r 2(a).

[143] *Constitutional Legislation (Repeal) Act 1985* (NSW), s 3; Twomey (n 52), 161–62.

[144] Twomey (n 52), 75–94; Twomey (n 123), 62–180, 360–67; A Twomey, 'The Making of the *Australia Acts* 1986' in G Winterton (ed), *State Constitutional Landmarks* (Sydney, Federation Press, 2006) 167.

[145] *Australia (Request and Consent) Act 1985* (Cth); *Australia Acts (Request) Act 1985* (NSW).

[146] 'Proclamation' (02.03.1986) in *Commonwealth of Australia Gazette* (1986) No S85; The Australia Act 1986 (Commencement) Order 1986, SI 1986/319 (Imp).

[147] Australia Act 1986 (Imp), s 1.

[148] *Australia Act 1986* (Cth), s 2; Australia Act 1986 (Imp), s 2; *Mobil Oil Australia Pty Ltd v Victoria* [2002] HCA 27; (2002) 211 CLR 1 (HCA), 22–23 [9] (Gleeson CJ), 34 [48] (Gaudron, Gummow and Hayne JJ) and the cases there cited; Twomey (n 123), 214–17.

[149] *Australia Act 1986* (Cth), s 5; Australia Act 1986 (Imp), s 5.

respecting any manner and form requirements applicable in relation to the constitution, powers or procedures of the State Parliament;[150] and

— to terminate (prospectively) the application of the Colonial Laws Validity Act 1865 (Imp);[151] and
— to terminate restrictions applying in relation to merchant shipping;[152] and
— to provide for the Queen's powers and functions in relation to the States (except the appointment and dismissal of the Governor) to be exercised only by the Governor (unless the Queen be personally present), and for the Queen to be advised by State (rather than UK) ministers;[153] and
— to abolish disallowance or reservation of, or withholding of assent to, laws, or suspension of their operation pending the signification of Her Majesty's pleasure;[154] and
— to terminate any responsibility of British ministers for the States;[155] and
— to terminate appeals to the Privy Council from Australian courts other than the High Court.[156]

Because of the parallel legislative scheme, involving the State, Commonwealth and Imperial Parliaments, an issue about which *Australia Act(s)* brought about these results arises. Some commentators assert that the *Australia Act 1986* (Cth) is the 'operative' legislation, the Australia Act 1986 (Imp) being considered legally superfluous and enacted for political and prudential reasons.[157] Others hold that the Imperial version is necessary to support, in particular, section 15(1),[158] or because the validity of the State

[150] *Australia Act 1986* (Cth), s 6; Australia Act 1986 (Imp), s 6.
[151] *Australia Act 1986* (Cth), s 3; Australia Act 1986 (Imp), s 3.
[152] *Australia Act 1986* (Cth), s 4; Australia Act 1986 (Imp), s 4.
[153] *Australia Act 1986* (Cth), s 7; Australia Act 1986 (Imp), s 7.
[154] *Australia Act 1986* (Cth), ss 8–9; Australia Act 1986 (Imp), ss 8–9.
[155] *Australia Act 1986* (Cth), s 10; Australia Act 1986 (Imp), s 10.
[156] *Australia Act 1986* (Cth), s 11; Australia Act 1986 (Imp), s 11.
[157] Goldring (n 131), 200.
[158] Section 15(1) provides that, subject to any power conferred by amendment of the *Commonwealth Constitution*, the Act and the Statute of Westminster 1931 (Imp) may be amended only by the Commonwealth Parliament, at the request or with the concurrence of the State Parliaments. Three issues arise. First, if, as is the orthodox view, the Commonwealth Parliament cannot bind itself by manner and form provisions (for possible exceptions, see GG Winterton, 'Can the Commonwealth Parliament Enact "Manner and Form" Legislation?' (1980) 11 *Federal Law Review* 167), the paramount force of the Imperial Act is required for s 15(1) to be effective. Second, it has been thought that s 15(1) might be used to amend s 8 of the Statute of Westminster, which precludes the Commonwealth Parliament's use of the power in s 2(2) of the Statute—to amend or repeal Imperial Acts—to amend the *Commonwealth Constitution* otherwise than by means of the s 128 referendum procedure. Such an operation of s 15(1) expands the powers of the Commonwealth Parliament and introduces

request Acts or the capacity of the Westminster Parliament to legislate for Australia is open to challenge.[159] The better view appears to be that the Imperial Act is legally essential.[160] Nonetheless, in *Sue v Hill*, a majority of the High Court relied on the Commonwealth version.[161] More recently (albeit after our period), the Court has expressly held that 'the Commonwealth rather than the Imperial statute is determinative'[162] and that '[t]he *Australia Act*, too, is to be traced to its Australian source—the Constitution of the Commonwealth'.[163]

New South Wales asserted its post-*Australia Acts* status and powers in the *Constitution (Amendment) Act 1987* (NSW). This Act:

— repealed restrictions (or express permissions that had been necessary in the colonial era) relating to wastelands of the Crown, merchant shipping, reservation, disallowance and Instructions to Governors (whether in Imperial or New South Wales legislation); and
— provided that the Governor, Lieutenant-Governor and Administrator should be commissioned under Her Majesty's Sign Manual and the Public Seal of New South Wales; and
— terminated the effect of the existing Governor's letters patent and Instructions;[164] and
— made further extensive provisions with respect to the Governor and the Executive Council.

an exception to the s 128 referendum procedure. Since it was itself not authorised by a referendum, this result could only have been brought about by the paramount force of the Imperial Act. Thirdly, in countenancing (in conjunction with s 15(3)) the possibility of an amendment to the *Commonwealth Constitution* conferring a power on the Commonwealth Parliament to amend the Act (or the Statute) otherwise than by the method set out in s 15(1), it might be thought that the s 128 amendment power has been limited: no other possibility—such as an amendment to the *Commonwealth Constitution* conferring power on a State Parliaments to amend the Act so far as it is part of the law of that State—is envisaged. Again, such an implied amendment to the *Commonwealth Constitution* would have to rely on the Imperial, not the Commonwealth, Act. See B O'Brien, 'The Australia Acts' in MP Ellinghaus, AJ Bradbrook and AJ Duggan (eds), *The Emergence of Australian Law* (Sydney, Butterworths, 1989) 337, 339–42; Carney (n 2), 71–74; L Zines, *The High Court and the Constitution*, 5th edn (Sydney, Federation Press, 2008) 421–25; Twomey (n 123), 386–411.

[159] The debate about the validity of the *Australia Act 1986* (Cth) and the Australia Act 1986 (Imp) is comprehensively treated in Twomey (n 123), 367–432.

[160] See Twomey, ibid, 413–15 and the authorities there cited.

[161] *Sue v Hill* [1999] HCA 30, (1999) 199 CLR 462 (HCA), 490–91 [59]–[61] (Gleeson CJ, Gummow and Hayne JJ), cp 528 [172] (Gaudron J), referring to the two Acts collectively.

[162] *Durham Holdings Pty Ltd v New South Wales* [2001] HCA 7, (2001) 205 CLR 399 (HCA), 409 fn 72 (Gaudron, McHugh, Gummow and Hayne JJ).

[163] *Attorney-General (WA) v Marquet* [2003] HCA 67, (2003) 217 CLR 545 (HCA), 570 [67] (Gleeson CJ, Gummow, Hayne and Heydon JJ). See also above, text to n 117.

[164] As Twomey notes, amended interim Instructions had come into force in February 1986: Twomey (n 52), 147.

An additional Part was inserted into the *Constitution Act 1902* (NSW) the following year, reaffirming the status and independence of the judiciary.[165] The final major constitutional change in our period was the introduction of fixed-term Parliaments in 1995.[166]

B. Constitutional History: Commonwealth

i. *Federation to the Statute of Westminster*

Although principally focused in the last decade of the nineteenth century, more than 50 years of consideration preceded the realisation of the federal idea in Australia.[167] Of the history that preceded Federation,[168] it is relevant for present purposes to note four features. First, after the rejection of British proposals in the late 1840s, the process was directed and driven in and by the Australian Colonies themselves.[169] In contrast to the Canadian precedent, the text of the Imperial Act had been drafted locally, rather than by Imperial officials;[170] although it was closely scrutinised (and very slightly amended) in 1900, the Imperial Government had—at least publicly—been only peripherally involved in the detail of drafting before then.[171] Second, Federation was achieved through the collaboration of the Colonies as polities: the participants at the 1890 Conference and the Conventions of 1891, 1897 and 1898, and especially the Premiers' Conferences of 1895, 1896 and 1899, represented their Colonies, and the referenda of 1899 and 1900 were conducted not nationally but in each federating Colony. Third, although organised into Colonial units, as just

[165] *Constitution (Amendment) Act 1992* (NSW), s 3, sch 1, item (4). The relevant Part was entrenched in 1995: *Constitution (Entrenchment) Amendment Act 1992* (NSW), s 3, sch 1.

[166] *Constitution (Fixed Term Parliaments) Amendment Act 1993* (NSW).

[167] A convenient timeline appears in H Irving (ed), *The Centenary Companion to Australian Federation* (Cambridge, CUP, 1999) viii–xii.

[168] The classical accounts are Quick and Garran (n 27), 79–261 and JA La Nauze, *The Making of the Australian Constitution* (Melbourne, Melbourne University Press, 1972).

[169] Irving (n 167), 4.

[170] La Nauze (n 168), 249.

[171] Quick and Garran (n 27), 229. In secret, however, the Secretary of State for the Colonies, Joseph Chamberlain, had furnished the Premier of NSW, George Reid, with two detailed memoranda prepared by the Colonial Office (with the assistance of the Crown Law Officers), setting out suggested amendments on matters concerning imperial interests, together with a third memorandum containing other drafting criticisms. In the course of the 1897–99 constitutional conventions, Reid moved many of these amendments, apparently also passing on some of the suggestions to the drafting committee and its chair, Edmund Barton. See further BK de Garis, 'The Colonial Office and the Commonwealth Constitution Bill' in AW Martin (ed), *Essays in Australian Federation* (Melbourne, Melbourne University Press, 1969) 94. The memoranda are reproduced in JM Williams, *The Australian Constitution: A Documentary History* (Melbourne, Melbourne University Press, 2005) 714–32.

observed, the participants nonetheless met as popular representatives: the participants at the 1897 and 1898 Conventions were elected, rather than appointed by the Colonial Parliaments as those at the 1891 Convention were.[172] Moreover, quite apart from non-governmental popular involvement through federation leagues and the People's Conventions of 1893 and 1896,[173] the proposed constitution was submitted for the approval (albeit not in final form and without direct legal effect) of the electors of each Colony at referenda.[174] Fourth, whatever *political* basis it had in any compact between the Colonies or as the expression of popular will, the *legal* process by which Federation was effected was an Act of the Imperial Parliament.

The *Commonwealth Constitution*—contained in, and deriving its legal authority from, the Commonwealth of Australia Constitution Act 1900 (Imp)—established a new, federal Colony within the British Empire. The Commonwealth was established as the national polity, while the six Australian Colonies became integers of the Federation as States, and it was anticipated that new States as well as Territories might later join or form within the union.[175] Legislative power in enumerated areas was conferred on the Commonwealth Parliament, comprising the Queen, a Senate (in which the original States were guaranteed equal representation) and a House of Representatives (elected on the basis of population, originally of States only but from 1922 including also the Northern Territory).[176] Commonwealth legislative power was, in a few instances, exclusive of that of the States but for the most part concurrent with it, though federal law prevailed to the extent of any inconsistency.[177] The new executive government was headed by the Governor-General as the Queen's representative, advised by an Executive Council, and administered by Ministers of State.[178] Judicial power was vested in the High Court and any additional courts the Parliament might create, or in any existing courts in which it might invest federal jurisdiction.[179] Appeals to the Privy Council were, at

[172] See, eg, *Australasian Federation Enabling Act 1895* (NSW), ss 8–15. This was not true of WA, where Parliament elected the representatives, though all electors were eligible for nomination: *Australasian Federation Enabling Act 1896* (WA), ss 7–22.

[173] See, in particular, Quick and Garran (n 27), 150–65.

[174] *Australasian Federation Enabling Act 1895* (NSW), ss 32–35 (as amended by *Australasian Federation Enabling Act Amendment Act of 1897* (NSW), s 2); *Australasian Federation Enabling Act 1899* (NSW), ss 3–7.

[175] *Commonwealth Constitution*, ch VI.

[176] ibid, ss 1, 51–52. A non-voting representative for the NT was established by the *Northern Territory Representation Act 1922* (Cth), ss 3, 5; he was later given the right to vote on disallowing NT Ordinances: *Northern Territory Representation Act 1936* (Cth), s 2.

[177] *Commonwealth Constitution*, ss 52, 109.

[178] ibid, ss 61–64.

[179] ibid, s 71.

the insistence of the Imperial Government,[180] retained, save that appeals concerning the constitutional powers inter se of the integers of the Federation were only permitted on the grant of a certificate by the High Court.[181] Chapter IV of the *Commonwealth Constitution* dealt with finance and trade, facilitating economic as well as political union. Otherwise than in respect of the legislative, executive and judicial powers granted to the Commonwealth, residual authority remained with the States, the constitutions, powers and laws of which were expressly preserved and continued.[182] Amendment of the *Commonwealth Constitution* was, by section 128, vested in the Commonwealth Parliament with the approval, at a referendum, of a majority of electors and a majority of electors in a majority of the States.[183]

The new Commonwealth was still legally a Colony, with all of the attributes that that status entailed. By section 2 of the Colonial Laws Validity Act 1865 (Imp), it could not enact laws repugnant to paramount Imperial laws (those extending to Australia by express words or necessary intendment).[184] Save under those heads of power necessarily implying otherwise,[185] it could not legislate extra-territorially.[186] Its laws were subject, in various instances, to disallowance or reservation[187] and, in exercising (or not) the power to assent, the Governor-General acted as the Imperial Government's representative in Australia and the Queen acted on the advice of the Government in London. The Commonwealth, like the federating Colonies and the States, had no international status or international legal personality distinct from that of the UK sufficient to appoint ambassadors or enter treaties—at least until 1919, when the process of acquiring international legal personality began, with Australia's separate signature of the Treaties of Versailles and of Saint-Germain-en-Laye and its concomitant founding membership of the League of Nations.[188]

180 Quick and Garran (n 27), 242–49.

181 *Commonwealth Constitution*, s 74.

182 ibid, ss 106–108.

183 For the possibility that s 128 is a manner and form provision binding the Westminster Parliament, see JA Thomson, 'Altering the Constitution: Some Aspects of Section 128' (1983) 13 *Federal Law Review* 323, 343–44 and the authorities there cited.

184 *Union Steamship Co of New Zealand Ltd v Commonwealth* (1925) 36 CLR 130 (HCA), 140–41 (Knox CJ), 152 (Isaacs J), 153–54 (Higgins J), 163 (Rich J), 163–64 (Starke J).

185 See, eg, *Commonwealth Constitution*, ss 51(i), 51(xix).

186 *Merchant Service Guild of Australasia v Commonwealth Steamship Owners' Association [No 3]* (1920) 28 CLR 495 (HCA), 503 (Knox CJ, Isaacs, Rich and Starke JJ).

187 See, eg, *Commonwealth Constitution*, ss 59, 74.

188 See *Commonwealth v New South Wales* (1923) 32 CLR 200 (HCA), 218 (Higgins J); *Jolley v Mainka* (1933) 49 CLR 242 (HCA), 281–84 (Evatt J); *Victoria v Commonwealth* (1996) 187 CLR 416 (HCA), 477–78 (Brennan CJ, Toohey, Gaudron, McHugh and Gummow JJ); *Treaty of Peace Act 1919* (Cth), Preamble. Along with Canada, South Africa, New Zealand and India, 'Australia' is indented under the 'British Empire' in the list of original members: *Treaty of Peace between the Allied and Associated Powers and Germany* (Cmd 153, 1919) (entered into force: generally and for Australia 10.01.1920), art 1, pt I, annex, para I; *Treaty of Peace between the Allied and Associated Powers and Austria* (Cmd 400, 1919) (entered into force: generally and for Australia 16.07.1920), art 1, pt I, annex, para I.

Three amendments to the *Commonwealth Constitution* were made during this period. The first was a technical one, providing for Senators' terms to commence on 1 July, better to coincide with elections to the House of Representatives, which were thought most likely to take place in March.[189] Secondly, the Commonwealth's power to take over State debts was extended to debts incurred after Federation.[190] The most significant change, however, was the 1927 Financial Agreement, endorsed through a new section 105A:[191] the Commonwealth took over the public debts and associated liabilities of the States (and the States undertook to make interest payments to the Commonwealth),[192] and the Australian Loan Council was established, with the consequence, in effect, that State Governments could thereafter only borrow money within the States.[193] Some 13 other alterations were approved by the Commonwealth Parliament but failed to secure the necessary majorities at referendum.[194]

Apart from formal constitutional alterations, this period saw a change in constitutional interpretation of permanent significance when, in 1920, the High Court abandoned the 'reserved powers' doctrine. This doctrine had held that Commonwealth legislative powers were to be construed narrowly, to avoid intruding into powers the Court considered to be impliedly reserved to the States. In the *Engineers' Case*, the Court adopted, instead, a principle of literal interpretation, reading the Commonwealth's legislative powers broadly, in light of their ordinary meaning and without reference to an undefined residue of State power.[195] For present purposes, two aspects of the decision are significant. First, the new stance on constitutional interpretation vastly increased the scope of Commonwealth legislative power. Second, as the judge and legal historian Sir Victor Windeyer expresses the point:[196]

> [T]he Constitution was read in a new light, a light reflected from events that had, over 20 years, led to a growing realization that Australians were now one people and Australia one country and that national laws might meet national needs … [T]he *Engineers'* case, looked at as an event in legal and constitutional history, was a consequence of developments that had occurred outside the law courts as well as a cause of further developments there.

[189] *Constitution Alteration (Senate Elections) 1906* (Cth).

[190] *Commonwealth Constitution*, s 105, as amended by *Constitution Alteration (State Debts) 1909* (Cth).

[191] *Constitution Alteration (State Debts) 1928* (Cth).

[192] *Financial Agreement Act 1928* (Cth), sch, pt III, subsequently validated by *Financial Agreement Validation Act 1929* (Cth), s 2.

[193] *Financial Agreement Act 1928* (Cth), sch, pt I, cll 3–5. The terms of the Agreement were subsequently varied on a number of occasions and the international borrowing restrictions were eventually removed: *Financial Agreement Act 1994* (Cth), s 4, sch, item 16(1).

[194] See Commonwealth of Australia, Parliamentary Library, *Parliamentary Handbook of the Commonwealth of Australia*, 31st edn (Canberra, 2008) pt 5.

[195] *Amalgamated Society of Engineers v Adelaide Steamship Co Ltd* (1920) 28 CLR 129 (HCA), 153–54 (Knox CJ, Isaacs, Rich and Starke JJ), 161–62, 164–65 (Higgins J).

[196] *Victoria v The Commonwealth* (1971) 122 CLR 353 (HCA), 396 (footnote omitted). See also Latham (n 101), 563–64.

ii. Statute of Westminster to the Australia Acts

Political developments in the early twentieth century saw the Commonwealth's colonial status diverge rapidly from reality as, along with the other Dominions, it grew in independence both within the Empire and, hastened by its participation in World War I, in the eyes of other nations.[197] As noted above, Australia participated in the 1919 peace treaties; despite some initial doubts about the extent of its sovereignty in international law,[198] by 1923 it was recognised that the Commonwealth could enter international treaties,[199] though the power to declare war and peace was not taken to be possessed separately from the Imperial Government until 1941.[200] Although evolutionary,[201] these political shifts were recognised, in particular, in the 1926 Imperial Conference's Balfour Declaration, according to which the Dominions were, along with the UK, held to be[202]

> autonomous Communities within the British Empire, equal in status, in no way subordinate one to another in any aspect of their domestic or external affairs, though united by a common allegiance to the Crown, and freely associated as members of the British Commonwealth of Nations.

While some changes were effected by intra-Imperial convention or practice within the international community, *legal* changes to the Commonwealth of Australia's colonial status were not effected until the federal Parliament adopted the Statute of Westminster 1931 (Imp) in 1942, with effect retrospective to (the declaration of war with Germany on) 3 September 1939.[203] Section 2 of the Statute, the most important, terminated the application of the paramountcy provision of the Colonial Laws Validity Act 1865 (Imp) in respect of future Commonwealth (but not State) laws. The remainder of

[197] See Imperial War Conference, 1917, *Extracts from Minutes of Proceedings and Papers Laid before the Conference* (Cd 8566, 1917), 5, resolution IX; Conference of the Prime Ministers and Representatives of the United Kingdom, the Dominions, and India, *Summary of Proceedings and Documents* (Cmd 1474, 1921), 14.

[198] Zines (n 158), 376.

[199] Imperial Conference, 1923, *Summary of Proceedings* (Cmd 1987, 1923), 13–15 and see generally A Twomey, 'International Law and the Executive' in BR Opeskin and DR Rothwell (eds), *International Law and Australian Federalism* (Melbourne, Melbourne University Press, 1997) 69, 69–74.

[200] Twomey (n 199), 74–75.

[201] *Kirmani v Captain Cook Cruises Pty Ltd [No 1]* (1985) 159 CLR 351 (HCA), 363 (Gibbs CJ); *Shaw v Minister for Immigration and Multicultural Affairs* [2003] HCA 72, (2003) 218 CLR 28 (HCA), 41 [24] (Gleeson CJ, Gummow and Hayne JJ); L Zines, *Constitutional change in the Commonwealth* (Cambridge, CUP, 1991), 1–2.

[202] Imperial Conference, 1926, *Summary of Proceedings* (Cmd 2768, 1926), 14.

[203] Statute of Westminster 1931 (Imp), s 10; *Statute of Westminster Adoption Act 1942* (Cth), s 3. Revealing the contemporary relationship between the Imperial and Commonwealth governments in foreign affairs, the Australian Prime Minister announced on that occasion that 'Great Britain has declared war upon [Germany] and that, as a result, Australia is also at war': National Film and Sound Archive, 'Menzies Speech: Declaration of War' (*NFSA title number 188388*, 03.09.1939), available at <http://aso.gov.au/titles/radio/menzies-speech-declaration-war>.

the Statute largely reflected changes that had already emerged by way of convention:[204] section 3 confirmed the Commonwealth Parliament's extra-territorial legislative competence; section 4 declared that the Imperial Parliament would no longer legislate for the Commonwealth otherwise than at its request and consent; and sections 5 and 6 freed the Commonwealth from certain restrictions relating to merchant shipping and courts of admiralty. Since, however, the Statute did not amend or repeal the *Commonwealth Constitution* or the Commonwealth of Australia Constitution Act 1900 (Imp), certain colonial-status limitations contained in those instruments continued to apply, notably in relation to disallowance and reservation. The important difference, however, was that the King was, in relation to these powers, thenceforth to be advised by ministers of the Commonwealth, not the Imperial, Government.[205] In accordance with this altered constitutional convention, the King was reluctantly obliged to appoint as Governor-General the sole nominee of his Australian Prime Minister, despite His Majesty's own misgivings in principle about appointing an Australian rather than an ostensibly more neutral Englishman.[206]

The significance of these developments in the Commonwealth's status as a Dominion after the Statute of Westminster 1931 (Imp) had already been revealed in relation to Western Australia's 1934 attempt to secede, a matter touching on both State and federal constitutional history and on broader considerations of community: 'it challenges dearly held beliefs about Australian nationalism, unity and destiny'.[207] Although discussed in State Parliament as early as 1906,[208] the secession movement in Western Australia crystallised in the referendum conducted on 8 April 1933,[209] at which the electors voted at a ratio of almost 2:1 in favour of secession.[210] The Western Australia Parliamentary Committee that prepared an address to His Majesty and petitions to the Imperial Parliament explained in its 489-page supplement:[211]

> The main reasons by which His Majesty's subjects in Western Australia are constrained to secede from the Commonwealth, and to resume the position which they previously enjoyed as a self-governing unit within the British Empire, are

[204] Zines (n 201), 5.

[205] Imperial Conference (n 202), 16; Imperial Conference, 1930, *Summary of Proceedings* (Cmd 3717, 1930), 26–27; Zines (n 201), 24.

[206] See RG Menzies, *Afternoon Light* (London, Cassell, 1967) 251–52; H Nicolson, *King George the Fifth: His Life and Reign* (London, Constable & Co, 1952) 477–82.

[207] GJ Craven, 'A Few Fragments of State Constitutional Law' (1990) 20 *University of Western Australia Law Review* 353, 365.

[208] Western Australia, Parliament, *The Case of the People of Western Australia* (Perth, Government Printer, 1934) 376–93 [592]–[631].

[209] Pursuant to *Secession Referendum Act 1932* (WA).

[210] 138,653 electors voted for secession and 70, 706 against: Western Australia, Parliament (n 208), 391 [625].

[211] ibid, 328 [522].

> that the combined effects of an Australian protective customs tariff and of free trade between the States of the Commonwealth, have inflicted grave injustice, great hardship, and severe distress upon the people of Western Australia; that the result of the combined effects of Australian protection and interstate free trade are such as to have most seriously endangered the whole economic structure and social fabric of the State; and that adequate and necessary relief from the ill effects of Australian protection and interstate free trade as aforesaid, cannot be obtained by the people of Western Australia otherwise than by their withdrawal from the Commonwealth.

The address and petitions themselves further referred to factors differentially and adversely affecting Western Australia, including its geographical isolation, the expansive interpretation of Commonwealth powers and the general centralisation of Australian government at Canberra.[212]

Western Australia's case for secession was by no means trivial or fanciful, as is indicated by the popular support at the referendum and by the sympathies of two of the other smaller States, Tasmania and South Australia[213]—though Western Australia electors, at the same time as approving the referendum on secession, voted in an anti-secession Premier.[214] Nonetheless, the new Government respected the referendum result and the Parliament enacted the *Secession Act 1934* (WA), authorising the address to His Majesty and petitions to each House of the Imperial Parliament seeking Imperial legislation to separate Western Australia from the Commonwealth and erect it as a self-governing Dominion. However, as Besant explains,[215] the import of the Imperial constitutional convention confining the Westminster Parliament's exercise of its undoubted legal powers in relation to Dominions—even before the Commonwealth adopted the Statute of Westminster 1931 (Imp)—had not been appreciated. The Houses of the Westminster Parliament, in what seems to be a move orchestrated by the Imperial Government,[216] decided, before receiving the petitions, to enquire into the preliminary question of the propriety of receiving them, having regard to constitutional practice and principle.[217] A Joint Select Committee, after hearing extensive legal argument from counsel for Western Australia and for the Commonwealth, affirmed in 1935 that secession was solely within the power of the Imperial Parliament, but also affirmed the existence of a constitutional convention according to

212 *Secession Act 1934* (WA), sch 2, item 15(e).

213 CW Besant, 'Two Nations, Two Destinies: A Reflection on the Significance of the Western Australian Secession Movement to Australia, Canada and the British Empire' (1990) 20 *University of Western Australia Law Review* 209, 216.

214 ibid, 214–15.

215 ibid, 237–49.

216 ibid, 258.

217 Joint Committee appointed to consider the petition of the State of Western Australia (n 130), vi [1]–[2].

which that Parliament would not interfere in the affairs of a Dominion or self-governing Colony otherwise than at the request of the Government or Parliament of the relevant Dominion or Colony.[218] Since the Imperial Parliament was being asked to amend the Commonwealth of Australia Constitution Act 1900 (Imp), the request could not properly come from Western Australia but ought to come from the Commonwealth, as the polity primarily concerned.[219] With the Imperial Parliament thus refusing to engage with the subject, agitation rapidly died out (despite some calls for unilateral secession),[220] and half a century was to pass before a self-determination referendum in Australia succeeded with legal effect.[221] Considered from the perspective of elucidating the constitutional relationship between the Empire and Australia, the Joint Committee's report has been described as a 'Declaration of Australian Independence'.[222]

In terms of formal constitutional alterations, Commonwealth legislative power in relation to welfare programmes was expanded by the insertion of section 51(xxiiiA) in 1946, after the High Court held the *Pharmaceutical Benefits Act 1944* (Cth) ultra vires.[223] In 1967, the restriction on the Commonwealth Parliament's power to make laws for Aboriginal people under section 51(xxvi) was removed, and the exclusion of Aboriginal people from being counted in determining population was repealed.[224] The last successful referenda were held in 1977. In the aftermath of the 1975 constitutional crisis, amendments to section 15 of the *Commonwealth Constitution* ensured that casual Senate vacancies would be filled from the same party as the out-going Senators (and that the replacements would serve out the remainder of the out-going Senators' terms).[225] Section 128 was amended to permit residents of Territories represented in the House of Representatives to vote in future referenda.[226] Finally, section 72 was amended to impose a compulsory retirement age of 70 for federal judges (or, in the case of courts other than the High Court, such lower age as the Parliament might prescribe).[227]

Beyond formal constitutional alterations, several High Court decisions in this period had significant consequences for the relationship between Commonwealth and State law. The States' financial autonomy (and consequently also, in some measure, their political independence), already

[218] ibid, viii [6]–[7].
[219] ibid, viii–ix [8]–[9].
[220] Besant (n 213), 294–99.
[221] In the Territory of Cocos (Keeling) Islands: below, n 440.
[222] Besant (n 213), 310.
[223] *Attorney-General (Victoria) v Commonwealth* (1945) 71 CLR 237 (HCA).
[224] *Constitution Alteration (Aboriginals) 1967* (Cth).
[225] *Constitution Alteration (Senate Casual Vacancies) 1977* (Cth).
[226] *Constitution Alteration (Referendums) 1977* (Cth).
[227] *Constitution Alteration (Retirement of Judges) 1977* (Cth).

restricted by the Loan Council arrangements agreed in the 1927 Financial Agreement, was essentially ended when, after World War II, the Court construed the Commonwealth's powers to tax and to make conditional grants to the States under sections 51(ii) and 96 of the *Commonwealth Constitution* in such a way as to deny the States, in political effect, the power to levy income tax, and to accord the Commonwealth virtually unlimited power to impose conditions on its grants to the States.[228] In 1948, the Commonwealth granted representation in the House of Representatives to electors in the Australian Capital Territory (here defined to include the Jervis Bay Territory) on the same limited basis as the Northern Territory.[229] Voting rights for Territory members were expanded in 1959 to all matters connected with their Territories,[230] and to full rights shortly after that.[231] In 1974, the two Territories were granted two Senators each.[232]

iii. After the Australia Acts

The principal focus of the *Australia Acts* was the States.[233] Nonetheless, Imperial connections with the Commonwealth were also severed: section 1 terminated altogether (prospectively) the Westminster Parliament's competence to legislate for the Commonwealth and the Territories as well as the States, and section 12 repealed the provisions of the Statute of Westminster 1931 (Imp) that had preserved that Parliament's competence to legislate at the request and consent of the Commonwealth.

The question of the legal source of authority for the *Commonwealth Constitution* (and, by analogy, for the State Constitutions) following the *Australia Acts* has been much debated.[234] As Lindell explains, while an

[228] See *South Australia v Commonwealth* (1942) 65 CLR 373 (HCA); *Victoria v Commonwealth* (1957) 99 CLR 575 (HCA); Zines (n 158), 483–86.

[229] *Australian Capital Territory Representation Act 1948* (Cth), ss 4, 6.

[230] *Australian Capital Territory Representation Act 1959* (Cth), s 3; *Australian Capital Territory Representation Act (No 2) 1959* (Cth), s 3; *Northern Territory Representation Act 1959* (Cth), s 3.

[231] *Australian Capital Territory Representation Act 1966* (Cth), s 3; *Northern Territory Representation Act 1968* (Cth), s 4.

[232] *Senate (Representation of Territories) Act 1973* (Cth), s 4, later upheld in *Western Australia v Commonwealth* (1975) 134 CLR 201 (HCA); *Queensland v Commonwealth* (1977) 139 CLR 585 (HCA).

[233] As to which Act is operative in Australian law, see above, text to nn 157–63.

[234] See, eg, GG Winterton, 'The Acquisition of Independence' in R French, G Lindell and C Saunders (eds), *Reflections on the Australian Constitution* (Annandale, NSW, Federation Press, 2003) 31; G Lindell, 'Further Reflections on the Date of the Acquisition of Australia's Independence' in R French, G Lindell and C Saunders (eds), *Reflections on the Australian Constitution* (Annandale, NSW, Federation Press, 2003) 51; RD Lumb, 'Fundamental Law and the Processes of Constitutional Change in Australia' (1978) 9 *Federal Law Review* 148; G Lindell, 'Why is Australia's Constitution Binding?—The Reasons in 1900 and Now, and the Effect of Independence' (1986) 16 *Federal Law Review* 29; GG Winterton, 'Extra-Constitutional Notions in Australian Constitutional Law' (1986) 16 *Federal Law Review* 223; M Moshinsky, 'Re-Enacting the Constitution in an Australian Act' (1989) 18 *Federal Law Review* 134;

explanation based on the legal authority of the Imperial Parliament at the relevant times continues to be sound, a desire to distance present realities from Australia's colonial past has led to calls for an alternative account, by reference to popular participation in the adoption of the *Commonwealth Constitution* and subsequent acquiescence in its operation as fundamental law.[235] Though it is reflected in opinions of some High Court judges,[236] others have differed,[237] and this view has never (at least in our period) been adopted as such in Australian law.

Of practical as well as theoretical significance is a final post-1986 development: the High Court's decision that '[t]here is but one common law in Australia which is declared by this Court as the final court of appeal'.[238] Though a single common law had been suggested from early on,[239] the possibility that there was a separate federal common law, or that the common law was institutionally distinct from State to State,[240] was put to rest only when the Privy Council ceased[241] to be part of the hierarchy of Australian courts.[242] An important concomitant of the Court's recognition of a single common law in *Lange* was the affirmation that '[t]he Constitution, the federal, State and territorial laws, and the common law in Australia together constitute the law of this country and form "one system

GG Winterton, 'Popular Sovereignty and Constitutional Continuity' (1998) 26 *Federal Law Review* 1; N Aroney, 'A Public Choice? Federalism and the Prospects of a Republican Preamble' (1999) 20 *University of Queensland Law Journal* 262; A Dillon, 'A Turtle by Any Other Name: The Legal Basis of the Australian Constitution' (2001) 29 *Federal Law Review* 241. These and other relevant sources are discussed in PC Oliver, *The Constitution of Independence: the Development of Constitutional Theory in Australia, Canada, and New Zealand* (Oxford, OUP, 2005) 266–78; Twomey (n 123), 423–32.

[235] Lindell, 'Why is Australia's Constitution Binding?—The Reasons in 1900 and Now, and the Effect of Independence' (n 234), 37.

[236] *Kirmani v Captain Cook Cruises Pty Ltd [No 1]* (1985) 159 CLR 351 (HCA), 383 (Murphy J), 410 (Brennan J), 442 (Deane J); *Australian Capital Television Pty Ltd v Commonwealth* (1992) 177 CLR 106 (HCA), 138 (Mason CJ); *Ridgeway v The Queen* (1994) 184 CLR 19 (HCA), 91 (McHugh J); *McGinty v Western Australia* (1996) 186 CLR 140 (HCA), 230, 237 (McHugh J). See also *Bistricic v Rokov* (1976) 135 CLR 552 (HCA), 566–67 (Murphy J); *China Ocean Shipping Co v South Australia* (1979) 145 CLR 172 (HCA), 236–37 (Murphy J).

[237] See, eg, *Australian Capital Television Pty Ltd v Commonwealth* (1992) 177 CLR 106 (HCA), 181 (Dawson J).

[238] *Lange v Australian Broadcasting Corporation* (1997) 189 CLR 520 (HCA), 563 (Brennan CJ, Dawson, Toohey, Gaudron, McHugh, Gummow and Kirby JJ). See further: *Lipohar v The Queen* [1999] HCA 65, (1999) 200 CLR 485 (HCA), 505–10 [43]–[59] (Gaudron, Gummow and Hayne JJ).

[239] See, eg, *R v Kidman* (1915) 20 CLR 425 (HCA), 435–36 (Griffith CJ).

[240] See K Foley, 'The Australian Constitution's Influence on the Common Law' (2003) 31 *Federal Law Review* 131, 132–35 and the references there cited.

[241] Subject to the continued existence of *Commonwealth Constitution*, s 74: above, n 138.

[242] *Kable v Director of Public Prosecutions (NSW)* (1996) 189 CLR 51 (HCA), 113–14 (McHugh J), 138 (Gummow J).

of jurisprudence"',[243] though this statement was made in the context of affirming that the Commonwealth and the States were not, inter se, to be understood as foreign or independent countries.[244]

C. Enacting Formulae

In the thirteenth century, the King initiated and enacted laws with the *advice* of Parliament.[245] As Holdsworth says, it was 'only gradually and in consequence of the growing importance of Parliament that a statute comes to be regarded as an enactment of the king and Parliament'.[246] Stubbs traces the evolution of the enacting words—'*petition*' of the Commons, '*assent* of the prelates, dukes, earls, barons and at the *insistence* and special *request* of the commons', '*by the advice and assent* of the lords spiritual and temporal, *and at the prayer* of the commons'—until the phrase 'by the authority of Parliament' becomes standard from 1445.[247] The formula still used by the Westminster Parliament is recognisable in the first Act of Henry VII's reign:[248]

> THE King ... at his Parliament holden at *Westminster* ... by the Assent of the Lords Spiritual and Temporal, and the Commons, in the said Parliament assembled, and by Authority of the said Parliament ...

The enacting formula thus expresses 'the Act's nature as a command of the sovereign legislature, namely the Queen in Parliament'.[249] The linguistic form 'be it enacted' may have its origins as a response to petitions to the King, but the jussive imperative now performs a 'certificatory

[243] *Lange v Australian Broadcasting Corporation* (1997) 189 CLR 520 (HCA), 564 (Brennan CJ, Dawson, Toohey, Gaudron, McHugh, Gummow and Kirby JJ), referring to *McArthur v Williams* (1936) 55 CLR 324 (HCA), 347 (Starke J); *Thompson v The Queen* (1989) 169 CLR 1 (HCA), 34–35 (Deane J) and also noting Commonwealth of Australia Constitution Act 1900 (Imp), s 5. The idea of an integrated Australian legal system was also expressed in *Fencott v Muller* (1983) 152 CLR 570 (HCA), 607 (Mason, Murphy, Brennan and Deane JJ); *Kable v Director of Public Prosecutions (NSW)* (1996) 189 CLR 51 (HCA), 102 (Gaudron J), 114 (McHugh J), 137–39 (Gummow J).

[244] A somewhat oblique provision preserving the 'continuity of the federal system, including the unified system of law, under this Constitution' also featured in the unsuccessful 1999 referendum proposing the establishment of a Republic: Constitution Alteration (Establishment of Republic) Bill 1999 (Cth), sch 3, item 6.

[245] W Holdsworth, *A History of English Law*, vol 2, 4th edn (London, Methuen, 1936), 435.

[246] ibid, 437.

[247] W Stubbs, *The Constitutional History of England*, vol 3, first published Clarendon Press 1897, 5th edn (New York, Barnes & Noble, 1967), 481–83 [441] (emphasis added). See also Holdsworth, *A History of English Law* (n 245), 438–40.

[248] Real Actions Act 1485 (Eng).

[249] FAR Bennion, *Bennion on Statutory Interpretation*, 5th edn (London, LexisNexis, 2008) 744.

function', meaning, '"Let it be recognized as having been enacted ..."'.[250] However, the enacting words are no mere ornament: they still represent the constitutional allocation of legislative power: 'the threefold expression of assent, advice, and authority may be regarded as the declaration of the function of the estates in legislation'.[251] Those who support popular sovereignty advocate the omission of the monarch from the legislative process.[252] In certifying the participation (*consent* not merely *advice*) of the appropriate actors, the enacting formula reveals central features of the legal system to which the law belongs and relates.

That this function has continuing relevance and is not merely an 'old fiction ... a venerable sham'[253] or an 'ancient form of servility'[254] is evident in the Scottish context. Power to make laws, known as 'Acts of the Scottish Parliament', is vested in the Scottish Parliament, which, critically (and unlike Australian Parliaments), does not include the Queen as an integer. However, Bills passed by the Parliament do not become Acts until they have received Royal Assent.[255] Expressing this relationship in an enacting formula resembling the traditional model is problematic,[256] and Acts of the Scottish Parliament in fact bear not enacting words but a simple declaration (clearly certificatory rather than performative) that 'The Bill for this Act of the Scottish Parliament was passed by the Parliament on [*date*] and received Royal Assent on [*date*]'.

i. New South Wales

The formulae used in early Acts of the Governor and Council in New South Wales vary somewhat along the following basic[257] pattern:[258]

> Now therefore be it [ordained and[259]] enacted, by [His Excellency] [Sir Thomas Brisbane,[260]] the Governor of [the Colony of[261]] New South Wales [*or* of the said Colony[262]], with the Advice of the Council

[250] BS Jackson, 'Who Enacts Statutes?' (1997) 18 *Statute Law Review* 177, 179–81.

[251] Stubbs (n 247), 482 [441].

[252] Carney (n 2), 32. This is already the case in the ACT: *Australian Capital Territory (Self-Government) Act 1988* (Cth), ss 8(2), 22(1); *Legislation Act 2001* (ACT), s 28.

[253] JO Pierce, 'Constitutional Phases of English History in the Seventeenth Century' (1903) 37 *American Law Review* 26, 32.

[254] WL Martin, 'The British Constitution' (1904) 12 *American Lawyer* 179, 200.

[255] Scotland Act 1998 (UK), s 28(1)–(2).

[256] See E Clive, 'Law-Making in Scotland: From APS to ASP' (1999) 3 *Edinburgh Law Review* 131, 137–39.

[257] Some Acts show greater variation: eg, the *Currency Act 1824* (NSW) simply provides 'Now therefore it is hereby enacted'.

[258] See, eg, *Male Convicts Punishment Act 1825* (NSW).

[259] See, eg, *Justices Indemnity Act 1825* (NSW).

[260] See, eg, *Deeds Registration Act 1825* (NSW). His Excellency appears to be the only Governor so named.

[261] See, eg, *Postage Act 1825* (NSW).

[262] See, eg, *Puisne Judge Act 1825* (NSW).

With the arrival of Governor Darling, the Council is frequently (but not consistently) accorded an active, rather than merely an advisory role, albeit elusively phrased ('by and with the advice'):[263]

> Be it therefore enacted by His Excellency the Governor of New South Wales *by and with* the advice of the Legislative Council

In the latter part of Governor Bourke's tenure, the Council's role is occasionally further emphasised:[264]

> Be it therefore enacted and declared, by His Excellency the Governor of New South Wales, with the advice *and consent* of the Legislative Council thereof

In 1855, the year before fully representative and responsible self-government was instituted, 'advice and consent' standardly appears in the enacting formula, but the prepositional phrase is more commonly 'with' than 'by and with'.[265] With the coming into force of the new constitution and its bicameral legislature, the enacting formula (after a couple of minor variations very early on) settled into the pattern it was to follow for over 130 years:[266]

> Be it [therefore] enacted by the Queen's Most Excellent Majesty by and with the advice and consent of the Legislative Council and Legislative Assembly of New South Wales in Parliament assembled and by the authority of the same, as follows:–

The substitution of the Queen for the Governor is a notable change, reflecting the enhanced status of the now fully representative and responsible legislature.[267] As part of the 1933 reforms relating to disagreement between the Council and the Assembly over supply Bills and deadlocks in relation to other Bills, section 5C was inserted into the *Constitution Act 1902* (NSW),[268] expressly providing that the formulae to be used in those situations would be:[269]

> BE it enacted by the King's Most Excellent Majesty, by and with the advice and consent of the Legislative Assembly of New South Wales in Parliament assembled, in accordance with the provisions of section 5A of the *Constitution Act 1902*, as amended by subsequent Acts, and by the authority of the same, as follows:

and:[270]

> BE it enacted by the King's Most Excellent Majesty, by and with the advice and consent of the Legislative Assembly of New South Wales in Parliament

[263] See, eg, *Hulks Regulation Act 1826* (NSW) (emphasis added).
[264] See, eg, *Sydney Jury Lists Act 1834* (NSW) (emphasis added).
[265] Some 23 Acts in 1855 use 'with' and 18 'by and with'.
[266] See, eg, *Constitution Act Amendment Act 1857* (NSW).
[267] Jenks (n 48), 238, cited in Twomey (n 52), 165. The change was not universal: Tasmanian laws are still (in 2015) enacted by the Governor, not the Queen.
[268] *Constitution Amendment (Legislative Council) Act 1932* (NSW), s 5.
[269] *Constitution Act 1902* (NSW), s 5C(1).
[270] ibid, s 5C(2).

> assembled, with the approval of the electors, in accordance with the provisions of section 5B of the *Constitution Act 1902*, as amended by subsequent Acts, and by the authority of the same, as follows:

There has been no cause for any save the first of these formulae to be employed.[271] Its use in 1996 was an exception to the language of the formula currently used, which appeared for the first time in September 1987:[272]

> The Legislature of New South Wales enacts:

This formula does not appear consistently until November 1987:[273] seven Acts in the intervening period use the old formula, while 12 use the new formula, presumably as a result of the time at which the relevant Bill was prepared. The change, which reflects the constitutional definition of the 'Legislature',[274] seems to have been made by the Government, and although a question was raised about it in Parliament, no answer appears to have been given.[275]

While constitutional amendments that do not need approval at a referendum use the new formula,[276] those that do require submission to the electors[277] retain the older language:[278]

> BE it enacted by the Queen's Most Excellent Majesty, by and with the advice and consent of the Legislative Council and Legislative Assembly of New South Wales in Parliament assembled, with the approval of the electors as required by the Constitution Act 1902, and by the authority of the same, as follows:

ii. Commonwealth

The proper enacting formula was the subject of considerable discussion at the first session of the Commonwealth Parliament. There was support for the straightforward 'Parliament' or 'Parliament [of the Commonwealth] of Australia'—for brevity, to reflect section 1 of the *Commonwealth Constitution* and to avoid according preference to one House by naming it before

[271] *Appropriation (Parliament) Act 1996* (NSW). Whether or not invalidity would result from the failure to employ the appropriate formula is a separate question (answered differently in different US States: see, eg, JG Sutherland, *Statutes and Statutory Construction*,vol I, 2nd edn (J Lewis ed, Chicago, Ill, Callaghan & Co, 1904) 115–22, §§69–72). That invalidity would follow from non-compliance with s 5C has been doubted: Carney (n 2), 95.

[272] *Supply Act 1987* (NSW).

[273] With and from the *Tow Truck Industry Act 1987* (NSW); the last Act to use the old formula was the *Non-Indigenous Animals Act 1987* (NSW).

[274] *Constitution Act 1902* (NSW), s 3.

[275] New South Wales, *Parliamentary Debates* (Legislative Council, 10.11.1987), 15548 (Hon Marie Bignold).

[276] See, eg, *Constitution (Legislative Assembly) Amendment Act 1990* (NSW).

[277] See, eg, by virtue of *Constitution Act 1902* (NSW), s 7A or 7B.

[278] See, eg, *Constitution (Legislative Council) Amendment Act 1991* (NSW), remarked upon in *Bignold v Dickson* (1991) 23 NSWLR 683 (CA), 690 (Kirby P).

the other.[279] Ultimately, because of its closer resemblance to the traditional form and to the language of the *Commonwealth Constitution*,[280] because it was thought to possess 'more dignity and more of a sonorous ring',[281] and because it allowed flexibility in the case of measures not assented to by both Houses or that required the additional approval of the electors, Commonwealth Attorney-General Alfred Deakin[282] preferred the formula that was, in the event, employed in ordinary legislation until 1972:[283]

> BE it [therefore[284]] enacted by the King's Most Excellent Majesty, the Senate, and the House of Representatives of the Commonwealth as follows:–

In fact, the formula used in the very first Act differed because, until the twenty-fourth Parliament, following British practice, an additional clause was included in appropriation Acts to reflect sections 53 and 54 of the *Commonwealth Constitution*.[285] Thus, the following formula was used in appropriation Acts from 1901 until the three Acts to which assent was given on 28 May 1963,[286] after which the standard enacting formula was used for appropriations,[287] too:[288]

> BE it enacted by the King's Most Excellent Majesty, the Senate, and the House of Representatives of the Commonwealth of Australia, for the purpose of appropriating the grant originated in the House of Representatives, as follows:–

As foreshadowed by Deakin, the formula was also differenced for constitutional alterations:[289]

> BE it enacted by the King's Most Excellent Majesty, the Senate, and the House of Representatives of the Commonwealth of Australia, with the approval of the electors, as required by the Constitution, as follows:–

[279] Commonwealth of Australia, *Parliamentary Debates* (Senate, 19.06.1901), 1192–98.

[280] WH Moore, 'The Australian Commonwealth Constitution, 1901–2' (1903) 5 *Journal of the Society of Comparative Legislation* 115, 118.

[281] Commonwealth of Australia, *Parliamentary Debates* (House of Representatives, 13.06.1901), 1080 (Mr McCay).

[282] Commonwealth of Australia, *Parliamentary Debates* (House of Representatives, 11.06.1901), 846–47. See also Commonwealth of Australia, *Parliamentary Debates* (House of Representatives, 12.06.1901), 1021–22; Commonwealth of Australia, *Parliamentary Debates* (House of Representatives, 13.06.1901), 1079–80.

[283] *Property for Public Purposes Acquisition Act 1901* (Cth). For an earlier variation omitting punctuation, see the *Acts Interpretation Act 1901* (Cth).

[284] Where the Act included a preamble: see, eg, *Naval Agreement Act 1903* (Cth).

[285] Commonwealth of Australia, *Parliamentary Debates* (House of Representatives, 14.06.1901) 1190; Commonwealth of Australia, *Parliamentary Debates* (House of Representatives, 21.06.1901) 1473–75. See also Moore, 'The Australian Commonwealth Constitution, 1901–2' (n 280), 119–20.

[286] *Processed Milk Products Bounty Act 1963* (Cth); *Supply Act 1963–64* (Cth); *Supply (Works and Services) Act 1963–64* (Cth).

[287] See, eg, the *Appropriation Act 1963–64* (Cth).

[288] *Governor-General's Establishment Act 1902* (Cth). For an earlier variation omitting punctuation and including 'and' after 'Majesty', see Act No 1 of 1901, the *Consolidated Revenue* (1901) (Cth).

[289] *Constitution Alteration (Senate Elections) 1906* (Cth).

In January 1973,[290] as part of a wide-ranging programme to substitute the word 'Australia' for 'Commonwealth', the Whitlam Government adopted a new formula:[291]

> BE IT [THEREFORE][292] ENACTED by the Queen, the Senate and the House of Representatives of Australia as follows:–

Deakin's more flexible formula having been abandoned, in contrast to British practice in the case of extraordinary legislative process,[293] there was no reference to the joint sitting or to section 57 of the *Commonwealth Constitution* in the enacting formula of Acts passed pursuant to the deadlock-resolution provision in 1974.[294]

Whitlam's change was, however short-lived.[295] While not wholly reversing the 1973 changes, the Fraser Government, over Whitlam's objections,[296] revived reference to 'the Commonwealth' from 1976:[297]

> BE IT [THEREFORE][298] ENACTED by the Queen, and the Senate and House of Representatives of the Commonwealth of Australia, as follows:–

An equivalent formula was used in the three constitutional alterations of 1977:[299]

> BE IT ENACTED by the Queen, and the Senate and House of Representatives of the Commonwealth of Australia, with the approval of the electors, as required by the Constitution, as follows:–

[290] The last Act to employ this formula was the *Repatriation (Torres Straight Islanders) Act 1972* (Cth).

[291] *Social Services Act 1973* (Cth).

[292] See, eg, *Royal Style and Titles Act 1973* (Cth).

[293] The formula used, eg, in the Hunting Act 2004 (UK) is 'BE IT ENACTED by The Queen's most Excellent Majesty, by and with the advice and consent of the Commons in this present Parliament assembled, in accordance with the provisions of the Parliament Acts 1911 and 1949, and by the authority of the same, as follows:–'. The words are substituted by the Clerk of the Parliaments in pursuance of the Parliament Acts 1911 and 1949 (UK), s 4(1): see Jackson (n 250), 186–88, 207.

[294] See *Commonwealth Electoral Act (No 2) 1973* (Cth); *Health Insurance Act 1973* (Cth); *Health Insurance Commission Act 1973* (Cth); *Representation Act 1973* (Cth); *Senate (Representation of Territories) Act 1973* (Cth); *Petroleum and Minerals Authority Act 1973* (Cth). This was remarked upon in *Victoria v Commonwealth* (1975) 134 CLR 81 (HCA), 139 (Gibbs J).

[295] The last Act to employ this formula was the *Captains Flat (Abatement of Pollution) Agreement Act 1975* (Cth).

[296] Commonwealth of Australia, *Parliamentary Debates* (House of Representatives, 25.02.1976), 282–83 (Mr Whitlam), 287–88 (Mr Ruddock), 290 (Mr Ellicott).

[297] *National Health Act 1976* (Cth).

[298] See, eg, *Australia (Request and Consent) Act 1985* (Cth).

[299] *Constitution Alteration (Referendums) 1977* (Cth); *Constitution Alteration (Retirement of Judges) 1977* (Cth); *Constitution Alteration (Senate Casual Vacancies) 1977* (Cth).

In November 1990, again as the result of an executive Government decision, without consultation with Parliament,[300] the current formula appeared for the first time:[301]

> The Parliament of Australia [therefore[302]] enacts:

This rather terse formula does not appear consistently until March 1991:[303] 50 Acts in the intervening period use the old formula, compared to 39 using the new formula, again presumably as a result of the time at which the relevant Bill was prepared. While there have been no constitutional alterations since 1977, Government Bills for such alterations adopt the new form, mutatis mutandis:[304]

> The Parliament of Australia, with the approval of the electors, as required by the Constitution, enacts:

D. Seals and Royal Title

From the time of Edward the Confessor, the great seal has been used 'to testify the royal will in the administration of justice, and in all matters of government'.[305] Closely connected with seals, since it figures prominently on them, is the royal title. Maitland reminds us that the seals are not 'mere ceremonial symbols like the crown and the sceptre; they are real instruments of government':[306] in English (and Australian) constitutional practice, certain acts may only be effected by document under seal. The practice followed until the late nineteenth century—by which a document signed with the Royal Sign Manual and countersigned by the Secretary of State authorised a document to be issued under the privy seal, which in turn instructed the Lord Chancellor to issue a document under the great seal—furnished the 'foundation' of ministerial responsibility.[307] Thus, with reference to two of the senses of 'the Crown' that the High Court

[300] Commonwealth of Australia, *Parliamentary Debates* (House of Representatives, 07.11.1990), 3426 (Mr Peacock); Commonwealth of Australia, *Parliamentary Debates* (Senate, 15.11.1990), 4371–72 (Senator Tambling); Commonwealth of Australia, *Parliamentary Debates* (Senate, 09.09.1992), 616 (Senator Watson).

[301] *Wool Tax (No 1) Further Amendment Act 1990* (Cth).

[302] See, eg, *Native Title Act 1993* (Cth).

[303] With and from the *Loan Act 1991* (Cth), to which assent was given on the same day as the last Act to use the old formula, the *Family Law Amendment Act 1991* (Cth).

[304] See, eg, Constitution Alteration (Establishment of Republic) Bill 1999 (Cth).

[305] J Campbell, *The Lives of the Lord Chancellors and Keepers of the Great Seal of England*, vol 1 (London, John Murray, 1845) 35.

[306] FW Maitland, *The Constitutional History of England* (Cambridge, CUP, 1908) 393.

[307] ibid, 203. See now Great Seal Act 1884 (UK), in particular, s 2(1).

has identified, the seal is an indication of the 'body politic'[308] concerned in an act, and the countersignature, by revealing the (member of the) government responsible for advising the monarch, indicates 'the capacity in which the Sovereign acts'.[309]

New South Wales, like the other Colonies, had its own great seal from the very beginning,[310] as did the Commonwealth.[311] These were, then, distinct bodies politic (the latter including members that were themselves bodies politic[312]).[313] However, it was not until 1926 in relation to the Commonwealth[314] and, as Twomey demonstrates,[315] not until 1986 in relation to the States[316] that local ministers advised the monarch in place of the Government in London. Thus, until then, while Governors-General and Governors generally affixed the (great or public) seals of their polities on the advice and with the countersignature of their local ministers,[317] the instruments appointing those vice-regal officers were made under the great seal of the UK, and the warrants under the Royal Sign Manual, using the UK version of the royal title, were countersigned by ministers of the Government in London.[318]

The royal title and the legislative bodies assenting to its amendment are a further legal reflection of the factual notion of community. Shortly after New South Wales was established, George III adopted the royal style and title 'George the Third by the Grace of God of the United Kingdom of Great Britain and Ireland King, Defender of the Faith'.[319] In 1876, when assuming the government of India from the East India Company, Queen Victoria adopted, for use outside the UK, the additional title 'Empress of

[308] *Sue v Hill* [1999] HCA 30, (1999) 199 CLR 462 (HCA), 498 [84] (Gleeson CJ, Gummow and Hayne JJ).

[309] Twomey (n 91), 748, describing the sense identified in *Sue v Hill* [1999] HCA 30, (1999) 199 CLR 462 (HCA), 499–500 [88] (Gleeson CJ, Gummow and Hayne JJ).

[310] Commission (02.04.1787) (n 9), 63.

[311] Letters Patent constituting the Office of the Governor-General and Commander-in-Chief of the Commonwealth of Australia (29.10.1900) (Imp) in Statute Law Committee (ed) (n 106), cl 2.

[312] FW Maitland, 'The Crown as Corporation' (1901) 17 *LQR* 131, 144.

[313] *Commonwealth v New South Wales* (1906) 3 CLR 807 (HCA), 813–14 (Griffith CJ); *Sue v Hill* [1999] HCA 30, (1999) 199 CLR 462 (HCA), 500–502 [89]–[91] (Gleeson CJ, Gummow and Hayne JJ).

[314] Imperial Conference, 1926, *Summary of Proceedings* (n 202), 17. See also Imperial Conference, 1930, *Summary of Proceedings* (n 205), 27.

[315] Twomey (n 91), 752–59.

[316] *Australia Act 1986* (Cth), ss 7, 13, 14; Australia Act 1986 (Imp), ss 7, 13, 14.

[317] *Amalgamated Society of Engineers v Adelaide Steamship Co Ltd* (1920) 28 CLR 129 (HCA), 152 (Knox CJ, Isaacs, Rich and Starke JJ). See, eg, New South Wales Constitution Act 1855 (Imp), sch 1, s 2.

[318] See Twomey (n 91), 754.

[319] A Proclamation (01.01.1801) (Imp) in A Pulling (ed), *Statutory rules and orders other than those of a local, personal, or temporary character, issued prior to 1890, and now in force*, vol I (London, HMSO, 1891), pursuant to Union with Ireland Act 1808 (Imp), s 1, art 1.

India'.[320] In 1901, Edward VII recognised the Dominions by adding (after 'Ireland') 'and of the British Dominions beyond the Seas'.[321] In 1927, on the recommendation of the Imperial Conference following the establishment of the Irish Free State,[322] George V changed 'the United Kingdom of Great Britain and Ireland and …' to 'Great Britain, Ireland, and …'.[323] All of these changes were effected by Imperial enactment. By the time India attained independence, the conclusions of the 1926 and 1930 Imperial Conferences had been enshrined in law, restricting the Westminster Parliament to legislating for the Dominions at their request and consent.[324] In particular, convention established in the preamble to the Statute of Westminster 1931 (Imp) required the assent of the Dominion Parliaments to changes to the royal style and titles. Accordingly, the several Parliaments concurrently assented to the omission of 'Emperor of India' from George VI's title by proclamation 'under the great seal of the Realm'.[325] The reprint of the 1948 proclamation does not record which Realm's seal was affixed, but that it was the UK seal is implicit in the title itself: 'George VI by the Grace of God of Great Britain, Ireland and the British Dominions beyond the Seas King, Defender of the Faith'.[326] Western Australia adopted legislation omitting 'Emperor of India' from official documents (but not purporting to effect any change in the title itself, this being achieved by the Imperial Act).[327]

Meeting in the margins of a 1952 economic conference, Commonwealth Prime Ministers agreed that, apart from its inaccuracy with respect to Ireland, the royal title failed to reflect the monarch's special position as Head of the Commonwealth.[328] It was agreed that each country should enact legislation adopting a title suitable for its own purposes (and assenting to equivalent legislation in other countries) but retaining a common element describing Her Majesty as 'Queen of Her other Realms and Territories and Head of the Commonwealth'.[329] Thus, reflecting the changed reality of Australia's status,[330] the sovereign acquired, by Australian (federal) legislation in 1953, a distinct Australian title for the first time: 'Elizabeth the Second, by the Grace of God of the United Kingdom, Australia and

320 A Proclamation (28.04.1876) (Imp), ibid, pursuant to Royal Titles Act 1876 (Imp).

321 A Proclamation (04.11.1901) (Imp) in A Pulling (ed), *Statutory rules and orders revised*, vol I (London, HMSO, 1904), pursuant to Royal Titles Act 1901 (Imp), s 1.

322 Imperial Conference, 1926, *Summary of Proceedings* (n 202), 15–16.

323 A Proclamation, SI 1927/422 (UK), pursuant to Royal and Parliamentary Titles Act 1927 (Imp), s 1.

324 Statute of Westminster 1931 (Imp), s 4.

325 Indian Independence Act 1947 (Imp), 7(2); *Royal Style and Titles Act (Australia) 1947* (Cth), s 3.

326 A Proclamation [1948] SR&O 4747 (Imp).

327 *Royal Style and Titles Act 1947* (WA), s 2.

328 The issue had been raised from 1947 but was not resolved for another five years: Twomey (n 52), 592.

329 Home Office, *The Title of the Sovereign* (Cmd 8748, 1953), 3.

330 *Re Patterson; Ex parte Taylor* [2001] HCA 51, (2001) 207 CLR 391 (HCA), 466–67 [226]–[227] (Gummow and Hayne JJ).

Her other Realms and Territories Queen, Head of the Commonwealth, Defender of the Faith'.[331] The Act empowered the Queen to issue her proclamation using whichever seal she appointed;[332] in the event, the proclamation was passed under the great seal of Australia.[333] This time, it was South Australia that enacted legislation prescribing the title to be used in legislative instruments.[334] Her Majesty's title to the end of our period—'Elizabeth the Second, by the Grace of God Queen of Australia and Her other Realms and Territories, Head of the Commonwealth'—derives from changes made in 1973.[335] The proclamation was issued under the great seal of Australia,[336] though the Act again permitted Her Majesty to appoint a seal by warrant.[337] South Australia and Western Australia legally recognised the change.[338]

E. Commonwealth and State Symbols

While the great seal and the royal title both have functions within the legal system, other reflections of community acknowledged in the legal system, such as arms, flags, honours and anthems, are less functional than symbolic. Nonetheless, these facts related to identity and community find reflections in the legal system.

i. Arms

New South Wales's arms were granted in 1906,[339] and include depictions of the St George's Cross and Southern Cross, a lion passant guardant (as in the arms of England), golden fleeces and wheatsheaves, the rising sun, and a British lion rampant guardant and a kangaroo for supporters.

[331] 'Proclamation' (28.05.1953) in *Commonwealth of Australia Gazette* (1953) No 34, 1547, pursuant to the *Royal Style and Titles Act 1953* (Cth), s 4(1), sch. The Commonwealth Act was reserved, and the Queen signified her Royal Assent on 03.04.1953. Unlike its UK counterpart, which retained the traditional practice of signifying a title in Latin and in English, Her Majesty's title in Australia is expressed uniquely in English: cp A Proclamation [1954] SR&O 2973 (UK), pursuant to Royal Titles Act 1953 (UK), s 1.

[332] *Royal Style and Titles Act 1953* (Cth), s 4(1).

[333] 'Warrant' (28.05.1953) in *Commonwealth of Australia Gazette* (1953) No 34, 1547.

[334] *Royal Style and Titles Act 1956* (SA), s 2.

[335] 'A Proclamation' (19.10.1973) in *Australian Government Gazette* (1973) No 152, 5, pursuant to *Royal Style and Titles Act 1973* (Cth), s 2(1). The Act, having been reserved, received the Royal Assent on 19.10.1973: 'Proclamation' (19.10.1973) in *Australian Government Gazette* (1973) No 152, 3.

[336] 'Royal Warrant' (19.10.1973) in *Australian Government Gazette* (1973) No 152, 4.

[337] *Royal Style and Titles Act 1973* (Cth), s 2(1).

[338] *Royal Style and Titles Act 1973* (SA), s 4; 'Proclamation' (04.12.1973) in *Government Gazette of Western Australia* (1973) No 91, 4479.

[339] 'Warrant granting Armorial Ensigns and Supporters for the State of New South Wales' (11.10.1906) in *New South Wales Government Gazette* (1907) No 24, 1346.

The State arms were recognised in local law when their misuse was made an offence in 1922.[340]

The Commonwealth was first granted arms and supporters in 1908.[341] Those original arms, combining the St George's Cross and the Southern Cross, were replaced by the current design, featuring the symbols of the States, in September 1912.[342] The seven-pointed Commonwealth (Federation) Star and the red kangaroo and emu supporters were retained. The mace used in the Commonwealth Parliament bears the great seal of Australia as well as the arms of the States.[343]

ii. Flags

On the union with Ireland in 1801, George III proclaimed the Union flag for use on land (no difference was, or is, made between civil, state and war flags) and the red ensign (featuring the Union flag in the canton) for use at sea, at that time both by merchant vessels and by naval vessels in the Red Squadron.[344] By Admiralty circular issued in 1866, it was directed that Colonial naval and government vessels should fly a blue ensign distinguished by the seal or badge of the Colony.[345] New South Wales's first badge featured the St George's Cross on a silver field.[346] The badge was amended in 1876 to its present form, incorporating the Southern Cross and lion passant guardant, as in the New South Wales arms.[347]

Following a competition initiated by the new federal Government[348] at the instigation of the Imperial authorities,[349] Edward VII approved the blue ensign defaced by the Commonwealth (Federation) star and the Southern Cross as the Flag of the Commonwealth.[350] This flag was

[340] *Unauthorised Documents Act 1922* (NSW), s 3. After our period, various symbols, including the State arms, were patriated under the *State Arms, Symbols and Emblems Act 2004* (NSW).

[341] 'Warrant granting Armorial Ensigns and Supporters to the Commonwealth of Australia' (07.05.1908) in *Commonwealth of Australia Gazette* (1908) No 39, 1181.

[342] 'Warrant granting Armorial Ensigns for the Commonwealth of Australia' (19.09.1912) in *Commonwealth of Australia Gazette* (1913) No 3, 46–48. In fact, since 1953, the arms have incorrectly represented the badge of WA: in that year, the black swan was reoriented to face the hoist (ie, notionally west) rather than the fly.

[343] Commonwealth of Australia, *Parliamentary Debates* (House of Representatives, 29.11.1951), 3089 (Mr Law).

[344] A Proclamation (n 319) (Imp). See also Merchant Shipping Act 1854 (Imp), s 105.

[345] Circular No 4–S (16.01.1866) in Great Britain, Admiralty (ed), *The Navy List corrected to the 20th December, 1865* (London, John Murray, 1866).

[346] Premier's Department of New South Wales, *Emblem Book of the State of New South Wales* (Sydney, New South Wales, Premier's Department, 2002), 6.

[347] 'Government Notification' (15.02.1876) in *New South Wales Government Gazette* (1876) No 55, 708.

[348] 'Design for a Federal Flag' (29.04.1901) in *Commonwealth of Australia Gazette* (1901) No 27, 89.

[349] Commonwealth of Australia, *Parliamentary Debates* (Senate, 09.10.1901), 5749 (Senator O'Connor).

[350] 'Miscellaneous' (29.12.1902) in *Commonwealth of Australia Gazette* (1903) No 8, 93. A seventh point was added to the Commonwealth (Federation) star in 1908 to represent

initially confined to use at sea by the Commonwealth Government, but usage gradually expanded to land,[351] though the Union flag continued to take precedence, and civilians were only permitted to use the Australian Red Ensign (described below).[352] The blue ensign was not legally adopted as the national flag, taking precedence over the Union flag, until 1954,[353] and popular preference for the Union flag (use of which was not precluded by the 1953 Act)[354] continued well into the 1970s.[355] In 1998, the legislation was amended to require the consent of a majority of electors for any change to be made to the Australian national flag.[356] The Torres Strait Islander Flag and the Australian Aboriginal Flag were first proclaimed under the *Flags Act 1953* (Cth) in 1995.[357]

While pre-Federation Imperial law had declared the red ensign to be the proper national colours for merchant vessels unless other colours were permitted by royal or Admiralty warrant,[358] an amendment to the Queen's Regulations and Admiralty Instructions in 1890 permitted Colonial merchant vessels to carry, in addition to the red ensign, a distinguishing flag bearing the badge of the Colony.[359] In 1903, the Admiralty permitted as national colours for vessels registered in the Commonwealth the red ensign defaced by the Commonwealth star and the Southern Cross;[360] this was confirmed by Commonwealth legislation in 1912.[361] In 1938, use of the red ensign so defaced was permitted as the proper colours for private vessels other than merchant ships.[362] This flag became the 'Australian Red Ensign' in 1954,[363] and the proper national colours for all civilian Australian ships in 1981.[364]

the Territories as well as the six original States: 'Warrant' (03.10.1908) in *Commonwealth of Australia Gazette* (1908) No 65, 1709.

351 E Kwan, 'National Parliament, National Symbols: From British to Australian Identity' (Senate Occasional Lecture Series, Canberra, 04.05.2007) 6.

352 ibid, 9.

353 *Flags Act 1953* (Cth), s 3.

354 ibid, s 8.

355 Kwan (n 351), 11.

356 *Flags Act 1953* (Cth), s 3(2), as inserted by *Flags Amendment Act 1998* (Cth), s 3, sch 1.

357 'Proclamation' (27.06.1995) in *Commonwealth of Australia Gazette* (1995) No S258, 1; 'Proclamation' (27.06.1995) in *Commonwealth of Australia Gazette* (1995) No S259, 1, pursuant to the *Flags Act 1953* (Cth), s 5.

358 Merchant Shipping (Colours) Act 1889 (Imp), s 1.

359 United Kingdom, Admiralty, *Queen's Regulations and Admiralty Instructions* (London, HMSO, 1890), art 86(3).

360 'Warrant' (04.06.1903) in *Commonwealth of Australia Gazette* (1903) No 38, 433. The Commonwealth (Federation) star had only six points in 1903; the seventh was added in 1908: 'Warrant' (n 350).

361 *Navigation Act 1912* (Cth), s 406.

362 'Warrant' (25.11.1938) in *Commonwealth of Australia Gazette* (1939) No 32, 842.

363 *Flags Act 1953* (Cth), s 4.

364 *Shipping Registration Act 1981* (Cth), s 30.

While both the British white ensign (from the hoist) and the distinctive flag of the Commonwealth (from the jack-staff) were flown when the Royal Australian Navy was established,[365] an Australian white ensign, matching the designs of the national flag and the Australian Red Ensign, was adopted in 1967.[366] Similarly, the Royal Australian Air Force flew a British Royal Air Force Ensign from 1922 to 1948. A sky-blue adaptation of the Australian national flag with the British Royal Air Force roundel in the lower fly was used from 1949 until 1982, when a distinctive Australian roundel featuring a red kangaroo was formally adopted.[367] An Ensign for the Australian Defence Forces collectively was proclaimed in 2000.[368]

iii. Honours and Advance Australia Fair

Throughout our period, the grant of honours was a prerogative of the monarch, as 'the fountain of all honour and dignity'.[369] A distinct Australian honours system, the Order of Australia, was established in 1975,[370] though Imperial honours could be awarded at the instigation of State governments until 1992.[371] At approximately the same time, an Australian national anthem was sought to replace *God Save the Queen*, which had been in use from the beginning of our period. The Whitlam Government adopted *Advance Australia Fair* as the national anthem in 1974, other than on specifically royal occasions; two years later, the Fraser Government broadened the use of *God Save the Queen* to include vice-regal, defence and loyal toast occasions, and instituted the 1977 national plebiscite at which *Advance Australia Fair* emerged as the most popular choice.[372] The anthem was not, however, directly given status within the legal system until proclaimed in 1984.[373]

[365] Imperial Conference, 1911, 'Memorandum of Conferences between the British Admiralty and Representatives of the Dominion of Canada and the Commonwealth of Australia' in Imperial Conference, 1911, *Papers laid before the Imperial Conference: Naval and Military Defence* (Cd 5746-II, 1911) 1, 1.

[366] 'Proclamation' (16.02.1967) in *Commonwealth of Australia Gazette* (1967) No 18, 1103, pursuant to the *Flags Act 1953* (Cth), s 5.

[367] 'Proclamation' (29.04.1982) in *Commonwealth of Australia Gazette* (1982) No S89, 1, pursuant to the *Flags Act 1953* (Cth), s 5.

[368] 'Proclamation' (12.04.2000) in *Commonwealth of Australia Gazette* (2000) No S190, 1, pursuant to the *Flags Act 1953* (Cth), s 5.

[369] *The Prince's Case* (1606) 8 Co Rep 13b (KB), 18b; 77 ER 496, 502.

[370] By 'Letters Patent' (14.02.1975) in *Australian Government Gazette* (1975) No S28, 1.

[371] Twomey describes the grant of Imperial honours after 1975: Twomey (n 123), 154–56, 355–58.

[372] Commonwealth of Australia, Parliamentary Library, *Parliamentary Handbook of the Commonwealth of Australia* (n 194), 412.

[373] 'Proclamation' (19.04.1984) in *Commonwealth of Australia Gazette* (1984) No S142.

F. Defence Forces

Responsibility for defence and control of armed force are matters connected with community and identity frequently reflected in legal systems—almost necessarily, according to Cicero's ideal allocation to the sovereign magistrates of power over the armed forces: 'In the field they shall hold the supreme military power; they shall be subject to no one; the safety of the people shall be their highest law'.[374]

Unsurprisingly, given the military autocracy over which he presided and the remoteness of the Colony, Governor Phillip's Commission gave him plenary power and authority in securing the territory and its dependencies against enemies, pirates and rebels.[375] So, too, did Governor Darling's 1825 Commission, when civil government was instituted.[376] While control of the military was thus essentially autochthonous, the forces under the Governors' command were, until 1870, Imperial troops serving in New South Wales on a rotational basis, and the command structure of which the Governors were part was also British.[377] The volunteer corps of citizen soldiers formed in the 1850s were initially outside government control,[378] but were later supplemented by a small professional staff, and gradually came to form regulated militias, paid by the Colonial Government and liable to be placed by the Governor under the command of regular officers.[379] Problems arose when New South Wales sent some such forces to the Sudan in 1885, since the Colonial legislation under which they were controlled had no extraterritorial effect, prompting Imperial legislation to fill the gap.[380] At around this time, an Australian military identity began to form, partly in connection with 'Australian' corps comprising native-born men, and partly in connection with 'a myth, a now-forgotten subspecies of the bush legend … about "buff-coloured boys" whose untutored ability to ride and shoot was revealing a natural talent of Australian colonists for war'.[381]

Protection by sea was provided for more directly, with the formation of Colonial naval forces following war scares in the mid-nineteenth century.[382]

374 Cicero, *De Legibus*, original c 46–43 BC (CW Keyes tr, Cambridge, Mass, Harvard University Press, 1928) III.iii.8.

375 Commission (02.04.1787) (n 9), 64.

376 Commission (n 62), 103.

377 J Grey, *The Australian Army: A History* (Melbourne, OUP, 2001) 5.

378 C Wilcox, 'Colonial Military Forces' in P Dennis and others (eds), *The Oxford Companion to Australian Military History*, 2nd edn (Melbourne, OUP, 2008) 143, 144.

379 *Volunteers Act 1854* (NSW).

380 Army Act 1881 (Imp), s 177. The contemporary understanding of the unity of the Crown, at least in military matters, is reflected in the Privy Council's advice that payment of a solider by the Imperial Government operated to discharge the debt due to him for his service, even though his contract was with the NSW government: *Williams v Howarth* [1905] AC 551 (PC), 554.

381 Wilcox (n 378), 146.

382 *Colonial Naval Service Act 1855* (NSW).

The Imperial Parliament legislated to allow Colonial legislatures to raise naval forces—without expense to the Imperial Government but liable to control by the Admiralty[383]—but only Victoria did so (after negotiating for the Imperial Government to pay for a warship).[384] Notwithstanding these local forces, defence of the Australian Colonies essentially rested with the Imperial Navy. Under the 1887 Anglo-Australian Naval Agreement, the Admiralty created the Auxiliary Squadron, Australia Station, with financial contributions from the Colonies but under solely Imperial control.[385]

Imperial interest in coordinating the different Colonial military forces led to an inspection by an Imperial General in 1889. While the Colonial Defence Committee considered that, in the extremely unlikely event of an attack on Australian territory, the Imperial Navy could offer adequate protection, it strongly endorsed the recommendation that Colonial military forces adopt a common system and prepare for concerted action across Colonial borders.[386] While an immediate aim was to put the Colonies in a position to contribute to Imperial military action outside Australia, in exchange for the protection offered by the Imperial Navy on which they were dependent, the realisation of a common need for defence became part of the Federation debate,[387] particularly since Imperial command of any joint Australian force (in Australia) would have been unacceptable to the Colonies.[388]

At Federation, defence became a Commonwealth responsibility,[389] with the command-in-chief vested in the Governor-General as the Queen's representative (but relevantly acting on the advice of Australian ministers).[390] Colonial units were transferred to the Commonwealth and amalgamated as the Commonwealth Military Forces and the Commonwealth Naval Forces in March 1901,[391] though they continued to be administered under pre-Federation Colonial laws until a comprehensive federal law was enacted in 1903.[392] That Act provided for Australian command, though forces could be placed under Imperial command in time of war.[393] The third service, the Royal Australian Air Force, was originally established

[383] Colonial Naval Defence Act 1865 (Imp).

[384] 'Colonial Naval Defence Act' in P Dennis and others (eds), *The Oxford Companion to Australian Military History*, 2nd edn (Melbourne, OUP, 2008).

[385] See *Australasian Naval Force Act 1887* (NSW); Imperial Defence Act 1888 (Imp).

[386] *Correspondence relating to the Inspection of the Military Forces of the Australasian Colonies by Major-General J Bevan Edwards CB* (C 6188, 1890), 31–32.

[387] Control and discipline of combined Colonial forces at King George Sound and Thursday Island were provided for in the *The Federal Garrisons Act 1893* (Federal Council of Australasia).

[388] J Mordike, *An Army for a Nation* (Sydney, Allen & Unwin, 1992) 15–19.

[389] *Commonwealth Constitution*, ss 51(vi), 51(xxxii), 52(ii) and 69, 114.

[390] ibid, s 68.

[391] 'Proclamation' (19.02.1901) in *Commonwealth of Australia Gazette* (1901) No 9, 21.

[392] *Defence Act 1903* (Cth).

[393] ibid, s 53.

under the *Defence Act 1903* (Cth) in 1921 but retrospectively established by statute in 1923, on the same basis as the other services and subject to the *Defence Act 1903* (Cth).[394]

Despite Commonwealth command, external defence was still in substance an Imperial matter, since Australia continued to rely on Imperial naval protection. A new Anglo-Australian Naval Agreement came into effect in 1903, under Imperial command, with more ships and a greater contribution from the Australian and New Zealand Governments.[395] The Imperial approach to defence was evident when, with the landing of troops of the Australian Imperial Forces at Gallipoli in 1915, Australian identity, military and national, acquired one of its most important anchors. With war 'seen both as a proving-ground for national character and as an experience that all nations must go through to forge a true sense of national identity and to prove themselves in the eyes of the world',[396] this engagement, encapsulating the compatible duality of Australian and Imperial identities, as well as (at least in the received account) values of egalitarian mateship, gave rise to the ANZAC (Australian and New Zealand Army Corps) legend, a defining component of Australian nationality and community identity.[397] It was not, in fact, until after World War II (and, in particular, after the failure of the Singapore strategy) that Australian strategic thinking moved away from an Imperial mind-set and towards closer collaboration with regional and United States forces, in particular through the ANZUS Treaty (still on foot in 2001) and under the umbrella of the South-East Asia Treaty Organization (dissolved in 1977).[398]

G. Summary

Section I.A exposed the constitutional and legal processes by which New South Wales developed from an autocratic penal Colony to a largely

[394] *Air Force Act 1923* (Cth).

[395] See *Naval Agreement Act 1903* (Cth).

[396] 'ANZAC Legend' in P Dennis and others (eds), *The Oxford Companion to Australian Military History*, 2nd edn (Melbourne, OUP, 2008) 37.

[397] See generally ibid and also P Brazil, 'Australian Nationality and Immigration' in KW Ryan (ed), *International Law in Australia*, 2nd edn (North Ryde, NSW, LBC, 1984), 210–11. Although ANZAC Day was officially recognised as early as 1916, it did not become a public holiday in NSW until 1924: *Banks and Bank Holidays (Amendment) Act 1924* (NSW), s 2(a) and, though long-since celebrated uniformly across the States, it was not recognised in Commonwealth legislation until declared to be the 'national day of commemoration to recognise and commemorate the contribution of all those who have served Australia (including those who died) in time of war and in war-like conflicts' in 1995: *Anzac Day Act 1995* (Cth), s 3.

[398] T Frame, 'Royal Australian Navy' in Dennis and others (eds) (n 396), 467–69. See *Security Treaty between Australia, New Zealand and the United States of America* (1952) 131 UNTS 83 (No 1736) (entered into force: generally and for Australia 29.04.1952); *Southeast Asia Collective Defense Treaty (with Protocol)* (1954) 209 UNTS 23 (No 2819) (entered into force: generally and for Australia 19.02.1955).

self-governing Colony with representative and responsible government within the Empire to, in turn, a State in the Australian Federation. It observed, in parallel, the evolution in Imperial institutions from agents of the Imperial government to 'amphibious' entities with multiple, overlapping roles in relation to the law in different parts of the Empire. Section I.B similarly traced the growth of the Commonwealth into a discrete polity with international legal personality, freed from the constraints of Empire as it was transformed from Colony to Dominion to independent nation. Sections I.C, D and E tracked the increasing dissociation from Imperial legal forms in legislation and governmental institutions, as reflected in enacting formulae, the royal title and symbols of government. Section I.F highlighted a particular aspect of legal constitutional and legal development, concerning control of armed force, which also gradually passed from Imperial into Australian hands.

The sum of the changes traced in this section reveals that the process of constitutional and legal change was gradual across the period, but that it occurred in perceptible fits and starts. Though it has been possible only to allude to or hint at the broader social and political background (connected, for example, with transportation, the squatter movement, immigration, the trade union movement, religious toleration and the changing dynamics of the Australian economy), it may also be observed that the motivation and agitation driving the changes, through whatever form they were ultimately given legal effect, was local, and that, after the mid-nineteenth century, relatively little opposition was encountered from Imperial authorities when reform measures were sought. These general conclusions aside, the significance of these constitutional and legal changes, and of the manner in which they were achieved, differs between Kelsen's and Raz's accounts of continuity and discontinuity of legal systems, such that substantive analysis of the consequences of these changes must be deferred to chapters four and six.

II. SPATIAL SCOPE

That space—principally but not exclusively territory—is a central phenomenon in the identity of legal systems is evident from references, both pre-theoretical and intra-systemic, to, for example, the 'law of England', 'law areas', 'the law of the land' or even 'federal jurisdiction'. This is so even though no account holds that every change in the spatial scope of a legal system entails discontinuity: expansion and contraction of spatial scope is uncontroversially a feature of continuous legal systems, though it may sometimes entail discontinuity instead. The acquisition, alienation, merger and separation of spaces in which legal authority is exercised often approximate changes in the personal, as well as the geographical, scope of legal systems. Space is relevant to non-legal notions of community and identity too—as the continuing controversy over the use of the name 'Macedonia' illustrates.[399] This section proceeds first by way of overview of, and then by examination of several of the phenomena connected with, changes in the spatial scope of Australian legal systems between 1788 and 2001.

A. Overview

New South Wales initially encompassed the whole of the Australian continent east of 135°E (roughly the continent's mid-point), together with the adjacent Pacific islands.[400] The proclamation of the Colony added more than 4.1 million square kilometres of territory to the British Empire.[401] The subsequent two centuries brought significant changes to the spatial scope of Australian legal systems, including by separation, merger, surrender, transfer from the UK, administration under international mandate or trusteeship agreement, and by original acquisition. The changes are summarised chronologically below:

1825	Western border of NSW moved west to 129°E[402]
1825	Colony of Van Diemen's Land separated from NSW[403]
1829	Colony of WA created adjacent to NSW[404]
1836	Province of SA separated from NSW[405]
1839	Boundaries of NSW redefined to include NZ[406]

[399] The on-going dispute is the subject of the *Interim Accord* (1995) 1891 UNTS 3 (No 32193) (entered into force: 13.10.1995).

[400] Instructions (n 11), 85.

[401] B Kingston, *A History of New South Wales* (Port Melbourne, CUP, 2006) 2.

[402] Commission (n 62), 100.

[403] Order in Council (14.06.1825) (Imp) in Watson (ed) (n 61), pursuant to the Justice, New South Wales Act 1823 (Imp), s 44.

[404] Government of Western Australia Act 1829 (Imp), s 1. Following a brief military and convict settlement at King George Sound under Major Lockyer between 1826 and 1831, established in fear of French settlement, land had been settled (outside any existing Colony) under the command of Lieutenant-General Stirling and Captain Fremantle: Instructions (30.12.1828), available at <http://foundingdocs.gov.au/item-sdid-5.html>.

[405] Letters Patent establishing the Province of South Australia (19.02.1836), available at <http://foundingdocs.gov.au/item-sdid-38.html>, pursuant to the South Australia Act 1834 (Imp), s 1.

[406] By letters patent dated 15.06.1839; see 'Proclamation' (14.01.1840) in *New South Wales Government Gazette* (1840) No 4, 65. It is unclear whether actions by NSW Governors in relation to NZ between 1814 and 1840 were within or outside their territorial jurisdiction: for a brief summary, see Carney (n 2), 57–58.

1841	Colony of NZ separated from NSW[407]
1844	NI transferred from NSW to Van Diemen's Land[408]
1846	Colony of North Australia separated from NSW[409]
1847	Colony of North Australia reincorporated into NSW[410]
1851	Colony of Victoria separated from NSW[411]
1856	Settlement of NI (with the Governor of NSW as Governor of NI) separated from Tasmania[412]
1859	Colony of Queensland separated from NSW[413]
1861	Western border of SA moved west to 129°E[414]
1862	Western border of Queensland moved west to 139°E[415]
1863	The part of NSW north of SA annexed to SA[416]
1872	Islands off the Queensland Coast administered by the Governor of Queensland (without but pending incorporation into Queensland)[417]
1879	Torres Strait Islands annexed to Queensland[418]

[407] By letters patent dated 16.11.1840, pursuant to the New South Wales and Van Diemen's Land Act 1840 (Imp), s 2: see 'Notice' (20.11.1840) in *New South Wales Government Gazette* (1841) No 26, 461.

[408] 'Letters Patent' (24.10.1843) in *New South Wales Government Gazette* (1844) No 85, 1142, pursuant to the Norfolk Island Act 1843 (Imp), s 1.

[409] By letters patent dated 17.02.1846, pursuant to the Australian Constitutions Act 1842 (Imp), s 51: see 'Proclamation' (09.11.1846) in *New South Wales Government Gazette* (1846) No 95, 1422.

[410] By letters patent dated 28.12.1847 and 03.04.1848: see 'Proclamation' (16.01.1849) in *New South Wales Government Gazette* (1849) No 13, 117.

[411] Australian Constitutions Act 1850 (Imp), s 1.

[412] Order in Council declaring Norfolk Island to be a separate British Settlement (24.06.1856) (Imp) in Pulling (ed) (n 319), vol V, pursuant to the Australian Waste Lands Act 1855 (Imp), s 5.

[413] 'Letters Patent erecting Moreton Bay into a Colony, under the name of Queensland' (06.06.1859) in *Queensland Government Gazette* (1859) vol 1 No 1, 1, pursuant to the power preserved in the New South Wales Constitution Act 1855 (Imp), s 7.

[414] Australian Colonies Act 1861 (Imp), s 1.

[415] 'Supplementary Commission' (13.03.1862) in *Queensland Government Gazette* (1862) vol 3 No 51, 295, pursuant to the Australian Colonies Act 1861 (Imp), s 2.

[416] Letters Patent altering the Boundaries of the Colonies of South Australia and New South Wales (06.07.1863) (Imp) in Pulling (ed) (n 321), pursuant to Australian Colonies Act 1861 (Imp), s 2. Local legislation provided for the sale or disposal of the newly acquired territory: *Northern Territory Act* (1863) (SA).

[417] 'Letters Patent appointing the Governor of the Colony of Queensland to be Governor of all Islands within Sixty Miles from the Coast of the said Colony, and authorising the Annexation of the aforesaid Islands to that Colony' (30.05.1872) in *Queensland Government Gazette* (1872) vol 13 No 80, 1270.

[418] 'Proclamation' (18.07.1879) in *Queensland Government Gazette* (1879) vol 25 No 10, 143, pursuant to the *Queensland Coast Islands Act 1879* (Qld); Queensland Coast, Islands and Waters Letters Patent dated 10 October 1878 (Imp).

1888	British New Guinea became a Crown Colony underwritten by Queensland, NSW and Victoria[419]
1897	NI administered by the Governor of NSW (without incorporation into NSW)[420]
1901	NSW, Tasmania, WA, SA, Victoria and Queensland (but not, for example, NI) incorporated as States in the Commonwealth[421]
1902/1906	British New Guinea placed by the UK under the authority of (1902), and accepted by (1906), the Commonwealth as the Territory of Papua[422]
1910	NT surrendered by SA to, and accepted by, the Commonwealth[423]
1910	Federal Capital Territory (ACT) surrendered by NSW to, and accepted by, the Commonwealth[424]
1914	NI placed by the UK under the authority of, and accepted by, the Commonwealth[425]
1915	Jervis Bay Territory surrendered by NSW to, and accepted by, the Commonwealth[426]
1920	Nauru became a League of Nations Mandate Territory (but not a Territory of the Commonwealth) administered by the Commonwealth together with the UK and NZ[427]

[419] See Letters Patent erecting British New Guinea into a separate Possession and Government (08.06.1888) (Imp) in Pulling (ed) (n 319); *The British New Guinea (Queensland) Act of 1887* (Qld).

[420] Order in Council making Provision for the Government of Norfolk Island [1897] SR&O 504 (Imp); Order in Council providing for the Administration of the affairs of Norfolk Island by the Governor, for the time being, of the State of New South Wales (18.10.1900) (Imp) in Pulling (ed) (n 321), pursuant to the Australian Waste Lands Act 1855 (Imp), s 5.

[421] 'A Proclamation' (17.09.1900) in *Commonwealth of Australia Gazette* (1901) No 1, 1, pursuant to the Commonwealth of Australia Constitution Act 1900 (Imp), s 3.

[422] Letters Patent for placing British New Guinea under the authority of the Commonwealth of Australia (18.03.1902) (Imp) in Statute Law Committee (ed) (n 106); *Papua Act 1905* (Cth), s 5; 'Proclamation' (01.09.1906) in *Commonwealth of Australia Gazette* (1906) No 47, 1141.

[423] 'Proclamation' (22.12.1910) in *Commonwealth of Australia Gazette* (1910) No 79, 1901, pursuant to the *Northern Territory Acceptance Act 1910* (Cth), s 6; *Northern Territory Surrender Act 1907* (SA), s 7.

[424] 'Proclamation' (05.12.1910) in *Commonwealth of Australia Gazette* (1910) No 75, 1851, pursuant to the *Seat of Government Acceptance Act 1909* (Cth), s 5; *Seat of Government Surrender Act 1909* (NSW), s 6. Certain misdescriptions were subsequently corrected: *Seat of Government Acceptance Act 1922* (Cth); *Seat of Government Surrender (Amendment) Act 1923* (NSW).

[425] *Norfolk Island Act 1913* (Cth), s 3; 'Proclamation' (17.06.1914) in *Commonwealth of Australia Gazette* (1914) No 35, 1043 and Order in Council placing Norfolk Island under the Authority of the Commonwealth of Australia (30.03.1914) (Imp) in Statute Law Committee (ed) (n 106), pursuant to the Australian Waste Lands Act 1855 (Imp), s 5.

[426] 'Proclamation' (01.09.1915) in *Commonwealth of Australia Gazette* (1915) No 103, 1710 pursuant to the *Jervis Bay Territory Acceptance Act 1915* (Cth), s 4; *Seat of Government Surrender Act 1915* (NSW), s 6.

[427] *Mandate for Nauru* (1921) 2 League of Nations Official Journal 93 (entered into force: generally and for Australia 17.12.1920); *Nauru Island Agreement Act 1919* (Cth), s 3, sch.

1921	Territory of New Guinea acquired by the Commonwealth[428] subject to a Class C League of Nations Mandate (denoting administration as an integral part of the mandatory's territory)[429]
1927	NT divided into the Territories of North Australia and Central Australia[430]
1931	Territories of North Australia and Central Australia reincorporated as NT[431]
1934	Territory of Ashmore and Cartier Islands placed by the UK under the authority of, and accepted by, the Commonwealth[432]
1936	Australian Antarctic Territory placed by the UK under the authority of, and accepted by, the Commonwealth[433]
1942	Imperial law (retrospectively from 1939) ceased to extend to or bind the Commonwealth (with limited exceptions)[434]
1945	Territory of Papua and Territory of New Guinea administered together as the Territory of Papua–New Guinea[435]
1947	Territory of Heard Island and McDonald Islands acquired by the Commonwealth from the UK[436]

[428] See *Jolley v Mainka* (1933) 49 CLR 242 (HCA), 249–50 (Starke J), 256 (Dixon J); cp 278–81 (Evatt J).

[429] *Mandate for the German Possessions in the Pacific Ocean Situated South of the Equator, other than German Samoa and Nauru* (1921) 2 *League of Nations Official Journal* 85 (entered into force: generally and for Australia 17.12.1920); 'Proclamation' (07.04.1921) in *Commonwealth of Australia Gazette* (1921) No 32, 639, pursuant to the *New Guinea Act 1920* (Cth), ss 4–5.

[430] *Northern Australia Act 1926* (Cth), s 36; 'Proclamation' (21.01.1927) in *Commonwealth of Australia Gazette* (1927) No 7, 137.

[431] *Northern Territory (Administration) Act 1931* (Cth).

[432] Order in Council placing the Ashmore Islands and Cartier Island under the Authority of the Commonwealth of Australia (23.07.1931) (Imp) in Statute Law Committee (ed) (n 106); 'Proclamation' (09.05.1934) in *Commonwealth of Australia Gazette* (1934) No 28, 761, pursuant to the *Ashmore and Cartier Islands Acceptance Act 1933* (Cth), s 5.

[433] Order in Council placing certain Territory in the Antarctic Seas under the Authority of the Commonwealth of Australia (07.02.1933) (Imp) in Statute Law Committee (ed) (n 106); 'Proclamation' (24.08.1936) in *Commonwealth of Australia Gazette* (1936) No 70, 1553, pursuant to the *Australian Antarctic Territory Acceptance Act 1933* (Cth), s 2.

[434] Statute of Westminster 1931 (Imp), ss 2, 4, 11; *Statute of Westminster Adoption Act 1942* (Cth), s 3.

[435] See *Papua–New Guinea Provisional Administration Act 1945* (Cth).

[436] Because of fears that publicity would precipitate claims to Antarctic territory, and because of doubts about the British claims to sovereignty, the transfer was effected by an exchange of notes in 1950, with acknowledgement of effect retrospective to 26.12.1947, when Australia had established occupation of the islands: A Kerr, *A Federation in These Seas* (Canberra, Attorney General's Department, 2009) 251–52. By the *Heard Island and McDonald Islands Act 1953* (Cth), s 3 the islands were 'declared to be a Territory of the Commonwealth'.

1947 Nauru became a UN Trust Territory (but not a Territory of the Commonwealth) administered by the Commonwealth together with the UK and NZ[437]

1947 Territory of New Guinea became a UN Trust Territory[438]

1949 Administrative union of the Territory of Papua and the Territory of New Guinea as the Territory of Papua and New Guinea[439]

1955 Territory of Cocos (Keeling) Islands placed by the UK under the authority of, and accepted by, the Commonwealth[440]

1958 Territory of Christmas Island placed by the UK under the authority of, and accepted by, the Commonwealth[441]

1968 UN Trusteeship Agreement in relation to Nauru ceased[442]

1969 Coral Sea Islands Territory declared by the Commonwealth[443]

1975 Territory of Papua and Territory of New Guinea relinquished[444]

1980 Legislative power over, and title to the sea-bed of, coastal waters vested by the Commonwealth in the States and the NT[445]

[437] *Trusteeship Agreement for the Territory of Nauru* (1947) 10 UNTS 3 (No 138) (entered into force: generally and for Australia 01.11.1947). Administration of Nauru continued under the tripartite Agreement with the UK and NZ, as amended in 1923 but not ratified until the *Nauru Island Agreement Act 1932* (Cth), s 2, sch. More direct control by Australia was provided for when the Agreement was amended in 1965: see, generally, the *Nauru Act 1965* (Cth) and, in particular, sch 2.

[438] *Trusteeship Agreement for the Territory of New Guinea* (1947) 8 UNTS 181 (No 122) (entered into force: generally and for Australia 13.12.1946).

[439] *Papua and New Guinea Act 1949* (Cth), ss 8–10.

[440] The Cocos Islands Order in Council 1955, SI 1955/1642, pursuant to the Cocos Islands Act 1955 (Imp), s 1 and 'Proclamation' (03.11.1955) in *Commonwealth of Australia Gazette* (1955) No 58, 3665, pursuant to the *Cocos (Keeling) Islands Act 1955* (Cth), s 5. The transfer was requested by Australia: *Cocos (Keeling) Islands (Request and Consent) Act 1954* (Cth), s 3. The political status of the Cocos (Keeling) Islands was finally settled by a self-determination referendum on 06.04.1984, in accordance with UNGA Res 1541 (XV) (15.12.1960), Annex, Principle IX(b), and pursuant to the *Referendum (Self-determination) Ordinance 1984* (CKI). Of the 261 electors, 229 voted for integration with Australia: 'Declaration of Results of Referendum' (07.04.1984) in *The Territory of Cocos (Keeling) Islands Government Gazette* (1984) No 8/84, noted by the General Assembly: UNGA Res 39/30 (05.12.1984).

[441] The Christmas Island (Transfer to Australia) Order in Council 1958, SI 1958/1515, pursuant to the Christmas Island Act 1958 (Imp), s 1 and 'Proclamation' (18.09.1958) in *Commonwealth of Australia Gazette* (1958) No 54, 3185, pursuant to *Christmas Island Act 1958* (Cth), s 5. The transfer was requested by Australia: *Christmas Island (Request and Consent) Act 1957* (Cth), s 3.

[442] 'Proclamation' (25.01.1968) in *Commonwealth of Australia Gazette* (1968) No 9, 581, pursuant to *Nauru Independence Act 1967* (Cth), s 4.

[443] *Coral Sea Islands Act 1969* (Cth), s 3. The Commonwealth's claim to the islands was based on original acquisition of territorial sovereignty at international law by occupation over a period of years: Commonwealth of Australia, *Parliamentary Debates* (House of Representatives, 29.05.1969), 2471–72 (Mr Barnes).

[444] *Papua New Guinea Independence Act 1975* (Cth), s 4.

[445] *Coastal Waters (Northern Territory Powers) Act 1980* (Cth), s 5; *Coastal Waters (Northern Territory Title) Act 1980* (Cth), s 4; *Coastal Waters (State Powers) Act 1980* (Cth), s 5; *Coastal*

1986	Imperial law ceased to apply (prospectively) in the Commonwealth, the States and the Territories[446]
1990	Limits of the (existing) territorial sea declared by the Commonwealth[447]
1994	Exclusive Economic Zone declared by the Commonwealth[448]
1997	Coral Sea Islands Territory expanded to include Elizabeth and Middleton Reefs[449]
1999	Limits of contiguous zone declared by the Commonwealth[450]

B. Separations and Mergers

When territory has been separated in Australia, it has usually been expressly provided, or else implied, that existing laws continue in the separated territory until modified, save to the extent that the separation itself effected modifications.[451] Exceptions were the separation of South Australia from New South Wales, when the new Province was separated out and erected free of all enacted laws relating to any part of Australia,[452] and the independence of Papua New Guinea, when all Australian and Imperial laws applying to the territory were repealed.[453]

In relation to the direct merger of one Australian territory into another, the norm has been continuity of laws, subject to modifications necessarily

Waters (State Title) Act 1980 (Cth), s 4. The legislation was part of the off-shore constitutional settlement following the High Court's decision that the sea boundaries of the States ended at the low-water mark: *Bonser v La Macchia* (1969) 122 CLR 177 (HCA), 185, 189 (Barwick CJ), 220–22 (Windeyer J); *New South Wales v Commonwealth* (1975) 135 CLR 337 (HCA), 367–71 (Barwick CJ), 378 (McTiernan J), 467–68 (Mason J), 491 (Jacobs J). Neither Act extended the limits of any State or the NT: *Coastal Waters (Northern Territory Powers) Act 1980* (Cth), s 7(a); *Coastal Waters (Northern Territory Title) Act 1980* (Cth), s 7(a); *Coastal Waters (State Powers) Act 1980* (Cth), s 7(a); *Coastal Waters (State Title) Act 1980* (Cth), s 8(a).

[446] *Australia Act 1986* (Cth), ss 1, 3, 12; Australia Act 1986 (Imp), ss 1, 3, 12.

[447] 'Proclamation' (09.11.1990) in *Commonwealth of Australia Gazette* (1990) No S297, 1, pursuant to the *Seas and Submerged Lands Act 1973* (Cth), s 7(1).

[448] 'Proclamation' (26.07.1994) in *Commonwealth of Australia Gazette* (1994) No S290, 1, pursuant to the *Seas and Submerged Lands Act 1973* (Cth), s 10B.

[449] *Environment, Sport and Territories Legislation Amendment Act 1997* (Cth), s 3, sch, item 20.

[450] 'Proclamation' (31.03.1999) in *Commonwealth of Australia Gazette* (1999) No S148, 1, pursuant to the *Seas and Submerged Lands Act 1973* (Cth), s 13B.

[451] No express provision was made in relation to the separations of Van Diemen's Land or North Australia from NSW. For express provisions for continuance of laws in relation to the other separations, see: Order in Council declaring Norfolk Island to be a separate British Settlement (n 412) (Imp), 131; Order in Council empowering the Governor of Queensland to make Laws, and to provide for the Administration of the said Colony (06.06.1859) (Imp) in Pulling (ed) (n 319), vol VI , cl 20; *Northern Australia Act 1926* (Cth), s 38(1).

[452] South Australia Act 1834 (Imp), s 1.

[453] *Papua New Guinea Independence Act 1975* (Cth), s 5.

effected by the merger and to the application in the incorporated territory of laws of the incorporating territory.[454] The unification of North Australia and Central Australia as the Northern Territory is revealed to be a merger of the latter into the former, since the laws of North Australia continued but were also applied to Central Australia.[455]

The Commonwealth's acquisition of territory—whether by surrender from the States, by Her Majesty's placing of territory under its authority or by other means of acquisition[456]—is not quite as straightforward as separation followed by merger because, apart from the territory of the seat of government contemplated by the Constitution,[457] there need not be any territory solely of the Commonwealth (that is, territory outside the States) at all. However, to the extent that Commonwealth law has a territorial[458] scope outside the territory of the States, that scope encompasses the Territories,[459] and the surrender of State territory to the Commonwealth is thus analytically similar, though not identical, to separation and merger. When this has occurred, express provision has generally been made continuing existing laws in the new Territories (subject to modifications necessarily effected by the surrender), but internal (continental) and external Territories have been treated differently, in that existing and future Commonwealth Acts are not applied to external Territories unless expressly stated.[460] The continuance of laws in Norfolk Island is not, however, to be taken at face value, since the Governor of New South Wales repealed all laws in force in Norfolk Island shortly before transfer to the Commonwealth, and provided that, subject to 32 laws enacted at

[454] Norfolk Island Act 1843 (Imp), s 2; *Queensland Coast Islands Act 1879* (Qld), s 1. So much is implicit in relation to NZ: *Extension of NSW Laws to New Zealand Act 1840* (NSW), s 1. No express provision was made in relation to the reincorporation of North Australia into NSW.

[455] *Northern Territory (Administration) Act 1910–1931* (Cth), s 16, as inserted by *Northern Territory (Administration) Act 1931* (Cth), s 5. The laws of the two Territories cannot have differed significantly at the time of reunification.

[456] *Commonwealth Constitution*, s 122.

[457] ibid, s 125. No such territory was acquired until 1910: above, text to n 423.

[458] On Commonwealth law's non-territorial spatial scope, see below, section II.C.

[459] The constitutional significance of the Commonwealth's acquiring territory has been questioned, with some suggestion that mere acquisition of territory does not constitute that territory as part of 'the Commonwealth', at least in relation to an external League of Nations mandate territory: *Capital Duplicators Pty Ltd v Australian Capital Territory* (1992) 177 CLR 248 (HCA), 286 (Gaudron J). See also Carney (n 2), 404–06 and the cases there cited. However, while the High Court has observed that there 'are different senses in which a place, or a community, or a body politic, may be said to be, or not to be, "a part of" another place, or community, or body politic', from the perspective of the legal system, what matters is the authority of the Commonwealth over the territory: *Bennett v Commonwealth* [2007] HCA 18, (2007) 231 CLR 91 (HCA), 108 [36] (Gleeson CJ, Gummow, Hayne, Heydon and Crennan JJ).

[460] *Seat of Government Acceptance Act 1909* (Cth), s 6; *Northern Territory Acceptance Act 1910* (Cth), s 7; *Norfolk Island Act 1913* (Cth), ss 4(1), 5; *Ashmore and Cartier Islands Acceptance Act 1933* (Cth), ss 6–7; *Cocos (Keeling) Islands Act 1955* (Cth), ss 8, 10; *Christmas Island Act 1958* (Cth), ss 7–8; *Coral Sea Islands Act 1969* (Cth), ss 4, 6.

that time and to any Imperial Order in Council, Norfolk Island was to be governed by all laws and statutes in force in England on 25 July 1828.[461] The continuance of laws in the Coral Sea Islands Territory ought to have been unnecessary, since the islands were unpopulated and acquired on the basis that they were *terra nullius*. Laws may have been continued out of an abundance of caution, but the UK had disclaimed any title or claim, and, while New South Wales might potentially have had a claim to them, its validity is doubtful.[462]

Several other Territories were treated somewhat differently. On the acquisition of New Guinea, German law was expressly repealed, native title and native customs and laws were continued (subject to the ordinances applicable in the Territory and so far as 'not repugnant to the general principles of humanity'), and certain Imperial, Commonwealth, Queensland and Papuan laws were adopted, together with English common law applicable to the circumstances of the Territory.[463] Thus, the guarantees required by the League of Nations mandate were adopted and, as with other external Territories, Commonwealth Acts were otherwise not to apply unless expressly stated.[464] While the Jervis Bay Territory was constituted a separate Territory on acceptance by the Commonwealth, it was 'annexed' to the Federal Capital Territory, to the extent that the laws there in force from time to time were 'applied' in the still legally distinct Jervis Bay Territory.[465] When the Territory of Heard Island and McDonald Islands was acquired, existing laws were terminated and those of the Australian Capital Territory applied in the Territory, with the further qualification that Commonwealth Acts would not apply unless expressly stated.[466] Similar 'application' of the law of an entire system (or subsystem) was subsequently effected in relation, for example, to the Christmas Island and Cocos (Keeling) Islands Territories, where all existing law except certain enumerated statutes was repealed and Western Australian law was applied.[467] Law so applied may be locally amended or repealed, and its application may be terminated by a House of the Commonwealth Parliament.[468]

[461] Proclamation (23.12.1913) (NI) in Commonwealth of Australia, Department of Territories (ed), *The Laws of Norfolk Island* (Canberra, Government Printer, 1965).

[462] See Kerr (n 436), ch 13.

[463] *Laws Repeal and Adopting Ordinance 1921* (NG), ss 4, 9–16.

[464] *Mandate for New Guinea* (n 429), arts 3–5; *New Guinea Act 1920* (Cth), ss 13, 15.

[465] *Jervis Bay Territory Acceptance Act 1915* (Cth), s 4(2), though s 4(3) also incorporated the provision of the *Seat of Government Acceptance Act 1909* (Cth), s 6, continuing existing laws until changed.

[466] *Heard Island and McDonald Islands Act 1953* (Cth), ss 4–5, 7.

[467] *Cocos (Keeling) Islands Act 1955* (Cth), ss 8–8A; *Christmas Island Act 1958* (Cth), ss 8–8A, inserted by the *Territories Law Reform Act 1992* (Cth), s 16. The Territory is taken to be caught by the geographical expressions 'Australia' and 'the Commonwealth': *Acts Interpretation Act 1901* (Cth), s 17(a).

[468] *Cocos (Keeling) Islands Act 1955* (Cth), s 8C; *Christmas Island Act 1958* (Cth), s 8C.

C. Unpopulated Territory and Non-territorial Space

With the exception of the Coral Sea Islands Territory mentioned in section II.B above, acquisition of territory regarded as unpopulated seems to have proceeded on the assumed basis that there was no pre-acquisition law to continue. For example, no express provision was made in relation to the annexation in 1863 of the part of New South Wales north of South Australia to the latter Province: doubtless in view of the lack of European settlement, the territory was essentially treated as comprising wasteland, and legislation simply provided for it to be governed by a Government Resident, appointed by the Governor of South Australia.[469] Similarly, no provision was made in relation to the Australian Antarctic Territory; though it lacks a permanent population, it is not inconceivable that pre-transfer UK law might have applied. Even if any such law existed and survived the transfer, it was extinguished in 1954, when the law of the Australian Capital Territory was applied to the Territory.[470]

The non-territorial spatial scope of Commonwealth law exceeds its territorial scope, in terms of sheer size, in virtue of the sovereign rights and jurisdiction exercised in Australia's vast Exclusive Economic Zone (EEZ).[471] Nonetheless, the material scope of Commonwealth law in that respect is limited to the matters permitted by the UN Convention on the Law of the Sea, essentially concerning the exploration, exploitation, conservation and management of the seabed, subsoil and superjacent waters.[472] There are no provisions in the treaty or in Australia's declaration of its EEZ addressing continuance of laws—but nor is it clear that there were any laws that could be continued. Included within the EEZ (to a distance of 12 nautical miles from the baselines) is the territorial sea, over which, together with the superjacent airspace and subjacent seabed, sovereignty is vested in the Commonwealth, again without any express provision relating to continuance of pre-declaration laws.[473] The same is true of the contiguous zone (the international waters to a distance of 12 nautical miles from the territorial sea), in which the Commonwealth may exercise the control necessary to prevent or punish infringement of customs, fiscal, immigration or sanitary laws within its territory or territorial sea.[474] While the 1980 off-shore settlement, vesting legislative power over, and title to, the sea-bed of coastal waters (within the territorial sea) in the States and the Northern Territory,[475] was also essentially silent as

[469] *Northern Territory Act* (1863) (SA), ss 12–13.
[470] *Australian Antarctic Territory Act 1954* (Cth), ss 5–6.
[471] *Seas and Submerged Lands Act 1973* (Cth), s 10A.
[472] ibid, s 3, sch, pt V.
[473] ibid, s 6.
[474] ibid, s 3, sch, art 33.
[475] Above, n 445.

to continuance of laws, the vesting of title was expressly subject to, for example, the *Great Barrier Reef Marine Park Act 1975* (Cth).[476]

D. Unincorporated Administration

In at least three instances, Australian law extended to territories not incorporated into any Australian polity. From the time that Her Majesty assumed sovereignty over British New Guinea until it was placed under the authority of, and (as the Territory of Papua) accepted by, the Commonwealth, the territory was governed, as a discrete possession, by an Administrator under instructions from the Governor of Queensland, with the administration underwritten by Queensland, New South Wales and Victoria.[477] The proposals for the administration of the territory did not expressly deal with continuance of laws, so those laws continued at common law, until changed by the new authority.[478] In contrast, express provision was made for the continuance of laws when Norfolk Island was placed under the authority of the Governor of New South Wales, without incorporation into that State.[479]

In Nauru, as in New Guinea, German law was expressly repealed, native title and native customs and laws were continued (subject to the ordinances applicable in the territory and so far as 'not repugnant to the general principles of humanity'), and certain Imperial, Commonwealth, Queensland and Papuan laws were adopted, together with English common law applicable to the circumstances of the territory.[480] In addition, all legislation made during the British occupation of the island was continued in force.[481] The mandate and the trust agreement[482] were thus fulfilled, although, unlike in New Guinea, only when direct administration began in 1965, just prior to independence, were there enacted the familiar provisions expressly continuing existing laws but limiting the application of Commonwealth Acts to those expressed to extend to the territory.[483] Continuance of laws was implied when New Guinea was jointly administered with Papua during World War II,[484] before that was made explicit in this

[476] *Coastal Waters (State Title) Act 1980* (Cth), s 4(3).

[477] *The British New Guinea (Queensland) Act of 1887* (Qld), schs 1–2.

[478] Blackstone (n 1), [108]–[109].

[479] Order in Council making Provision for the Government of Norfolk Island [1897] SR&O 504 (Imp), cl 6; Order in Council providing for the Administration of the affairs of Norfolk Island by the Governor, for the time being, of the State of New South Wales (n 420) (Imp), cl 6.

[480] *Laws Repeal and Adopting Ordinance 1922* (Nauru), ss 3, 9–11, 13–16.

[481] ibid, s 12.

[482] *Mandate for Nauru* (n 427), art 2; *Trusteeship Agreement for Nauru* (n 437), art 5(2)(a).

[483] *Nauru Act 1965* (Cth), ss 61, 63–64. By intergovernmental agreement authorised by Commonwealth law, certain appeals from the Supreme Court of Nauru may still be brought to the High Court: *Nauru (High Court Appeals) Act 1976* (Cth), s 5.

[484] See *Papua–New Guinea Provisional Administration Act 1945* (Cth), ss 6–8.

case, too, along with the non-application of Commonwealth Acts unless expressly stated, when the joint administration of the distinct Territories was made permanent in 1949.[485]

E. Summary

Once again, until the role of spatial considerations in a given account of continuity and discontinuity of legal systems is established, it is not germane to draw conclusions about continuity and discontinuity, save in purely factual terms. From that factual perspective, however, this section has revealed the significant territorial expansions and contractions between 1788 and 2001 from the perspective of the Imperial and Australian polities to whose control the territories were subject. Particular attention was drawn to the effect on the laws applicable in given places of separation and merger of territory, its derivative or original acquisition and its unincorporated administration, together with instances of uninhabited territory and non-territorial spaces. Significant dimensions of continuity have been respected in most cases, but other changes imported fundamentally different associations at different points in time.

III. PERSONAL SCOPE

The set of people subject to a legal system changes constantly, through the operation of the legal system both on the natural processes of birth and death and on legal processes such as naturalisation. As with changes in the spatial scope of legal systems, no account holds that every change in the set of people subject to a system entails discontinuity, yet some changes may do so. Non-legal phenomena of membership and community identity are most closely reflected in forms of legal membership such as allegiance, nationality and citizenship. Additional legal instantiations of these features may be found in the law relating to the franchise and oaths of allegiance. This section sets out legal reflections of membership and community in these institutions as they evolved in Australia between 1788 and 2001.

A. Allegiance, Nationality and Citizenship

The legal notions of allegiance, nationality and citizenship are key reflections of pre-legal ideas of community membership. These reflections are,

[485] *Papua and New Guinea Act 1949* (Cth), ss 32–33.

however, not necessarily exact: individuals exist independently of their status within the legal system, so their lack of status within the system need not necessarily indicate a lack of membership of a community.[486] In other words, community membership as reflected in allegiance, nationality and citizenship may be both over- and under-inclusive, in view, for example, of marginal (or marginalised) cases such as temporary visitors to a territory, who owe 'local' allegiance[487] but who are not, in substance, members of the community. Nonetheless, while some judges legitimately assert that there is 'no specific criterion identified for membership of the community constituting the Australian body politic',[488] the centrality of these legal concepts is attested in others' findings that '[t]he Australian community, through Parliament, decides who will be admitted to what the *Australian Citizenship Act* now describes as the formal membership of the community represented by citizenship, "a common bond, involving reciprocal rights and obligations"'.[489] In historical context, the legal notion of allegiance is also significant in forming, along with the jurisdiction of the Privy Council, one of only two elements of 'Imperial fundamental law', imported automatically into all Colonies but not susceptible to local alteration save where authorised by Imperial statute.[490]

i. Allegiance, Naturalisation and Denization

In 1788, the principle of English law that applied in Australia to relate individuals to the legal system was not nationality or citizenship but allegiance. The *locus classicus* for this principle was *Calvin's Case*,[491] a test case contrived to establish whether a man born in Scotland after James I acceded to the English throne was an alien in England. The judges held that allegiance, the reciprocal bond of obedience (to the sovereign) and protection (of the subject),[492] took four forms, of which only two are relevant.[493] Natural allegiance was acquired by birth to parents under

[486] DA Wishart, 'Allegiance and Citizenship as Concepts in Constitutional Law' (1986) 15 *Melbourne University Law Review* 662, 665.

[487] *Calvin's Case* (1608) 7 Co Rep 1a (Exch Ch), 6a; (1608) 77 ER 377, 384.

[488] *Nolan v Minister for Immigration and Ethnic Affairs* (1988) 165 CLR 178 (HCA), 189 (Gaudron J).

[489] *Re Minister for Immigration and Multicultural Affairs; Ex parte Te* [2002] HCA 48, (2002) 212 CLR 162 (HCA), 172 [26] (Gleeson CJ), citing the preamble inserted by the *Australian Citizenship Amendment Act 1993* (Cth), s 3.

[490] Latham (n 101), 520.

[491] *Calvin's Case* (1608) 7 Co Rep 1a (Exch Ch), 77 ER 377. The law before *Calvin's Case*, as far as it can be discerned, is summarised in C Parry, *Nationality and Citizenship Laws of the Commonwealth and of the Republic of Ireland* (London, Stevens & Sons, 1957) 28–40.

[492] *Calvin's Case* (1608) 7 Co Rep 1a (Exch Ch), 5b ff; 77 ER 377, 383 ff.

[493] The other two were local allegiance, owed by an alien temporarily present in the dominion, and legal allegiance, arising by oath sworn in the leet (a process said to have been instituted by King Arthur): ibid, 7 Co Rep 6b–7a; 77 ER 384–85; Parry (n 491), 41–42.

the actual obedience of the King,[494] within the King's dominions and at a time when the kingdom was under the allegiance of the relevant King, and was—being a consequence of natural not human law—incapable of divestment or change.[495] Acquired allegiance, which Coke calls denization, was acquired after birth, could be absolute or limited, and was effected by Act of Parliament, letters patent (made by the King personally[496]) or conquest.[497]

The judges held that allegiance was owed to the King personally rather than to the kingdom.[498] Accordingly, those born in Scotland before the union of the Crowns remained aliens in England; and as to *postnati*, should the union be broken, the status of natural born subjects would endure and a subject in the affected territory would thereafter owe allegiance to two sovereigns.[499] However, this central holding and its consequence for the separation of the Crowns did not survive: Parry traces naturalisation and denization of both *antenati* and *postnati* in the seventeenth century to show that the doctrine was ignored in the context of the union of the British and Dutch Crowns under William III,[500] and it was expressly abandoned by the time the Crowns of the UK and Hanover were separated on Queen Victoria's accession.[501] However, the distinction between allegiance by birth and allegiance by naturalisation or denization persisted. Allegiance was entailed by birth in the Colonies just as in England.[502] Nonetheless, already in the seventeenth century, the American Colonies had begun to assert control over membership of the political communities they constituted through local processes of denization and naturalisation.[503]

The first local law on the topic in Australia was an 1828 New South Wales statute empowering the Governor to grant letters of denization to foreigners who intended to settle in the Colony, upon recommendation

494 Recall that James I also claimed dominion over, eg, France, but was not in actual possession of it.

495 *Calvin's Case* (1608) 7 Co Rep 1a (Exch Ch), 5a, 6a, 9b, 18b, 25a; 77 ER 377, 383, 384, 388, 399, 407; Parry (n 491), 41.

496 *Calvin's Case* (1608) 7 Co Rep 1a (Exch Ch), 25b; 77 ER 377, 407–08.

497 ibid, 7 Co Rep 6a; 77 ER 383–84; Parry (n 491), 41–42. On the subsequent treatment of the last, conquest, situation, see ibid, 72–73.

498 *Calvin's Case* (1608) 7 Co Rep 1a (Exch Ch), 10a, 14b; 77 ER 377, 389, 394. While in the main clarifying rather than restating the law, on this point, 'the judges were probably adopting a thesis which was unhistoric as a result of their anxiety to reach a socially and politically desirable result': Parry (n 491), 41.

499 *Calvin's Case* (1608) 7 Co Rep 1a (Exch Ch), 27a–28a; 77 ER 377, 409–10; Parry (n 491), 43.

500 Parry (n 491), 45–47, 53.

501 *Re Stepney Election Petition; Isaacson v Durant* (1886) LR 17 QBD 54, 65–66 (Lord Coleridge CJ, Hawkins and Mathew JJ).

502 *Craw v Ramsey* (1668) Vaugh 274 (CP), 279; (1668) 124 ER 1072, 1074.

503 Parry (n 491), 56, 74–76.

by the Secretary of State for the Colonies.[504] The letters of denization were only effective within New South Wales.[505] The Legislative Council was not concerned with questions of any discrete New South Wales identity but simply sought to encourage foreigners to settle in Australia.

The first general British naturalisation Act, of 1844, applied only to aliens resident in Great Britain and Ireland,[506] as was confirmed by an Act of 1847, by which the Imperial Parliament also confirmed the force of all past and future Colonial laws concerned with naturalisation, within the limits of the Colony concerned.[507] The 1844 Act was re-enacted in New South Wales, mutatis mutandis, by an 1847 Act that also deemed any inconsistent English law or statute dealing with aliens not to extend to or be in force in New South Wales.[508] As this proviso prefigured, and as the 1847 Imperial Act invited them to do, the Australian Colonies adapted local naturalisation laws in the period up to Federation: for example, excluding Chinese people from naturalisation,[509] or providing for naturalisation without further residence by a person already naturalised in another Australian Colony.[510]

The closer links between the Australian Colonies are reflected in naturalisation law in the margins of Federation. Europeans naturalised in any Colony to which the Federal Council of Australasia Act 1885 (Imp) extended were, in 1897, deemed to be naturalised in any other such Colony, subject to any applicable residence requirements.[511] Then, enacted by the new federal Parliament pursuant to section 51(xix) of the *Commonwealth Constitution*,[512] the *Naturalization Act 1903* (Cth) provided for naturalisation of

[504] *Denization Act 1828* (NSW), s 1. On the curiosity of providing not for naturalisation but denization, which could only be granted by the sovereign, and the argument that no delegation was involved because of the requirement for recommendation by the Secretary of State, see Parry (n 491), 523, 527. Parry does not notice, however, that the Governor's Instructions at the time prohibited the enactment of laws relating to naturalisation: above, text to n 61. Denization was also provided for in Van Diemen's Land by *An Act for enabling the Lieutenant-Governor to grant Letters of Denization in certain cases* (1834) 5 Wm IV c 4 (VDL).

[505] *Denization Act 1828* (NSW), s 2.

[506] Aliens Act 1844 (Imp), s 6.

[507] Aliens Act 1847 (Imp). See also the Naturalization Act 1870 (Imp), s 16.

[508] *Aliens Act 1847* (NSW), ss 4, 15.

[509] *Chinese Immigrants Regulation and Restriction Act of 1861* (NSW), s 9.

[510] *An Act to afford to Aliens who have been naturalized in Great Britain, or in any of the Australasian Colonies, certain privileges within the Province of South Australia* (1860) 23 & 24 Vict c 20 (SA), s 1. Victoria made a similar provision but with respect to those naturalised in any continental Colony in Australia, Africa or America, or in Tasmania or NZ: *The Aliens Statute 1865* (Vic), s 9. When SA attempted to provide for re-naturalisation of those naturalised under the Imperial legislation and naturalisation not expressly limited to the Province, the measure was disallowed: see Parry (n 491), 525 and the references indicated there in fn 19, suggesting that the Secretary of State's view that a person naturalised in the UK was to be treated as a natural-born subject in the Colonies was disputed even within the Colonial Office.

[511] *Australasian Naturalisation Act 1897* (Federal Council of Australasia), s 3.

[512] The Commonwealth Constitution itself makes no reference to nationality or citizenship but only to 'subjects of the Queen': see, eg, *Commonwealth Constitution*, ss 34, 117, in the

any European person resident for two years or naturalised in the UK.[513] The Act excluded the future operation of State laws[514] and was effective throughout, but only within, the Commonwealth.[515]

The status conferred by naturalisation under these statutes was, subject to certain persistent disabilities, that of a natural-born subject. The core concept giving rise to that status remained allegiance.[516] As Wishart notes,[517] however, by the time of the Naturalization Act 1870 (Imp), allegiance had ceased to be founded on natural law, since that Act abandoned the principle that allegiance was incapable of divestment by the subject.[518] While nationality within the Commonwealth was still British,[519] and while allegiance was blind to subdivisions within the Empire, the discrete communities of those subdivisions were nonetheless apparent. In *Potter v Minahan*, O'Connor J noted that

> [a] person born in Australia, and by reason of that fact a British subject owing allegiance to the Empire, becomes by reason of the same fact a member of the *Australian community* under obligation to obey its laws, and correlatively entitled to all the rights and benefits which membership of the community involves [...][520]

Similarly, Isaacs J acknowledged that, while allegiance was the only tie that bound a person to the King, it was a different (and, in the immigration context, relevant) question whether the person was 'a constituent part of the community known as the Australian people'.[521]

ii. Nationality Under the Common Code

The development of a legal concept of Australian nationality was delayed by the Nationality and Status of Aliens Act 1914 (Imp), which

former case explicitly encompassing those naturalised for at least five years. On the terminology used in s 117, see Wishart (n 486), 675–76.

513 *Naturalization Act 1903* (Cth), s 5.

514 ibid, s 13.

515 ibid, s 8; *Markwald v Attorney-General* [1920] 1 Ch 348 (CA), 361–32 (Lord Sterndale MR), 368 (Warrington LJ), 371 (Younger LJ). Locally naturalised people were nonetheless treated as British protected persons except in their former national country: Brazil (n 397), 213.

516 *Potter v Minahan* (1908) 7 CLR 277 (HCA), 304–305 (O'Connor J); *Gavin Gibson & Co Ltd v Gibson* [1913] 3 KB 379(KB), 388 (Atkin J).

517 Wishart (n 486), 699.

518 Naturalization Act 1870 (Imp), ss 3, 4, 6; *Singh v Commonwealth* [2004] HCA 43; (2004) 222 CLR 322 (HCA), 390 [174] (Gummow, Hayne and Heydon JJ).

519 *Attorney-General for the Commonwealth v Ah Sheung* (1906) 4 CLR 949 (HCA), 951 (Griffith CJ, Barton and O'Connor JJ).

520 *Potter v Minahan* (1908) 7 CLR 277 (HCA), 305 (O'Connor J) (emphasis added).

521 ibid, 308 (Isaacs J). As a matter of law, the relevance of the 'community' to the status of alienage for the purposes of Commonwealth constitutional law was later doubted: *Re Patterson; Ex parte Taylor* [2001] HCA 51, (2001) 207 CLR 391 (HCA), 472–73 [247] (Gummow and Hayne JJ).

created a 'common code' of nationality and naturalisation for the Empire. The Imperial statute and amendments in 1925, 1936 and 1946 were adopted by re-enactment in the *Nationality Act 1920* (Cth).[522] In its Australian incarnation, the Act defined as British subjects: those who were natural-born British subjects (principally those born within His Majesty's dominions and allegiance);[523] those who had the status of[524] natural-born British subjects because they were naturalised under the Act (principally on the basis of five years' residence within His Majesty's dominions and allegiance)[525] or under equivalent legislation in the rest of the Empire;[526] and those who became His Majesty's subjects by reason of annexation of territory.[527] Although nowhere exactly stated, nationality was equated with being a British subject.[528] In this wholly statutory context, allegiance plays only a minor role: its inclusion in the phrase 'His Majesty's dominions and allegiance' simply deals with the case of dominions of another sovereign occupied by the King, or dominions of the King occupied by another sovereign.[529]

The common code preserved Dominion legislatures' powers to enact purely local naturalisation laws, as well as to discriminate between classes of British subjects.[530] This reflected the first resolution on naturalisation agreed at the 1911 Imperial Conference, upon which the code was based: 'Imperial nationality should be world-wide and uniform, each Dominion being left free to grant local nationality on such terms as its Legislature thinks fit'.[531] A stronger acknowledgement of their entitlement to determine their own membership was the fact that the scheme of Imperial naturalisation only applied to a self-governing Dominion if it adopted part II of the Act.[532] As Brazil remarks,[533]

> by asserting a right to lay down basic principles of British nationality in parallel with British legislation the Australian Parliament and the other Dominion Parliaments that did likewise had begun to move away from the colonial phase under which the only appropriate laws were regarded as laws relating to local naturalisation.

[522] Parry (n 491), 532–33.
[523] *Nationality Act 1920* (Cth), s 6(1).
[524] ibid, s 11.
[525] ibid, s 7.
[526] ibid, s 15.
[527] ibid, s 5(1).
[528] See ibid, ss 9, 18, 20(2), 21.
[529] Wishart (n 486), 701.
[530] British Nationality and Status of Aliens Act 1914 (Imp), s 26.
[531] Imperial Conference, 1911, *Minutes of Proceedings of the Imperial Conference, 1911* (Cd 5745, 1911), 16.
[532] British Nationality and Status of Aliens Act 1914 (Imp), s 9.
[533] Brazil (n 397), 214.

The price of negotiating and adopting the 'common code' of 1914,[534] with naturalisation effective throughout the Empire and the common status of a British subject, was the denudation of that status of any meaningful incident, apart from the (admittedly not insignificant) right to enter the UK. This reflected the fifth resolution agreed at the 1911 Conference: 'Nothing now proposed would affect the validity and effectiveness of local laws regulating immigration and the like or differentiating between classes of British subjects'.[535] Accordingly, to effect population discrimination, Colonial Governments resorted to devices other than nationality: while no longer precluded from naturalisation as they had been under the *Naturalization Act 1903* (Cth), non-European British subjects were still prevented from entering Australia on the basis of immigration law.[536] Parry observes two major consequences of the common code's compromise position. First, 'the vaunted "common status" of British subjects did not connote outside the United Kingdom any substantial equality in relation to, in particular, the right to enter or settle in any particular part of British territory'.[537] Second, and critically for present purposes, 'if the "common status" of British subjects thus had virtually no meaning in the law of many localities, insistence upon it inhibited the development of any coherent concept of membership of local communities'.[538]

By stressing the unity of the Crown and the bond of allegiance common throughout the Empire, the 1914 code obscured legal recognition of the discrete identities of parts of the Empire. These discrete identities continued to develop, especially in the increasingly autonomous Dominions. A 1929 conference on Dominion legislation and merchant shipping accepted that common allegiance was not inconsistent with separate nationalities.[539] The 1930 Imperial Conference (which agreed the Statute of Westminster 1931 (Imp)) reiterated that the common status should be recognised throughout the Commonwealth of Nations (as the Empire had become), but resolved[540]

> [t]hat it is for each Member of the Commonwealth to define for itself its own nationals, but that, so far as possible, those nationals should be persons possessing the common status, though it is recognised that local conditions or

[534] The code was not adopted without divergence across the Empire: Parry (n 491), 84.

[535] Imperial Conference, 1911, *Minutes of Proceedings of the Imperial Conference, 1911* (n 531), 16.

[536] *Re Patterson; Ex parte Taylor* [2001] HCA 51, (2001) 207 CLR 391 (HCA), 439 [146] (Gummow and Hayne JJ). See the *Immigration Act 1901–1920* (Cth), s 3(a), with reference to a dictation test, which, by operation of the *Immigration Restriction Act 1901* (Cth), s 3, and the *Immigration Restriction Amendment Act 1905* (Cth), s 5, was a test given in a European language only.

[537] Parry (n 491), 85.

[538] ibid, 86.

[539] Secretary of State for Dominion Affairs, *Report of the Conference on the Operation of Dominion Legislation and Merchant Shipping Legislation, 1929* (Cmd 3479, 1930), 25 [78].

[540] Imperial Conference, 1930, *Summary of Proceedings* (n 205), 22.

> other special circumstances may from time to time necessitate divergences from this general principle.

In the same year, Australia, as a member of the League of Nations, participated in the conference that produced the Convention on Certain Questions relating to the Conflict of Nationality Laws.[541] By 1936, divergence from the common code—in relation, for example, to the nationality of married women[542]—manifested the patriation of nationality, reflected also in Latham CJ's view 'that it is within the province of Australian law to determine who are to be regarded in Australia as "Australian nationals"'.[543] The people of Australia were recognised separately from the people of Great Britain (and the other Dominions) in George VI's coronation oath in 1937.[544] At the Imperial Conference held shortly afterwards, British nationality was regarded as entirely separate from 'membership', the neutral term[545]

> denoting a person whom [a] Member of the Commonwealth has, either by legislative definition of its nationals or citizens or otherwise, decided to regard as 'belonging' to it, for the purposes of civil and political rights and duties, immigration, deportation, diplomatic representation, or the exercise of extra-territorial jurisdiction.

Nonetheless, compared, in particular, to South Africa and Canada, Australia took few initiatives to mark out an Australian identity by reference to legal status (as distinct from the practical effect of, for example, the 'White Australia' immigration policy): as Brazil notes, it is possible that 'nationalistic aspirations were real and deep in fact, but found expression in other forms and symbols, from the ANZAC legend to cricket contests with England'.[546]

iii. Citizenship

With World War II over, the defects of the 1914 common code could be addressed and, commencing on Australia Day 1949,[547] Australian law for the first time provided for Australian citizenship: by birth, descent, registration (in the case of citizens of Commonwealth countries) or

[541] Brazil (n 397), 210, 215. See *Convention on Certain Questions relating to the Conflict of Nationality Laws* (1930) 179 LNTS 89 (No 4137) (entered into force: generally 01.07.1937; for Australia 08.02.1938).

[542] Parry (n 491), 532; Wishart (n 486), 680.

[543] *The King v Burgess; Ex parte Henry* (1936) 55 CLR 608 (HCA), 650 (Latham CJ).

[544] Imperial Conference, 1937, *Summary of proceedings* (Cmd 5482, 1937), 9–10.

[545] ibid, 25.

[546] Brazil (n 397), 210.

[547] Celebrated nationally by 1935 but not yet a public holiday: E Kwan, 'Celebrating Australia: A History of Australia Day' (2007), available at <http://www.australiaday.org.au/australia-day/history/>, 2.

naturalisation.[548] It was, moreover, an exclusive title: like Canada, but unlike the UK, Australian law provided for the loss of citizenship upon the subsequent acquisition of the citizenship of another country, even another Commonwealth country.[549] The oath of allegiance was to be administered in public and 'accompanied by proceedings designed to impress upon applicants the responsibilities and privileges of Australian citizenship'.[550]

The 'common clause' retained the status of 'British subjects' or 'Commonwealth citizens'—now a derivative status, referring to those holding the citizenship of Australia or another Commonwealth country.[551] This common status has been described as 'the statement in law of the principle of "common allegiance" upon which so much emphasis was placed during the Imperial Conferences of 1926 and 1930'.[552] By the 1948 Act and its Imperial equivalent, allegiance itself, as a foundational legal concept (invoked as recently as 1946)[553] was 'altogether swept away, together with all other rules of the common law respecting nationality'.[554] Allegiance became the consequence and not the cause of nationality,[555] and, moreover, the Crown having become 'separate and divisible for each self-governing dominion or province or territory',[556] Australians now owed allegiance 'not as British subjects but as subjects of the Queen of Australia'.[557] This had important consequences for two considerations of membership as reflected in Australian law. First, there was a concomitant contraction in the range of individuals caught by the expression 'subject of the Queen' in

[548] *Nationality and Citizenship Act 1948* (Cth), pt III.

[549] ibid, s 17; Parry (n 491), 552. This remained the case until the section was repealed by the *Australian Citizenship Legislation Amendment Act 2002* (Cth), s 3, sch 1, item 1.

[550] *Nationality and Citizenship Act 1948* (Cth), s 41. The point was especially important to the then Minister for Immigration: Commonwealth of Australia, *Parliamentary Debates* (House of Representatives, 30.09.1948), 1064–65 (Mr Calwell).

[551] *Nationality and Citizenship Act 1948* (Cth), s 7; British Nationality Act 1948 (Imp), s 1.

[552] Wishart (n 486), 686. See *Re Patterson; Ex parte Taylor* [2001] HCA 51, (2001) 207 CLR 391 (HCA), 441–42 [151] (Gummow and Hayne JJ), citing *McM v C (No 2)* [1980] 1 NSWLR 27 (NSWSC), 44 (McLelland J).

[553] *Joyce v Director of Public Prosecutions* [1946] AC 347 (HL(E)).

[554] Parry (n 491), 92, approved in *Re Patterson; Ex parte Taylor* [2001] HCA 51, (2001) 207 CLR 391 (HCA), 441–42 [151] (Gummow and Hayne JJ).

[555] *Re Patterson; Ex parte Taylor* [2001] HCA 51, (2001) 207 CLR 391 (HCA), 466 [226] (Gummow and Hayne JJ); Parry (n 491), 99.

[556] *R v Foreign Secretary; Ex parte Indian Association* [1982] 1 QB 892 (CA), 917 (Lord Denning MR); see also 920–22 (Kerr LJ), 928 (May LJ). See also *R v Secretary of State for the Home Department; Ex parte Bhurosah* [1968] 1 QB 266 (CA), 284 (Lord Denning MR, Danckwerts and Diplock LJJ agreeing); *Nolan v Minister for Immigration and Ethnic Affairs* (1988) 165 CLR 178 (HCA), 184 (Mason CJ, Wilson, Brennan, Deane, Dawson and Toohey JJ); *Re Patterson; Ex parte Taylor* [2001] HCA 51, (2001) 207 CLR 391 (HCA), 466–67 [227] (Gummow and Hayne JJ); *Shaw v Minister for Immigration and Multicultural Affairs* [2003] HCA 72, (2003) 218 CLR 28 (HCA), 42 [28] (Gleeson CJ, Gummow and Hayne JJ).

[557] *Pochi v Macphee* (1982) 151 CLR 101 (HCA), 109 (Gibbs CJ, Mason and Wilson JJ agreeing).

sections 34 and 117 of the *Commonwealth Constitution*.[558] Secondly, in light of the Commonwealth Parliament's constitutional power to make laws with respect to 'aliens',[559] there was a broadening of the range of individuals whom the legal system regarded as non-members. At common law, aliens were the counterparts to subjects: those 'born out of the liegeance of the king, and within the liegeance of some other state'.[560] As is made clear above, allegiance and alienage had undergone significant change between 1788 and 1901, but alienage at all times included those owing allegiance to another sovereign or owing allegiance to no sovereign.[561] Consequent on the position from 1949, however, that nationality gave rise to allegiance rather than the other way around and that allegiance was due to the Queen of Australia, in Australian constitutional law, 'alien' came to signify, at least, 'any person who was born outside Australia, whose parents were not Australians, and who has not been naturalized as an Australian', and thus to include other British subjects resident in Australia.[562]

As Wishart notes, the marginalisation of the status of British subjects was viewed in the Commonwealth Parliament as 'the consequence of the disintegration of the Empire', and the separation of peoples as 'a corollary of nationhood'.[563] In 1969, the common clause was amended to provide that citizens of Australia or other Commonwealth countries *had the status of*, rather than *were*, British subjects.[564] That status was retained—for the

[558] *Nolan v Minister for Immigration and Ethnic Affairs* (1988) 165 CLR 178 (HCA), 185–86 (Mason CJ, Wilson, Brennan, Deane, Dawson and Toohey JJ); *Street v Queensland Bar Association* (1989) 168 CLR 461 (HCA), 525 (Deane J); *Re Patterson; Ex parte Taylor* [2001] HCA 51, (2001) 207 CLR 391 (HCA), 432 [123]–[124] (McHugh J), 467 [228]–[229] (Gummow and Hayne JJ); *Shaw v Minister for Immigration and Multicultural Affairs* [2003] HCA 72, (2003) 218 CLR 28 (HCA), 38 [14] (Gleeson CJ, Gummow and Hayne JJ).

[559] *Commonwealth Constitution*, s 51(xix).

[560] *Daubigny v Davallon* (1793) 2 Anst 462 (Exch), 468; 145 ER 936, 938 (Macdonald CB per curiam); *Calvin's Case* (1608) 7 Co Rep 1a (Exch Ch), 16a; (1608) 77 ER 377, 396.

[561] *Singh v Commonwealth* [2004] HCA 43, (2004) 222 CLR 322 (HCA), 389–94 [173]–[177], 395 [190] (Gummow, Hayne and Heydon JJ).

[562] *Pochi v Macphee* (1982) 151 CLR 101 (HCA), 109–10 (Gibbs CJ, Mason and Wilson JJ agreeing); *Nolan v Minister for Immigration and Ethnic Affairs* (1988) 165 CLR 178 (HCA), 184–86 (Mason CJ, Wilson, Brennan, Deane, Dawson and Toohey JJ); *Shaw v Minister for Immigration and Multicultural Affairs* [2003] HCA 72, (2003) 218 CLR 28 (HCA), 40 [22], 42 [27]–[28] (Gleeson CJ, Gummow and Hayne JJ), 87 [190] (Heydon J), though a majority of the High Court for a time thought otherwise: see *Re Patterson; Ex parte Taylor* [2001] HCA 51, (2001) 207 CLR 391 (HCA). Subsequent decisions have held that a person born to foreign citizens, albeit in Australia, may be an alien, whether or not the person was also a foreign citizen: *Singh v Commonwealth* [2004] HCA 43, (2004) 222 CLR 322 (HCA), 342 [32] (Gleeson CJ), 400 [205] (Gummow, Hayne and Heydon JJ), 419 [272] (Kirby J); *Koroitamana v Commonwealth* [2006] HCA 28, (2006) 227 CLR 31 (HCA), 38–39 [14] (Gleeson CJ), 46 [49]–[50] (Gummow, Hayne and Crennan JJ), 54 [80] (Kirby J).

[563] Wishart (n 486), 683. The Bill recognising this was described by the Acting Leader of the Opposition in terms of 'isolationism', as 'separatist in nature' and as effecting the 'liquidation of the British Empire': Commonwealth of Australia, *Parliamentary Debates* (House of Representatives, 18.11.1948), 3230–34 (Mr Harrison).

[564] *Citizenship Act 1969* (Cth), s 6.

purposes of existing statutes but with minimal other incidents—even after it had ceased to exist in every other Commonwealth jurisdiction,[565] until its ultimate abolition in 1987.[566] The status was, for example, one of the qualifications to vote, until the *Commonwealth Electoral Act 1918* (Cth) was amended to refer to 'Australian citizens' in 1981.[567]

Although citizenship under federal legislation is, since 1987, the dominant legal manifestation of the membership relationship between individuals and legal systems in Australia, its dominant position is not indelible, universal or exclusive—just as its history shows it was not inevitable. The notion is statutory, not constitutional, and its scope and incidents are matters for Parliament.[568] Further, just as there were British protected persons who were members of the legal system(s) of the Empire but were never regarded as British subjects or nationals,[569] certain non-citizens—British subjects resident in Australia before 26 January 1984—still enjoy, in limited respects, a special position in Australian law.[570]

B. Franchise

In a system where norm-subjects are able to participate in norm-creation, the extent of the franchise is an important and general reflection of pre-legal concepts of community, membership and participation. The franchise 'is critical to representative government, and lies at the centre of our concept of participation in the life of the community, and of citizenship'.[571] While this need not be true of every legal system (and was not true of the

[565] Brazil (n 397), 222.

[566] *Australian Citizenship Amendment Act 1984* (Cth), ss 7, 33, which, pursuant to the proclamation made under s 2(2), came into force on 01.05.1987.

[567] *Statute Law (Miscellaneous Amendments) Act 1981* (Cth), s 32.

[568] *Re Minister for Immigration and Multicultural Affairs; Ex parte Te* [2002] HCA 48, (2002) 212 CLR 162 (HCA), 173 [31] (Gleeson CJ), 180 [58] (Gaudron J), 188–89 [90], 192 [108]–[109] (McHugh J); *Koroitamana v Commonwealth* [2006] HCA 28, (2006) 227 CLR 31 (HCA), 46 [48] (Gummow, Hayne and Crennan JJ), 47 [54]–[55] (Kirby J). Parliament can, eg, decline to extend citizenship to inhabitants of external territories: *Re Minister for Immigration and Multicultural Affairs; Ex parte Ame* [2005] HCA 36, (2005) 222 CLR 439 (HCA), 458 [33] (Gleeson CJ, McHugh, Gummow, Hayne, Callinan and Heydon JJ).

[569] See Parry (n 491), 89–91.

[570] See, eg, *Commonwealth Electoral Act 1918* (Cth), s 93(1)(b)(ii).

[571] *Roach v Electoral Commissioner* [2007] HCA 43, (2007) 233 CLR 162 (HCA), 174 [7] (Gleeson CJ); see also at 199 [83] (Gummow, Kirby and Crennan JJ). See also *Kean v Kerby* (1920) 27 CLR 449 (HCA), 459 (Isaacs J). Strictly, Australian constitutions do not provide for (any particular model of) representative government; rather, they institute a system of government that incorporates representative elements (such as the requirement in ss 7 and 24 of the *Commonwealth Constitution* that certain members of Parliament be 'directly chosen by the people'). Other elements of that system of government may be inconsistent with an abstract conception of representative government: eg, a monarchy that is hereditary or vice-regal representatives and executive officers—and some members of Parliament—that are appointed.

UK or of Australia before the end of the nineteenth century), it does have particular resonance in relation to Australia, where representative institutions took root comparatively early, and where many electoral reforms of the nineteenth and twentieth centuries made their first, or very early, appearances.

i. New South Wales

When representative government was introduced into New South Wales, voting was limited to male subjects of the Queen (including Aboriginal inhabitants of the Colony), aged at least 21 years, not attainted or convicted of treason, felony or other infamous offence (an offence of dishonesty)[572] in any part of the Queen's dominions, and seised of or entitled to freehold within the relevant electoral district worth at least £200 (clear value) or occupying a house worth at least £20 pa for at least the six months preceding the election.[573] The property values were reduced to £100 and £10 respectively in 1850, at the same time that leaseholders worth at least £10 pa were permitted to vote.[574] The same qualifications were provided for when responsible and representative government was established with the bicameral Parliament in 1855, save that the property qualification could, additionally, be met by holding a crown pastoral licence including the right to vote, having earned a salary of at least £100 pa for at least six months before registration, or having paid at least £40 for board and lodging (or £10 for lodging alone) for the same room for at least six months before registration.[575]

Comprehensive local legislation enacted in 1858 enfranchised all male subjects of the Queen, aged at least 21 years, resident in New South Wales for at least three years, if enrolled and not disqualified or incapable of voting,[576] if, in the preceding six months, they: had been resident in the relevant district; held a freehold or leasehold (of at least three years' duration) in the district to the clear value of at least £100 or £10 pa respectively; occupied premises in the district to the annual value of at least £10; or held a crown pastoral lease.[577] Certain resident holders of miner's rights or licences were also entitled to vote,[578] and, once the University of Sydney

[572] See *Roach v Electoral Commissioner* [2007] HCA 43, (2007) 233 CLR 162 (HCA), 190–92 [59]–[62] (Gummow, Kirby and Crennan JJ).

[573] Australian Constitutions Act 1842 (Imp), ss 5–7.

[574] Australian Constitutions Act 1850 (Imp), s 4.

[575] New South Wales Constitution Act 1855 (Imp), sch 1, s 11.

[576] Disqualified, on the grounds of an unsound mind, receipt of charitable aid, attainder or conviction for treason, felony or an infamous offence, or incapable, because in military or police service: *The Electoral Act of 1858* (NSW), ss 11–12.

[577] ibid, s 9.

[578] ibid, s 13.

had accumulated a sufficiently large body of graduates, certain staff and graduates of the University were permitted to vote for one additional member of the Assembly.[579]

The qualifications as revised in 1880 provided for voting by male subjects aged at least 21 years, 'absolutely free', enrolled and not disqualified or incapacitated (as under the 1858 Act), who were, for the preceding six months, resident in a district and who held freehold or leasehold to the clear value of at least £100 or £10 pa respectively, occupied premises to the annual value of at least £10, or held a crown pastoral lease or licence.[580] By the 1893 scheme, all male subjects resident in New South Wales for at least a year and in the relevant district for the preceding three months, aged at least 21 years, absolutely free and not disqualified, were entitled to be enrolled and, if enrolled, to vote.[581]

These qualifications and disqualifications (apart from that excluding police voting)[582] were retained in the consolidating legislation enacted shortly after Federation.[583] In 1902, the franchise was extended to women.[584] The military disqualification was removed in 1911.[585] By the 1912 consolidation, the residence criterion was six months within the Commonwealth and three months' residence in New South Wales (as a natural-born or naturalised subject), and one month in the relevant district, but the other elements were unchanged.[586] In 1921, enrolment was made compulsory.[587]

When, in 1928, New South Wales agreed to maintain joint electoral rolls with the Commonwealth, voting, too, became compulsory,[588] and the franchise was extended to subjects of the King who had lived in Australia

[579] ibid, ss 3, 15.

[580] *Electoral Act of 1880* (NSW), ss 11–12.

[581] *Parliamentary Electorates and Elections Act of 1893* (NSW), ss 23–24. Grounds of disqualification were naval, military or police service, unsoundness of mind, receipt of charitable aid, past conviction of an offence that, if committed in NSW, would entail death or penal servitude, current imprisonment, imprisonment without the option of a fine for three months in the preceding six months, or conviction in the preceding year for certain character offences (ranging from bribery to drunkenness, or aggravated assault on a wife).

[582] Removed by the *Franchise Extension Act 1896* (NSW), s 1.

[583] *Parliamentary Electorates and Elections Act 1902* (NSW), ss 21–22.

[584] *Women's Franchise Act 1902* (NSW), s 2. Women were not, however, permitted to be nominated or elected: s 4. Women were not eligible for election to the Legislative Assembly until 1918, or to the Legislative Council until 1926: *Parliamentary Elections (Amendment) Act 1918* (NSW), s 8, sch (amendment to s 79); *Constitution (Amendment) Act 1925* (NSW), s 2.

[585] *Parliamentary Elections (Amendment) Act 1911* (NSW), s 3(1)(c).

[586] *Parliamentary Electorates and Elections Act 1912* (NSW), s 20.

[587] ibid, s 52A, inserted by the *Parliamentary Electorates and Elections (Amendment) Act 1921* (NSW), s 2(9).

[588] *Parliamentary Electorates and Elections Act 1912* (NSW), s 120A, as inserted by the *Parliamentary Electorates and Elections (Amendment) Act 1928* (NSW), s 30(a). In 1979, this requirement was embodied in the *Constitution Act 1902* (NSW), s 11B: *Constitution (Amendment) Act 1979* (NSW), s 2, sch 1, item (4); *Parliamentary Electorates and Elections (Constitution) Amendment Act 1979* (NSW), s 2, sch 1, item (15).

for at least six months, New South Wales for at least three months and in an electoral subdivision for at least one month, who were not disqualified by reason of unsound mind, attainder of treason, or serving a sentence for any offence punishable under the law of New South Wales or any of the King's dominions by imprisonment for one year or longer.[589] As Twomey points out, the Commonwealth and New South Wales qualifications were not identical: unlike New South Wales law, the uniform federal franchise excluded any 'aboriginal native of Australia Asia Africa or the Islands of the Pacific except New Zealand', unless entitled under section 41 of the *Commonwealth Constitution*.[590] The reference to the King's dominions in the disqualification based on imprisonment for one year or longer was removed in 1969.[591] The voting age was lowered from 21 to 18 the following year.[592] The period of residence in New South Wales (apart from residence in the electorate) was removed in 1977.[593] Consequent on the abolition of the status in Commonwealth statutes, the references to subjects of the King were amended in 1982 to refer to Australian citizens and certain British subjects already enrolled.[594] From 1987 to the end of our period, all Australian citizens (and those who would have the status of British subjects if that status had not been abolished and who were enrolled immediately before 26 January 1984) aged over 18 and not disqualified (as previously) were entitled to enrol and, when enrolled, to vote.[595]

ii. Commonwealth

Sections 8 and 30 of the *Commonwealth Constitution* provide that, until the Parliament otherwise provides, the qualifications for electors shall be the qualifications prescribed for electors of the more numerous House of each State Parliament (excluding plural voting). The Parliament provided

[589] *Parliamentary Electorates and Elections Act 1912* (NSW), ss 20–21, as amended by the *Parliamentary Electorates and Elections (Amendment) Act 1928* (NSW), s 15(a).

[590] *Commonwealth Franchise Act 1902* (Cth), s 4; Twomey (n 52), 326. Section 41 of the *Commonwealth Constitution* provides that no adult person who has or acquires a right to vote at elections for the more numerous House of the Parliament of a State may be excluded from the Commonwealth franchise. At the time the federal franchise was enacted, this exception operated in favour of, inter alia, all Aboriginal Australians in those States, including NSW, where they were entitled to vote. However, the guarantee only protects an adult enjoying a right to vote under a State law in force when the (comprehensive) Commonwealth franchise was established: *R v Pearson; Ex parte Sipka* (1983) 152 CLR 254 (HCA), 261, 264 (Gibbs CJ, Mason and Wilson JJ), 278–80 (Brennan, Deane and Dawson JJ). Accordingly, by 2001, it was of historical interest only.

[591] *Parliamentary Electorates and Elections (Amendment) Act 1969* (NSW), s 3(a).

[592] *Parliamentary Electorates and Elections (Amendment) Act 1970* (NSW), s 2.

[593] *Parliamentary Electorates and Elections (Further Amendment) Act 1977* (NSW), s 3, sch 1, item (2)(a).

[594] *Parliamentary Electorates and Elections (Amendment) Act 1982* (NSW), s 3, sch 1, item (1).

[595] *Parliamentary Electorates and Elections Act 1912* (NSW), s 20, as amended by the *Parliamentary Electorates and Elections (Amendment) Act 1987* (NSW), s 4, sch 1, item (3).

otherwise in 1902, establishing (subject to section 41 of the *Commonwealth Constitution*[596]) as qualified to vote (subject to disqualifications) any person, male or female, married or unmarried, who was aged at least 21 years, had lived in Australia for at least six months, was a subject of the King and was enrolled.[597] Disqualification arose if a person was of unsound mind, attainted of treason, convicted and subject to a sentence of at least one year's imprisonment for an offence in any part of the King's dominions, or, as noted above, belonged to one of what the marginal note calls the 'coloured races'.[598] The same qualifications and disqualifications applied under the 1918 Act, with a temporary extension for those serving in the armed forces not otherwise qualified.[599] The racial disqualification was mitigated somewhat in 1925, enfranchising natives of British India and any person who obtained British nationality by naturalisation under Commonwealth or State law.[600] From 1932, section 30FD of the *Crimes Act 1914* (Cth) disqualified from enrolment and voting for seven years the committee members of an association declared to be unlawful.[601]

The racial disqualification was further mitigated in 1949 in favour of Australian Aborigines who were entitled to vote for the lower House of a State Parliament or who had served in the defence force.[602] The remaining racial exclusions were removed in 1961 and 1962, and an exclusion for holders of temporary entry permits and prohibited immigrants was substituted.[603]

The voting age was lowered to 18 in 1973.[604] In 1981, the status criterion was amended to refer to 'Australian citizens' or British subjects who were enrolled before 26 January 1984.[605] The prisoner disqualification was amended in 1983 to exclude those convicted and under sentence for an offence punishable by five years' imprisonment or longer under

[596] Above, n 590.

[597] *Commonwealth Franchise Act 1902* (Cth), s 3.

[598] ibid, s 4.

[599] *Commonwealth Electoral Act 1918* (Cth), s 39.

[600] *Commonwealth Electoral Act 1925* (Cth), s 2.

[601] Inserted by the *Crimes Act 1932* (Cth), s 7.

[602] *Commonwealth Electoral Act 1918* (Cth), s 39, as amended by the *Commonwealth Electoral Act 1949* (Cth), s 3(b). At the same time, s 3(a) substituted the term 'British subjects' for 'natural-born or naturalized subjects of the King'.

[603] *Commonwealth Electoral Act 1918* (Cth), s 39, as amended by the *Commonwealth Electoral Act 1961* (Cth), s 4; *Commonwealth Electoral Act 1962* (Cth), s 2.

[604] *Commonwealth Electoral Act 1918* (Cth), s 39, as amended by the *Commonwealth Electoral Act 1973* (Cth), s 3.

[605] *Commonwealth Electoral Act 1918* (Cth), s 39(b), as amended by the *Statute Law (Miscellaneous Amendments) Act 1981* (Cth), s 32 (as itself amended by the *Statute Law (Miscellaneous Amendments) Act (No 1) 1982* (Cth), s 215). For entry into force, see 'Proclamation' (13.10.1983) in *Commonwealth of Australia Gazette* (1983) No S247, 1. The formulation was altered to take account of changes to citizenship legislation in 1985: *Commonwealth Electoral Act 1918* (Cth), s 93, as renumbered by the *Commonwealth Electoral Legislation Amendment Act 1984* (Cth), s 5 and amended by the *Statute Law (Miscellaneous Provisions) Act (No 2) 1985* (Cth), s 3, sch 1.

Commonwealth or State law, and those convicted of treason or treachery.[606] At the same time, the residence qualification for enrolment was removed and, instead, the entitlement to vote made conditional on having a 'real place of living' in the relevant Division within three months preceding the polling day (with exceptions for certain Antarctic, overseas and itinerant electors).[607] That condition was removed in 1987.[608]

In the last decades of our period, some Justices of the High Court suggested that the phrase 'chosen by the people' in sections 7 and 24 of the *Commonwealth Constitution* now precludes the Parliament's legislating for less than universal adult suffrage.[609] The Justices advancing this view suggest that the meaning of the words depends on the temporal and social context of the legislation, and that the 'fact' or 'common understanding' of membership of the Australian community is now such as to render anything less than universal adult citizen suffrage (with only minor exceptions) something other than a choice by the people. While both this interpretation of sections 7 and 24 and the method adopted to reach it are disputed, it is significant as a legal reflection of (partly) non-legal norms of community membership.

iii. Norfolk Island

Brief mention may be made of the franchise in the external Territory of Norfolk Island towards the end of our period. Self-government, through a Legislative Assembly of nine members, was conferred on Norfolk Island in 1979.[610] To qualify to be an elector, a person was required: to be an Australian citizen, or otherwise have the status of a British subject; have attained 18 years; be a Norfolk Island resident or holder of a non-temporary entry permit; and have been ordinarily resident in Norfolk Island during the preceding six months.[611] A person convicted and under sentence of imprisonment of one year or longer for an offence against a Commonwealth, State

[606] *Commonwealth Electoral Act 1918* (Cth), s 39(6), as amended by the *Commonwealth Electoral Legislation Amendment Act 1983* (Cth), s 23. An attempt, after our period, to disqualify all prisoners, regardless of the duration of their sentence, was held to be unconstitutional in *Roach v Electoral Commissioner* [2007] HCA 43, (2007) 233 CLR 162 (HCA).

[607] *Commonwealth Electoral Act 1918* (Cth), ss 39(4), (7), as amended by the *Commonwealth Electoral Legislation Amendment Act 1983* (Cth), s 23.

[608] *Commonwealth Electoral Amendment Act 1987* (Cth), s 44, sch.

[609] *Attorney-General (Cth); Ex rel McKinlay v Commonwealth* (1975) 135 CLR 1 (HCA), 36 (McTiernan and Jacobs JJ); *McGinty v Western Australia* (1996) 186 CLR 140 (HCA), 166–67 (Brennan CJ), 201 (Toohey J), 221–22 (Gaudron J); *Langer v Commonwealth* (1996) 186 CLR 302 (HCA), 342 (McHugh J). See also, subsequently to our period, *Roach v Electoral Commissioner* [2007] HCA 43, (2007) 233 CLR 162 (HCA), 174 [7] (Gleeson CJ), 198–99 [83] (Gummow, Kirby and Crennan JJ).

[610] *Norfolk Island Act 1979* (Cth), s 19(1).

[611] *Legislative Assembly Ordinance 1979* (NI), s 6(1) (made by the Governor-General under the *Norfolk Island Act 1979* (Cth), s 69(1)).

or Territory law was disqualified.[612] In 1985, the Legislative Assembly amended the Ordinance so as to enfranchise Australian citizens or British subjects aged over 18 who had resided in Norfolk Island for three years (continuously, or, in total, for at least two years and six months in the previous three years) and who satisfied the Administrator of an intention to live in Norfolk Island indefinitely.[613] In 1986, the citizenship requirement was removed entirely, and, in 1991, the residence requirement was amended, such that the franchise encompassed any person aged over 18 who had been present in Norfolk Island for 900 days during the preceding four years.[614]

Thus, from 1986 to the end of our period, membership of the Norfolk Island community, as reflected in the electoral franchise, operated on the basis of long-term residence, without reference to allegiance, nationality or citizenship, which, whatever their other differences, had been central elements in the franchise laws of all Australian polities since the beginning.[615] This distinctive feature was the subject of litigation after our period, when the Commonwealth Parliament inserted into the governing *Norfolk Island Act 1979* (Cth) an Australian citizenship qualification.[616] That law was challenged (unsuccessfully) by plaintiffs who complained that it 'selects as a criterion one which is not a defining characteristic a person must possess in order to be a member of the Norfolk Island community or one of the people of Norfolk Island; it excludes from electoral rights a substantial number of people who are part of the people of Norfolk Island'.[617]

C. Oaths of Allegiance

On commencing his tenure, Governor Phillip was required to take the oath of abjuration in the form: 'I AB do truly and sincerely acknowledge, profess, testify, and declare, in my Conscience, before God and the World, That our Sovereign Lord King *George* is lawful and rightful King of this Realm, and all his Majesty's Dominions and Countries thereunto belonging'.[618]

612 *Legislative Assembly Ordinance 1979* (NI), s 6(2).

613 *Legislative Assembly (Amendment) Act 1984* (NI), s 2.

614 *Statute Law Revision (Status) (No 3) Act 1986* (NI), s 3, sch, item 3; *Legislative Assembly Amendment Act 1991* (NI), s 6.

615 In relation to NI representative bodies 1897–1914, see *Bennett v Commonwealth* [2007] HCA 18, (2007) 231 CLR 91 (HCA), 117–20 [68]–[69], [71], [73]–[76] (Kirby J).

616 *Norfolk Island Amendment Act 2004* (Cth), s 3, sch 1, pt 1.

617 *Bennett v Commonwealth* [2007] HCA 18, (2007) 231 CLR 91 (HCA), 109 [38] (Gleeson CJ, Gummow, Hayne, Heydon and Crennan JJ).

618 Treason Act 1766 (Imp), s 1. He was also required to make the assurance in the form there provided, as well as the declaration provided in the Popish Recusants Act 1672 (Eng), s 9, an oath of office in the usual form and the oath prescribed for governors of plantations in the Navigation Act 1660 (Imp), s 2: Commission (02.04.1787) (n 9), 62–63.

A variety of forms of oath was employed after the grant of a local legislature. Members of the early New South Wales Legislative Council took an official oath to 'faithfully advise and assist the Governor or Acting Governor of the Colony of *New South Wales* and its Dependencies'.[619] The first local denization legislation, somewhat curiously, used the form provided in the Security of the Sovereign Act 1714 (Imp), instead of the amended form used since 1766.[620]

Under the constitutional reforms of 1842, Legislative Councillors swore (or affirmed) to 'be faithful and bear true Allegiance to Her Majesty Queen *Victoria* as lawful Sovereign of the United Kingdom of *Great Britain* and *Ireland*, and of this Colony of *New South Wales*, dependent on and belonging to the said United Kingdom'.[621] Contemporary local naturalisation legislation simply required an oath to 'be faithful and bear true allegiance to Her Majesty Queen Victoria'.[622] This was, however, updated in 1853 to refer to 'Her Majesty Queen Victoria as lawful Sovereign of the United Kingdom of Great Britain and Ireland and of this Colony of New South Wales dependent on and belonging to the said United Kingdom'.[623] The same 'dependent on and belonging to' formulation was set out in the 1855 Constitution (drafted in the same year) for Members of the Legislative Council and Legislative Assembly.[624]

The formulation becomes opaque, however, when substituted in 1900 by an oath (or affirmation) of allegiance in the simple form, 'I,   , do swear that I will be faithful and bear true allegiance to [Her] Majesty [Queen Victoria], Her Heirs and Successors according to law. So help me God'.[625] Only the Executive Councillor's oath referred to a polity, swearing to give counsel and advice 'for the good management of the public affairs of New South Wales'.[626]

The simpler 1900 formulation reflected contemporary moves towards uniformity in the UK,[627] and was reflected in the formulation provided in the schedule to the *Commonwealth Constitution*: 'I, *AB*, do swear [solemnly and sincerely declare and affirm] that I will be faithful and bear true allegiance to [Her] Majesty [Queen Victoria], [Her] heirs and successors according to law. [SO HELP ME GOD!]'. The constitutional reference, in

619 Justice, New South Wales Act 1823 (Imp), s 32.

620 *Denization Act 1828* (NSW), s 2.

621 Australian Constitutions Act 1842 (Imp), ss 25–26. The formulation was extended to other Colonies by the Australian Constitutions Act 1850 (Imp), s 12.

622 *Aliens Act 1847* (NSW), s 8.

623 *Naturalization Act 1853* (NSW), s 2.

624 New South Wales Constitution Act 1855 (Imp), sch 1, ss 33–34. So, too, in local legislation: see, eg, *Colonial Naval Service Act 1855* (NSW), s 5.

625 *Oaths Act 1900* (NSW), s 4(1), sch 2.

626 ibid, ss 5, 10, sch 5.

627 The Parliamentary Oaths Act 1866 (Imp), s 1; Promissory Oaths Act 1868 (Imp), s 2; Naturalization Act 1870 (Imp), s 9.

1901 at least, extended 'to Her Majesty's heirs and successors *in the sovereignty of the United Kingdom*'.[628] The oath of allegiance required of Commonwealth officers and those to be naturalised followed the constitutional form.[629] Oaths of allegiance and office in similar form, referring only to 'Her Majesty and Her Majesty's Heirs and Successors', were provided in post-*Australia Acts* amendments to the New South Wales constitution.[630]

D. Summary

The significance of the evolution of norms of social and community membership reflected in the materials surveyed in this section is analysed in chapters four and six. Nonetheless, from an essentially factual perspective, the changes highlighted in subsection III.A exposed initial tensions in the construction of community membership, with effect limited to particular Colonial units, the development of closer links between the societies of the Australian Colonies from the mid-nineteenth century, and the breaking apart of the governing notions of allegiance and then, in turn, nationality, in order to give effect to local membership criteria with legal incidents. The depiction of the franchise in section III.B revealed a progressive extension of the vote to those with an interest in community decision-making, from land-owners, to pastoral leaseholders to residents. Preferential treatment for residents of other Australian Colonies was observed prior to Federation, and exclusions based on disqualifying features such as executive service were gradually removed, such that, by the end of the period, certain judges of the High Court of Australia considered that universal adult citizen suffrage had become an established social fact governing the interpretation of the *Commonwealth Constitution*. In contrast, section III.C showed that the form of oaths of allegiance and office became somewhat more opaque as a consequence of generalisation and standardisation.

IV. CONCLUSIONS: CHANGES IN AUSTRALIAN LAW 1788–2001

It is not the purpose of this chapter to offer any judgements on continuity or discontinuity: to do so would involve applying one or other theoretical account, which is the subject of subsequent chapters. Nonetheless, between 1788 and 2001, profound change is visible in respect of all the

[628] Commonwealth of Australia Constitution Act 1900 (Imp), s 2 (emphasis added).

[629] See, eg, *Papua–New Guinea Provisional Administration Act 1945* (Cth), s 14; *Nationality and Citizenship Act 1948* (Cth), s 16, sch 2.

[630] *Constitution Act 1902* (NSW), s 9E, inserted by the *Constitution (Amendment) Act 1987* (NSW), s 2, sch 1, item (3).

features considered. In some cases, it is possible to discern a broad periodisation. The relevant constitutional history, for example, was considered in periods of military autocracy, limited local legislative authority, representative and responsible government as separate Colonies, colonial States within a colonial Commonwealth, colonial States within an independent Commonwealth and independent States in an independent Commonwealth. Much of the other material considered under the rubric of the nature and material scope of Australian law follows a roughly similar pattern, although changes in governmental forms and symbols are frequently radically unsynchronised with changes in constitutional law. Australian law's reflections of changing community identities, considered under the rubrics of spatial and personal scope, follow their own discrete patterns—somewhat arbitrary in the former case and, in the latter, shadowing changes in the nature and scope of Australian law but at some remove in time. What emerges is a set of features, the changes to which over time are much more complex and often more fundamental than the simple substitution of timbers in Theseus's ship.[631] Where, when and how propositions of continuity or discontinuity can be made in relation to this matrix of features, and how convincing those propositions are, are questions that may now be addressed.

[631] Plutarch, 'Theseus' in *Plutarch's Lives*, vol I, original 1st century AD (B Perrin tr, London, Heinemann, 1914) XXIII.1.

3

Kelsen: Authorised Constitutional Change

THIS CHAPTER CRITICALLY reconstructs Kelsen's account of the continuity and discontinuity of legal systems[1] during his 'classical' phase. This is generally taken to refer to the period from 1921 to 1960;[2] the key expression of Kelsen's account (in English) is, therefore, to be found in his *General Theory of Law and State* and *Pure Theory of Law*. Notwithstanding this focus on his classical phase, reference will also be made to the consequences of Kelsen's rethinking of fundamental doctrines during his final, radical or 'sceptical' phase,[3] with particular reference to his incomplete and only posthumously published *General Theory of Norms*. This chapter systematically examines the modes of authorised constitutional change implicated in Kelsen's account, and interrogates the exceptions and qualifications to the model it presents. This analysis, at the level of theory, is preliminary to the further elaboration and testing of Kelsen's account conducted in chapter four, where the account reconstructed here is applied to the historical instance of Australia between 1788 and 2001.

Sections I and II of this chapter explain the model's concepts of norms, validity, hierarchy and basic norm. The reconstruction of these core elements of the model is assisted by reference to salient criticisms and suggested modifications drawn from the extensive literature examining Kelsen's theory of law. Particular attention is given to the model's account of multiple, independent and total and partial legal systems, as it will be suggested that the operation of these parts of the model plays a more prominent role in its account of continuity than has been appreciated.

[1] Kelsen's preferred term, 'legal orders', is relevantly synonymous with 'legal systems'.

[2] See SL Paulson, 'Introduction' in SL Paulson and BL Paulson (eds), *Normativity and Norms: Critical Perspectives on Kelsenian Themes* (Oxford, OUP, 1998) xxiii, xxiii–xxiv. For discussion of the periodisation of Kelsen's work, see SL Paulson, 'Four Phases in Hans Kelsen's Legal Theory? Reflections on a Periodization' (1998) 18 *OJLS* 153; SL Paulson, 'Arriving at a Defensible Periodization of Hans Kelsen's Legal Theory' (1999) 19 *OJLS* 351 and the references there cited.

[3] For a survey of the significant changes to Kelsen's thought in the final period, see M Hartney, 'Introduction: The Final Form of The Pure Theory of Law' in H Kelsen, *General Theory of Norms* (M Hartney tr, Oxford, Clarendon Press, 1991); SL Paulson, 'Kelsen's Legal Theory: the Final Round' (1992) 12 *OJLS* 265.

Section IV turns to the account of continuity and discontinuity itself, examining the central criterion of authorised constitutional change and identifying three exceptions, before addressing Kelsen's alternative account of continuity by reference to international law. Finally, section V deals (at the abstract level of theory) with four sets of problems with Kelsen's account of continuity.

At the outset, it is important to note some general features of Kelsen's legal theory. Famously, it aims to be a 'pure' theory: it seeks to give an account of law and legal systems without reference to 'alien' elements, such as psychology, sociology, ethics and political theory.[4] While it is a general theory, not an interpretation of a particular legal system, its scope is limited to systems of positive law[5] that are 'by and large effective'.[6] In essence, Kelsen's theory is descriptive in its aim and cognitive in its approach: it is an account of how to explain and understand existing legal systems.

I. FRAMEWORK: NORMS AND LEGAL ORDERS

In Kelsen's account, a legal system is a system of norms regulating human behaviour.[7] A norm functions as a standard of behaviour;[8] its forms (for Kelsen) include command, permission and authorisation (power to create norms).[9] Positive norms are the objective normative meaning of an act of will.[10] They are created by an act of will;[11] this establishes their positivity. Norms are, however, distinct from the acts of will that create them: they are distinguished by the property of 'validity';[12] validity is the 'specific existence' of norms.[13] The validity of norms can have spatial, temporal, personal and material spheres.[14]

Kelsen's account deals with existing legal systems. This limitation of scope is reflected in what Kelsen describes as a condition of validity: to be valid, the norm must belong to a system of norms that is, on the whole,

[4] H Kelsen, *Pure Theory of Law, Reine Rechtslehre*, first published 1960, 2nd edn (M Knight tr, Berkley, Ca, University of California Press, 1967) 1.

[5] ibid.

[6] H Kelsen, 'Professor Stone and the Pure Theory of Law' (1965) 17 *Stanford Law Review* 1128, 1142.

[7] Kelsen, *Pure Theory* (n 4), 4.

[8] ibid, 17.

[9] ibid, 4–5.

[10] ibid, 8–9.

[11] ibid, 16.

[12] ibid, 10–11.

[13] H Kelsen, *General Theory of Law and State* (A Wedberg tr, New York, Harvard University Press, 1945) 30.

[14] Kelsen, *Pure Theory* (n 4), 12–15.

efficacious.[15] The human behaviour the system regulates must actually conform to it, at least to some minimum degree.[16] If the system as a whole ceases to be effective, no (valid) norm can be said to exist. Effectiveness and validity do not coincide: efficacy is a necessary but not a sufficient condition of validity.[17] In Kelsen's theory, a norm may be immediately valid (if created in accordance with the relevant authorising norm in the context of a generally efficacious legal system), but, if the minimum degree of effectiveness never follows, it loses validity.[18]

Validity is closely connected with the idea of a normative *system* in Kelsen's account. The reason for the validity of a norm, as an 'ought', is always another (valid) norm.[19] Kelsen distinguishes two ways in which one norm can be the reason for the validity of another; each way necessarily gives rise to a system or order of norms.[20] A system or order is present where a set of norms has a unity 'constituted by the fact that they all have the same reason for their validity; and the reason for the validity of a normative order is a basic norm … from which the validity of all norms of the order [is] derived'.[21] First, a norm may be the reason for the validity of a second norm because the second norm can be derived from the first by inference from the general to the specific.[22] One of Kelsen's examples is the norm 'You must not hurt your neighbor', which may be derived in this way from the more general norm 'You shall love your neighbor'.[23] Mapping the inferences will produce a set of norms that form a system with, at its hierarchical summit, a basic norm in the form of the most general norm from which the others are derived. Kelsen terms a normative order of this kind 'static'.[24]

Second, a norm may be the reason for the validity of a second norm because it authorises the creation or application of the second norm. Each norm in such a system is created according to the provisions of another norm.[25] The basic norm of this kind of system establishes a norm-creating authority; specific acts of will of that authority (or of an authority authorised by an act of will of that authority) create norms of the system.[26] Kelsen calls a system of this kind, which incorporates a process of creation and

15 Kelsen, *General Theory of Law and State* (n 13), 42.
16 Kelsen, *Pure Theory* (n 4), 11, 210–11.
17 Kelsen, *General Theory of Law and State* (n 13), 119; Kelsen, *Pure Theory* (n 4), 212.
18 Kelsen, *Pure Theory* (n 4), 11.
19 Kelsen, *General Theory of Law and State* (n 13), 111; Kelsen, *Pure Theory* (n 4), 193.
20 Kelsen, *Pure Theory* (n 4), 195–97.
21 ibid, 31.
22 Kelsen, *General Theory of Law and State* (n 13), 112.
23 ibid.
24 ibid.
25 ibid, 132.
26 ibid, 113.

application of norms, 'dynamic'.[27] Since law regulates its own creation,[28] a legal system is a dynamic normative system: 'The basic norm of a legal order is the postulated ultimate rule according to which the norms of this order are established and annulled, receive and lose their validity.'[29] The dynamic character of legal systems is also linked to their positivity, since, while an authorising norm is the reason for the validity of another norm, the creation of a norm requires an act of will.

Finally, legal systems are distinguished from other (dynamic) normative systems by coercion: law is a coercive order;[30] it has a monopoly on the use of force.[31] Archetypally, therefore, rules of law are norms stipulating sanctions,[32] and a norm is only a legal norm if it purports to regulate human behaviour 'by providing an act of coercion as [a] sanction'.[33] Kelsen realises that not all products of the law-creating process will generate legal norms in this sense.[34] His theory therefore accommodates a category of 'dependent' norms: these do not themselves stipulate sanctions but are essentially connected with norms that do; the connection is that the dependent norm is one of the conditions of the norms stipulating coercive acts.[35] Norms of constitutional law[36] and norms establishing definitions[37] are dependent norms of this type.

II. HIERARCHY AND BASIC NORM

The scheme of a dynamic normative order leads to a hierarchy of norms, where an authorising norm is depicted as superior to norms whose creation it authorises. Sketched from superior to subordinate legal norms, a system of positive legal norms consists of: the constitution, comprising rules regulating the creation of general norms;[38] general norms, which determine law-applying organs and their procedures; and individual norms, created by the judicial and administrative acts of law-applying organs.[39] It is the scheme of internal justification—validity—that produces

[27] Kelsen, *Pure Theory* (n 4), 70. Kelsen adopted the hierarchical theory from Adolf Merkl: Paulson, 'Four Phases in Hans Kelsen's Legal Theory? Reflections on a Periodization' (n 2), 164; A Jakab, 'Problems of the *Stufenbaulehre:* Kelsen's Failure to Derive the Validity of a Norm from Another Norm' (2007) 20 *Canadian Journal of Law and Jurisprudence* 35, 35–36.

[28] Kelsen, *Pure Theory* (n 4), 71.

[29] Kelsen, *General Theory of Law and State* (n 13), 113.

[30] ibid, 19.

[31] ibid, 21; Kelsen, *Pure Theory* (n 4), 35–36.

[32] Kelsen, *General Theory of Law and State* (n 13), 30.

[33] ibid, 123; Kelsen, *Pure Theory* (n 4), 25, 33.

[34] Kelsen, *General Theory of Law and State* (n 13), 123.

[35] Kelsen, *Pure Theory* (n 4), 51, 54–58.

[36] ibid, 51.

[37] ibid, 57–58.

[38] Kelsen, *General Theory of Law and State* (n 13), 124.

[39] ibid, 128; Kelsen, *Pure Theory* (n 4), 222–24.

the hierarchy, and the hierarchy that produces the systematic character of the legal order.[40] This is because at the top of the hierarchy sits the basic norm, which 'constitutes, as a common source, the bond between all the different norms of which an order consists'.[41]

Kelsen's hierarchy is constructed on the basis of by and large effective norms connected in such a way that the creation of each norm is determined or authorised by another norm.[42] Kelsen's failure fully to explain the idea of determination or authorisation—he simply characterises it as creation by an act of will in accordance with a delegation of norm-creating power[43]—leads many commentators to criticise his theory for omitting a key element. Hart (in a distinct but related context) argues that, in order to show that one norm authorises a second norm, it is not sufficient to show that the first norm provides that a norm of a certain description is valid (including a norm described by reference to the competence of norm-creating and norm-enforcing organs) and that the second norm satisfies that description. Hart gives the example of a Soviet Laws Validity Act of the Westminster Parliament that purports to validate the law of the Soviet Union; he suggests that the lack of recognition of, or appeal to, this statute as determining or affecting the validity of Soviet law by the law-enforcing organs in Soviet territory shows that the 'relationship of validating purport' is not, of itself, sufficient: it must be supplemented by some independent criterion (for Hart, recognition).[44] The only criterion available in Kelsen's model is effectiveness, and, to a certain (and perhaps a large) extent, effectiveness will demonstrate which norms succeed in authorising the norms they purport to authorise. This is perhaps most obviously the case in relation to constitutional norms, the effectiveness of which is, in Kelsen's model, implicated in every application of a sanction.

As Kelsen describes it, we proceed from individual norms to their authorising general norms, thence to the constitution, thence to any prior constitution that authorised the current constitution and, ultimately, we[45]

> reach some constitution that is the first historically and that was laid down by an individual usurper or by some kind of assembly. The validity of this first

[40] MP Golding, 'Kelsen and the Concept of "Legal System"' in RS Summers (ed), *More Essays in Legal Philosophy: General Assessments of Legal Philosophies* (Oxford, Blackwell, 1971) 69, 77.

[41] Kelsen, *General Theory of Law and State* (n 13), 111; Kelsen, *Pure Theory* (n 4), 195, 205; H Kelsen, *General Theory of Norms, Allgemeine Theorie der Normen*, first published 1979 (M Hartney tr, Oxford, Clarendon Press, 1991) 255.

[42] Kelsen, *General Theory of Law and State* (n 13), 132–36; Kelsen, *Pure Theory* (n 4), 233–36.

[43] Kelsen, *General Theory of Law and State* (n 13), 113.

[44] HLA Hart, 'Kelsen's Doctrine of the Unity of Law' (1970) in *Essays in Jurisprudence and Philosophy* (Oxford, OUP, 1983) 309, 336–39. Dworkin agreed on this point: RM Dworkin, 'Comments on the Unity of Law (A Response)' in HE Kiefer and MK Munitz (eds), *Ethics and Social Justice* (Albany, NY, State University of New York Press, 1970) 200, 205.

[45] Kelsen, *General Theory of Law and State* (n 13), 115.

> constitution is the last presupposition, the final postulate, upon which the validity of all the norms of our legal order depends. It is postulated that one ought to behave as the individual, or the individuals, who laid down the first constitution have ordained. This is the basic norm of the legal order under consideration.

By 'the final postulate', Kelsen indicates that it is axiomatic that those who created the first constitution were empowered to do so.[46] The basic norm is, in the classical Kelsenian model, a cognitive device. The first constitution is, ex hypothesi, not created in accordance with any authorising norm and so its validity, and therefore that of all norms of the system it constitutes, remains to be explained. In order to explain how it is that participants in the legal system regard the system's norms as valid, we must assume the basic norm: a non-posited source of validity authorising the creation of the norms of the first constitution.[47] The basic norm is an act of thought, not an act of will,[48] and participants regard it is valid because it is presupposed to be valid; it is presupposed to be valid because without this presupposition, the legal scientist (or the legal officials to whom laws are addressed)[49] could not interpret any act as a legal act.[50] We are free not to presuppose the basic norm, but it is only in doing so that we can interpret the subjective meaning of an act of will as its objective meaning—as having normative force.[51] Kelsen confirms this epistemological function in describing the basic norm as the 'transcendental-logical condition' of the normative interpretation of positive law.[52] The basic norm closes up the arch of legal logic in Kelsen's legal science, which is the 'practical discipline which expounds as a logical unity any effective régime of force'.[53]

The choice of postulating the basic norm as a device to explain how we can interpret law as normative is motivated or necessitated by the purity of Kelsen's theory: it enables us to interpret law as a system of objectively

[46] JW Harris, 'The Basic Norm and the Basic Law' (1994) 24 *Hong Kong Law Journal* 207, 210; MS Green, 'Hans Kelsen and the Logic of Legal Systems' (2003) 54 *Alabama Law Review* 365, 405. Kelsen does not use the term 'axiom'.

[47] Green (n 46), 388.

[48] Kelsen later modifies this view, holding that it is an act of will but a fictitious one: Kelsen, *General Theory of Norms* (n 41), 256. Kelsen goes still further when, having reconceptualised norms as the meaning of acts of will alone, he posits the fiction of an imaginary authority whose act of will has the basic norm as its meaning: N Duxbury, 'Kelsen's Endgame' (2008) 67 *CLJ* 51, 55–56, referring to H Kelsen, 'The Function of a Constitution' in RHS Tur and W Twining (eds), *Essays on Kelsen*, 'Die Funktion der Verfassung', first published 1964 (I Stewart tr, Oxford, Clarendon Press, 1986) 111, 117.

[49] JW Harris, 'Kelsen, Revolutions and Normativity' in E Attwooll (ed), *Shaping Revolution* (Aberdeen, Aberdeen University Press, 1991) 1, 12.

[50] Kelsen, *General Theory of Law and State* (n 13), 116, 396; Kelsen, *Pure Theory* (n 4), 204; Kelsen, *General Theory of Norms* (n 41), 256.

[51] Kelsen, *Pure Theory* (n 4), 204; Kelsen, *General Theory of Norms* (n 41), 256.

[52] Kelsen, *Pure Theory* (n 4), 218; Kelsen, *General Theory of Norms* (n 41), 257.

[53] JW Harris, 'When and Why Does the Grundnorm Change?' (1971) 29 *CLJ* 103, 131.

valid (binding) norms without regard to critical morality.[54] The basic norm, however, marks the limit of the pure theory, because the validity of the basic norm itself is presumed because of its content, and not derived from the validity of an authorising norm.[55] Unlike the legal norms that it authorises, the basic norm is a 'presupposed norm; it is not positive law, but only its condition'.[56]

Consistently with its epistemological role, the content of the basic norm is ascertained inductively through consideration of the (effective) norms of the legal system.[57] In other words, examining the laws to which the behaviour of individuals by and large conforms, and the way in which those laws are created and applied, reveals the assumption on which we have to proceed in order to explain that behaviour as conformity to norms, rather than mere compliance with acts of will. The basic norm is ascertained from the description of an existing legal system. Essentially, therefore, the content of the basic norm is nothing more than the authorisation of the initial norm-creating authority, or the identification of an initial norm-creating fact.[58] In this core sense (and ignoring, for the moment, the relevance of international law), Kelsen frames the general form of the basic norm as follows: 'Coercive acts [o]ught to be performed under the conditions and in the manner which the historically first constitution, and the norms created according to it, prescribe.'[59] The basic norm of any given system, however, points to an actual constitution and system of norms that is by and large effective, underscoring the construction of the basic norm as the underlying premise that makes possible the interpretation of a particular set of (efficacious) legal materials as normative (and, in Kelsen's sense, valid).[60]

Kelsen attributes three further content elements to the basic norm. First, he sometimes builds in a reference to the use of force, rendering express in the form of the basic norm that it is the basic norm of a *legal* system, which Kelsen holds is distinguished from other dynamic normative systems by

[54] Kelsen, 'The Function of a Constitution' (n 48), 117; H Kelsen, 'On the Pure Theory of Law' (1966) 1 *Israel Law Review* 1, 6–7. In his final phase, Kelsen characterises the basic norm as a 'fiction', abandoning the neo-Kantian explanation set out here: Kelsen, *General Theory of Norms* (n 41), 256; Paulson (n 3), 269–70.

[55] Kelsen, *General Theory of Law and State* (n 13), 401.

[56] ibid; Kelsen, *Pure Theory* (n 4), 194–95.

[57] Kelsen, *General Theory of Law and State* (n 13), 120, 437; Kelsen, *Pure Theory* (n 4), 46–47, 86–87; Kelsen, 'Professor Stone and the Pure Theory of Law' (n 6), 1142; Kelsen, 'The Function of a Constitution' (n 48), 115.

[58] Kelsen, *General Theory of Law and State* (n 13), 405; Kelsen, *Pure Theory* (n 4), 196; Kelsen, *General Theory of Norms* (n 41), 255, 257.

[59] Kelsen, *Pure Theory* (n 4), 201.

[60] ibid, 201–02.

its preoccupation with coercion by force.[61] Note that Kelsen purports to describe, rather than prescribe, the link between law and coercion as a universal feature of legal systems. Accordingly, if that description is proved to be inaccurate, the inclusion of coercion as a content element of the basic norm will be an unsuccessful theoretical move, because the basic norm will not be distilled from, and will not constitute as a system, the set of all laws: it will refer only to those connected with the imposition of sanctions. In other words, assuming that Kelsen includes reference to coercion on a descriptive basis, the basic norm will fail to describe the legal materials accurately; and, alternatively, if the inclusion of coercion is stipulative not descriptive, the stipulation will be susceptible to challenge because, while it makes the account work, it will nevertheless appear as an artificially and misleadingly limited account of the relevant legal materials.

The second content element that sometimes features in Kelsen's explanation of the basic norm is the incorporation of the effectiveness criterion. This second additional element is evident, along with the first, when Kelsen states the general form of the basic norm as: 'Force ought to be exerted under the conditions and in the manner prescribed by the by and large effective constitution and by the by and large effective general and effective individual norms created according to the constitution.'[62] Incorporating express reference to the requirement of a minimum degree of effectiveness in this way simply restates one of the parameters of Kelsen's legal theory: that it concerns *existing* legal systems. Its inclusion is innocuous in so far as it draws attention to the methodology by which the basic norm is distilled and to the limits of the system it constitutes. However, we ought to clarify Kelsen's line of thought here and understand effectiveness as a limit that results from the way the examination of a particular set of legal materials is conducted, not a free-standing requirement arising from that examination.

Third, Kelsen understands the basic norm to import a guarantee that laws can be understood as meaningful, or, more precisely, that materials submitted to legal cognition can be interpreted as a meaningful whole, without using logically non-contradictory sentences.[63] Kelsen justifies this feature not by direct reference to the character of norms as part of a normative system but (at least in the main argument that emerges in his classical phase) indirectly, through the logical principle of non-contradiction that applies to statements describing those norms.[64] Because it is not logically possible for the statement 'the law requires *A*' to be true at the same

[61] ibid, 208.
[62] ibid.
[63] Kelsen, *General Theory of Law and State* (n 13), 406; Kelsen, *Pure Theory* (n 4), 208.
[64] Kelsen abandoned this argument, and other arguments for the same position, in his post-classical period: below, section III.D.

time that the statement that 'the law requires *not-A*' is true, Kelsen says that the principle of non-contradiction applies to norms within a given normative system.[65]

Kelsen offers two explanations for why this principle is embedded in the basic norm. On the one hand, he characterises the principle of non-contradiction as entailed by the notion of 'legality' or the 'rule of law', by which he means 'the idea that a certain consequence is linked to a certain factual condition, that, if this consequence is linked to this condition, only this consequence and none other (or no consequence) may follow'.[66] Kelsen maintains that the idea of legality cannot function without the principle of non-contradiction, and that the idea of legality is inherent in the basic norm because the basic norm has the form of a legal rule.[67] On the other hand, Kelsen also says that contradiction would impede effectiveness and that, since the basic norm stipulates effectiveness as a condition of validity, it also prohibits contradiction.[68] As with the inclusion of effectiveness, inclusion of the principle of non-contradiction as a content element of the basic norm is perhaps better understood as expressing a feature of the basic norm that necessarily results from the methodology employed in its construction, rather than as a free-standing content element that is discoverable in the basic norm established by reference to any set of legal materials. It is a consequence of Kelsen's approach to interpreting legal materials, not something that is universally found in all legal materials.

In his later (posthumous) work, Kelsen abandons the principle of non-contradiction between norms.[69] Although he did not expressly address the point, it follows that, in Kelsen's final form, the basic norm would not refer to or incorporate the principle.

III. MULTIPLE LEGAL SYSTEMS

It is relevant to examine how Kelsen teases out the implications of his pure theory in relation to the existence of multiple legal orders within a given territory or population. Kelsen addresses three situations where multiple legal orders are potentially implicated: independent legal systems, total and partial legal systems, and the relationship between municipal and international legal systems.

[65] Kelsen, *Pure Theory* (n 4), 74.
[66] Kelsen, *General Theory of Law and State* (n 13), 406.
[67] ibid.
[68] Kelsen, *Pure Theory* (n 4), 208.
[69] Kelsen, *General Theory of Norms* (n 41), 211–25. Note, though, that he maintains the applicability of the principle to statements about norms: ibid, 223.

A. Independent Systems

A lynchpin of the theory during his classical phase is Kelsen's conclusion that '[i]t is logically not possible to assume that simultaneously valid norms belong to different, mutually independent systems'.[70] The reason it would be illogical lies in the potential for contradiction between the norms of two valid independent systems and the logical impossibility of such contradiction that Kelsen discerns. One reason the potential for contradiction arises is because Kelsen suggests the systems must be unlimited in scope: any limitation implies a higher norm that reveals the two systems to be partial subsystems of a total system.[71] On the basis that it is, from a cognitive point of view, impossible for an actor simultaneously to be required to *A* and *not-A*, Kelsen holds that only one system can be valid: one can adopt the view (presuppose the basic norm) of either system but not both; the validity of one system excludes the validity of all others.[72] Notwithstanding the incompatibility of different legal systems, Kelsen notes that the same individuals may constitute organs in more than one system: in a personal union of this kind, the individual or individuals do not constitute the same organ in each capacity.[73]

B. Total and Partial Systems

To comprise a system or 'order', norms must share the same reason for validity.[74] This means that the basic norm of the total legal system must ultimately sustain all the norms within the sphere of validity of the total legal system, including those in the sphere of validity of the partial legal system.[75] It also means that the norms of the partial legal system share a common (relative) basic norm. To constitute total and partial systems, there must be a hierarchy: the partial legal system is subordinated to the

[70] Kelsen, *General Theory of Law and State* (n 13), 363. Cp Green (n 46), 405. As to late Kelsen, see below, section III.D.

[71] Kelsen, *General Theory of Law and State* (n 13), 408. This step is open to challenge. Kelsen does not, in this context, explain why a system's basic norm might not entail a fundamental temporal, spatial, personal or material limitation. For example, the basic norm that may be distilled from the materials of the German legal system reveals such a limitation: Basic Law for the Federal Republic of Germany (Germany), art 79(3). The reason for Kelsen's position may be his theory of the alternative, according to which such a limitation is merely apparent: below, section IV.C. In any event, since the possibility of contradiction, even between systems of limited scope, cannot necessarily be excluded, the main line of Kelsen's reasoning holds.

[72] Kelsen, *General Theory of Law and State* (n 13), 407–10; Kelsen, *Pure Theory* (n 4), 329. The point is emphasised in Dworkin (n 44), 201; Green (n 46), 405–06.

[73] Kelsen, *General Theory of Law and State* (n 13), 309.

[74] ibid, 111; Kelsen, *Pure Theory* (n 4), 31.

[75] Kelsen, *General Theory of Law and State* (n 13), 304; Kelsen, *Pure Theory* (n 4), 315–16.

total legal system 'because [the total legal system] contains a norm which determines the creation of the norms of the [partial legal system], and hence the latter has the reason of its validity in the former'.[76] These conceptual parameters aside, it appears that Kelsen's model conceives of total and partial legal systems on the basis of territory. While Kelsen describes *partial legal communities* recognised on the basis that norms share the same territorial sphere of validity or the same personal sphere of validity, *partial legal systems* are only recognised to arise on the basis of (prescribed) territorial subdivisions.[77] Since a legal system is a dynamic normative order,[78] decentralisation must be dynamic as well as static: there must be norm-creating and norm-applying organs regulating the norms within the territorial sphere of validity of the partial legal system, not merely norms than happen to have coterminous territorial spheres of validity.[79] Accordingly, the criteria that emerge for a partial legal system are norms that: first, trace their validity to the basic norm of the total legal system; second, trace their validity to the basic norm of the total system through a (relative) basic norm of the partial legal system (which is a positive norm of the total legal system); third, share a territorial sphere of validity that is part (only) of the territorial sphere of validity of the basic norm of the total legal system; and, fourth, are created and applied by organs, the competence of which is limited to the territorial sphere of validity of the partial legal system. Kelsen suggests that, aside from a purely theoretical case, the total legal system must contain some positive norms (applicable across the total territorial sphere of validity) and not merely consist of the basic norm of the total legal system that provides the basis for understanding the partial legal systems as parts of that total legal system.[80]

Kelsen understands a federal legal system to operate as a complex of total and partial legal systems,[81] being distinguished from a relatively decentralised unitary system on the basis that the integers of the federation possess more, and more important, norm-creating powers, including powers in relation to their constitutions.[82] The subjects of a partial legal system constitute a partial legal community. In Kelsen's characterisation, each partial legal system has a constitution, but the federal (central) constitution—which also constitutes only a partial legal order—is simultaneously the constitution of the whole federal (total) legal system.[83]

76 Kelsen, *Pure Theory* (n 4), 332. See also Kelsen, *General Theory of Law and State* (n 13), 373.
77 Kelsen, *General Theory of Law and State* (n 13), 304–306; Kelsen, *Pure Theory* (n 4), 315, 317.
78 Above, text to n 29.
79 Kelsen, *General Theory of Law and State* (n 13), 308–10; Kelsen, *Pure Theory* (n 4), 317.
80 Kelsen, *Pure Theory* (n 4), 316.
81 Kelsen, *General Theory of Law and State* (n 13), 317.
82 ibid, 317–18.
83 ibid, 317.

A supreme federal court is also competent to decide conflicts between the integers and a federal executive can execute sanctions against them.[84]

As just noted, Kelsen holds that the central constitution must also be the constitution of the total legal system. However, it is not obvious that this should be so where previously independent legal systems join a federation. In a substantive (rather than a formal) sense, there will be a constitution of the whole, which will include the constitution of the central integer, but it will equally include at least part of the substantive constitutions of the State integers. It is, of course, possible for the substantive constitution of the whole federal system to be comprised in the formal constitution of the central integer, where that formal constitution also contains the (formal and) substantive constitutions of the States.[85] Assuming, however, that the formal constitution of the central integer does not include the substantive constitutions of the State integers, the substantive constitution of the central integer must logically include at least part of the (substantive) constitutions of the States, and the substantive constitutions of the States must also include at least part of the (substantive) constitution of the central integer. This is a necessary consequence of the allocation of norm-creating power between integers in a federation: at a minimum, the autonomy of each integer with respect to its own constitution (which Kelsen holds is a necessary feature of a federal arrangement) limits the norm-creating power of every other integer and is therefore part of its substantive constitution. It is therefore unwarranted of Kelsen to identify the constitution of the central integer with the constitution of the whole federation. If he means the formal constitution, that is not justified as a matter of logic and is disproved in practice.[86] If he refers to the substantive constitution of the central integer, he fails to do justice to the interconnectedness of the substantive constitutional arrangements in a federation.

C. International Law and the Universal Legal System

Kelsen gives two accounts of municipal legal systems. The first, as set out to this point, ignores international law. According to the second, however, all positive law belongs to one universal legal system, of which international law and municipal legal systems are partial legal systems.[87] This—monist—thesis is grounded in Kelsen's contention that simultaneously

[84] ibid, 320.

[85] See, eg, Constitution of India (India).

[86] Below, 141–42.

[87] Kelsen, *Pure Theory* (n 4), 315. See also H Kelsen, 'The Pure Theory of Law and Analytical Jurisprudence' (1941) 55 *Harvard Law Review* 44, 66–70; Kelsen, *General Theory of Law and State* (n 13), 325–26, 351.

valid but independent norms and normative systems are impossible.[88] On the basis that international and municipal legal systems are part of the same system, Kelsen examines which has primacy. He concludes that interpretation of the legal materials is consistent both with a basic norm giving primacy to international law and with a basic norm giving primacy to one municipal legal system. The choice, he says, is ultimately a question of ideological or political perspective.[89] In terms of his account of municipal legal systems, the consequence of adopting the primacy of international law model is that what would otherwise appear as the basic norm of a municipal legal system is, in Kelsen's view, a rule of positive international law. That is, Kelsen asserts that a rule of (customary) international law provides that a social order is a municipal legal order when it is a relatively centralised coercive order regulating human behaviour, inferior only to the international legal order, and efficacious for a certain territory.[90]

D. Late Kelsen

In his posthumous *General Theory of Norms*, Kelsen abandons the view that logic applies to norms, and expressly acknowledges both that there is no contradiction (but merely an antithesis or opposition) between norms requiring an actor to *A* and *not-A* and that two valid normative systems may conflict.[91] Unfortunately, the consequences of this change of position are not fully worked out in Kelsen's unfinished work. At the very least, the conclusion that mutually independent legal systems may not simultaneously be valid no longer holds. Further, without this underlying premise to tie all valid norms into one system, it may be that Kelsen's picture of total and partial legal systems has to compete with an analysis of independent but overlapping legal systems with independent basic norms. Finally, as Hartney observes, although Kelsen removes the central plank of his monist argument, he does not revisit the relationship between international law and municipal legal orders in light of his change of position.[92] It is in part because the consequences of Kelsen's change of heart about the nature of

[88] Kelsen, *General Theory of Law and State* (n 13), 379–80. Above, section III.A.

[89] Kelsen, *General Theory of Law and State* (n 13), 388; Kelsen, *Pure Theory* (n 4), 346; H Kelsen, 'Sovereignty and International Law' (1960) 48 *Georgetown Law Journal* 627, 638–40.

[90] Kelsen, *General Theory of Law and State* (n 13), 121, 221, 351, 367; Kelsen, *Pure Theory* (n 4), 214, 289.

[91] Kelsen, *General Theory of Norms* (n 41), 213–16. Kelsen's classical view that valid norms belonging to the same system could not contradict one another (even if it were logically impossible to comply with both) was criticised by various commentators: see, eg, Hart (n 44), 325–32.

[92] Hartney (n 3), xlix.

norms are not worked out that this book focuses on his classical period and notices this final position only in passing.

IV. CONTINUITY

Kelsen's account of the continuity of legal systems over time is essentially an account of continuity of the basic norm. This strategy and outcome result from the fact that Kelsen's legal system is a system of norms, the existence of which is a matter of validity, and the validity of which stems from the basic norm. The unity of a system of norms, Kelsen frequently observes, consists in those norms' sharing a single basic norm. There is continuity over time as long as the basic norm is, at all instances in that time period, the same. If, at any point, a different basic norm must be presupposed, there is discontinuity. To the question, 'When is a legal system that exists in a given place at a given time the same legal system that exists in that place at another time?'[93] Kelsen's account answers, 'When the basic norm that the legal scientist must presuppose in order to understand the legal systems as binding is the same at each (and each intervening) point in time.'

Since the basic norm is a construction of legal science framed in terms of (by reference to) a historically first constitution, Kelsen's account of continuity is often understood as taking a historically first constitution as the criterion of identity of a legal system over time. To observe that there is continuity of a system's basic norm over time is to observe that the norms of the system trace their validity through the same historically first (normative) constitution in all instances over the given time period. Accordingly, we arrive at the central thesis about change in Kelsen's account: a change in the set of norms comprising a legal system at a given moment in time does not entail that a different legal system exists at the next moment in time, as long as the change was authorised, ultimately, by the historically first constitution (to which the basic norm refers). Since an unauthorised change—that is, the unauthorised introduction of a new norm that the legal scientist observes to be effective—at a sub-constitutional

[93] So far as Kelsen's account is concerned, the question cannot be framed in terms of a legal system's existing *among a particular people* at a particular time since, for the Kelsenian legal scientist, there is no such thing as social community considered otherwise than as people subject to a common order regulating their mutual behaviour: Kelsen, *General Theory of Law and State* (n 13), 20–21, 182–83; Kelsen, *Pure Theory* (n 4), 150, 286–87; H Kelsen, 'Law, State, and Justice in the Pure Theory of Law' (1948) in *What is Justice? Justice, Law, and Politics in the Mirror of Science* (Berkeley, Ca, University of California Press, 1957) 288, 290–93. The unity of a territory and a people is derived from the legal system: Kelsen, *General Theory of Law and State* (n 13), 255. That unity consists in the behaviour of those people in that territory, oriented towards and governed by that system. Accordingly, for Kelsen, the sociological concept of a state or a community presupposes the juristic concept: ibid, 183–92.

level in the hierarchy of norms entails a constitutional change (if it were a change consistent with and cognisable by reference to the constitution, it would not be unauthorised), the relevant changes will necessarily involve changes to constitutional norms. Broadly speaking, the thesis thus equates continuity with authorised constitutional change and discontinuity with unauthorised constitutional change. This is, however, not always true in Kelsen's model.

A. Revolutions, Authorisation and Effectiveness

It is in the course of explaining the basic norm and its relation to effectiveness that Kelsen introduces his analysis of revolutions. A revolution, in Kelsen's sense, is an *unauthorised* but *effective* (constitutional) change.[94] There are two aspects to Kelsen's analysis: authorisation, which ultimately engages the intellectual process of identifying the basic norm, and effectiveness, which, as a condition of validity and therefore existence, determines the set of legal materials that are in issue.

The chain of validity linking norms to higher norms that authorise their creation ends with a norm of positive law (a constitutional norm, in substance) that authorises norm-creation but is not itself authorised:[95]

> In this way we eventually arrive at a historically first constitution that cannot have been created in this way and whose validity, therefore, cannot be traced back to a positive norm created by a legal authority; we arrive, instead, at a constitution that became valid in a revolutionary way, that is, either by breach of a former constitution or for a territory that formerly was not the sphere of validity of a constitution and of a national legal order based on it.

Where an unauthorised positive (constitutional) law is encountered, recourse must be had to the basic norm to understand the normativity of the law. Only by identifying the presupposition that makes sense of the legal materials we recognise as binding—the basic norm—can we understand normativity. The constitutional norms that are effective after a revolution are, ex hypothesi, unauthorised and, as ultimate authorising norms, constitute the most important set of legal materials from which the basic norm must, inductively, be ascertained. Where a change consists in establishing (effective but) unauthorised constitutional norms, the intellectual process of distilling what is presupposed will reveal a(n authorising) basic norm that differs from the basic norm that the process revealed when applied to the legal materials existing before the change.

[94] Kelsen, *Pure Theory* (n 4), 209.

[95] ibid, 200. This passage (in particular, its last phrase) is discussed in detail below, text to ch 4, n 103.

As Kelsen observes, 'it is never the constitution merely but always the entire legal order that is changed by a revolution'.[96] In contrast, where a new set of (effective) constitutional norms is created in an authorised fashion, that intellectual process will reveal the same basic norm as it revealed when applied to the pre-existing legal materials. The fact that revolutionary norms are unauthorised according to the source of authority initially presupposed requires the jurist to presuppose a new source of authority consistent with the revolutionary norms.

The second aspect to Kelsen's analysis is effectiveness. Efficacy is a condition of the validity of norms, and this is a cornerstone of Kelsen's account of law as a positive, hierarchical normative system. Accordingly, while norms generally remain valid (that is, they exist) until invalidated in a manner determined by the legal system, an enduring loss of efficacy denies a condition of their validity and entails their non-existence.[97] It follows that part of what a successful revolution brings about is, relevantly, a change in the set of legal materials that are to be considered when ascertaining the basic norm. The old constitution loses its effectiveness (its norms cease to exist); the new constitution becomes effective (its norms come into existence); and application of the intellectual process of ascertaining the basic norm to different material (the new constitutional norms) produces a different basic norm.[98]

The presence of this effectiveness aspect complicates Kelsen's account of continuity. Whether constitutional norms authorise change *by reference to efficacy* is a contingent matter: some constitutional norms may allow for the validity of norms that emerge by custom and for the invalidity of those (and perhaps also posited) norms by desuetude or the emergence of inconsistent custom; others may not. Those that do so may provide for efficacy as a criterion of validity in relation to sub-constitutional norms only, or they may provide for it in relation to constitutional norms as well. However, because one of the parameters of Kelsen's account is that it deals only with valid (existing) norms, and because 'by and large' efficacy of the system is a condition of validity, enduring[99] ineffectiveness[100]

[96] Kelsen, *General Theory of Law and State* (n 13), 118.

[97] ibid, 117; Kelsen, *Pure Theory* (n 4), 209. The loss could be general—the whole system ceases to be effective—or specific—'[i]t must be assumed that any legal norm, even a statutory norm, may lose validity by desuetudo': Kelsen, *General Theory of Law and State* (n 13), 119. The loss of efficacy must, however, be an enduring loss: the effect on a single norm is likened to the application of a customary norm of repeal, and Kelsen appears to hold that a norm of desuetude is implied in all legal systems: ibid; see also Kelsen, *Pure Theory* (n 4), 11.

[98] Kelsen, *General Theory of Law and State* (n 13), 216; Kelsen, *Pure Theory* (n 4), 210.

[99] Kelsen takes great pains to stress that effectiveness and validity are not the same; he uses desuetude to illustrate this by observing that a posited norm was valid as soon as it was posited (and, therefore, before it could become effective)—but he still accepts that 'an enduring lack of effectiveness … ends the validity': Kelsen, *General Theory of Law and State* (n 13), 119; Kelsen, *Pure Theory* (n 4), 11.

[100] Enduring effectiveness, as opposed to ineffectiveness, is considered below.

is *necessarily* a mode of change, regardless of what the positive law of the system provides on the subject: it results in the subtraction of elements from the set of legal norms to be considered from one point in time to another.

While Kelsen's discussion of desuetude expressly deals only with 'general' and 'individual' norms, categories he distinguishes in the hierarchy from 'constitutional' norms,[101] it is not possible to understand him as excluding ineffectiveness as a mode of change in relation to constitutional norms. Not only does Kelsen include efficacy in the basic norm as a parameter of his analysis from the dualist perspective,[102] and as a requirement of positive international law (which is, relative to a municipal legal system, a basic norm) from the international-law monist perspective,[103] but, as Teles points out, he expressly contemplates custom as a law-creating fact directly authorised by the basic norm (for example, of systems such as UK and international law, where no historically first constitution is discernible).[104]

Accordingly, Teles makes the point that Kelsen's theory cannot exclude the possibility of a basic norm that authorises a historically first constitution that expressly authorises change by reference to an effectiveness criterion such as *constitutio posterior derogat priori*.[105] Honoré gives the example of a Roman practice, according to which whoever is proclaimed by the army and the Senate is emperor, even if the person proclaimed had treasonously murdered the previous emperor.[106] In this situation, emergence of a new constitution simply by its becoming effective amounts to *authorised* constitutional change, the basic norm authorises a succession of constitutions (without regard to validity criteria other than effectiveness—manifested here in the proclamation by the army and the Senate) and, accordingly, there is continuity not discontinuity. Subject to Hart's argument about relationships of validating purport[107] and to an account of change in the practice that reveals the efficacy of the change (for example, if proclamation by the army but not by the Senate comes to suffice), it is, in fact, difficult to see that there could ever be discontinuity in this

[101] Cp Kelsen, *Pure Theory* (n 4), 213 and 221 ff.

[102] Above, text to n 62.

[103] Above, text to n 90.

[104] MG Teles, 'Revolution, *Lex Posterior* and *Lex Nova*' in E Attwooll (ed), *Shaping Revolution* (Aberdeen, Aberdeen University Press, 1991) 69, 72–73, referring to Kelsen, *Pure Theory* (n 4), 226.

[105] Teles (n 104), 72. In a slightly different context, Honoré also notices the possibility of a temporal limitation on the validity of constitutional norms according to their own terms—as with interim or provisional constitutions, which may expressly contemplate their own substitution by permanent instruments: AM Honoré, 'Reflections on Revolutions' (1967) 2 *Irish Jurist* 268, 273–74. Of course, the rules of change here are usually less open than Teles's formulation, since they generally authorise adoption of new constitutional norms according to a prescribed process.

[106] Honoré (n 105), 274.

[107] Above, text to n 44.

situation. Further, the fact that Kelsen does not recognise desuetude or loss of efficacy of a constitutional norm as entailing discontinuity is part of the reason his account has been considered unable to explain gradual and peaceful separations of legal systems. If Kelsen's account considered that the fading into history of unused constitutional powers amounted to a 'revolution', this aspect of the notorious objection concerning lawful separation[108] would disappear.

While Kelsen's account necessarily countenances enduring *ineffectiveness* as a mode of 'authorised' constitutional change, the position in relation to enduring *effectiveness* is less clear. As noted above, Kelsen acknowledges that custom may be authorised as a law-creating fact, indirectly, by constitutional norms and, directly, by the basic norm—but these are merely contingent possibilities. Many commentators have understood Kelsen's account not to include enduring effectiveness as a *necessary* mode of (authorised) constitutional change in the same way as enduring ineffectiveness. Raz criticises Kelsen's model on the basis that it would find discontinuity between a system whose historically first constitution included no authorisation of customary law creation, and a system valid for the same people and territory and including the same institutions but at a later point in time, when the courts have, by gradual evolution of custom, come to be authorised to create law or when a mistake has come to be accepted and enforced.[109] Maher observes that the initially unauthorised development of custom is a significant and widespread legal phenomenon, and similarly criticises Kelsen's account for finding discontinuity (in a circumstance in which, he says, political and social scientists would not).[110] He also observes problems in Kelsen's account where, contingently, the basic norm does authorise custom: if only a particular customary norm is authorised, any change in that custom will entail discontinuity unless customary change is also constitutionally authorised, but if customary change is constitutionally authorised, the authorisation is vacuous, since any custom that develops will be validated.[111]

This, ultimately, is why the better interpretation of Kelsen's account seems to be, as has been assumed, that it does not include enduring effectiveness as a necessary mode of (authorised) constitutional change in the same way as enduring ineffectiveness. The elision of effectiveness and validity that would result—albeit delayed by whatever period is necessary for the change to count as enduring—would undermine Kelsen's whole account. There is, however, a thin textual foundation for an interpretation

108 Below, section V.C.

109 J Raz, *The Concept of a Legal System: An Introduction to the Theory of Legal System*, 2nd edn (Oxford, Clarendon Press, 1980) 109.

110 G Maher, 'Analytical Jurisprudence and Revolution' in JL Curiel (ed), *Memoria del X Congreso Mundial Ordinario de Filosofía del Derecho y Filosofía Social*, vol V (Mexico City, Universidad Nacional Autónoma de México, 1981) 343, 345–46.

111 G Maher, 'Custom and Constitutions' (1981) 1 *OJLS* 167, 172.

encompassing enduring effectiveness as a mode of authorised constitutional change. Kelsen expressly analyses the emergence of customary law inconsistent with earlier statutory law, and holds that it terminates validity 'even in relation to a formal constitutional law that expressly excludes the application of customary law'.[112] However, since Kelsen at this same point refers to the 'canceling effect' of customary law, it is not clear that he intended more than desuetude. In the case of desuetude, Kelsen addresses the distinction between effectiveness and validity by canvassing the effect of a loss of efficacy on validity but not a gain of efficacy: he reiterates his central claim that a norm is valid if it has been created in an authorised fashion and not annulled.[113] Moreover, it is difficult to read Kelsen as contemplating enduring effectiveness as a *necessary* mode of authorising constitutional change when he merely says that 'the constitution *may* also establish custom as a law-creating fact'.[114]

B. Exception: Termination of Systemic Validity

We must notice one exception to Kelsen's account of continuity. Kelsen says that *authorised* constitutional change (which does not entail discontinuity in the basic norm) *will* result in discontinuity of a legal system where it implies the 'termination of the validity of the national order as a whole'.[115] The example Kelsen gives is of the Austrian legal system's merging into the German legal system, by constitutional means, in 1938 (and putatively in 1918, though that union was prevented from coming into existence by the Treaty of Saint-Germain-en-Laye).[116] While it appears in his *General Theory of Law and State*, Kelsen does not expressly restate this exception in his *Pure Theory of Law*, where he adopts an international-law monist view according to which the temporal sphere of validity of a legal system is determined by rules of international law.[117] It is, as has been observed, inconsistent with his general account of continuity by reference to the basic norm,[118] and the basis for the exception is nowhere explained.[119]

[112] Kelsen, *Pure Theory* (n 4), 227.

[113] Kelsen, *General Theory of Law and State* (n 13), 119–20.

[114] Kelsen, *Pure Theory* (n 4), 225 (emphasis added).

[115] Kelsen, *General Theory of Law and State* (n 13), 220.

[116] ibid. For the Treaty, which established the Republic of Austria and so prevented the merger into the German Reich from coming into effect, see *Treaty of Peace between the Allied and Associated Powers and Austria* (Cmd 400, 1919) (entered into force 16.07.1920).

[117] Kelsen, *Pure Theory* (n 4), 289.

[118] The exception is not inconsistent with Kelsen's (monist) account of continuity by international law by reference to 'essential' territory (below, section IV.D): it is the sole example, in fact, of an 'essential' territorial change.

[119] DN MacCormick, 'Constitutional and Administrative Law (Book Review)' [1972] *PL* 174, 178; G Maher, 'The Identity of the Scottish Legal System' [1977] *Juridical Review* 21, 25–26; DN MacCormick, 'Does the United Kingdom Have a Constitution? Reflections on MacCormick v Lord Advocate' (1978) 29 *Northern Ireland Legal Quarterly* 1, 17–18.

Nor is it clear that the example is appropriate: the choice of constitutional means to merge into another legal system is designed precisely to ensure continuing validity of the system, not to imply its termination.

The exception reaches towards noticing a change in *ultimacy*. Notwithstanding that the process appears to be an authorised constitutional change from the perspective of the Austrian legal system, Kelsen's exception suggests that the proper interpretation is that, post-merger, the ultimate constitutional norms of the merged legal system are those of the pre-existing German legal system *and they retain their character as ultimate and non-authorised norms*, even in relation to the part of their territorial sphere of validity that was previously the territory of the Austrian legal system. On this reading, the Austrian legal system, by constitutional means, *purports* to incorporate (German) norms authorising previously non-authorised (Austrian) constitutional norms. What is implied is the termination of the ultimacy of the constitutional norms of the pre-merger Austrian system. The unexpressed step in Kelsen's reasoning in the case of merger is a denial that norms that are valid across a total territory can be valid for different reasons in different parts of the territory. This is consistent with the general structure of the Kelsenian hierarchy of norms, according to which a norm may authorise the creation of many norms but is itself authorised by only a single norm.[120] In other words, the constitutional norms of the German legal system cannot, after the merger, be non-authorised and ultimate in relation to the pre-merger German territory, and yet authorised (by constitutional norms of the pre-existing Austrian legal system) in relation to the pre-merger Austrian territory. If that were true, validity of norms with an undifferentiated territorial sphere of validity would be conferred by different basic norms in relation to different parts of the territory. At the time of *General Theory of Law and State*, Kelsen adhered to the view that simultaneously valid norms must be part of the same normative system,[121] so this result would be untenable.

Kelsen's exception can be understood consistently with his account of continuity if the process of constitutional change is understood to be formal only. In substance, a different set of ultimate constitutional norms (those of the merged legal system) is understood to be the source of validity for all norms, even those previously understood to derive their validity from the pre-merger Austrian constitution. This is, perhaps, what Kelsen

[120] Kelsen, *General Theory of Law and State* (n 13), 123–24. Because of the way Kelsen constructs norms, it will often be the case that a norm includes, as conditions, other legal norms that may be authorised according to several different chains of validity, such that the norm in question may be considered *jointly* authorised by all of these authorities. The point is that it is not *severally* authorised.

[121] Above, section III.A.

means by describing the change as one that implies the termination of the validity of the system as a whole. Interpreting the post-merger set of legal materials—*and ignoring the constitutional surrender of authority as irrelevant*—will reveal a basic norm that differs from the basic norm that would have been revealed in relation to the pre-existing Austrian legal system. In essence, this charitable interpretation reads Kelsen as saying that, while it may *appear* to be authorised in the sense that it does not breach any constitutional norm, acceptance of norms superior to (or, we might add, simply different from) the ultimate, non-authorised constitutional norms of a legal system is never, in substance, an authorised change. It is a kind of revolution.

Of course, the example might be viewed differently. Instead of interpreting the change as inserting the non-authorised constitutional norms of the German legal system above the previously non-authorised norms of the Austrian system, they could be inserted below, as it were. The non-authorised constitutional norms of the Austrian legal system would purport to authorise the previously non-authorised constitutional norms of the German legal system. Although it is the 'merged' partner, it is conceivable that Austrian law claims the authority to authorise the norms of the German constitution in this way: this is consistent with Kelsen's argument in relation to the primacy of national law model of his monist construction of law.[122] One important feature of the epistemological device of the basic norm, also revealed in Kelsen's argument in the context of choosing between monist models, is that the effective legal norms may be consistent with both a basic norm authorising German ultimate non-authorised constitutional norms to govern the merged system and a basic norm authorising Austrian ultimate non-authorised constitutional norms. Unless a suitable case were presented in which the point could be tested—and if the Austrian constitutional norms simply purport to give effect to the German constitutional norms it is difficult to see how a relevant controversy could arise—the ultimate positive law basis of validity of an individual norm enforced by a court will not be clear. Harris notices this problem and suggests a solution consistent with Kelsen's theory (but never considered by him): taking into account 'confident predictions' about which of the competing bases for validity the courts' practice would reveal to be effective in an appropriate case.[123] It is, however, difficult to see how these predictions could be made without reference to some kind of ideological choice. Kelsen, as Harris reminds us, fiercely denies that politics or ideology is involved in presupposing the basic norm.[124] However, Kelsen expressly

[122] Kelsen, *Pure Theory* (n 4), 341–42.

[123] Harris (n 46), 228–29. Raz adopts a similarly counterfactual approach in his doctrine of recognition: below, ch 5.III.B. See also Hart (n 44), 340.

[124] Harris (n 46), 228, referring to Kelsen, *Pure Theory* (n 4), 218, fn 82.

considers that the choice *between* candidate basic norms *is* an ideological one when he discusses his two monist models of the universal legal system.[125] The set of effective norms is inconclusive in each instance, so a similar kind of choice might be required here.

Let us assume that the Kelsenian model is intended to unfold according to the interpretation of this exception first sketched above and to deny the admissibility of the alternative Austrian-centric reading of the situation. The key move in this interpretation is ignoring the apparent authorisation of the constitutional change; this move renders the situation identical to the core case of revolution by unauthorised constitutional change and sidelines any Austrian authorisation claim. This would make sense of the Kelsenian account, but, if this move cannot be justified and the exception simply stipulates that this kind of constitutional change is to be understood as unauthorised even though it seems—and, importantly, may be understood by all those involved—to be authorised, then the exception ends up being anomalous and unexplained.

Within the Kelsenian framework, there are several possible ways to justify the move of treating as unconstitutional this particular kind of change even though it appears to be constitutional. First, we might turn to efficacy. If, in the merged system, recourse is had to the German constitutional norms in a way that conflicts with recourse to the Austrian constitutional norm purporting to authorise them, we can say that the norm authorising the merger no longer exists and need not be taken into account in deriving the basic norm. However, given that the norm would, ex hypothesi, sit behind the German constitutional norms, conflict is at best contingent and generally extremely unlikely, and, as noted above, where a basic norm consistent with either approach is possible, nothing is gained.

Second, in a variation on the efficacy argument, we could construe the norm authorising the merger as operating at a single moment in time and being spent—ceasing, according to its own terms, to have any authorising force after effecting the merger. Again, this is at best a contingent possibility and an interpretation that may be inconsistent with the understanding of those involved in creating the norm, and possibly even with its terms. Further, to confine the validating effect of the norm authorising the merger in this way would be a radical departure from the general position in Kelsen's account: validity or authority is otherwise determined at the time of norm-creation, and persists even after the temporal sphere of validity of the authorising norm has ceased, until the norm validly created expires on its own terms or is repealed.[126]

Third, in a further refinement of the same line of thought, it might be argued that the norm authorising the merger is not a norm at all but merely

[125] Above, n 89.
[126] Below, section V.A.

a political act, upon which no normative force was conferred by the basic norm of the pre-merger Austrian system, because the content of the norm would deny the (continuing) normative force of the basic norm. In other words, implying termination of the validity of the legal system as a whole is inconsistent with the power of change conferred by the constitutional norms, so there is only the *appearance* of constitutionality. Again, the interpretation risks inconsistency with what the actors understand themselves to be doing—they conceive of themselves as effecting change by constitutional means—but it gives weight to Kelsen's argument that systemic invalidity is implied in their act.

Finally, again varying the argument slightly, we might discredit the alternative according to which the pre-merger Austrian basic norm authorises the post-merger German constitutional norms with reference to Hart's observation that a purported authorisation is, by itself, unconvincing: something more is required to show actual authorisation.[127] While this is consistent with the underlying sense of Kelsen's exception—that, *really*, this change is not relying on the pre-merger constitutional norms—it encounters the difficulty that in no other circumstance does Kelsen require anything more than effectiveness and, as it were, authorising purport.

At the end of the day, Kelsen notices, with this first exception, a potential weakness of his account, but his attempt to address it is unconvincing absent an articulation of its rationale and explanation of its consistency with the reasoning underlying the primary thesis of continuity based on authorised constitutional change.

C. Deemed Constitutionality: Constitutional Norms with an Alternative Character

Kelsen reduces the scope for discontinuity according to the model of unauthorised constitutional change by interpreting some constitutional norms as having an 'alternative' character. The situation Kelsen contemplates is one where constitutional norms confine the norm-creating power of a legislature—by, for example, prescribing a certain procedure or prescribing certain limitations as to the content of norms that may be created—but where the legislature itself is the only institution that may determine the question of the constitutionality of a measure it creates. Kelsen says:[128]

> If a statute enacted by the legislative organ is considered to be valid although it has been created in another way or has another content than prescribed by

[127] Above, text to n 44.

[128] Kelsen, *General Theory of Law and State* (n 13), 156. See also Kelsen, *Pure Theory* (n 4), 272–74.

> the constitution, we must assume that the prescriptions of the constitution concerning legislation have an alternative character. The legislator is entitled by the constitution either to apply the norms laid down directly in the constitution or to apply other norms which he himself may decide upon.

Kelsen adopts this interpretation on the basis that a statute so enacted could not otherwise be regarded as valid. If the 'alternative character' Kelsen discerns in the constitutional norm—obey this limitation or do not obey this limitation—is an accurate characterisation of the constitution of a given legal system, then the apparent constitutional limitation is not relevantly a norm at all, in Kelsen's sense.[129] An Act of the Parliament at Westminster purporting to deprive that Parliament of the power to enact laws with respect to dogs would, in UK constitutional theory, be ineffective;[130] one aspect of the doctrine of continuing parliamentary sovereignty is that the courts will not regard it as lawful to question the validity of an Act of Parliament once they have identified it as such;[131] accordingly, a subsequent Act dealing with dogs would be upheld. Accordingly, while the Act purporting to limit the powers of the Parliament would appear on the statute book, no corresponding norm would form part of the materials comprising the UK legal system in Kelsen's account, because it would not be a norm. If it is not a norm, it is not a constitutional norm, breach of it does not entail unauthorised constitutional change and Kelsen's model of continuity according to authorisation of constitutional change remains intact.

The same conclusion follows even if the constitutional norm is clearly expressed in prescriptive terms and all of the participants in the legal system understand it to impose a limit on the norm-creating power of the legislature. In other words, where a legislature, whose enactments are not subject to review for constitutionality, knowingly breaches a limitation purportedly imposed on its enactment by the constitution, in the (cynical) knowledge or expectation that its enactment will nevertheless be obeyed and it is, in fact obeyed, Kelsen's model understands this to be constitutionally authorised action.

Kelsen applies a similar line of reasoning in relation to the creation of individual norms, such as judicial decisions that do not conform to the

[129] It may still be a norm if, as Kelsen notes, it is a condition of the imposition of a sanction on, eg, a person or organ that has participated in the creation of the norm: Kelsen, *General Theory of Law and State* (n 13), 158; Kelsen, *Pure Theory* (n 4), 274–75. However, if it can only be framed as a condition of the sanction imposed on that person or organ, the norm is not one that governs the validity of the subordinate norm.

[130] In the sense, not that it would not be complied with in practice, but that it would not validly have the legal force and normative effect that it purported to have.

[131] *Pickin v British Railways Board* [1974] AC 765 (HL(E)); but see *R(Jackson) v Attorney General* [2005] UKHL 56, [2006] 1 AC 262 (HL(E)), 281 [27] (Lord Bingham), 288–89 [49]–[51] (Lord Nicholls).

relevant general norms (where, for example, a court makes an order it has no power to make), concluding that the principle of res judicata means that an ultimate court purporting to apply the general norm and yet creating a non-conforming individual norm is presented with an alternative, permitting the court to adhere to the governing norm or not to adhere to it.[132] How, then, does his theory of the alternative apply when the two situations are combined: a legislature's norm-creating powers are limited by a constitutional norm, the constitutionality of norms purportedly created by the legislature may be finally determined by an ultimate court and that court determines that a purported norm is constitutional, even though it was created in breach of the constitutional limitation? Kelsen expressly acknowledges that where such a court upholds the validity of the norm and it therefore becomes effective, 'then we are faced with a revolutionary change of the constitution'.[133] Similarly, he says that the execution of orders of an ultimate court improperly constituted of usurpers effects a revolutionary change, although, for reasons that he does not explain, 'only a revolutionary partial change'.[134]

There is an obvious unexplained inconsistency in Kelsen's account here. Where a court (or an organ executing individual legal norms) determines a norm to have been validly created notwithstanding a constitutional exclusion of the legislature's (or any other organ's) norm-creating power to do so, there is a revolution. However, where the legislature has power to make that determination and does so, there is not. Moreover, where an ultimate court creates individual norms in breach of general norms, there is no revolution. Why does Kelsen not attribute to the norm empowering the ultimate court to determine the constitutionality of legislation (or the norm empowering the executing organ to give effect to individual legal norms) the same alternative character he attributes to the legislature in that situation and to that court in other, non-constitutional situations? Why is *that* putative constitutional limitation a norm while the others, at the end of the day, are not (in virtue of their alternative character)? The obvious answer is that recognising the alternative character of the norm empowering an ultimate court to determine constitutionality would dissolve the distinction between effectiveness and authorisation of constitutional change: efficacy would be a criterion of constitutional authorisation and, given that Kelsen's account deals only with effective norms, *there could be no unauthorised constitutional change.*

In the result, this analysis suggests that, if the presence of constitutional norms with an alternative character is considered an inherent feature of legal systems, it is exposed to be an arbitrary fiction, deeming some

[132] Kelsen, *General Theory of Law and State* (n 13), 158–59; Kelsen, *Pure Theory* (n 4), 267–70.
[133] Kelsen, *Pure Theory* (n 4), 275.
[134] ibid, 276.

unauthorised constitutional changes to be authorised but not others. The explanation may nevertheless have force in some situations, including that described in relation to the Westminster Parliament above. Accordingly, it is submitted that the alternative character of a norm is only a contingent feature, and that what it demonstrates, in those legal systems where it is established, is the absence of a relevant norm (in Kelsenian terms). In other situations, as where an unsupervised legislature knowingly and cynically exceeds a constitutional limitation on its norm-creating power, a power that it and other participants in the legal system acknowledge, the alternative should not be assumed to exist: to do so this would conceal the use of efficacy as the criterion of continuity in place of authorised constitutional change. Rather, a (Kelsenian) revolution should be acknowledged.

D. Continuity by International Law

The account of continuity set out so far ignores international law.[135] Kelsen's picture when international law is factored in is simpler. Kelsen reports a positive rule of international law according to which:[136]

> The legal order remains the same as long as its territorial sphere of validity remains essentially the same, even if the order should be changed in another way than that prescribed by the constitution, in the way of revolution or *coup d'état*. A victorious revolution or a successful *coup d'état* does not destroy the identity of the legal order which it changes.

In place of constitutional authorisation, *territory* (or essential territorial identity) appears as the criterion of continuity: continuity in time is based directly on (essential) territorial identity over time.[137] Accordingly, discontinuity exists only where a national legal order becomes effective over 'a territory which, together with the individuals living thereon, has until now belonged to no State at all, or to two or more States, or has formed only part of the territory and the population of one State'.[138] Continuity is determined directly by these rules of international law, and not by authorisation in accordance with the constitution of the national legal system, since efficacy rather than (national) constitutional authorisation is the criterion of validity for national constitutional change: 'A norm of general international law authorizes an individual or a group of individuals, on the basis of an effective constitution, to create and apply as a legitimate

[135] Kelsen, *General Theory of Law and State* (n 13), 116.
[136] ibid, 220–21.
[137] ibid, 220. This criterion does, however, appear to presume some continuity of population (and perhaps of some legal norms).
[138] ibid, 219.

government a normative coercive order.'[139] The underlying account is, in a sense, still one of authorised constitutional change—but the authorisation comes from international law, which, from a superior position in the hierarchy to the national constitution, sanctions revolutions and coups as valid modes of constitutional change, subject to the essential territorial integrity criterion.[140]

Thus, pursuant to Kelsen's account of continuity by international law, unauthorised constitutional change that does not disturb the overall efficacy of the legal system within a given territory, such as a coup d'état, does not entail discontinuity. What does entail discontinuity is the establishment of a legal system in previously uninhabited territory, in territory that was formerly an undifferentiated part of an existing legal system, or in territory that encompassed what was formerly part of the territories of two or more existing legal systems. In each situation, the territory is different and the effective national legal system has changed. The link to a *national legal system*—a relatively centralised coercive order regulating human behaviour, inferior only to the international legal order, and efficacious for a certain territory[141]—is key, but the identity of the state (the personification of that national legal system) is, in Kelsen's model, a function of its territorial sphere of validity.

Of course, from the monist perspective, the continuity discussed here is that of a partial, not a total, legal system. The only true (as opposed to 'relative') basic norm sits not behind the constitution of the municipal legal system but behind the ultimate positive rules of the single universal legal system—and that basic norm remains unchanged throughout. Kelsen in fact uses the situation of continuity despite unauthorised constitutional change in a municipal legal system—citing the intuitive acceptance of continuity between the Tsarist and bolshevist Russian legal systems—to argue that his thesis about the unity of international and national law is correct.[142]

V. PROBLEMS WITH KELSEN'S ACCOUNT

In setting out Kelsen's account of continuity, we have already discussed problems associated with relationships of validating purport, the merger of legal systems, the relationship between efficacy and continuity, the

[139] Kelsen, *Pure Theory* (n 4), 215; see also ibid, 337–38.

[140] In this branch of the account, 'authorisation' is compatible with international law's also authorising (municipal law) norms forbidding coups and revolutions.

[141] Kelsen, *General Theory of Law and State* (n 13), 121, 221, 351, 367; Kelsen, *Pure Theory* (n 4), 214, 289.

[142] Kelsen, *General Theory of Law and State* (n 13), 368–69.

termination of systemic validity, the possible alternative character of constitutional norms and the application of monist accounts of continuity according to international law. In the literature examining Kelsen's work, further criticisms are levelled, focusing principally on constructing the hierarchy, potential circularity in the basic norm and problems associated with reference to a historically first constitution.

A. Constructing the Hierarchy

There is an ambiguity in Kelsen's authorising norms. The hierarchical model assumes that it is possible to identify an authorising norm for any norm of the system; however, the original authorising norm may have ceased to exist (in the ordinary and legal senses of 'exist').[143] Another norm may, at the present time, (purport to) authorise the subordinate norm, or there may be no presently existing authorising norm at all—where, for example, an organ at one time authorised to enact regulations is later replaced by a new organ with the same regulation-creating power, or is abolished entirely, but the regulations remain in force. However, if there is a new present authorising norm, Kelsen's model would regard the subordinate norm as a different norm, since, when fully stated, the conditions for its existence refer to a different authorisation. There is, accordingly, no account of change at the upper levels of the hierarchy. If there is no presently existing authorising norm, the model demands the continuing relevance of the original authorising norm: the problem is, as Finnis expresses it, that Kelsen does not distinguish between norms that authorise norm-creation at the present time and norms that authorised the creation of norms at some past time but no longer exist, though they are in some sense present as the source of validity of the norms they authorised when they did exist.[144] To resolve this ambiguity and avoid the spectre of reliance on those superseded, non-existent but somehow present (and thus also, in a sense, existing) norms, Finnis recognises a general principle that a norm remains valid until it expires according to its own terms or terms implied at its creation, or until it is repealed in accordance with conditions of repeal in force at the time of repeal.[145] There is no reason not to read Kelsen's account charitably: to understand that, in order to explain authorising norms with temporal spheres of validity that are narrower than those of the norms they authorise, the account assumes a principle that validly created norms remain valid until expiry or repeal.

[143] Golding (n 40), 96.

[144] JM Finnis, 'Revolutions and Continuity of Law' (1971) in *Philosophy of Law—Collected Essays: Volume IV* (Oxford, OUP, 2011) 407, 421.

[145] ibid, 423.

This reading leaves Kelsen's technical notion of existence intact: to extend the notion of existence to encompass the attenuated form in which the authorising norm 'exists' after its own temporal sphere of validity has ended would go too far (and Finnis does not suggest this). What Finnis's observation highlights is that Kelsen's account of dynamic normative orders focuses exclusively on validity (authorisation) *at the time of norm-creation*. The application of Kelsen's account may illustrate a situation where accommodating *retrospective* authorisation may be advantageous.[146]

B. Circularity in Ascertaining the Basic Norm

The second criticism is that there appears to be some circularity in deriving a basic norm inductively from legal materials where it is the basic norm that identifies which legal materials are part of the system.[147] Applied to the continuity context, the problem is this: if the criterion of authorised constitutional change excludes the possibility of a rule *constitutio posterior derogat priori* in a basic norm at one time,[148] we appear to presume discontinuity by ascertaining a different basic norm at a subsequent time, on the basis of materials that we construe as not authorised by the original constitution.

Both in general and in relation to continuity specifically, this criticism may be exaggerated. We must recall that Kelsen's project deals only with existing legal systems: he enters in medias res to explain how it is that we are able to understand effective legal norms as imposing obligations. In particular, Kelsen does not hold that a revolution derogates from previous law; rather, he holds that the validity of previous law is lost when effectiveness is lost (and a new basic norm is presupposed).[149] The materials upon which we rely to ascertain a basic norm are effective legal norms, identified by tests of obedience and enforcement in cases of disobedience;[150] on the basis of the rough picture of the laws officials apply and their reasons for applying them, we infer and identify the laws they assume and continue to refine the picture, working along the chain of authorisations through historically valid and effective norms and constitutions until, via the historically first constitution, we ultimately identify a basic norm.[151] Rather than

[146] Below, text to ch 4, n 34.

[147] J Stone, *Legal System and Lawyers' Reasonings* (London, Stevens & Sons, 1964) 130; Raz (n 109), 102.

[148] See also above, text to n 105.

[149] Teles (n 104), 71.

[150] Harris (n 53), 120. Harris also suggests that obedience and enforcement may be the subject of *predictions* as well as observation, but this seems to be a development of Kelsen's account: ibid, 121.

[151] Golding (n 40), 97–98.

regarding this process as circular, which it might be if we selected the initial (or putatively post-revolutionary) materials according to the basic norm we sought to identify, we ought perhaps to ask whether Kelsen's method involves unstated recourse to prima facie indicia of membership to distinguish between effective legal norms at the initial stage or to discard outliers at the refinement stage. The most obvious criteria, consistent with the parameters of Kelsen's account, are the territorial, temporal, personal and material spheres of validity of norms and commonality in norm-creating or norm-applying institutions. While Kelsen's account may be saved from circularity, the failure to nominate such criteria expressly deprives us of an important feature of the account.

C. Historically First Constitutions

Three major problems have been identified in relation to historically first constitutions. The first is that, in the understanding of participants and observers other than Kelsenian legal scientists, the beginning of a legal system may not be a historically first constitution in Kelsen's sense of a constitution established by revolutionary means. The possibility of a legal system's dividing into two independent systems by a process of constitutionally authorised change is illustrated by the course of colonial independence during the twentieth century. In Kelsen's model, pursuing the chains of validity in this situation reveals the same basic norm that authorised the undivided legal system—in other words, it will treat as part of the legal system a variety of legal materials that participants do not consider part of the system and, ultimately, it will fail to accord any separate identity to the divided legal systems at all.[152]

Harris, however, argues that Kelsen's account does not require us to trace validity through all laws of validating purport: he interprets Kelsen as requiring only that there be a presupposed origin of normative empowerment rooted in history. Drawing on the choice that Kelsen permits between international and municipal monist understandings of the universal legal system,[153] Harris suggests that Kelsen's theory allows us to choose any presupposed basic norm, the presupposition of which would make no difference to the content of the law.[154] In other words, we are free to stop pursuing a chain of authorisation at any historical constitution the presupposition of which would render it possible to understand all the existing laws as objectively binding (valid). So interpreted, the historically

[152] Raz (n 109), 102–03; Finnis (n 144), 413–15, 420.
[153] Above, n 89.
[154] Harris, (n 46), 212.

first constitution might not be absolutely chronologically first, in the sense that its validity cannot be established by reference to any authorising norm, but could, instead, be relatively first, in the sense that it is the first constitution we reach the presupposition of which achieves the cognitive aim for which Kelsen created the basic norm. This may be an attractive amendment but it is not what Kelsen's account provides: in the passages set out above,[155] it is clear that we only presuppose a basic norm when we have to—when there is no authorisation for a total (national) legal system in positive law. Moreover, since Harris allows that we may pursue the chain of validity further back than what we might term the minimally first constitution—in other words, we can choose between basic norms authorising any historical constitution that will enable us to understand all existing laws as binding—it is still possible, consistently with his interpretation of Kelsen's account, for a basic norm to be presupposed that does not identify divided legal systems.

Second, Kelsen's recourse to the historically first constitution in effect assumes the unity of that constitution as a set of norms: the account achieves or attributes this unity by presupposing a single basic norm that authorises a set of norms comprising the historically first constitution. However, it is not clear precisely why and how the norms of the original constitution are to be understood as a set (otherwise than in virtue of the conclusion that they are all authorised by the basic norm).[156] Ross notes that systemic unity implies either one highest authority or a plurality of coordinated authorities at the highest level,[157] and, if Kelsen's model addresses a historically first constitution that includes coordinate authorising norms, his account fails to identify what (other than the basic norm) reveals them to be coordinate. A related problem is highlighted by Golding, who points out that there may be several norms that are candidates for authorising a particular law, and that there is no a priori reason to assume that all officials presuppose one and the same basic norm.[158]

At the level of theory, there are no obvious solutions to these first two criticisms, relating to historically first constitutions: the charges levelled at Kelsen's account appear sound. However, the implications of these criticisms in practice may be less pronounced than might be supposed; in fact, the application of the model may even reveal subtleties that suggest solutions to these problems. The analysis of these criticisms is, therefore, reprised in chapter four.

The third problem that commentators have frequently discerned is that the focus on validity and the historically first constitution misses out

[155] In particular, above, text to n 95.

[156] Raz (n 109), 100 ff; Finnis (n 144), 426.

[157] A Ross, 'On Self-Reference and a Puzzle in Constitutional Law' (1969) 78 *Mind* 1, 3, fn 1.

[158] Golding (n 40), 98–99.

important information—that it is a formal criterion of continuity and one that ignores deeper continuities,[159] in particular in terms of institutional actors,[160] historical, moral, political or sociological identity,[161] and commonality of education, religion, recreation, language and economy.[162] A related criticism is that Kelsen's account does not accord with reality because, for example, its equal treatment of revolutions and coups d'état is 'out of step with the reality of coups in post-colonial societies that do not aim at destruction of the entire legal order, but only at usurpation of political offices'.[163] The fact that (pre-revolution) judges in post-revolutionary courts appeal to considerations of necessity, justice and policy, which Kelsen would have dismissed as irrelevant, also shows the unreality of his account.[164] Of course, these are criticisms of Kelsen's project and methodology, not its execution or internal coherence. The parameters of Kelsen's approach—the demands of 'purity' for legal theory—exclude reference to these broader considerations as criteria of change, and his account certainly did not purport to offer practical guidance to judges in revolutionary courts.

VI. CONCLUSIONS

This chapter has presented a critical reconstruction of Kelsen's account of continuity and discontinuity of legal systems, with particular attention to the working out of the core notion of authorised constitutional change and to three exceptions implied more or less expressly in the model. It concluded that, within the parameters of Kelsen's account, enduring ineffectiveness is necessarily an exception amounting to authorised constitutional change, whether or not desuetude is provided for as a matter of legal doctrine within the positive-law legal system. Upon examination of the nature and scope of the termination of systemic validity exception, it was concluded that this qualification to the model was unconvincing in abstract theoretical terms without further explication by reference to a principle of ultimacy, and, even then, was difficult to reconcile with

[159] Maher (n 110), 347; J Bell, 'Legal Revolutions and the Continuity of Public Law' in E Attwooll (ed), *Shaping Revolution* (Aberdeen, Aberdeen University Press, 1991) 119, 121.

[160] Stone (n 147), 135.

[161] NHM Roos, 'The Identity of Legal Systems in the Light of some Paradoxes of Constitutional Law' in E Attwooll (ed), *Shaping Revolution* (Aberdeen, Aberdeen University Press, 1991) 56; Harris (n 53), 112; Maher (n 119), 35–36; M Tayyab, 'Jurisprudence of Successful Treason: Coup d'Etat & Common Law' (1994) 27 *Cornell International Law Journal* 49, 108–09.

[162] Maher (n 119), 36–37.

[163] Tayyab (n 161), 107.

[164] Maher (n 110), 349–50.

the central tenets of Kelsen's account. It was observed that the exception deeming there to be constitutionality of change in relation to constitutional norms with an alternative character would, in some situations, amount to an arbitrary fiction, though it may be both coherent and persuasive in other cases. Possible answers (or charitable interpretations of ambiguous explanations) were elucidated regarding problems in constructing the hierarchy of norms where superior norms have ceased to exist and in the apparent circularity encountered in ascertaining the basic norm. However, it was not possible to discern, at the theoretical level, answers to other objections to Kelsen's reasoning connected with historically first constitutions, which are central to his account of the continuity and discontinuity of legal systems. These problems were, therefore, identified as particular points of interest for the application chapter that follows.

4

Application of Kelsen's Account

THIS CHAPTER APPLIES Kelsen's account of continuity and discontinuity, as reconstructed in chapter three, to the specific instance of Australia between 1788 and 2001. Section I identifies and traces a hierarchy of legal norms to locate a historically first constitution and a basic norm. Section II focuses on the particular problems presented by arguably unconstitutional legislation between 1788 and 1823, suggesting possible further elaborations of Kelsen's model. Section III situates the position of pre-Federation New South Wales in the model's account of total and partial legal systems, and explores the implications of the model—somewhat underdeveloped on the point—for the continuity and discontinuity of partial legal systems. Section IV turns to issues of merger in an attempt to understand Federation in terms of Kelsen's account, and engages with several of the exceptions to the criterion of authorised constitutional change that were analysed in chapter three. Section V considers the effect of Australia's emergent nationhood around the time of the Statute of Westminster 1931 (Imp), and argues that a proper understanding of the account requires closer attention than has previously been afforded to the interconnection of the notions of historically first constitutions and total and partial legal systems. After briefly dealing with continuity and discontinuity to the end of our period in section VI, section VII applies Kelsen's alternative account of continuity and discontinuity by reference to international law. The application of Kelsen's account in this chapter reveals that some of the problems identified at the abstract theoretical level are surmountable in practice. It also uncovers subtleties in Kelsen's model and important gaps in the analysis, both of which necessitate a degree of amplification in order to apply the account to the concrete case of Australia. While the application demonstrates in practice some of the criticisms in theory, other conclusions that result from the application of the account as amplified are potentially surprising.

I. NORMS AND CONSTITUTIONS IN NEW SOUTH WALES IN 1788

A. Locating the Basic Norm

An application of Kelsen's account (ignoring, for the moment, the alternative of continuity by international law) begins by identifying the norms purporting to regulate human behaviour by providing an act of coercion as a sanction (legal norms) that are generally obeyed or enforced in cases of disobedience (effective norms).[1] Accordingly, the first theoretical criticism of Kelsen's model that is encountered in applying the model is one noticed at the end of the last chapter: the account's failure to explain how the set of effective legal norms that comprise a legal system can be identified independently of the basic norm ostensibly identified by inference from them.[2]

It is submitted that this criticism is less momentous in practice than it may appear in theory. Launching the enquiry in medias res as Kelsen's model contemplates, it is apparent that legal materials are connected, factually, by institutions and formal sources that may readily be identified as creating or applying effective legal norms. Moreover, there is a strong territorial underpinning to Kelsen's model, discernible in the effectiveness parameter and in the notion of the territorial sphere of validity of a system. Accordingly, by looking at the sanctions imposed in New South Wales for breaching standards of behaviour, and by paying attention to references to the institutions and sources that create and apply them in and for the territory of New South Wales, an initial corpus of norms quickly becomes apparent to the Kelsenian legal scientist. Of course, this initial corpus may be both over- and under-inclusive. However, at least in the case of colonial New South Wales, this initial approximation provides an adequate starting point. Subsequent refinement of the set of norms is possible if the legal scientist adopts something like Rawls's 'reflective equilibrium' device,[3] treating the set as provisional and subject to revision in the course of tracing patterns of authorisation of effective norms and describing a basic norm. In the case of New South Wales between 1788 and 1823, effective legal norms can be readily identified as expressed in Imperial law (principally prerogative but some of it also statutory), English common law received in the Colony, local gubernatorial legislation and local common law.[4] The Kelsenian legal scientist identifies these norms by recognising them as norms that purport to regulate human behaviour by providing an act of coercion as a sanction and that are generally obeyed or enforced in cases of disobedience, and, at least provisionally, considers them to belong to a relevant set on the basis of connections to common institutions and formal sources. Accordingly, while the tools provided by Kelsen's account are perhaps weak, they are nonetheless sufficient, and the analysis need not entail (vicious) circularity by presupposing a basic norm to identify the norms from which the basic norm is to be inferred.

[1] Above, ch 3.I.
[2] Above, ch 3.V.B.
[3] J Rawls, *A Theory of Justice*, revised edn (Oxford, OUP, 1999) 18–19, 42–45.
[4] Above, ch 2.I.A.i.

Next, applying the model of a dynamic normative order, patterns of authorisation for the creation and application of norms can be discerned: regulations governing the conduct of convicts, for example, were authorised by Phillip's Instructions, and, in turn, the Instructions were, like the Commission that accompanied and referred to them, made in the exercise of prerogative powers, themselves authorised by norms of Imperial common law. The authorisation for the authorising Imperial norms is ultimately conferred by a '"constitution" in the transcendental-logical [as opposed to the positive] sense':[5] that is, despite the absence of posited Imperial constitutional norms expressly authorising courts in Great Britain to apply customary law and authorising the Imperial Parliament to create norms by legislation, such authorising constitutional norms can and should (as a matter of legal science) nonetheless be understood to exist and to be referred to directly by the system's basic norm.

Authorisation for the norms comprising the Imperial constitution in 1788 may, in turn, be traced through earlier constitutions to the Union of England and Scotland, and perhaps as far back as the Glorious Revolution.[6] However, to pursue the enquiry further back through the context of Reformation and early modern Britain would be a diversion from this book's focus on an application of accounts of continuity to Australia between 1788 and 2001. What matters for present purposes is that the constitution, obedience to which the Kelsenian scientist discerns when examining the legal materials on hand in New South Wales in 1788, is ultimately an Imperial one; so, too, is the basic norm that the scientist must presuppose for systemic validity to follow. Two issues require consideration in consequence: first, whether settlement entailed discontinuity in the Imperial legal system and, second (assuming no discontinuity), whether settlement entailed the creation of a New South Wales partial legal system within the total Imperial legal system.

B. Discontinuity at Settlement?

Notwithstanding the authorisation by Imperial constitutional norms, did settlement itself entail discontinuity with the Imperial legal system: in other words, did the settlement of New South Wales create a historically first constitution, on the basis that it established a constitution and associated national legal system 'for a territory that formerly was not the sphere

[5] H Kelsen, *Pure Theory of Law, Reine Rechtslehre*, first published 1960, 2nd edn (M Knight tr, Berkley, Ca, University of California Press, 1967) 226.

[6] On whether a Kelsenian revolution took place in 1707, see, eg, G Maher, 'The Identity of the Scottish Legal System' [1977] *Juridical Review* 21.

of validity of a constitution and of a national legal order based on it'?[7] Prior to 1788, the territory comprised in Phillip's Commission was not the territorial sphere of validity of a (single) constitution and associated national legal system. At settlement, the Imperial authorities regarded the territory as relevantly—that is, for the purposes of constitutional law doctrines about the applicability of English law—uninhabited (*terra nullius*),[8] but even setting aside that contemporary classification in light of later acceptance not merely of habitation but of sophisticated social ordering amongst Aboriginal peoples,[9] the relevant question concerns continuity with Imperial law, not (potential) discontinuity in Aboriginal legal systems. Critically, there is no question of a new *national* legal system's creation in New South Wales in 1788: rather, the territorial sphere of validity of an existing national legal system—that of Imperial law—was extended. Territorial change may be relevant to continuity by international law[10] but, unless a new *national legal system*—a state, in the sense of international law—is created, it is immaterial from the dualist perspective. As—according to the reconstruction of the account pursued here—the extension occurred without breach of the constitution of the Imperial legal system, the Kelsenian legal scientist must conclude that settlement itself did not disrupt the continuity of the Imperial legal system.

C. New South Wales as a Partial Legal System

As to the second issue, it was established above that the criteria for a partial legal system are: a basic norm of the total legal system; a relative basic norm of the partial legal system (that is also a posited norm of the total legal system); a territorial sphere of validity that is part (only) of the territorial sphere of validity of the total legal system; and norm-creating and norm-applying organs, with competence limited to the territory of the partial legal system.[11] It is submitted that the subset of norms local to New South Wales—including, for example, specific norms, such as orders made by the New South Wales criminal and civil courts, and general norms, such as gubernatorial regulations made in relation to convicts—comprise a New South Wales partial legal system. These norms are ultimately valid in virtue of the Imperial basic norm identified above. In 1788, a complex of norms derived from Imperial statute and common law[12] 'determine[d] the

[7] Kelsen, *Pure Theory* (n 5), 200.
[8] Above, text to ch 2, n 7.
[9] *Milirrpum v Nabalco Pty Ltd* (1971) 17 FLR 141 (NTSC), 267 (Blackburn J). See, generally, *Mabo v Queensland [No 2]* (1992) 175 CLR 1 (HCA).
[10] Below, section VII.
[11] Above, ch 3.III.B.
[12] Above, ch 2.I.A.i.

creation of the norms'[13] of the New South Wales partial legal system and, in thus providing the grounds for validity of the partial system's norms, comprise the relative basic norm for the partial legal system. The territorial sphere of validity of Colonial law was defined in Phillip's Instructions[14] (albeit severely limited in practice by the efficacy parameter), and the territory so delimited defined the scope of the Governor's legislative and executive powers under his Commission[15] and of the courts under the Charter.[16] Accordingly, settlement entailed the creation of a New South Wales partial legal system within the total Imperial legal system.

II. CONTINUITY AND UNCONSTITUTIONAL GUBERNATORIAL ORDERS IN NEW SOUTH WALES

Patterns of authorisation by Imperial legal norms can be discerned for all of the effective legal norms in New South Wales in the period 1788–1823, with the exception of certain of the early Governors' general orders, such as those imposing taxes and regulating wage disputes. While many contemporary and subsequent commentators hold that these were ultimately not unconstitutional,[17] the alternative conclusion involves understanding the legal situation in a way that reveals much about Kelsen's account of continuity and discontinuity. If these orders were ultra vires, as has been thought (both at the time and since),[18] there is—subject to an important argument presented below[19]—no authorising norm until 1819: in that year, Imperial legislation confirmed the necessary powers prospectively and barred actions based on any past illegality.[20] If it is right that these general orders (or some of them) were, for a time, unlawful but effective, Kelsen's model holds that there was a partial technical revolution: this result obtains because the constitutional change was unauthorised but effective, and because none of the exceptions to this principle (enduring ineffectiveness,[21] termination of systemic validity[22] and deemed constitutionality as the

[13] Kelsen, *Pure Theory* (n 5), 332.

[14] Instructions (25.04.1787) in FM Bladen (ed), *Historical Records of New South Wales*, vol I, pt 2 (Sydney, Government Printer, 1892) 85.

[15] Commission (02.04.1787), ibid, 62.

[16] Charter for Establishing Courts of Civil and Criminal Jurisdiction on the Eastern Coast of New South Wales (02.04.1787) in F Watson (ed), *Historical Records of Australia*, vol 1, Series IV (Sydney, Library Committee of the Commonwealth Parliament, 1922) 6.

[17] Above, ch 2, n 22.

[18] Above, 13–14.

[19] Below, 133–35.

[20] Above, ch 2, n 26.

[21] Above, ch 3.IV.A.

[22] Above, ch 3.IV.B.

result of constitutional norms with an alternative character)[23] applies. It is useful to observe that the unauthorised constitutional change comprises two elements: the promulgation of the orders and their enforcement by the Colonial courts. The first entails arrogation of norm-creating power without an authorising norm; the second entails the failure to comply with a norm requiring the courts to annul unconstitutional legislation.

In the classical exposition of Kelsen's account, on the hypothesis that they are unconstitutional (and their creation unauthorised), the orders could nonetheless be norms of the system: something that presents itself as a norm and is subject to a legal procedure by which an organ is authorised to determine whether or not it is a norm is, ab initio, a norm—but an annullable norm.[24] Kelsen explains that the decision that such a putative norm is null has a constitutive character despite its declaratory form:[25]

> There must be something legally existing to which this decision refers. Hence, the phenomenon in question cannot be something nul *ab initio*, that is to say, legally nothing. It has to be considered as a norm annulled with retroactive force by the decision declaring it nul *ab initio*.

Only in a case where there is no legal procedure for determining whether the putative norm is a norm or not—Kelsen gives the example of a patient in an insane asylum purporting to issue a statute[26]—will there genuinely have been no norm ab initio. The model thus tolerates a certain degree of temporary unconstitutional action: the unconstitutional norms are not authorised by a norm-creating power but are to be conceived then and there as indirectly imbued with normative force through the power of (retrospective) annulment, a power that is authorised and is ultimately referable to the system's basic norm. Where an unconstitutional norm thus susceptible to annulment is not actually annulled, or the decision is taken not to annul it, the norm becomes effective, and Kelsen's account holds that there is a partial revolutionary constitutional change.[27] While Kelsen explains that the principle of legitimacy—of authorised creation—is limited by the principle of effectiveness in the case of norms that have an alternative character, that character is only recognised in a norm-creating

[23] Above, ch 3.IV.C. The presence of the courts means that the Governor was not uniquely empowered to determine the constitutionality of his own legislation in the same way as an assembly whose legislation is unreviewable. The Governor sat as an appellate court, but it was possible to appeal to the Privy Council (above, 14).

[24] H Kelsen, *General Theory of Law and State* (A Wedberg tr, New York, Harvard University Press, 1945) 159–61; Kelsen, *Pure Theory* (n 5), 276–78.

[25] Kelsen, *General Theory of Law and State* (n 24), 161.

[26] Kelsen, *Pure Theory* (n 5), 277–78.

[27] ibid, 275.

power vested in an organ that has the sole power to determine its compliance with that norm,[28] and so the exception does not apply here.

The significance of Kelsen's qualifying the revolutionary change involved as 'partial'[29] is not clear. It appears to be an acknowledgement of the potential triviality of the change involved. The enforcement of arguably unconstitutional gubernatorial legislation for a period of 30 years is perhaps more trivial than a coup d'état: certainly the change did not aim to destroy or supplant the entire legal system. However, the consequence in Kelsen's account must be the same: the whole legal system changes. Since norms simultaneously valid in the same territory may not belong to independent legal systems in Kelsen's model,[30] the norms that appear—and were understood at the time—to be authorised by Imperial norms must also be understood as authorised, like the norms of the impugned general orders, by local customary constitutional norms (applied by the Colonial courts) that coincidentally authorised the application of norms expressed in the Imperial sources. These customary constitutional norms would thus comprise the historically first constitution of the New South Wales legal system, sustained by a basic norm presupposed for this purpose.

The conclusion (putting aside the possibility of retrospective authorisation discussed below) that a technical revolution accompanied the enforcement of unconstitutional gubernatorial orders invites attention to extra-systemic continuities and discontinuities that, as noted at the end of the last chapter, Kelsen's account is famously criticised for ignoring.[31] If a technical revolution is produced by a proper application of Kelsen's account, a severe incongruity results between Kelsen's intra-systemic criterion of discontinuity and the extra-systemic indicia of community. Nothing in the economic or social history of the Colony to 1823 detailed in chapter two, and nothing in its political history apart from the enforcement of the Governors' general orders, indicates community discontinuity. Discontinuity here, in the Kelsenian sense that regards the legal system as a whole and results from unauthorised constitutional change and the presupposition of a new basic norm, is counter-intuitive. As the defence of the impugned orders by successive Governors—and the subsequent century of Imperial and local developments—makes abundantly clear, any affirmation of an autonomous, autochthonous constitutional root for Australian law from 1788 is wholly unrealistic, and illustrates the fragility and artificiality of an account based solely on unauthorised constitutional change.

28 Above, ch 3.IV.C.
29 Kelsen, *Pure Theory* (n 5), 276.
30 Above, ch 3.III.A.
31 Above, 118–19.

A. Possibility of Retrospective Authorisation

The central notion of the basic norm in Kelsen's model arguably ties validity of individual norms too closely to continuity of the system as a whole. In this instance, the result is brought about by the intersection of two features of Kelsen's account: first, the insistence that all legal norms in a system are ultimately valid for the same reason (a single basic norm); and, second, the focus on authorisation at the point of norm-creation. The insistence that all valid legal norms in a given territory belong to one legal system, sustained by a single basic norm, makes it impossible to account for occasional (and, in the long view, temporary) aberrations of the kind represented by the consistent enforcement of unconstitutional general orders within a broader stream of continuity. It is a strength of Kelsen's account that it deals with the subset of unconstitutionally promulgated norms that are subsequently annulled without disrupting continuity; however, it is a weakness of the account that all unconstitutionally created norms that are tolerated or endorsed entail discontinuity in the system as a whole, regardless of the potentially minimal practical significance of the norms in issue. As explained above, acceptance of enduring effectiveness as a form of authorised constitutional change would avoid this result—but at the cost of eliding effectiveness and validity.[32] The doctrine of norms with an alternative character is another aspect of Kelsen's model that attempts to account for this kind of problem—but its scope of application is narrow. Again, that limitation of scope is necessary to ensure that efficacy does not become the criterion of authorisation, with the result that there could never be unauthorised constitutional change.[33]

The problem might be expressed in terms of the time at which the creation of a norm is authorised: Kelsen's account of validity within a dynamic normative order focuses uniquely on authorisation by the authorising norm at the moment of creation or application of the authorised norm. *Retrospective* authorisation finds no place—presumably because it would entail the existence, for a time, of effective legal norms that were, ex hypothesi, not sustained by the basic norm. However, the possibility of retrospective annulment—a possibility that, conceived as set out above, entails indirect authorisation ab initio through the power to annul an unconstitutional norm after promulgation—may offer a way around this problem by analogy.[34] According to this analogy, a norm that was unauthorised when created could nevertheless be considered part of the system

[32] Above, 105–06.

[33] Above, 112.

[34] Although it is retrospective authorisation that is in issue here, it may also be noted that Kelsen's account permits retrospective norms more generally: see, eg, Kelsen, *General Theory of Law and State* (n 24), 43–44, 146, 149.

ab initio if a competent organ authorised it retrospectively (or retrospectively widened the norm-creating power purportedly relied upon at the time of creation). In a sense the norm empowering that organ would have an alternative character: requiring the organ to apply the existing applicable norms governing norm-creation or to apply different norms. However, some control mechanism would, again, be necessary to prevent the slide into mere effectiveness as the criterion of authorisation and validity. Most obvious methods of control designed to ensure that retrospective authorisation only applies to peripheral and temporary aberrations or incidental incremental changes would likely entail recourse to substantive considerations of sociology, ethics and political theory, which are clearly precluded by the 'purity' parameter of Kelsen's account. However, as with the analogy to retrospective annulment on which the thought is based, the need for *actual* authorisation by the organ—rather than the mere *potential* for authorisation that exists because of the power—would be a small but perhaps significant control that is not excluded by Kelsen's methodology. Unless actually upheld by a competent organ, the norm, even if otherwise effective, would not be retrospectively authorised. Even with this control, however, there would be cause for unease about the elision of effectiveness and validity: an organ such as a common law court, which operates largely by custom, might well exercise a power of retrospective authorisation by mere practice. However, in this example, two elements must be dissociated: the possibility of retrospective authorisation, on the one hand, and, on the other, constitutional law norms governing the norm-creating and norm-applying powers of courts that are customary in nature and that thereby sanction effectiveness as a method of constitutional change. The latter is possible in Kelsen's account (but, as argued above, only as a contingent feature of particular systems, not a necessary feature of all).[35] To discount the complication introduced by customary constitutional norms, let us suppose that the Imperial legislation in 1819 barring actions based on the otherwise unlawful general orders provided retrospective statutory authority for those orders. Kelsen's unmodified account, with its focus on authorisation at the time of norm-creation, would hold the general orders as valid only from 1819 (with the consequence of discontinuity outlined above). However, if space were made for retrospective authorisation (along the lines of retrospective annulment), the orders would be valid ab initio, no discontinuity would follow, and no blurring of effectiveness and validity would arise. If Kelsen's model can accommodate norms with an alternative character as well as retrospective annulment, the suggestion of retrospective authorisation sketched above is not immediately implausible.

However, the complication of customary constitutional norms, and the blurring of efficacy and validity that they may entail, remains. If, to take

[35] Above, 103–04.

the other available conclusion, the Governors' general orders are understood to have been lawful rather than unlawful, because the local New South Wales courts, in recognising and applying them, effected a change to the customary norms of constitutional law (which those norms authorised the courts to do), then no distinction between efficacy and validity is maintained. As noted above, authorised constitutional change is rendered vacuous as a criterion of continuity or discontinuity, since all effective change will be authorised and discontinuity will never follow.[36] This criticism of Kelsen's model is as unyielding in practice as it is in theory.

B. Regularisation and Multiple Sufficient Basic Norms

In any event, towards the end of the period of gubernatorial autocracy, the situation in relation to the impugned general orders was regularised. Applying Kelsen's account of continuity to these facts gives rise to two potential problems. A Kelsenian legal scientist undertaking a search for the historically first constitution and basic norm of the legal system in force in New South Wales, who began with the materials he found in 1823, would find no trace of the unconstitutional general orders and, accordingly, the pattern of authorised norm-creation would lead only to Imperial norms. The first problem is that, if the proper conclusion of the scientist's investigation in 1818 was an autochthonous basic norm, there is a danger that the scientist of 1823 would compare the basic norm derived in his time to that derivable from the norms in 1788, conclude that they were identical, and then conclude that there was continuity between them. Of course, the diligent legal scientist would recognise that continuity depends on derivation of the same basic norm at all intervening points in time and conduct an appropriately comprehensive analysis of all norms, historical and contemporary. Even if the scope of this analysis is not infinite, the practical burden imposed on the legal scientist is significant. Although of second-order importance, difficulty of application is a relative disadvantage where a choice of competing theoretical accounts is available.

The second problem is more substantive. Assuming, again, that applying Kelsen's model in 1818 results in the identification of a local New South Wales basic norm, is that also the basic norm to be identified by the Kelsenian legal scientist in 1823? Once the unconstitutional Governors' orders had taken root, a new basic norm had to be inferred that sustained all of the norms of the system, including apparently Imperial norms.[37]

[36] Above, text to ch 3, n 111.

[37] Not, however, including any Imperial norms inconsistent with the validity of the impugned gubernatorial orders.

The Imperial basic norm of 1788 could not itself be presupposed because it would not sustain the unconstitutional Governors' orders; however, the basic norm newly presupposed also had to sustain the apparently Imperial norms then in force. Once the Governors' orders were regularised, however, it is not clear how the Kelsenian legal scientist examining the set of norms of 1823 would choose between the revolutionary basic norm, which, ex hypothesi, could sustain all of the applicable Imperial law, and the Imperial basic norm of 1788. The principal difficulty with Kelsen's model exemplified here is the problem of multiple sufficient basic norms: the set of norms and associated patterns of authorisation can be traced both to a basic norm requiring obedience to the historically first constitution of the Empire and to a basic norm requiring obedience to the putative historically first constitution of New South Wales (which happens also to authorise application of pre- and post-revolutionary Imperial norms).

Relying on something like the device of 'confident predictions' advocated by Harris,[38] the Kelsenian legal scientist might conclude that New South Wales law, after regularisation of the Governors' orders, *re-joined* the Imperial legal system. Presupposition of the basic norm of the Imperial legal system would be entirely consistent with the set of norms examined in 1823 and fulfils the epistemological, 'transcendental-logical'[39] function of the basic norm. Reintegration is far from implausible: it fits better with the historical creation of all of the norms of the system of 1823 (and subsequently), and a survey of contemporary participants—the basis for the scientist's 'confident predictions'—would have indicated that they did not consider New South Wales law ever to have been separated from Imperial law anyway. Moreover, concluding that reintegration had occurred would avoid the absurdity of discerning a legal system (with the territorial scope of New South Wales) sustained by a basic norm that, on the one hand, confers validity (by reference) on a set of norms that are independently sustained (elsewhere) by the basic norm of a second (Imperial) legal system—but, on the other hand, confers validity on no other norms whatsoever. While the conclusion that Australian law was, between 1788 and 1823, in turn, part of the Imperial legal system, then a revolutionary New South Wales legal system and then a reintegrated Imperial legal system is not inherently implausible, it must be said that the frequency and apparent effortlessness of these points of discontinuity compounds the air of unreality that characterises the postulated autochthonous phase itself.

On the other hand, the Kelsenian legal scientist might elect to apply an 'inertia principle' or 'presumption of continuity', and decline to depart from the basic norm presupposed while the Governors' orders were in

[38] Above, text to ch 3, n 123.

[39] Kelsen, *Pure Theory* (n 5), 218; H Kelsen, *General Theory of Norms, Allgemeine Theorie der Normen*, first published 1979 (M Hartney tr, Oxford, Clarendon Press, 1991) 257.

force, unless the materials analysed require a different presupposition. Hart's criticism based on the hollowness of relationships of validating purport is then foregrounded.[40] Norms of the Imperial legal system purport to authorise norms of New South Wales law, as, ex hypothesi, do norms of New South Wales constitutional law sustained by the presupposed local basic norm; merely purporting to confer validity, Hart points out, cannot actually confer validity, and the only other tool available in Kelsen's model, effectiveness, is incapable of discriminating between basic norms that purport to authorise identical sets of effective norms.

The short point is that Kelsen's account offers inadequate explanation of how the central move—presupposition of the basic norm—is to be made. Reasonable suggestions may be made to supplement the account, but these may, as just illustrated, result in diametrically different conclusions. The theoretically straightforward move of presupposing a basic norm to 'clos[e] up the arch of legal logic'[41] in Kelsen's account encounters an apparently insurmountable obstacle when, in practice, multiple sufficient basic norms are available to fulfil the epistemological function.

III. CONTINUITY AND PRE-FEDERATION NEW SOUTH WALES AS A PARTIAL LEGAL SYSTEM

As detailed above,[42] the period between 1823 and 1901 saw the advent of representative and responsible government (and adoption of the insignia of self-government) in New South Wales, the end of transportation, local control over natural resources, significant changes to the size and shape of the territory, local laws on denization and citizenship, the creation and extension of the franchise, and the formation of a local military and navy. These profound alterations to the material, spatial and personal scope of the law in force in New South Wales were effected by Imperial legislation, local legislation and changes in the common law made by courts constitutionally authorised to make them. Accordingly, in terms of Kelsen's model, there was, prima facie, continuity in New South Wales from settlement to Federation, with the possible exception of the unconstitutional gubernatorial orders considered in the last section. However, the detail of the application reveals two more subtle issues in applying Kelsen's account to partial legal systems, notwithstanding the apparently straightforward conclusion of continuity by authorised constitutional change.

[40] Above, text to ch 3, n 44.
[41] JW Harris, 'When and Why Does the Grundnorm Change?' (1971) 29 *CLJ* 103, 131.
[42] Above, ch 2.I.A.ii.–I.A.iii.

A. Continuity of Partial Legal Systems

The first issue is that, save in one special case, Kelsen's model does not expressly deal with the criterion for continuity *of partial legal systems*. The account of total and partial legal systems is underdeveloped in important respects. For present purposes, it is appropriate to note two features of the content of relative basic norms of partial legal systems. First, it appears that the relative basic norm refers directly to—and, in fact, comprises—the historically first constitution of the partial legal system. It is possible, of course, for the basic norm of a total legal system to refer directly to constitutional norms, too: Kelsen uses the example of a system where no posited law authorises custom as a law-creating fact, and describes the basic norm authorising custom as a constitution in the transcendental-logical sense.[43] Kelsen indicates that the relative basic norm 'determines the creation of the norms of the [partial legal system]'.[44] In other words, it cannot simply be a presupposition of the kind, 'One ought to behave as the constitution prescribes'.[45] Rather, the posited norm of the total legal system that is—or the normative content of which is—also the relative basic norm of the partial legal system must directly authorise norm-creation and norm-application by particular organs; the relative basic norm of a partial legal system must comprise its constitution (or at least its historically first [substantive] constitution). Kelsen's statement elsewhere that partial legal systems have their own constitutions[46] is consistent with this reconstruction: the partial legal system *does* have a constitution—only it is comprised *in* the basic norm rather than in posited norms of the partial legal system *sustained by* that system's (relative) basic norm. If a true basic norm were in issue, the constitution would be a constitution in the transcendental-logical sense Kelsen describes. Since the basic norm of the partial legal system is only relative—it exists in posited law of the total legal system—the constitution of the partial legal system might be thought to be *quasi*-transcendental-logical. It serves the epistemic function for which a basic norm is presupposed, but it is in fact not presupposed but posited. Further, the constitution comprised in the relative basic norm may authorise its amendment by the organs of the partial legal system, in which case there can be a posited constitution as well as the quasi-transcendental-logical historically first constitution comprised in the relative basic norm.

The second feature to note about the content of the relative basic norm is that it appears that it may prescribe criteria for continuity of the partial

[43] Kelsen, *Pure Theory* (n 5), 226.
[44] ibid, 332. See also Kelsen, *General Theory of Law and State* (n 24), 373.
[45] Kelsen, *Pure Theory* (n 5), 201.
[46] Kelsen, *General Theory of Law and State* (n 24), 317.

legal system other than constitutionally authorised change. In determining the creation of the partial legal system and prescribing its first constitution, the relative basic norm may determine the temporal sphere of validity of that system as well as its territorial, material and personal spheres of validity. So much appears from the one special case in which Kelsen adverts to the criterion for continuity of a partial legal system: where national (municipal) legal systems are considered to be partial legal systems within a universal total legal system.[47] Here, Kelsen indicates that the temporal sphere of validity of a national legal system is determined by international law[48] and, specifically, by a norm providing the criterion of essential territorial identity explained above.[49] Kelsen does not suggest that international law *must* adopt this criterion: he merely describes this as the criterion adopted. Accordingly, we may infer that the criterion of continuity of a partial legal system is contingent: the total legal system may provide constitutionally authorised change as the criterion, but it might equally provide for continuity on some other basis—including, as Kelsen's example shows, essential territorial identity.

If the reconstruction of Kelsen's model of total and partial legal systems proposed in the last two paragraphs is accepted, then the criterion of continuity for Colonial partial legal systems within the Imperial total legal system need not be authorised constitutional change. The problem of the unconstitutional gubernatorial orders discussed in the previous section might be sidestepped if, for example, the Imperial law relative basic norm of the New South Wales partial legal system provided for continuity on the basis of essential territorial identity.[50] As with the application of this criterion in Kelsen's model of continuity by international law,[51] effectiveness rather than authorisation would then, in substance, be an authorised mode of constitutional change in the New South Wales partial legal system.[52] There would be no question of unconstitutionality in the early Governors' general orders. In applying Kelsen's account, it is therefore essential to determine what criterion Imperial law provided for continuity of the New South Wales partial legal system.

The norm Kelsen attributes to international law in the case of national legal systems—authorising an individual or group to create and apply a government for a territory on the basis of an effective constitution

[47] Nothing turns here on whether the monist account accords primacy to international law or to a single municipal legal system.

[48] Kelsen, *General Theory of Law and State* (n 24), 350–51; Kelsen, *Pure Theory* (n 5), 290.

[49] Above, ch 3.IV.D.

[50] It is submitted that the insights that discussion reveals remain relevant in the absence of the partial legal system complication.

[51] Below, section VII.

[52] Above, text to ch 3, n 140.

alone[53]—would be inconsistent with the foundational importance of the rule of law in Imperial law, and is controverted in Imperial law's response to Southern Rhodesia's unilateral declaration of independence.[54] On the one hand, insistence on the rule of law is not so inflexible a principle in Imperial law as to engender discontinuity upon the slightest unlawful but tolerated act, as the universal attitude of assuming continuity in the face of the unconstitutional gubernatorial orders in New South Wales attests. On the other hand, that (arguably) unconstitutional state of affairs was not permitted to continue once concerns had been raised. Accordingly, what emerges as the applicable norm of Imperial law appears to be a two-fold criterion. There is temporal continuity in a partial legal system for which Imperial law provides discrete constitutional norms while: (i) the rule of law is by and large observed in the territory; and (ii) Her Majesty's Government in the UK has responsibility for the government of the territory.

The first limb of this criterion encapsulates a slightly watered-down version of Kelsen's authorised constitutional change criterion that is compatible with actions that are strictly unconstitutional but that are, in the interests of preserving law and order, undertaken in good faith, under colour of law and otherwise in substantial compliance with the regular law. The Privy Council appeared to articulate such a criterion in *Madzimbamuto v Lardner-Burke*,[55] and that criterion would be satisfied in the context of the marginal and temporary aberrations under the unlawful gubernatorial orders tolerated in New South Wales. The second limb is reflected in the way in which partial legal systems within the Empire are standardly terminated.[56] The rule of law, as well as constitutional norms sourced in Imperial law, may continue to exist in a territory, but Imperial law acknowledges no component partial legal system in territory for the government of which Her Majesty's Government in the UK no longer accepts responsibility. Both limbs reflect the territorial (or territorial-communal) underpinnings to the notion of a partial legal system. Application of this more nuanced understanding of Kelsen's model to New South Wales demonstrates continuity from settlement to Federation, of both the New South Wales partial legal system and also the total Imperial legal system, notwithstanding the unconstitutional gubernatorial orders and regardless of the series of more than half a dozen constitutions provided for New South Wales by Imperial law before Federation.

[53] Kelsen, *Pure Theory* (n 5), 215; see also ibid, 337–38.

[54] See *Madzimbamuto v Lardner-Burke* [1969] 1 AC 645 (PC), 723–25, 729 (the Board). See also Southern Rhodesia Act 1965 (Imp), s 1; Southern Rhodesia Constitution Order 1965, SI 1965/1952 (Imp), s 2.

[55] *Madzimbamuto v Lardner-Burke* [1969] 1 AC 645 (PC), 729–31 (the Board), 732, 737 (Lord Pearce). See JM Finnis and AR Carnegie, 'Constitutional Law' [1969] *Annual Survey of Commonwealth Law* 1, 72–74.

[56] See, eg, Sierra Leone Independence Act 1961 (Imp), s 1(2)(a).

B. Decentralisation and Constitutional Conventions

The second issue connected with the application of Kelsen's account to partial legal systems concerns the changes to the nature and material scope of the law applicable in New South Wales, which demonstrate increasing decentralisation over time. The total Imperial legal system is (at least as regards New South Wales) to be considered unitary rather than federal so long as the component partial legal systems lacked substantial constitutional autonomy.[57] In applying Kelsen's account, it is thus appropriate to ask whether the grants to the Australian Colonies of control over their own constitutions in the second half of the nineteenth century amount to 'legislative act[s] of a unitary State [the Empire] transforming itself into a federal State by increasing the degree of its decentralization'.[58] The requisite autonomy need not be complete: certain limiting constitutional principles are countenanced.[59]

The New South Wales Constitution Act 1855 (Imp) empowered New South Wales to amend its own constitution, but, as the Commonwealth of Australia Constitution Act 1900 (Imp) and, later, the Australia Act 1986 (Imp) make clear, the Imperial Parliament retained competence to amend, or abrogate entirely, the constitutions of these local legal systems.[60] However, the Privy Council notes that this competence was in practice strictly constrained: according to a strong convention present in Imperial constitutional practice, the Imperial Parliament would not exercise the power save at the request and consent of the local legal system concerned.[61] Significantly, though, this convention was not law: conventions are 'customs, practices, maxims, or precepts which are not enforced or recognised by the courts, [and which] make up a body not of laws, but of constitutional or political ethics'.[62] Accordingly, conventions find no place in

[57] Kelsen, *General Theory of Law and State* (n 24), 317–19. Kelsen discerns a spectrum, however, and factors such as the presence of local courts might suggest the Colonial legal systems were further toward the federal end of the spectrum than mere 'autonomous provinces': cp ibid, 316. On the other hand, the lack of Colonial participation in central decision-making (for example, by representation in the Imperial Parliament) suggests the relationship was well short of those at the federal end of the spectrum.

[58] ibid, 324.

[59] ibid, 318.

[60] As occurred, eg, in Southern Rhodesia: Southern Rhodesia Act 1965 (Imp); Southern Rhodesia Constitution Order 1965, SI 1965/1952 (Imp).

[61] See *Madzimbamuto v Lardner-Burke* [1969] 1 AC 645 (PC) and (especially in relation to the States), the authorities cited above, ch 2, n 130. See also *British Coal Corporation v The King* [1935] AC 500 (PC), 520 (the Board); *Manuel v Attorney-General* [1983] 1 Ch 77 (CA), 103–08 (Cumming-Bruce, Eveleigh and Slade LJJ).

[62] AV Dicey, *Introduction to the Study of the Law of the Constitution*, 1st edn 1885, 10th edn (London, Macmillan, 1959) 417. See also *Re Resolution to Amend the Constitution* [1981] 1 SCR 753, 774–75 (Laskin CJ, Dickson, Beetz, Estey, McIntyre, Chouinard and Lamer JJ), 883 (Martland, Ritchie, Dickson, Beetz, Chouinard and Lamer JJ).

Kelsen's model, which consists exclusively of legal norms. The exclusion of these non-legal norms, which qualify norms of constitutional law (and which are often critical to a proper understanding of the constitution), is necessitated by the purity and dynamic normative order parameters of Kelsen's account. If account is taken of the convention about the Imperial Parliament's exercise of its legal competence to alter or revoke the constitutions of the Australian Colonies, a structure closer to the federal end of the autonomy spectrum is more plausible; no such characterisation is possible if the politically potent but legally impotent constitutional convention is ignored. The exclusion of politics and relevant social practice in Kelsen's model thus complicates its application, even at the basic level of characterising the system along the spectrum from unitary to federal. Even if the characterisation of New South Wales law as a partial legal system is not impugned (it would be a partial legal system whether the overall structure were unitary or federal), the exclusion of non-legal norms (and perhaps also certain relevant non-norms) should be considered a weakness of the account.

IV. CONTINUITY AND MERGER: STATE LEGAL SYSTEMS AT FEDERATION

The most significant change in Australian law after the establishment of the Colonies was Federation, on 1 January 1901.[63] This, too, was effected by authorised modes of constitutional change, principally the enactment of the Commonwealth of Australia Constitution Act 1900 (Imp)—though

[63] The Federal Council of Australasia, established pursuant to Federal Council of Australasia Act 1885 (Imp), was an important staging-post on the route to Federation. The Council was a voluntary institution, from which it was possible to secede at any time, and it never secured the participation of all of the Australian Colonies (in particular, NSW never joined). It was created to facilitate a coordinated response to events in the Pacific (notably the settlement by other European powers of islands to which convicted criminals could be transported), and fulfilled an essentially political and advisory role. It had no executive or judiciary and controlled no discrete revenue or expenditure. It had limited inter-Colonial legislative competence, for the most part exercisable only at the request of two or more Colonies and only effective for the requesting Colonies. It is submitted that the Council ought best be characterised as an institution provided by Imperial law for legislative cooperation on certain topics: in other words, it operated more in the fashion of an intra-imperial confederacy than a federation; the mechanisms of the Council supplemented existing Imperial and State legal systems rather than created a new partial legal system within the Imperial legal system. See generally A Deakin, 'The Federal Council of Australasia' (1895) 6 *Review of Reviews for Australasia* 154; J Quick and RR Garran, *The Annotated Constitution of the Australian Commonwealth* (Sydney, Angus & Robertson, 1901) 109–15. This brief phase in Australian constitutional history nonetheless remains relevant in relation to the Commonwealth's power to make laws with respect to 'the exercise … of any power which can at the establishment of this Constitution be exercised only by the Parliament of the United Kingdom or by the Federal Council of Australasia': *Commonwealth Constitution*, s 51(xxxviii).

consequential changes were effected by, for example, the local *Constitution Act 1902* (NSW) and the revised letters patent made pursuant to the Imperial prerogative power. Prima facie, the Kelsenian legal scientist would conclude that a new partial legal system, the Australian legal system, was formed within the Empire and that that partial legal system was itself federal, with the Commonwealth and the States as component partial legal systems. However, the detailed application of Kelsen's account again reveals potential complications. Consideration must be given to:

— whether there was continuity between the Colonial and State legal systems; and
— whether Kelsen's account of federations accurately models the federal project as executed in Australia (and the related issue whether territorially overlapping coordinate partial legal systems within the total Imperial legal system are possible); and
— whether any equivalent to the termination of systemic validity exception applies in the case of merger of partial legal systems; and
— how well Kelsen's model of continuity squares with historical and intuitive—pre-theoretical, conventional but informed—understandings of Federation in Australia.

A. Continuity Between Colonial and State Partial Legal Systems

First, were the State legal systems continuous with the Colonial legal systems that preceded them? As argued above, a relative basic norm for the New South Wales Colonial partial legal system in 1900 can readily be discerned, consisting of a complex of constitutional norms including, for example, the 1855 constitution (as amended) and norms connected with paramountcy of, and repugnancy to, Imperial law[64] and with Imperial prerogative power. A critical issue is whether that constitution included the norms of change applicable to the statutory and prerogative norms that otherwise controlled the creation and application of norms of the local New South Wales partial legal system. In other words, the New South Wales Constitution Act 1855 (Imp) is clearly part of the New South Wales constitution in 1900, but is the norm according to which the Imperial Parliament may amend Acts by subsequent legislation also part of the constitution and relative basic norm of the New South Wales partial legal system? It is irrelevant, of course, that this norm is not limited to the territory of New South Wales and that it derives its validity from the Imperial basic norm, not the relative basic norm of the New South Wales partial legal system: the same is true of all of the constitutional norms of that

[64] Principally contained in the Colonial Laws Validity Act 1865 (Imp).

partial legal system. It is submitted that the norm of change is impliedly part of the New South Wales constitution, both in theory and in practice. At the theoretical level, the constitutional norms regulating law-creation are dependent norms[65] and, accordingly, exist as conditions of validity implicated in the complete statement of an individuated norm. In practice, the implication of norms of change into a Colonial constitution is illustrated, for example, by the Imperial norm that a prerogative grant of representative institutions to a Colonial legal system could be revoked only by the Imperial Parliament, unless a power of revocation was expressly reserved to the Crown.[66] It is thus clear that the norms of change applicable to the (Imperial) constitutional norms of the New South Wales partial legal system were also part of the complex of norms forming its constitution (and relative basic norm). The changes to New South Wales constitutional law brought about at Federation,[67] largely concerning the system's material sphere of validity, were effected by the Commonwealth of Australia Constitution Act 1900 (Imp) and were, accordingly, authorised by the New South Wales constitution. The rule of law was not infringed by, or as a result of, the changes, and Her Majesty's Government in the UK continued to take responsibility—albeit with some imprecisely defined reduction in scope—for the government of the States after Federation.[68] There is, therefore, continuity between the New South Wales Colonial legal system and the New South Wales State legal system, according to both the two-fold criterion specific to continuity of Colonial partial legal systems proposed above and to the generic notion of continuity by authorised constitutional change.

B. Australian and Commonwealth Legal Systems and Territorial Overlap

Federation, however, also involved the creation of a new Commonwealth partial legal system—'Commonwealth' signifying the law of the central legal system in Australia, as opposed to the State legal systems—and also a new Australian legal system—'Australian' signifying the total, federally-structured legal system of which the Commonwealth and State legal systems were to be component parts. The Commonwealth of Australia Constitution Act 1900 (Imp) did not merely establish a new set of Imperial norms that were to operate independently as part of (the constitutions of)

[65] Above, text to ch 3, n 36.
[66] *Sammut v Strickland* [1938] AC 678 (PC), 704, referring to *Campbell v Hall* (1774) Lofft 655 (KB), 98 ER 848.
[67] Above, ch 2.I.A.iv.
[68] Above, text to ch 2, n 131.

the several partial Colonial legal systems—in the same fashion as, for example, the Colonial Laws Validity Act 1865 (Imp) or the Judicial Committee Act 1833 (Imp) and the Judicial Committee Act 1844 (Imp). Rather, the federal project was, in the words of the Secretary of State, designed to ensure that the Australian Colonies would no longer to 'be a congeries of States, each of them separate from and entirely independent of the others, … [b]ut … in the words of the preamble of the Bill … "an indissoluble federal Commonwealth firmly united for many of the most important functions of government"'.[69]

At Federation, each of Commonwealth and Australian (Commonwealth and State) law met the criteria for constituting a partial legal system within the total Imperial legal system.[70] The norms of Commonwealth law and of Australian law were ultimately valid in virtue of the Imperial basic norm. Commonwealth law had a constitution and relative basic norm, principally, though not comprehensively, encapsulated in the Commonwealth of Australia Constitution Act 1900 (Imp). On Kelsen's account, the constitution of the Commonwealth partial legal system, as the central component legal system in a federal structure, was simultaneously the constitution of the total Australian legal system.[71] The territorial sphere of validity of both Commonwealth and Australian law was defined by reference to the sum of the territorial spheres of validity of the State systems, together with any additional territory subsequently acquired. The total territory so delimited defined the territorial jurisdiction of the legislative, executive and judicial organs of Commonwealth law and Australian law.

Unless otherwise accounted for (for example, by merger of the State legal systems into the Australian legal system as foreshadowed above and argued below), one consequence of the creation of these Australian and Commonwealth legal systems is that the territorial spheres of validity of apparently coordinate partial legal systems within the total Imperial legal system—the new Commonwealth and Australian legal systems on one hand and the ex hypothesi continuing State legal systems on the other—would overlap. Is this possible in Kelsen's model? The starting point is that legal norms simultaneously valid in a given territory must be part of the same normative system.[72] This principle is not violated in the case of the overlapping territorial spheres of validity of a total legal system and a subordinate partial legal system because the partial legal system, being authorised by norms of the total legal system, shares the same historically

[69] United Kingdom, *Parliamentary Debates (Fourth Series)*, vol 83 (HC, 14.05.1900), col 46 (Mr Chamberlain).

[70] See above, ch 3.III.B.

[71] See Kelsen, *General Theory of Law and State* (n 24), 317.

[72] Above, text to ch 3, n 70. See also, on the principle that the national legal system enjoys exclusive validity for a certain territory, Kelsen, *General Theory of Law and State* (n 24), 210–11.

first constitution and basic norm.[73] The same is true in Kelsen's account of federal systems, where, he says, the constitution of the central partial legal system is simultaneously the constitution of the total legal system, such that norms of the partial state constitutions are, again, authorised by the constitution and basic norm of the total (federal) legal system. However, on the above view of post-Federation Australian legal systems, Kelsen's federal analysis does not, prima facie, hold. The constitution of the New South Wales State partial legal system, continuous with the New South Wales Colonial partial legal system, would not be authorised by the constitution of the Commonwealth partial legal system (simultaneously the constitution of the Australian legal system) but directly by norms of the Imperial legal system. Ultimately, of course, all of the Australian, Commonwealth and State legal systems were sustained by the same Imperial basic norm, but their respective *relative* basic norms were different. Moreover, the two territorially overlapping systems were coordinate in hierarchical terms: neither was subordinate to the other. If Kelsen's view of the relationship of constitutions in a federal structure is accurate, it is by no means clear that his model contemplates or can accommodate this situation.

The account envisages decentralisation in a hierarchical sense, with the territorial spheres of validity of each subordinate level of decentralisation being part only of the territorial spheres of validity of the superior partial systems. To have coordinate partial legal systems with overlapping territorial spheres of validity—as this view of post-Federation Australia would require—is nowhere countenanced. In view of the strongly territorial and hierarchical conceptualisation of total and partial legal systems in Kelsen's model, overlapping partial legal systems must share the same relative basic norm (and historically first constitution) to avoid violating the principle that simultaneously valid norms in a given territory must be part of the same normative system—merely sharing the same ultimate basic norm is not enough. In other words, overlapping legal systems must stand in a relationship of (relative) total legal system to subordinate partial legal system, or of partial legal system to *subordinate* partial legal system. The above analysis of partial legal systems with overlapping territorial spheres of validity (the Australian, Commonwealth and State legal systems) but with constitutions that are independently subordinate to the constitution of the total legal system (the Imperial legal system) thus appears to violate this principle. The source of the problem is Kelsen's simplistic identification of the constitution of the total legal system with the constitution of the central partial legal system in a federation. It was suggested above that, at a theoretical level, the logical interrelation of central

[73] Kelsen, *Pure Theory* (n 5), 315.

and State partial legal systems in a federation implicates the constitutions of the State legal systems in the constitution of the total legal system just as much as it does the constitution of the central legal system.[74] Application of Kelsen's account to Australia illustrates this suggestion in practice. The problem is dissolved if it is recognised that the constitution of the Australian legal system is not identical to the constitution of the Commonwealth (central) legal system but comprises a complex of the constitutional norms of the Commonwealth legal system *and the State legal systems*. In this way, all of the legal systems derive their validity from the relative basic norm of the Australian legal system, which comprises what was termed above a quasi-transcendental-logical constitution: the complex of Imperial laws conferring norm-creating and norm-applying powers on the institutions of the Commonwealth and State legal systems. This correction to Kelsen's model of federal legal systems means that the relationship between the constitutions of the Australian legal system and the State legal systems is that of (relative) total legal system to subordinate partial legal system, and the problem of overlapping territorial spheres of validity of coordinate (rather than superior and subordinate) partial legal systems disappears.

C. Termination of (Partial) Systemic Validity?

How does Kelsen's account of continuity of partial legal systems square with the analysis according to which Colonial legal systems, which were partial legal systems of the total Imperial legal system, are transformed into partial legal systems of the Australian legal system and so become (for several decades) partial legal systems of a partial legal system within the total Imperial legal system? Does this change in status affect the continuity of the Colonial/State legal systems? The change in status has no impact in the application of either the two-fold criterion applicable to the continuity of Colonial partial legal systems within Imperial law, or the generic notion of continuity by authorised constitutional change. It should be noted, however, that the subordination to Australian law altered the criterion of continuity for State legal systems as partial legal systems—the new criterion may be understood as continuity so long as the State remains in the Federation—but, in common with the many changes to the material scope of validity of State legal systems that Federation entailed, the alteration did not affect the rule of law or the UK Government's responsibility for the government of the States. The question therefore becomes whether the termination of systemic validity exception applies in the case of partial legal systems.

[74] Above, 99.

As explained above,[75] change implying termination of systemic validity was framed as an exception to the general account of continuity by authorised constitutional change. The example informing Kelsen's discussion is merger: this is directly relevant to the Australian Colonial legal systems' joining in the federal Australian legal system. It is submitted that a termination of systemic validity exception does not apply in relation to the continuity of partial legal systems, either as a supervening, theoretically necessary element of Kelsen's account of continuity or as a doctrinal feature of Imperial law's provision for the temporal sphere of validity of Colonial partial legal systems. At the level of Kelsen's theory, the exception is expressly framed in terms of the 'termination of the validity of the national legal order as a whole'.[76] As stressed above, Kelsen repeatedly characterises a *national* legal system as a *total*, rather than a partial, legal system,[77] so the exception does not, in terms, apply. Further, Kelsen immediately goes on to discuss merger of the Austrian into the German legal systems from the point of view of international law—viewing the Austrian legal system and the merged German-Austrian legal system as partial legal systems of a total universal legal system that includes international law. Kelsen holds that the merger, implying termination of systemic validity of the Austrian partial legal system, is irrelevant from the point of view of international law: it applies its own norm about the temporal continuity of partial legal systems based on essential territorial identity.[78] By close analogy, therefore, the termination of systemic validity exception does not apply where the continuity of a partial legal system is in issue. At a theoretical level, this conclusion accords with the subordinate status of such a system and with the dual position of the basic norm giving unity to the partial system as both a posited norm of the total legal system and a quasi-transcendental-logical constitution of the partial legal system. The conclusion is also intuitively correct in its concrete application to New South Wales in light of the two-fold Imperial criterion of continuity proposed. The Imperial legal system made different constitutional provision for New South Wales at different stages in the history of that legal system, replacing autocratic constitutional norms with norms providing representative and responsible self-government. It is submitted that the reorganisation of the New South Wales partial legal system as part of a federal partial legal system is a change of the same kind and equally entails continuity, not discontinuity.

[75] Above, ch 3.IV.B.
[76] Kelsen, *General Theory of Law and State* (n 24), 220.
[77] ibid, 100. See also ibid, 304; Kelsen, *Pure Theory* (n 5), 315.
[78] Kelsen, *General Theory of Law and State* (n 24), 220.

D. Federation and Merger in Practice

Is the theoretical explanation according to which the Colonial legal systems (partial legal systems within the Imperial legal system) were transformed into partial legal systems of the Australian legal system (partial legal systems within a partial legal system within the total Imperial legal system) consistent with what happened at Federation in practice? The new status of State legal systems as partial legal systems of an Australian partial legal system within the total Imperial legal system is reflected in Western Australia's 1934 petition in support of secession, which sought Western Australia's restoration 'to its former status as a separate and distinct self-governing colony in the British Empire'.[79] The characterisation of the Australian constitution as a complex of norms, including the constitutional norms of the Commonwealth legal system but also those of the State legal systems, is not entirely obscured by the understandable contemporary focus on the *Commonwealth Constitution*. Quick and Garran relate the view that the Imperial Parliament, by the Commonwealth of Australia Constitution Act 1900 (Imp) and the *Commonwealth Constitution*, established an Australian 'political community', conveyed to it 'quasi-sovereign powers' and allocated one part of those powers to federal institutions, while the balance was 'reserved' to the States—the powers comprising the balance being 'such as are defined in the Constitutions of the States, granted to them by the Imperial Parliament before the union'.[80] Then, echoing the language of section 106 of the *Commonwealth Constitution*, they state the traditional view that, by the *Commonwealth Constitution*, 'the State constitutions were confirmed and continued in existence, subject to the grants of power made by the Constitution to the Federal organs of government'.[81]

[79] *Secession Act 1934* (WA), sch 2, item 19.

[80] Quick and Garran (n 63), 927.

[81] ibid. This was how the effect of ss 106–108 of the *Commonwealth Constitution* was understood until the 1970s: above, text to ch 2, n 113. On the view adopted since then—that s 106, eg, *confers* constitutions on the States rather than merely *acknowledges* their continuing existence by force of their original authorising norms—virtually every legal norm of the State legal systems changed at Federation. While their content remained the same, in theoretical terms, each norm that existed and appeared (and was, contemporaneously, understood) to be authorised by pre-Federation sources was repealed and replaced by a new norm authorised by the *Commonwealth Constitution*. As noted above, ch 3.V.A, the inability of Kelsen's model of dynamic normative orders to account for changes at the upper levels in the hierarchy, without also affecting all the subsidiary norms they authorise, conceals very substantial aspects of continuity. In substance, the content that was continued by ss 106–108 was continued unchanged, yet Kelsen's model forces the conclusion that almost every norm was changed, because the source of their validity was different. Uncertainty about which view of ss 106–108 is correct—say, in 1985—leaves the Kelsenian legal scientist faced with the problem of relationships of validating purport also described above, text to n 40. In construing the hierarchy of authorisation for, say, the *Constitution Act 1902* (NSW), the scientist must choose between the competing authorising norms of the *Commonwealth Constitution* and the New South Wales Constitution Act 1855 (Imp).

Although not expressing the point in terms, this characterisation reflects an understanding that the constitutional law of the total Australian legal system includes Imperial constitutional norms of the State legal systems. When any potential confusion introduced by the language of 'reservation' and 'continuance' is removed, the view expressed by these authors, both leaders in the Federation movement, accords precisely with the understanding reflected in Kelsen's model.

Finally, it may be noted that the conclusion that the constitution of the Australian legal system is not simply the constitution of the Commonwealth legal system but also includes the constitutional norms of the State legal systems accounts for the otherwise anomalous situation of the continuing direct links that were, by design, retained between Imperial institutions and State legal systems.[82] As these State constitutional norms are also elements in the complex comprising the constitution of the (relative total) Australian legal system, a hierarchical relationship between Imperial law and Australian law and between Australian law and State law is preserved. The residual links—remaining until the *Australia Acts*—are part of the Australian legal system as a partial legal system of the Imperial legal system; they are also, via the Australian legal system, part of the State legal systems, which are partial systems of the Australian legal system. In principle, however, the links are not direct but indirect; the norms retaining these links are coordinate with the norms expressed in the *Commonwealth Constitution* that impact upon the State legal systems. The presence within the complex of constitutional norms of the Australian legal system of a power to amend or repeal the Imperial norms sustaining those links confirms this picture.[83]

V. DISCONTINUITY: TOTAL AND NATIONAL LEGAL SYSTEMS AND THE STATUTE OF WESTMINSTER

A. Total (National) Legal Systems and Historically First Constitutions

Because their spheres of validity are generally conceived by Kelsen as limited only by international law, his model expressly and repeatedly equates *national* legal systems with *total* (as opposed to partial) legal systems: a national legal system is the 'total legal order constituting the State'.[84] The

[82] Above, 25–26. The additional complications as to the relationship between the Imperial, Australian and State legal systems illustrated by WA's attempt at secession would be overlooked in an application of Kelsen's model, since these rested principally on matters of constitutional convention, not legal norms: above, 136–37.

[83] *Commonwealth Constitution*, s 51(xxxviii).

[84] Above, n 77.

model conceives of the state as the community constituted by a national legal system,[85] which is a centralised legal system efficacious for a certain territory and subordinated only to international law.[86] The idea of a total (national) legal system is thus intrinsically linked to international law and to the international 'personality' of the (national) state as a juristic person with internal rights and duties (under national law) and external rights and duties (under international law).[87] Since national legal systems are total legal systems, it follows that, on acquiring international legal personality, the Australian legal system becomes a total legal system and ceases to be a partial legal system within a total (national) Imperial legal system.

As set out above,[88] the Commonwealth became a subject of international law no later than 1942. An exact date is notoriously difficult to identify.[89] Nonetheless, Kelsen himself adverts to membership of the League of Nations[90] as well as to separation of part of a territory by treaty[91] as relevant indicia. Australia was a founding member of the League of Nations separately from the Empire,[92] and Kelsen, as has been noted, expressly regarded the Statute of Westminster 1931 (Imp) as a treaty creating new national legal systems.[93] For simplicity, 1942—when the Statute came into force in relation to Australia (ignoring the deemed retrospectivity)[94]—is the date used in the remainder of this book.[95] Applying Kelsen's account, it follows that, on acquiring international legal personality, the Australian legal system, which had been a partial legal system within the total Imperial legal system, became a national—and thus a total—legal system. The significance of this shift for present purposes arises because of the model's explanation of a historically first constitution:[96]

> In this way we eventually arrive at a historically first constitution that cannot have been created in this way and whose validity, therefore, cannot be traced back to a positive norm created by a legal authority; we arrive, instead, at a

[85] Kelsen, *General Theory of Law and State* (n 24), 181.

[86] ibid, 121, 221, 351, 367; Kelsen, *Pure Theory* (n 5), 214, 289–90.

[87] Kelsen, *Pure Theory* (n 5), 290–91.

[88] Above, text to ch 2, n 200.

[89] PC Oliver, *The Constitution of Independence: the Development of Constitutional Theory in Australia, Canada, and New Zealand* (Oxford, OUP, 2005) 331–32. See also the authorities cited above, ch 2, n 234.

[90] Kelsen, *General Theory of Law and State* (n 24), 227–28.

[91] ibid, 230.

[92] Above, text to ch 2, n 188.

[93] Kelsen, *General Theory of Law and State* (n 24), 324.

[94] Above, text to ch 2, n 203.

[95] It may be observed in passing that there were conventional constitutional changes that marked the Commonwealth's increasing independence before 1942, such as those recognised at the 1926 Imperial Conference: above, text to ch 2, n 203. However, as these shifts in constitutional convention were merely political, the Kelsenian legal scientist must ignore them, notwithstanding any consequent artificiality: above, 136–37.

[96] Kelsen, *Pure Theory* (n 5), 200 (emphasis added).

> constitution that became valid in a revolutionary way, that is, either by breach of a former constitution or for a territory that formerly was not the sphere of validity of a constitution and of a *national legal order* based on it.

If the last phrase is understood at face value, the constitution of the Australian legal system would, from 1942, count as a historically first constitution. If this understanding is correct, as is argued below, one of the core objections to the model—that it cannot account for the separation of parts of legal systems by constitutional means—is significantly weakened. On this understanding, the transformation of a partial legal system into a total legal system—to reiterate, a *national* legal system, one that constitutes a state and is the subject of rights and duties in international law—is a phenomenon that creates a historically first constitution. In the first part of the explanation of historically first constitutions extracted above, Kelsen suggests that the process of tracing authorisation of norms through superior norms in the hierarchy only ceases when it is no longer possible to identify an authorising norm. What, then, if the transformation from partial to total (national) legal system occurs by constitutionally authorised means? This is, of course, relevant to Australia; Kelsen expressly holds that the Statute of Westminster 1931 (Imp) transformed a federal state (the Empire) into a confederacy of *states*, a set of *national* legal systems in a relationship consisting of international legal norms, with the Statute of Westminster itself embodying international law at the same time as national law.[97]

Does Kelsen mean that a historically first constitution is one that is *unauthorised* for one of only two reasons: *breach* of a former constitution, or *absence* of a constitution? This is what has usually been supposed. Finnis adverts to the ambiguity in the phrase 'formerly was not the sphere of validity of a constitution and of a national legal order based on it': it may refer to formerly uninhabited territory, or to territory that was formerly *only part* of an undifferentiated territorial sphere of validity.[98] Finnis ultimately interprets the passages in such a way that the transformation of a partial legal system to a total legal system does not count as a historically first constitution:[99]

> [O]n the Kelsenian analysis back to a historically first constitution, the 'Pakistani legal system' seems to be no more than a sub-unit in the British legal system, from which it cannot be freed save by way of some violation of British law.

There are strong grounds in favour of this interpretation: the strongest is that Kelsen's model is focused on authorisation, and the constitution of the new total legal system *was* authorised.

[97] Kelsen, *General Theory of Law and State* (n 24), 324.

[98] JM Finnis, 'Revolutions and Continuity of Law' (1971) in *Philosophy of Law—Collected Essays: Volume IV* (Oxford, OUP, 2011) 407, 413–14.

[99] ibid, 414.

There might, however, also be strong reasons not to treat the principle of authorised constitutional change as overriding. Textually, Kelsen refers to 'territory that formerly was not the sphere of validity of a constitution *and of a national legal order* based on it'.[100] The italicised phrase is significant: the territory of a *partial* legal system is not the territorial sphere of validity of a *national* legal system because all national legal systems are *total* legal systems. Prima facie constitutional authorisation in the case of lawful transformation into a national legal system cannot be denied. However, as set out above, constitutional authorisation is the primary but not the sole criterion of continuity. On the one hand, for example, the model builds in exceptions in the case of enduring ineffectiveness and constitutional norms with an alternative character: here, apparently unconstitutional change is effectively deemed to be constitutional and does not count as discontinuity—the principle of legitimacy (authorised constitutional change) is limited by the principle of efficacy.[101] On the other hand, authorised constitutional change that implies termination of systemic validity was expressly recognised as an exception, and counts as discontinuity.[102] It was argued above that the termination of systemic validity exception—the example was merger of one system into another—reached towards a change in ultimacy. Critically, the issues encountered in the case of the separation of a partial legal system are identical to those to which the termination of systemic validity exception is addressed. Ultimacy is just as much in issue in de-merger (separation) as it is in merger. If the principle of ultimacy limits the principle of legitimacy in the case of merger (termination of systemic validity), it is submitted that it is not incoherent or inapposite to resolve the ambiguity in Kelsen's explanation of historically first constitutions in a way that similarly treats the principle of ultimacy as limiting the principle of legitimacy in the case of de-merger (transformation to national legal system). The reference to the territorial sphere of validity of a national legal system in the last part of the explanation should thus be understood to indicate—in terms—that transformation of a partial legal system into a total (national) legal system entails discontinuity: it is an exception to the general rule that authorised constitutional change entails continuity.

A potentially complicating factor is the role played by international law in Kelsen's model. The merger discussion and the termination of systemic validity exception that appeared in *General Theory of Law and State* are not restated in *Pure Theory of Law* because, by that time, Kelsen's model is exclusively framed in terms of an international-law monist relationship

[100] Kelsen, *Pure Theory* (n 5), 200 (emphasis added).
[101] Above, ch 3.IV.A, IV.C.
[102] Above, ch 3.IV.B.

between municipal (national) and international law. From that monist perspective, the merger issue (like questions of continuity of legal systems generally) is resolved directly by reference to rules of international law. However, this role for international law tends to strengthen the reading of the explanation of historically first constitutions as including an exception for 'de-merged' states. In *General Theory of Law and State*, Kelsen indicates that a national legal system can emerge:[103]

(a) for territory (and population) that was formerly that of one state—the territorial sphere of validity of a (prior existing) national legal system; or
(b) for territory that was formerly not that of any state—not the whole nor any part of the territorial sphere of validity of any legal system; or
(c) for territory that was formerly that of two or more states—as to distinct areas of territory, the whole or part of the territorial sphere of validity of two or more national legal systems; or
(d) for territory that was formerly only part of the territory of one state—not the territorial sphere of validity of a national legal system and, accordingly, either part of an undifferentiated territory of a national legal system, or the territorial sphere of validity of one or more partial legal systems within a total (national) legal system.

From the monist perspective, the first situation entails continuity, pursuant to a rule of international law, whether or not there is authorised constitutional change.[104] From the dualist perspective, authorised constitutional change entails continuity in this first situation, but revolutionary (non-authorised) constitutional change entails discontinuity. This corresponds to the first limb of Kelsen's explanation of historically first constitutions (unauthorised because of breach of a former constitution). Situations (b)-(d) entail discontinuity from the monist perspective, because international law applies the criterion of essential territorial identity. It is submitted that these situations are what Kelsen has in mind in the second limb of his explanation of historically first constitutions, and that they also entail discontinuity from the dualist perspective, on the ground that the territory formerly was not the sphere of validity of a constitution and of a national legal order based on it. In other words, understanding the explanation of historically first constitutions in light of the four possible situations in which a national legal system may emerge, the second limb states three situations in which a constitution counts as historically first, even though it came into existence as a result of authorised constitutional change. The first limb gives a situation where the monist and dualist perspectives result

[103] Kelsen, *General Theory of Law and State* (n 24), 219.
[104] Above, ch 3.IV.D.

in different conclusions, while the second limb groups together three situations where discontinuity results from both perspectives.

The reach towards the principle of ultimacy here is expressed in the qualification 'national legal order', by which Kelsen indicates a legal system subject only to international law—a total rather than a partial legal system. The transformation from partial to total (national) legal system gives the norms of that system the character of ultimacy; the system is now subordinate only to international law. In doing so, the transformation also denies the characteristic of ultimacy to the norms (considered in their national-legal matrix) that, historically, authorised that constitution. It was argued above that underlying the termination of systemic validity exception (but not clearly expressed) was the denial that norms that are valid across a total territory could be valid for different reasons in different parts of the territory.[105] By parallel reasoning, in the case of situation (d), the constitutional norms of the newly created national legal system cannot be valid for the same reason as the norms in the rest of the territory of which it was formerly part, or else it would still be part of that territory and legal system:[106] it would be a partial, not a total (national), legal system—and the example expressly concerns a national legal system.

If this reconstruction (or, if it be preferred, charitable interpretation) of Kelsen's model is correct, a major weakness is avoided. However, while the transformation to national legal system exception is intelligible, it suffers from the same problem as its counterpart in the termination of systemic validity exception. In neither case does Kelsen convincingly articulate the underlying rationale, or explain how the exception is consistent with his primary thesis of continuity based on authorised constitutional change. Of course, the same criticism is also levelled at the exception concerning constitutional norms with an alternative character, where the principle of legitimacy (authorised constitutional change) is limited by the principle of effectiveness. These exceptions could be (uncharitably) characterised as ad hoc adaptations of the model designed to accommodate the facts of existing legal materials. However, it is submitted that Kelsen's explanation of what counts as a historically first constitution, including the transformation to national legal system exception, is not purely ad hoc or stipulative. It takes as its primary element the idea of *non-authorisation*, because of the breach or absence of an authorising constitution, but also takes into account *ultimacy* in the sense of being the most extensive (total) legal system subject to (and, as personified in the state, a subject of) international law.

[105] Above, ch 3.IV.B.

[106] This follows from Kelsen's adherence to the principle that simultaneously valid norms must be part of the same normative system: above, ch 3.III.A.

B. Application of the Transformation to National Legal System Exception

Returning to Australia, it thus appears possible to apply Kelsen's account with the consequence (actually flagged by Kelsen expressly)[107] that the Statute of Westminster 1931 (Imp) brought about relevant (Kelsenian) discontinuity between the Imperial legal system and the Australian legal system. This conclusion accords with the realities of Commonwealth law and the growing political and social independence of Australia from the broader Empire at the time. It may be observed that the residual 'direct' links between the Imperial and State legal systems that persisted after the Statute of Westminster do not require a different characterisation. It was argued above that the relevant Imperial norms were part of the complex of norms comprising the constitution of the Australian legal system from its establishment in 1901. This constitution was described above as quasi-transcendental-logical, as it directly comprised the empowering norms necessary to understand the norms of the then partial Australian legal system as valid but those norms were, in fact, posited norms of the Imperial legal system (which had its own transcendental-logical or quasi-transcendental-logical constitution). As explained above, upon Australian law's becoming a total (national) legal system in 1942, the complex of constitutional norms, now also including the Statute of Westminster, is to be understood as a historically first constitution. The Imperial constitutional norms of the State legal systems that, it was argued, were just as much part of the constitution of the Australian legal system as those of the Commonwealth legal system at Federation, remain part of the complex forming the Australian constitution at the time of the transformation to national legal system. The Australian constitution having become a constitution in the transcendental-logical sense, those norms are now part of the complex basic norm of Australian law. Nor is it problematic for Kelsen's account that these norms provide a continuing role for institutions that are, ex hypothesi, part of a distinct national legal system: the model recognises an exception to the principle of the exclusive territorial validity of national legal systems in the case of powers provided by treaty.[108] This exception applies here because the existing Imperial links were retained by section 9(2) of the Statute of Westminster, which Kelsen understands to be both national law and international law.

[107] Kelsen, *General Theory of Law and State* (n 24), 324.
[108] ibid, 212.

C. Alternative Analyses

The foregoing reconstruction of a transformation to national legal system exception turns on an apparently novel reading of Kelsen's explanation of historically first constitutions—one that recognises a qualification to the focus on authorised constitutional change that lies at the core of the model. It also draws on a reconstruction of Kelsen's account of total and partial legal systems and, in particular, the equation of national and total legal systems. It was expressly acknowledged above that Kelsen's account is underdeveloped on this point[109] and, accordingly, it may be that the identification of the transformation to national legal system exception rests upon challengeable foundations. If the reconstruction of Kelsen's model and the associated analysis developed above is rejected, three alternative accounts must be considered. First, if the transformation to national legal system exception is rejected, continuity falls to be considered in accordance with the two-fold Imperial criterion advocated above.[110] As explained above, His Majesty's Government in the UK ceased to be responsible for the government of Australia itself in 1930.[111] An application of this norm therefore points to relevant discontinuity. Discontinuity is as intuitively sound a conclusion if it results from this analysis as if it results from the transformation to national legal system analysis.

Second, if both the transformation to national legal system exception and the account of continuity of partial legal systems are rejected, the alternative is a straightforward application of the criterion of authorised constitutional change. All changes of the first half of the twentieth century having been constitutionally authorised, they do not entail discontinuity with the Imperial legal system. Even if the constitutional situation is characterised as one in which the Queen of Australia (possessed of power pursuant to Australian constitutional law) is simply the same person as the Queen of the UK, the relevant changes were still brought about in an authorised fashion and so entail continuity with the Imperial legal system. That conclusion is intuitively unsound. The development of community identity in Australia is traced above, as reflected in laws relating to allegiance, nationality and citizenship, the franchise, and oaths of allegiance and office. Notwithstanding considerable particular aspects of continuity, discontinuity is the inescapable intuitive conclusion to be drawn from the

[109] Above, section III.A.

[110] Above, 135.

[111] Above, text to ch 2, n 205. So much is also reflected in the assumption behind the express termination of the UK Government's responsibility for the government of the States in the Australia Act 1986 (Imp), s 10, despite the continued exercise of residual functions within the legal system by the monarch on the advice of the UK Government in the interim: above, 25–26.

cumulative evolutionary changes in politics, society and economy over this period, from local democracy and popular and local institutional control of government and constitutional change to the exclusion of Imperial authorities, to markers of distinct social groups that defend and support themselves and conceive of themselves as groups with shared group identities and with distinct entitlements and responsibilities.

Finally, if the reconstruction and application developed above is rejected, there remains the further alternative suggested by Harris, to the effect that the Kelsenian legal scientist may presuppose any basic norm authorising a historically *sufficient* constitution. This would permit the scientist in, say, 1950 to select the constitution of 1942 as historically first and to presuppose a sustaining basic norm accordingly. All legal norms existing then or after can trace their validity through that constitution: it is therefore sufficient. The resulting discontinuity would be intuitively acceptable, as it would if it arose at this time on the other bases proposed. Although a further sufficient prior constitution (or several) lies behind the constitution of 1942, the Kelsenian legal scientist may choose to terminate his analysis there, Harris suggests. As explained above,[112] Harris's reasoning draws on the ideological choice that—exceptionally—Kelsen permits the legal scientist between monist models; a similarly exceptional permission to take account of extra-legal considerations ought to be open between multiple historically sufficient constitutions, Harris proposes. A desire to emphasise discrete Australian identity and independence from its colonial past was noted above in relation to views about the legal source of authority for the *Commonwealth Constitution*.[113] The recent preference of the High Court to look no further than Australian legal sources[114] similarly suggests a place for Harris's suggestion in practice. The practice of participants may also provide a theoretical grounding for the legal scientist's choice, either through the fact of choice itself or through the rationales offered for that choice. These are frequently ideological, as with the democratic flavour of the popular sovereignty argument made by some in justifying the choice of the constitution of 1901.[115] However, applied in this way, the basic norm risks degenerating from a 'pure' logically necessary postulate to an 'impure' empirical or ideological choice, contingent on the views of participants at a given time. What happens when the participants (or the legal scientists acting on the facts of their practice) change their choice of historically sufficient constitution? Is there continuity or discontinuity? In 1972, no judge thought to cease his enquiry into the validity

[112] Above, text to ch 3, n 153.

[113] Above, text to ch 2, n 235.

[114] Above, ch 2, n 117.

[115] See, eg, *Nationwide News Pty Ltd v Wills* (1992) 177 CLR 1 (HCA), 72 (Deane and Toohey JJ); *Theophanous v Herald & Weekly Times Ltd* (1994) 182 CLR 104 (HCA), 171 (Deane J).

of Australian law when Australian sources ran out. From 1976, Murphy J opined that the constitution of 1901 was sufficient,[116] and others have variously proposed 1931, 1939, 1942 or 1986.[117] All of these choices were expressed in the last 35 years, yet Harris's suggestion does not explain how the Kelsenian legal scientist should respond to these changing data.

VI. CONTINUITY AFTER THE STATUTE OF WESTMINSTER

Arguably, the most obvious factual, practical challenge to the analysis developed in the last two sections is to account for the Australia Act 1986 (Imp), the implications of which might appear inconsistent with the proposed understanding of State legal systems as subordinate to the Australian legal system rather than to the Imperial legal system, and which might appear redundant if there were discontinuity in 1942 by reason of the transformation to national legal system exception (to Kelsen's general account of continuity by virtue of authorised constitutional change). However, as argued above, the constitution of the Australian legal system may readily be understood to include the Imperial norms relevant to the links terminated by the Australia Act 1986 (Imp) and also the norms of change pursuant to which the Act was promulgated.[118] There is thus no difficulty in regarding the Australia Act 1986 (Imp) as valid in virtue of the basic norm of the Australian constitution. It may also be valid in the Imperial or UK legal system in virtue of that system's basic norm, but the territorial sphere of validity of the constitution sustained by the Imperial basic norm on this analysis excludes Australia. The only relevant source of validity in Australia is the basic norm sustaining the historically first Australian constitution of 1942. It is relevant to recall that Kelsen's model acknowledges that the same individual or organ may act in different legal systems, albeit in different capacities,[119] and that it permits the exercise of power—and thus, by implication, also the termination of such exercise—by organs of another national legal system as an exception to the principle of the exclusive territorial validity of national legal systems.[120] The enactment of the Australia Act 1986 (Imp) by the Westminster Parliament, essentially as an agent for an Australian principal (or principals), and the tendering

[116] *Bistricic v Rokov* (1976) 135 CLR 552 (HCA), 566–67 (Murphy J); *Robinson v Western Australian Museum* (1977) 138 CLR 283 (HCA), 343–44 (Murphy J); *China Ocean Shipping Co v South Australia* (1979) 145 CLR 172 (HCA), 236–37 (Murphy J); *Kirmani v Captain Cook Cruises Pty Ltd [No 1]* (1985) 159 CLR 351 (HCA), 383–84 (Murphy J).

[117] Above, ch 2, n 234.

[118] Above, 145. See also text to n 64.

[119] Above, ch 3, n 73.

[120] Above, n 108.

of advice to the Queen on the settlement by both her Commonwealth and her UK responsible ministers afford intuitive credibility to this analysis.[121]

On the basis that there was a historically first Australian constitution in 1942, none of the changes to the nature or material, spatial or personal scope of the legal systems comprising Australian law after 1942 indicates discontinuity according to Kelsen's model or implies discontinuity at an intuitive level. Since the termination of residual Imperial links left the States undisturbed as components of the Federation, the *Australia Acts* do not entail any discontinuity in those partial legal systems. Other intra-systemic developments, such as the emergence of a single common law, were constitutionally authorised and so entail continuity. Extra-systemic changes—especially those connected with defence, nationality, citizenship and the franchise, but also the symbolic changes connected with arms, flags and honours—similarly reinforce continuity of the federal Australian legal system. If the reconstruction advocated above is rejected and an unmodified criterion of authorised constitutional change is applied, then the resulting continuity is, in virtue of these changes, even less intuitively acceptable, particularly after 1986, than it was suggested it would be in 1942.[122]

VII. CONTINUITY BY INTERNATIONAL LAW

Kelsen provides five examples of how the criterion of essential territorial identity in his account of continuity by international law is to be applied. Four are set out above,[123] providing that there is continuity if the territory is unchanged (even if constitutional change is unauthorised) and discontinuity if a national legal system (a state) is formed in territory that was formerly uninhabited, territory that was formerly that of two or more states, or territory that was formerly only part of the territory of one state. The fifth example is merger of one national legal system (and its territory) into another, which appears to count as discontinuity for the subsumed state but continuity for the subsuming state: the latter's territorial sphere of validity is enlarged but the change is not 'essential'.[124] No specification of what changes count as relevantly 'essential' is provided beyond these five examples.

[121] The often unappreciated involvement of UK ministers and of the Queen herself, at both the formal and substantive levels, in the negotiation of the *Australia Acts* is detailed in A Twomey, *The Australia Acts 1986: Australia's Statutes of Independence* (Leichhardt, NSW, Federation Press, 2010) 62–180.

[122] Above, 152–53.

[123] Above, text to n 103 and ch 3, n 138.

[124] Kelsen, *General Theory of Law and State* (n 24), 220.

As argued above,[125] annexation of uninhabited territory to an existing legal system is different from erection of a new legal system in formerly uninhabited territory. Therefore, even if New South Wales were regarded (incorrectly) as uninhabited in 1788, settlement did not, in virtue of this fact alone, entail discontinuity with the Imperial legal system. On Kelsen's model according to international law, it might, however, reasonably be supposed that application of the criterion of essential territorial identity has a quantitative dimension. Although Phillip's Commission purported to annex to the territorial sphere of validity of the Imperial legal system an additional territory of 3.8 million square kilometres (4.1 million, if New Zealand is included), Kelsen's account of continuity by international law is concerned only with territory over which the legal system 'is permanently effective'.[126] In the case of New South Wales at settlement, this was a far smaller territory than that claimed in Phillip's Commission. The territorial sphere of validity of the Imperial legal system thus 'remains essentially the same',[127] in quantitative terms, on the establishment of the penal settlement at Sydney in 1788.

Nonetheless, the territorial claims of Imperial law in Australia were not entirely hollow: while little or no attempt was made to apply its norms to Aboriginal people before 1816,[128] military discipline and control of convicts, for example, clearly followed the individuals concerned wherever they were. The territorial area of effective control gradually expanded with the establishment of new settlements, and, while vast areas of remote Australia remained unsupervised, it may be argued that, in the absence of any substantial competitor, effective control was established over the whole continent by the second half of the nineteenth century. If considered moment by moment, the gradual accretions to the area of permanently effective control comprising the territorial sphere of validity of the Imperial legal system might occasion no essential changes. However, the cumulative expansion over, say, 75 years is significant. Is the territorial change to be measured in absolute terms, or proportionally to the size of the pre-existing territorial sphere? Is there a qualitative dimension to the criterion of essential territorial identity: would the loss of London and the Home Counties be more likely to indicate that the Imperial legal system's territorial sphere of validity had essentially changed than the loss of Van Diemen's Land? A purely territorial criterion appears crude, and Kelsen's model seems less than fully developed on this point.

125 Above, section I.B.

126 Kelsen, *Pure Theory* (n 5), 337.

127 Kelsen, *General Theory of Law and State* (n 24), 221.

128 Proclamation (04.05.1816) in F Watson (ed), *Historical Records of Australia*, vol 9, Series I (Sydney, Library Committee of the Commonwealth Parliament, 1917) 142–44; AC Castles, *An Australian Legal History* (Sydney, LBC, 1982) 515–17; Australian Law Reform Commission, *The Recognition of Aboriginal Customary Laws* (Rep No 31, 1986) 34–36 [39]–[41].

Assuming there is no discontinuity in the Imperial legal system by reason of the territorial changes in Australia between 1788 and 1900, Federation must not, it seems, be understood to effect any change either. The reorganisation of partial legal systems within the total Imperial legal system is of no consequence from the perspective of the territorial international law continuity analysis. The same conclusion must apply to the surrender, transfer, separation and mergers of Territories within Australia (the Australian Capital Territory, Jervis Bay Territory, Northern Territory, etc) and within the Empire (Papua, Norfolk Island, Ashmore and Cartier Islands, Australian Antarctic Territory, etc), at least until the Statute of Westminster 1931 (Imp). The position may be less clear in relation to Nauru and New Guinea. Nauru was never, as such, a Territory of Australia, but the law of the Australian partial legal system (and therefore also that of the total Imperial legal system) applied there for nearly 50 years.[129] New Guinea was accepted pursuant to a League of Nations mandate that denoted administration as part of Australian territory. Kelsen's model distinguishes between the territorial sphere of validity of a legal system in a strict, narrow sense and other areas in which the legal system may execute coercive acts, pursuant to, but within the confines strictly allowed by, international law. Such areas include the high seas and land that is the territory of no state.[130] The application of Australian law in Nauru and New Guinea was, in virtue of their status as mandate territories, circumscribed by particular rules of international law. However, these restrictions on the material scope of the legal system were few, and are closer to those applicable (in Kelsen's model) to any national legal system as a function of international law than they are to the kind of limited competence that applies to the high seas and unclaimed territory.[131] Accordingly, it should be concluded that mandate territories fell within the territorial scope of Australian law and, therefore, that of the total system of Imperial law of which it comprised (at least until the Statute of Westminster 1931 (Imp)) only a partial legal system.

[129] Above, text to ch 2, n 463.

[130] Kelsen, *General Theory of Law and State* (n 24), 211.

[131] The mandates accorded plenary power but required the mandatory, for example, to promote the well-being and social progress of the inhabitants, to prohibit slavery, forced labour and arms trafficking, to refrain from supplying intoxicating spirits to the inhabitants and from militarising the territories, and to ensure freedom of movement and religion: *Mandate for Nauru* (1921) 2 *League of Nations Official Journal* 93 (entered into force: generally and for Australia 17.12.1920), arts 2–5; *Mandate for the German Possessions in the Pacific Ocean Situated South of the Equator, other than German Samoa and Nauru* (1921) 2 *League of Nations Official Journal* 85 (entered into force: generally and for Australia 17.12.1920), arts 2–5, and the more modern (and less prescriptive) *Trusteeship Agreement for the Territory of New Guinea* (1947) 8 UNTS 181 (No 122) (entered into force: generally and for Australia 13.12.1946), arts 3–8; *Trusteeship Agreement for the Territory of Nauru* (1947) 10 UNTS 3 (No 138) (entered into force: generally and for Australia 01.11.1947), arts 3–7.

However, as provided in the fourth of Kelsen's examples, relating to the creation of a national legal system in part only of the territory of an existing state, continuity of the Imperial legal system is affected by the emergence of Australia as an international legal person distinct from the Empire. Although the point is nowhere clarified in Kelsen's account, it may be doubted that there was discontinuity in the *Imperial* legal system. By analogy to the uninterrupted continuity of the subsuming state in the case of merger, the criterion of essential territorial identity operates in the case of separation of part of an existing state to deny continuity between the former total legal system and the new national legal system, but not to deny continuity between the former total legal system and the rump of that system after the separation. Australian law and the Imperial legal system would be discontinuous, but the (rump) Imperial legal system would be continuous before and after the emergence of Australia as a discrete international legal person. As argued above,[132] with effect from 1942, the Australian legal system was established as a national legal system in territory that was 'formerly only part of the territory and the population of one State'.[133] Accordingly, an application of Kelsen's account of continuity by international law identifies 1942 as the date of discontinuity. As adverted to above, there is a necessary connection in Kelsen's model between international law and the concept of a national legal system, such that, in circumstances like those in which Australian independence was achieved, it should not surprise us to find that Kelsen's model identifies discontinuity at the same point on both his account of continuity without international law and his account of continuity by international law.

The subsequent changes to the territorial sphere of validity of the Australian legal system by the acquisition or loss of Territories between 1942 and 2001[134] occasioned no change to the system's essential territorial integrity. Certainly, the system's territorial sphere of validity expanded by mergers (usually creating partial legal systems in each Territory) and contracted by separations, but the Australian legal system was in each case the subsuming or the remaining legal system, and, accordingly, as explained above, its essential territorial identity—and therefore its continuity—is not impugned. To the extent that other quantitative or qualitative changes, not expressly detailed in Kelsen's account, affect essential territorial identity, the changes to the territorial sphere of validity of Australian law between 1942 and 2001 must, again, be understood as leaving the continuity of the Australian legal system undisturbed. Whatever criteria of area, population or importance might be applied, the changes were comparatively

[132] Above, 146.
[133] Kelsen, *General Theory of Law and State* (n 24), 219.
[134] Above, ch 2.II.A.

insignificant and the territorial sphere of validity of Australian law ought to be understood as remaining essentially the same. The only exceptions that must be noted are the quantitatively significant non-territorial changes to the spatial scope of the Australian legal system, such as the declaration of the EEZ or the contiguous zone. These are spaces where Australia exercises limited rights accorded by international law outside its territorial boundaries and, as noted above,[135] are expressly outside the ambit of Kelsen's model.

The conclusions to which an application of Kelsen's account of continuity by international law leads—that a discretely identifiable Australian legal system came into existence in 1942 and continued to exist (at least) until 2001—are intuitively satisfactory. Attention to criteria other than essential territorial identity—in particular, criteria connected with the personal scope of Australian law—may suggest some harshness in the conclusions based solely on territory, but the conclusions reached on that basis are far from intuitively implausible. The application of Kelsen's account does, nonetheless, reveal the need for further explication of the central concept of essential territorial identity. The present analysis has benefitted from rare direct consideration by Kelsen in relation to the Statute of Westminster 1931 (Imp), which, if absent, could have complicated matters and rendered its conclusions less certain.

VIII. CONCLUSIONS

This chapter has applied Kelsen's model of continuity and discontinuity to the case of Australia between 1788 and 2001. While section I suggested that criticisms at the theoretical level connected with ascertaining a legal system's basic norm may be surmountable in practice, section II revealed other difficulties associated with the model's approach to understanding legal materials by entering in medias res. One such difficulty was choosing between multiple sufficient basic norms; Harris's notion of relying on confident predictions and an alternative inertia principle were both found to be unsatisfactory resolutions to this problem. Where two or more basic norms could be ascertained by inductive reasoning on the basis of available legal material, presupposition of a basic norm thus proved less straightforward in practice than it might appear from Kelsen's theory. Section II countenanced the possibility of accommodating a degree of temporary unconstitutional action within the model by examining the notions of retrospective annulment and retrospective authorisation, applying the latter in particular to the problem of unconstitutional changes in New

[135] Above, n 130.

South Wales between 1788 and 1819 to avoid the counter-intuitive technical revolution that Kelsen's account would otherwise produce.

Section III grappled with continuity and discontinuity of partial legal systems, noticing significant gaps in Kelsen's model and establishing the key insight that continuity of partial legal systems need not, in Kelsen's account, be governed by the same principles of authorised constitutional change that apply to total legal systems. Accordingly, it became necessary to establish a criterion for the continuity or discontinuity of the New South Wales partial legal system as a matter of Imperial law. Both the theory and this doctrinal point required examination of the unitary or federal character of the relationship between the Imperial total legal system and the New South Wales partial legal system over time. This, in turn, gave rise to examination of the applicable constitutional conventions, exclusion of which from Kelsen's account was found to produce a distorted understanding of the relationship.

Section IV engaged with a set of puzzles connected with explaining Federation in terms of Kelsen's model of total and partial legal systems. Kelsen's conception of the relationship between total and central partial legal systems in a federation proved unnecessarily narrow and simplistic, and the confusion produced incoherence in relation to coordinate partial legal systems with overlapping territorial spheres of validity. In examining continuity and discontinuity in the context of the transformation of a partial New South Wales legal system into a subordinate partial legal system of an Australian partial legal system (of the Imperial total legal system), it was argued that the termination of systemic validity exception does not apply to the merger of partial legal systems by constitutionally authorised means. On balance, notwithstanding serious unresolved problems, the account as reconstructed and amplified was, if applied in its own terms, found to accord with contemporary and subsequent understandings of how Federation unfolded in Australia.

Section V again focused attention on the important equation in Kelsen's model of national legal systems and total legal systems. It argued that the key to a persistent challenge to the model of authorised constitutional change was revealed in the characterisation of a national legal system (that of an international legal person) as a total, rather than a partial, legal system. The interaction between this feature of the account and its model of what counts as a historically first constitution was considered, apparently for the first time, and the relationship between these elements and the core criterion of constitutionally authorised change was examined. In light of other exceptions to the principle of authorised constitutional change elucidated in chapter three, section V argued that ambiguity in Kelsen's exposition of historically first constitutions should be resolved by understanding the account to provide a (fourth) transformation to national legal system exception. In this section, and also in section VI, analysing the period after the Statute of Westminster 1931 (Imp), it was concluded that only an entirely unreconstructed and unmodified understanding of Kelsen's model would produce the unsound conclusion that Australian law continued to be part of an Imperial legal system.

Section VII applied Kelsen's alternative account of continuity and discontinuity by international law. It revealed respects in which the criterion of essential territorial integrity was underdeveloped. However, when amplified consistently with other parts of the account, it was demonstrated that Kelsen's analysis reached the same conclusion—of discontinuity between Imperial and Australian legal systems no later than 1942.

In terms of the principal objectives of this book—testing the explanatory power of theoretical accounts of continuity and discontinuity, and developing our understanding of the evolution of Australian legal systems—it is submitted that the overall conclusions to be drawn from the analysis of Kelsen's model are these. First, if understood as this chapter and chapter three argue it should be understood, Kelsen's account of continuity and discontinuity is more subtle than has often been supposed; and while it is by no means perfect, it is capable, with some notable exceptions at the level of theoretical justification, of providing a satisfactory explanation of the evolution of legal systems in Australia that accords with both contemporary and subsequent understandings. Second, systematic application to the case of Australia and the particular phenomena it presents generated a significant range of insights into the operation of the model and the adequacy of its factual fit with Australian law over the period. This analysis did more than illustrate some of the problems identified at the theoretical level: it countered some of those problems or put them in proper perspective; it revealed further problems and, in context, suggested possible solutions; and it exposed hidden strengths, as well as hidden weaknesses or omissions in the account. Finally, the process of applying Kelsen's account directed attention to a range of specific legal materials and theoretical understandings that give substance to intuitive understandings of the evolution of legal systems in Australia. While application of the model did not ultimately demand fundamental reconsideration of those intuitions, the scrutiny to which it subjected episodes such as the early Governors' general orders and the achievement of Federation usefully enhanced reflection on these developments.

5

Raz: Continuity of Social Form

THIS CHAPTER OFFERS a critical reconstruction and amplification of Raz's account of continuity and discontinuity as synthesised from his account of legal systems, principally developed in *The Concept of a Legal System: An Introduction to the Theory of Legal System* and *Practical Reason and Norms*. The chapter first explains, in sections I and II, the governing taxonomy of laws and relations between laws, and the characteristic features of institutionalised normative systems that constitute the central elements in Raz's model of legal systems. Section III develops an understanding of the device of authoritative recognition, which holds together the model's account of momentary legal systems. Section IV turns to the model's account of continuity and discontinuity, exposing the framework that Raz sketches and developing the conceptual tools that that framework implies, in anticipation of the application of the account in chapter six. Whereas there is an extensive literature examining Kelsen's account of continuity and discontinuity, relatively little academic analysis has been undertaken in relation to Raz's account. Accordingly, the reconstruction and amplification that this chapter offers (consistently with other parts of Raz's work and with appropriate reference to associated scholarship) is itself a key contribution of this book, both in terms of advancing understanding of the account for its own sake and of facilitating its application in chapter six.

Raz's account is designed to explain three uncontroversial features of law:[1]

> The three most general and important features of the law are that it is normative, institutionalized, and coercive. It is normative in that it serves, and is meant to serve, as a guide for human behaviour. It is institutionalized in that its application and modification are to a large extent performed or regulated by institutions. And it is coercive in that obedience to it, and its application, are internally guaranteed, ultimately, by the use of force.

The model explains that law's normativity and institutionalised character are logical features, but that its coercive character is a factual, not a logical, necessity, given certain assumptions about human nature.[2]

[1] J Raz, *The Concept of a Legal System: An Introduction to the Theory of Legal System*, 2nd edn (Oxford, Clarendon Press, 1980) 3.

[2] J Raz, *Practical Reason and Norms*, 2nd edn (Oxford, OUP, 1990) 158–59.

Raz's model of legal systems is constructed on the basis of three key insights. First, legal systems are always aspects of political systems: complex forms of social life, such as states, churches or tribes.[3] Second, legal systems are institutionalised normative systems: systems that are established by norms and that have as their function the creation and application of norms.[4] Third, legal systems comprise 'intricate webs of interconnected laws'.[5] This insight captures Raz's contentions, first, that legal systems include both laws that are norms (legal norms) and laws that are not norms, and, second, that all laws that are not norms are connected to legal norms by relations between laws (internal relations). The second and third insights are the basis for the elaboration of the larger part of the model's structure and are addressed below. The first insight, which Raz himself suggests may be insufficiently emphasised in the account,[6] is, in relation to the criteria for the existence and continuity of legal systems, ultimately accorded primacy over the autonomous, internal features that Raz derives from the other two insights. Nevertheless, Raz warns against overemphasising social considerations:[7]

> It is too easy to underestimate the importance of those autonomous considerations which do contribute to a doctrine of identity. They are part of the essence of law, part of those qualities which are present in all legal systems and in virtue of which they are legal systems. They are also among the features which explain the special role the law has in the political system.

Success in this goal of accommodating both intra- and extra-systemic considerations is of particular interest in evaluating the model's account of continuity. That account incorporates consideration of changes both to laws and to non-legal norms. Accordingly, it is necessary and convenient to set out the principal features of Raz's account of the autonomous features of legal systems before turning to his account of continuity.

I. TAXONOMY OF LAWS AND INTERNAL RELATIONS

This section sets out the taxonomy of laws and internal relations in Raz's model, which informs the model's account of the identity of both

[3] Raz, *Concept of a Legal System* (n 1), 188, 211; J Raz, 'The Identity of Legal Systems' (1971) in *The Authority of Law*, 2nd edn (Oxford, OUP, 2009) 78, 100. On the social functions of law, see J Raz, 'The Functions of Law' (1973) in *The Authority of Law*, 2nd edn (Oxford, OUP, 2009).

[4] Raz, *Practical Reason and Norms* (n 2), 123.

[5] Raz, *Concept of a Legal System* (n 1), 183.

[6] ibid, 211.

[7] ibid, 212. (Omitted footnote reads: 'The necessary content of law, i.e. its being open, comprehensive, and supreme, is of course also crucial to the understanding of its role in the political system.')

momentary legal systems[8] (the membership question) and diachronic legal systems (the continuity question). It also outlines Raz's structural explanation of rights, which, to some degree, cuts across the model's essential reduction of legal systems to configurations of laws and internal relations, by reference to considerations of interest or value. Those considerations, too, are implicated in the model's account of continuity.

A. Laws

Raz's model classifies laws into four types: duty-imposing laws, power-conferring laws, permission-granting laws and laws that are not norms.[9] This classification is based on normative function.[10] The theory of norms underlying the model draws on Raz's concept of reasons for action, and treats norms as exclusionary reasons or permissions, or as logically related to exclusionary reasons or permissions.[11] Duty-imposing, power-conferring and permission-granting laws correspond to three types of norms—mandatory norms, power-conferring norms and permissions—while laws in the fourth category, laws that are not norms, have no direct normative (reason-guiding) function at all.

i. Duty-imposing Laws

Duty-imposing laws are mandatory norms.[12] That is, they comprise exclusionary reasons—reasons to refrain from acting on certain other

[8] 'A momentary legal system contains all the laws of a system valid at a certain moment': ibid, 34.

[9] This reconstruction of Raz's model omits another named type of laws: sanction-stipulating laws. Sanction-stipulating laws were included in an early exposition of Raz's model, where the normativity of law turned on critical reactions, principally in the form of sanctions: ibid, 152–56, 185–86. Raz's later development of the concept of a legal system holds that sanctions are factually necessary, given certain features of human nature, but are not logically necessary components of legal systems: Raz, *Practical Reason and Norms* (n 2), 158–59. The abandonment of the sanction-based explanation is noted in Raz, *Concept of a Legal System* (n 1), 224, fn 19; see also Raz, *Practical Reason and Norms* (n 2), 134, 154–62, 210, fn 7. In any event, it is not clear that sanction-stipulating laws, which have no place in a taxonomy based on normative function, were ever intended to be understood as a separate category. They were of two kinds: the first a subspecies of duty-imposing law that makes the application of a sanction a duty, and the second a subspecies of permission-granting law that permits the application of a sanction without making it a duty: Raz, *Concept of a Legal System* (n 1), 155, 174.

[10] Raz ultimately preferred the terms 'normative type' and 'logical type': Raz, 'The Functions of Law' (n 3), 165. The term 'normative function', retained here, is taken from a section in the original essay omitted in the republished version: see J Raz, 'On the Functions of Law' in AWB Simpson (ed), *Oxford Essays in Jurisprudence (Second Series)* (Oxford, Clarendon Press, 1973) 278, 280–87.

[11] Raz, *Practical Reason and Norms* (n 2), 142.

[12] Raz, *Concept of a Legal System* (n 1), 147.

reasons—accompanied by reasons to perform the norm-acts.[13] Accordingly, every law that requires the performance or omission of an action is both a reason for the performance or omission of that action and also an exclusionary reason for not acting on conflicting reasons that are not themselves legally recognised reasons.[14] Raz contends that duty-imposing laws necessarily exist in every legal system.[15]

ii. Power-conferring Laws

Power-conferring laws are power-conferring norms.[16] That is, they regulate behaviour 'by stipulating certain consequences of certain acts, which sometimes make it advantageous to perform these acts and sometimes make it advantageous not to perform them'.[17] Raz's argument that laws regulating behaviour in this way are norms draws on his concept of normative power,[18] an ability to affect exclusionary reasons or exclusionary permissions:[19]

> An act is the exercise of a normative power if, and only if, it is recognized as effecting a normative change [the creation, repeal or change in application of a norm] because, among other possible justifications, it is an act of a type such that it is reasonable to expect that, if recognized as effecting a normative change, acts of this type will be generally performed only if the persons concerned want to secure this normative change.

Acts that are the exercise of normative power are thus guided by a norm: agents will perform those acts if they wish to affect a norm in the way facilitated by the power, and will not perform them if they do not. Power-conferring norms thus qualify mandatory or permissive norms, such that an explanation of those mandatory or permissive norms necessitates reference to the related power-conferring norms.[20] A power to dispose of wastelands by Crown grant, for example, guides the behaviour of the relevant minister, who adopts the procedure of Crown grant in order to transfer land ownership. The transferee's rights in respect of the land cannot be fully understood without reference to the transfer by the minister in exercising that power. Power-conferring laws necessarily exist in Raz's model since there must, at the very least, exist laws conferring power on primary norm-applying organs to make binding applicative determinations.[21]

[13] Raz, *Practical Reason and Norms* (n 2), 39, 58–59.
[14] ibid, 144.
[15] Raz, *Concept of a Legal System* (n 1), 155.
[16] ibid, 157.
[17] ibid, 162.
[18] Raz, *Practical Reason and Norms* (n 2), 101–102. See also Raz, *Concept of a Legal System* (n 1), 156–62.
[19] Raz, *Practical Reason and Norms* (n 2), 103.
[20] ibid, 112.
[21] Below, 172–73.

Raz describes two types of power-conferring laws, both of which he asserts exist in every legal system (though he does not specifically defend that claim).[22] Regulative power-conferring laws confer 'regulative' power in relation to duty-imposing laws:[23] they affect the application of duty-imposing laws by, for example, conferring power to transfer property, to marry people or to declare a state of emergency.[24] While regulative power-conferring laws confer power to affect the application of existing norms, legislative power-conferring laws confer power to create new norms.[25] Although not expressly stated, it follows from Raz's definition of normative power as including power to affect the *application* of norms as well as their creation and repeal that legislative power-conferring laws can confer power to make laws that are not norms. Raz contends that a law providing 'All the legal norms of the system apply only to acts performed in a certain territory' is not a norm.[26] It is a law because (according to Raz's model) any acceptable set of principles of individuation will result in the proposition's being stated separately and not being incorporated into the expression of every norm of the system. It does not guide behaviour because that function is performed by the duty-imposing laws (and associated power-conferring and permission-granting laws) that require the application of the norms of the system, though it determines or qualifies the scope of the guidance they provide. In affecting the application of norms, and being made with the intention of so affecting them, such a law qualifies as an exercise of normative power, which may be conferred by power-conferring laws.

iii. Permission-granting Laws

Permission-granting laws are norms that grant 'exclusionary permissions'.[27] An exclusionary permission is a type of 'strong' permission: permission granted by a permission-granting norm, as distinct from a 'weak' permission, entailed by the absence of norms prohibiting an action.[28]

[22] Raz, *Concept of a Legal System* (n 1), 164. It has been suggested that Raz's model takes them as necessary to account for laws applying to officials, not backed by sanctions: P Pickert, 'The Concept of a Legal System (Book review)' (1975) 20 *American Journal of Jurisprudence* 154, 160. The force of this explanation is diminished once a sanction-based account of the normativity of law is excluded from Raz's model: see above, n 9.

[23] Raz, *Concept of a Legal System* (n 1), 162.

[24] ibid, 163.

[25] ibid.

[26] ibid, 145.

[27] This explanation of permission-granting laws as norms follows Raz, *Practical Reason and Norms* (n 2), 85–97, in preference to the earlier explanation, according to which permission-granting laws were not norms: Raz, *Concept of a Legal System* (n 1), 170–75.

[28] Raz, *Practical Reason and Norms* (n 2), 86. Raz adopts this analysis of permissions as norms in preference to an earlier analysis based on sanctions: see Raz, *Concept of a Legal System* (n 1), 224, fn 19.

According to Raz, strong permissions may be based on exclusionary reasons, but, since exclusionary reasons are generally accompanied by first-order reasons for action, the action will most often be required, not merely permitted.[29] More importantly, then, strong permissions may be based on exclusionary permissions. Exclusionary permissions entitle but do not require an agent to perform an action, notwithstanding reasons for not performing it: performing the permitted action will not be against reason, but nor will failing to perform it.[30] They are permissions to perform the norm-act and second-order permissions not to act on reasons for not performing the norm-act that are not themselves legally recognised reasons.[31] Accordingly, permission-granting laws do not alter the reasons that prohibit an action but entitle the agent not to act in accordance with those reasons.[32] Raz suggests but does not claim that permission-granting laws exist in every legal system.[33] Permission-granting laws cease to exist when every duty-imposing law they modify ceases to exist.[34]

iv. Laws that Are not Norms

An important consequence of the individuation of laws in Raz's model—as foreshadowed above in relation to power-conferring laws—is that not all laws are norms.[35] Some laws do not directly perform any normative function at all; their sole relevance is in their relations to laws that are norms. According to Raz, laws concerning status and juristic persons and laws determining the necessary conditions for the application of legal norms do not guide behaviour and are not norms, though they affect the interpretation and application of legal norms.[36] Raz does not purport to identify all laws that are not norms, or to identify any categories within the classification of laws that are not norms.[37] Nonetheless, it is clear that, in Raz's model, all legal systems contain laws that are not norms. Raz asserts (albeit without proving) that all legal systems institute some rights and that some of the laws instituting rights are not norms.[38] All legal systems also contain laws that are not norms as a result of being institutionalised normative systems. Many of the laws establishing primary norm-applying organs will not be norms: laws establishing what constitutes a determination of the organ may be an example.

29 Raz, *Practical Reason and Norms* (n 2), 89–90.
30 ibid, 90.
31 ibid, 144.
32 ibid, 96–97.
33 Raz, *Concept of a Legal System* (n 1), 174–75.
34 ibid, 175.
35 ibid, 168.
36 ibid, 145, 183.
37 ibid, 168.
38 ibid, 183.

B. Internal Relations

Raz notes that the variety of internal relations between laws in a given system depends on how those laws are individuated and the 'richness, complexity, and variety of the content of the legal system'.[39] Nevertheless, certain necessary kinds of relations follow from the types of laws Raz contends exist in every legal system. Although not expressly so explained by Raz, the basis for this classification of relations is their 'normative connection' (just as the basis for the classification of laws was their normative function). Raz describes 'genetic' and 'regulative' relations. To these must be added two further relations, one necessary and one contingent, implied but not named in Raz's model: they are here termed 'applicative' and 'permissive' relations.[40]

i. Genetic Relations

Genetic relations express the normative connection between power-conferring laws and laws created by the exercise of the power conferred. The necessary existence of legislative power-conferring laws entails the presence of genetic relations in all legal systems. Relations between legislative power-conferring laws and laws created in the exercise of powers conferred by them are genetic relations.[41]

ii. Regulative Relations

Regulative relations express the normative connection between power-conferring laws and laws the application of which is affected by the exercise of the power conferred. This connection reflects the fact that the regulated norm would be incompletely expressed without reference to the power-conferring norm. The necessary existence of regulative power-conferring

[39] ibid, 140.

[40] This reconstruction omits a fifth, 'punitive' relation that Raz describes, between duty-imposing laws and sanction-stipulating laws stipulating sanctions for their breach: ibid, 156. The identification of punitive relations arises from the sanction-based explanation of law's normativity, and may be omitted in consequence of its abandonment: see above, n 9. In any event, since sanction-stipulating laws are either duty-imposing laws or permission-granting laws, there is no special normative connection attaching to them: the relation between a sanction-stipulating law and the duty-imposing law for the breach of which it stipulates a sanction is factual, not normative, in nature. Also in connection with punitive relations, Raz refers to 'operative relations' as existing between sanction-stipulating laws and all laws other than legislative power-conferring laws: ibid, 186. This term does not denote a distinct relation but refers generically to the relations used in depicting an operative structure of legal systems. Operative relations are regulative, applicative, permissive or punitive relations. Since sanctions are not logically required, it is not logically necessary that all laws other than legislative power-conferring laws be linked to sanction-stipulating laws by operative relations.

[41] ibid, 164.

laws entails the presence of regulative relations in all legal systems.[42] Relations between duty-imposing laws and regulative power-conferring laws conferring power to regulate, for example, when, how and by whom a duty must be performed, are regulative relations.[43]

iii. Permissive Relations

Raz deals briefly with an unnamed relation when he observes that every permission-granting law has a necessary internal relation to one or more duty-imposing laws, since every permission-granting law, by definition, modifies the application of at least one duty-imposing law.[44] As explained above, permission-granting laws do not alter the internal scope of application of the duty-imposing laws they modify, and so are not simply more complete statements of those duty-imposing laws.[45] Nor, though they grant permissions, do permission-granting laws confer normative power as Raz describes it.[46] The relation is not, therefore, a regulative relation. Nor is the relation an applicative relation (below), because it modifies the application of duty-imposing laws in a distinct fashion. In the case of applicative relations, a law's application, in the sense of its sphere of operation, is determined or controlled in some way: it is an internal question of the scope of the norm. Where there is a permission-granting law, a law's application, in the sense of whether the law need be complied with at all, is rendered optional: this is the normative connection special to this relation, which may be termed a 'permissive relation'.[47] Further, the relation between permission-granting laws and the duty-imposing laws whose application they modify is a relation between norms, whereas applicative relations exist between norms and laws that are not norms. Since Raz postulates but does not assert the necessary existence of permission-granting laws in all legal systems, permissive relations are also contingent rather than necessary.

iv. Applicative Relations

Since Raz's model holds that every legal system contains laws that are not norms, there must exist relations between those laws and the duty-imposing,

[42] ibid, 162.

[43] ibid, 164. Though Raz does not say so expressly, regulative power-conferring laws can regulate other power-conferring laws; the relations between those regulative power-conferring and power-conferring laws are also regulative relations.

[44] ibid, 172.

[45] Above, section I.A.iii.

[46] See above, text to n 19.

[47] This distinction corresponds to that drawn between internal and external applicability in PE Navarro and JJ Moreso, 'Applicability and Effectiveness of Legal Norms' (1997) 16 *Law and Philosophy* 201.

power-conferring or permission-granting laws they affect. 'Applicative relations' express this normative connection, which reflects the fact that laws that are not norms affect laws that are. The closest Raz comes to recognising applicative relations is in noting that it is their relations with power-conferring and duty-imposing laws that make laws instituting status and juristic persons (which are laws that are not norms) part of legal systems.[48] Some of those relations with power-conferring and duty-imposing laws are regulative relations.[49] They relate laws that are norms to *laws conferring power to determine* the application of those laws (whether or not the power is exercised). However, other relations may be discerned that broadly resemble regulative relations but, instead, relate laws that are norms to *laws that are not norms but nevertheless actually determine* their application. The absence of normative power marks the distinction. Adapting one of Raz's examples, there is a regulative relation between a law conferring power to store uranium and a law taxing those who store uranium, but a different relation between a law defining an area as 'industrial' and a law taxing storage of uranium in industrial areas.[50] It is suggested that relations between status-defining laws and laws (norms) the interpretation or application of which they (partly) determine comprise, in practice, a significant category of relations.

Not every law that is not a norm stands in an applicative relation to another law. It is possible for a law that is not a norm to be entirely isolated: a law might provide that the colour 'z-blue' is defined in a certain way, without any other law relating to the colour z-blue. Such laws are nevertheless part of the legal system, because they stand in genetic relations to the legislative power-conferring laws that confer power to create them.

C. Rights and Other Legal Phenomena

Raz's model reduces legal phenomena to configurations of laws and internal relations. However, the model acknowledges that some phenomena are not completely described when so reduced. Rights are one such phenomenon. Although he does not demonstrate the point by argument, Raz contends that all legal systems institute some rights.[51]

In outline, Raz conceives of rights as relations between right-holders and right-objects, such as persons, physical objects and abstract legal entities.[52] Rights are instituted and defined by laws that are investitive,

[48] Raz, *Concept of a Legal System* (n 1), 183. In relation to equivalent rules of games, see Raz, *Practical Reason and Norms* (n 2), 117.

[49] Raz, *Concept of a Legal System* (n 1), 183.

[50] Adapted from an example explaining normative power: Raz, *Practical Reason and Norms* (n 2), 102.

[51] Raz, *Concept of a Legal System* (n 1), 183.

[52] ibid, 176.

divestitive and constitutive.[53] Investitive laws specify how rights are acquired, divestitive laws how they are disposed of and constitutive laws the consequences of being a right-holder (such as being the subject of a duty). Laws instituting rights are of the ordinary kinds: duty-imposing, power-conferring and permission-granting laws and laws that are not norms.[54]

Raz observes, however, that rights have another 'dimension':[55] three generalising functions of rights are not captured in an analysis of investitive, divestitive and constitutive laws and their relations to other laws. First, right-concepts are a means of relating regulative power-conferring laws to the power-conferring laws and duty-imposing laws they regulate.[56] Merely identifying the regulative relation does not sufficiently explain the conceptual connections between the regulative power-conferring, power-conferring and duty-imposing laws in question and the other laws that together institute the relevant right. Second, rights provide a way of abstracting conditions common to duty-imposing and power-conferring laws establishing rights, and of identifying those conditions in laws that are not norms but that are internally related to these duty-imposing and power-conferring laws.[57] This is a descriptive feature, which has a normative counterpart in a third function: rights 'form a potential source of new laws, an authorization to the courts to generate new rules for their protection'.[58]

Although not advanced in these terms by Raz, rights and other more complex legal phenomena are explicable in terms of the nature of legal systems in the model. Raz fundamentally conceives of legal systems as institutionalised normative systems, and of norms as reasons for action. Some reasons for action are values,[59] and all normative theory draws on a theory of value.[60] In Raz's conception, a person has a right if (amongst other things) an aspect of the person's well-being (his interest) is a sufficient reason for holding another person to be under a duty.[61] The notion of well-being or interest in this account of rights also draws on a theory of value. Accordingly, analysis of rights can be understood as organising law in a way that refers to values. Commonality may exist between laws

[53] ibid, 176–77.
[54] ibid, 182.
[55] ibid, 226.
[56] ibid, 181.
[57] ibid.
[58] ibid, 226.
[59] Raz, *Practical Reason and Norms* (n 2), 25, 34.
[60] ibid, 11.
[61] J Raz, 'The Nature of Rights' in *The Morality of Freedom* (Oxford, OUP, 1988) 165, 166. Raz expressly applies this account of rights generally to legal rights: see J Raz, 'Legal Rights' in *Ethics in the Public Domain: Essays in the Morality of Law and Politics*, rev edn (Oxford, Clarendon Press, 1995) 254.

because of the interests whose values they presuppose and promote, whether or not there are recognised relations between the laws themselves. Similarly, values may be realised and protected in particular ways, which may entail relations between aspects of laws independently of the internal relations (if any) between them. It may be that other aspects of practical reasoning—rationality or analogical reasoning—are features of institutionalised normative systems that explain complicated legal phenomena, the dimensions of which are not completely described in terms of laws and relations between laws. However, explaining these phenomena, including rights, is beyond the scope of Raz's model and, accordingly, of this book.

II. INSTITUTIONALISED NORMATIVE SYSTEMS

The presence of norm-creating and norm-applying institutions is the defining feature of institutionalised normative systems, and is essential to their criteria for existence, systemic validity and membership. With respect to existence, the primary criterion is efficacy: general[62] conformity to the norms of the system by norm-subjects, and endorsement and enforcement of the norms by norm-applying institutions.[63] In Raz's model, general—and even universal—conformity by *non-officials* is insufficient.[64] In contrast, it suffices that primary norm-applying organs (explained below) regularly enforce legal norms in appropriate cases.[65] Similarly, the presence of these institutions is related to the systemic validity of institutionalised normative systems, since systemic validity turns on these systems' being practised.[66] Norm-creating and norm-applying institutions are central in terms of membership, because all norms of institutional normative systems have internal relations with norms establishing those institutions,[67] thus permitting the identification of a set of related norms.

Raz identifies a subclass of norm-applying institutions necessarily present in institutionalised normative systems.[68] 'Primary norm-applying organs' are a defining feature of these systems because they provide an institutionalised and authoritative means of settling disputes.[69] These

[62] Observance by all norm-subjects is not necessary; the standard of conformity required is not high: Raz, *Practical Reason and Norms* (n 2), 125. Moreover, the observance of all norms is not required: all norms are relevant but not equally relevant: Raz, *Concept of a Legal System* (n 1), 206.

[63] Raz, *Practical Reason and Norms* (n 2), 126.

[64] ibid, 125.

[65] ibid, 131.

[66] ibid, 128.

[67] ibid, 126–27.

[68] ibid, 133–34.

[69] ibid, 137.

organs are institutions that have 'power to determine the normative situation of specified individuals, which are required to exercise these powers by applying existing norms, but whose decisions are binding even when wrong'.[70] Their decisions—'binding applicative determinations'[71]—are binding, because they have normative force,[72] and applicative, because they consist in the application of existing[73] norms to determine rights and duties in concrete situations.[74] Primary norm-applying institutions fulfil the system-unifying function indicated at the end of the last paragraph. Raz reasons as follows: norms guide the behaviour of norm subjects; the determinations of primary norm-applying organs, applying existing norms that those organs are bound to apply, must coincide with the guidance given to the norm subjects; therefore, 'if the system's guidance and evaluation are to coincide it must be regarded as containing only those norms which its primary organs are bound to apply'.[75]

In virtue of being *institutionalised* normative systems, legal systems in Raz's model necessarily exhibit four structural features: '(1) … they contain norms establishing primary institutions, (2) … a law belongs to them only if the primary institutions are under a duty to apply it … (3) … they have limits'[76]—that is, there are norms that are part of the system and others that are not—and (4) '[s]ince primary institutions are norm-applying there must be norms for them to apply'.[77] Further, in virtue of legal systems' being institutionalised *normative* systems, Raz's model holds, first, that in any given momentary legal system, every act that is not specifically prohibited is permitted[78] and, second, an act can only create or affect the application of laws pursuant to a power-conferring law.[79] These consequences follow from legal norms' characteristic methods of guiding behaviour: by prescription or permission,[80] on the one hand, and by conferring powers, on the other.

[70] ibid, 136. The model contemplates refinement of this description to take account of appeals, retrials, etc, and the exercise by primary norm-applying organs of functions other than that of making binding applicative determinations: ibid. That the determinations are ultimately binding even if wrong reflects a 'special feature' of primary norm-applying organs' applicative determinations: they exclude conflicting reasons both from outside, and also from within, the system: ibid, 145.

[71] ibid, 136.

[72] A determination has normative force as long as any change to the normative situation it effected would have been binding: ibid, 135.

[73] ibid, 139.

[74] ibid, 136–37.

[75] ibid, 142.

[76] J Raz, 'The Institutional Nature of Law' (1975) in *The Authority of Law*, 2nd edn (Oxford, OUP, 2009) 103, 115.

[77] Raz, *Practical Reason and Norms* (n 2), 138.

[78] Raz, *Concept of a Legal System* (n 1), 170.

[79] ibid, 171.

[80] If the law does neither, the behaviour is unguided and thus permitted in the weak sense: ibid.

Raz identifies three features distinguishing legal systems from other institutionalised normative systems: comprehensiveness, supremacy and openness. Importantly, legal systems may possess each of these features to varying degrees.[81] Comprehensiveness denotes legal systems' claim to the authority to regulate any type of behaviour (including by permission).[82] Supremacy is an elaboration of one aspect of comprehensiveness and denotes legal systems' claim to authority to regulate *other* institutionalised normative systems within their subject-communities (including, again, by permission).[83] It follows from the supremacy claim that legal systems are necessarily incompatible to the extent that they make competing supremacy claims with respect to the same subject-community.[84] Openness refers to legal systems' characteristic maintenance and support of other forms of social grouping, including by giving binding force within the legal system to norms from outside.[85] For example, legal systems may give binding force to the norms of private associations, or, in the context of conflict of laws, to the laws of another legal system. Although legal systems may achieve openness by requiring courts to recognise and enforce norms of other systems, Raz considers that these 'adopted norms' are not part of those (adopting) legal systems themselves.[86]

III. RECOGNITION

As noted above,[87] primary norm-applying organs play a central role in identifying the laws that are part of the system: in Raz's model, membership is based on 'authoritative recognition' by primary norm-applying organs.[88] A law is part of the legal system if the system's primary norm-applying organs are bound to recognise and apply that law in accordance with their own custom and practice,[89] with the qualification that norms adopted from other normative systems and given effect to by the legal

[81] Raz, *Practical Reason and Norms* (n 2), 150.
[82] ibid, 150–51.
[83] ibid, 151.
[84] ibid, 152.
[85] ibid, 152–53.
[86] ibid, 153. See further J Raz, 'Incorporation by Law' (2003) in *Between Authority and Interpretation: On the Theory of Law and Practical Reason* (Oxford, OUP, 2009) 182, 193–94. The ordinary criterion for membership of institutionalised normative systems is not sensitive to this difference: adopted norms, as well as autochthonous norms, would qualify as norms that primary norm-applying organs are bound to apply. Accordingly, the model's criterion is refined to exclude norms that belong to another normative system, or that are voluntarily created by norm-subjects pursuant to powers conferred by the system to enable them to organise their own affairs: Raz, *Practical Reason and Norms* (n 2), 153.
[87] Above, text to n 67.
[88] Raz, *Concept of a Legal System* (n 1), 190.
[89] ibid, 193, 211.

system, but not incorporated into it, are excluded.[90] The laws that primary norm-applying organs are bound to apply include the norms addressed to them (rules of recognition and other ultimate rules constituted by the practice of those organs) and the laws addressed to ordinary individuals that the norms addressed to the primary organs require those organs to apply.[91] Rules of recognition are norms requiring primary norm-applying organs to apply certain norms.[92] They are necessary for the existence of primary norm-applying organs and must exist in all legal systems. Raz contends that there can be more than one rule of recognition.[93] The additional ultimate rules practised by primary norm-applying organs—apart from rules of recognition—include, for example, laws guiding their discretion in deciding unregulated disputes.[94] Unlike rules of recognition, these are not necessarily entailed by the existence of primary norm-applying organs and need not exist in every legal system. Raz's model draws heavily on Hart's notion of a rule of recognition but, in basing the unity of a legal system on the principle of authoritative recognition by primary norm-applying organs rather than on a single rule of recognition, and by pointing to several kinds of ultimate rules, the model overcomes two difficulties: that of assuming a single rule of recognition, and that of accounting for the power of courts to resolve disputes where there is no existing rule they are duty-bound to apply.[95]

A. Recognising Relations Between Laws

Although Raz describes recognition of laws and not of relations between laws, his model should be understood as requiring that primary norm-applying organs recognise relations as well. This is because recognition

[90] Above, n 86. Recognition thus entails discriminating between laws of the system and external norms given effect to by the system, in order to preserve the 'distinction between standards that the courts have to apply and those that are the law of the land [which] is vital to our ability to identify the law as the political institution it is': Raz, 'Incorporation by Law' (n 86), 199.

[91] Raz, *Practical Reason and Norms* (n 2), 148.

[92] ibid, 147.

[93] ibid.

[94] Raz, 'The Identity of Legal Systems' (n 3), 96.

[95] Raz, *Concept of a Legal System* (n 1), 200; G MacCormack, '"Law" and "Legal System"' (1979) 42 *MLR* 285, 290. See also JM Finnis, 'Revolutions and Continuity of Law' (1971) in *Philosophy of Law—Collected Essays: Volume IV* (Oxford, OUP, 2011) 407, 427–28, discussing the difficulties in regarding as a unit a Hartian rule of recognition that consists of a set of duty-imposing, power-conferring and law-identifying rules, both at a given point in time and, since the set is subject to amendment, over time. Hart says only that the set is unified by the hierarchical arrangement of the criteria of recognition: HLA Hart, *The Concept of Law*, 2nd edn (Oxford, OUP, 1994) 105–06; HLA Hart, 'The Morality of Law (Book Review)' (1965) 78 *Harvard Law Review* 1281, 1293.

takes the form of binding applicative determinations, the fundamental concern of which is the application of *norms*. Laws that are not norms are also recognised and applied, but incidentally to the application of laws that are norms. A law that is not a norm cannot, in itself, be applied to resolve a dispute. It is the relations between laws that are norms and laws that are not norms that make the application of laws that are not norms possible. Accordingly, for the test of recognition to function as the criterion of identity, legal systems must consist of, and only of:

(a) the legal norms recognised by the primary norm-applying organs; and
(b) the relations recognised by the primary norm-applying organs between legal norms, and between legal norms and laws that are not norms; and
(c) the laws that are not norms but have recognised relations to legal norms.

Without recognition of relations, there is no principled way to move from the recognition of norms to the recognition of laws that are not norms. Accordingly, rules of recognition must bind primary norm-applying organs to apply laws, in some instances, by reference to the relations between them and other (recognised) laws. This explication of Raz's notion of recognition is consistent with his contention that recognition of a legislative power-conferring law entails recognition of the laws created in exercise of the power it confers,[96] which might include laws that are not norms.[97]

B. What Recognition Entails

Raz explains that recognition is a counterfactual idea: 'Saying of a primary organ that it recognizes a law means that, had the question been raised before it, in the proper exercise of its powers it would have acted on that law'.[98] In emphasising the significance of what primary norm-applying organs do in making their binding applicative determinations, Raz's model requires a prediction grounded in the (norm-guided) practice of those institutions—a practice necessarily belonging to the diachronic legal system.[99] While this counterfactual test produces a 'hazy border line to the set of laws' comprising the system, it has nonetheless been thought to reflect reality in so doing.[100]

[96] Raz, *Concept of a Legal System* (n 1), 196.
[97] Above, 166.
[98] Raz, *Concept of a Legal System* (n 1), 196.
[99] ibid.
[100] Pickert (n 22), 156.

Recognition should be understood as a practice that does not involve the exercise of normative power (something capable of effecting normative change).[101] The difference is illustrated by contrasting the activities of recognition, on the one hand, and of making binding applicative determinations, on the other. Making a binding applicative determination involves effecting a normative change: determining the normative situation of particular individuals.[102] If recognition entailed normative power in this way, it would amount to declaring what the law *is*—it would be legislative power. The role of recognition as an activity of primary norm-applying organs is not legislative: it involves identifying what *existing* laws apply, not making laws to apply to the situation. Recognition is an intellectual process—like writing or speaking—in which those organs engage in the course of making binding applicative determinations. Of course, primary norm-applying organs may also exercise legislative power, but they must recognise the laws they create before applying them.[103]

Understanding recognition as a practice that is not normative is significant because it explains an important contention Raz makes in relation to systems that have several norm-applying organs:[104]

> Of equal importance is the fact that one primary organ's recognition of the norms creating another primary organ (or a court) gives considerable support to the supposition that the first organ will recognize all the laws recognized by the second, *though it does not entail it.*

Assuming (contrary to the reconstruction of Raz's model presented here) that recognition entails the exercise of normative power, there would be a genetic relation between the law conferring power to recognise and any law recognised by an organ, in the same way as there is a genetic relation between a law conferring power to legislate and any legislation enacted. Since recognition of laws by any primary norm-applying organ would therefore entail genetic relations between the law establishing that organ and the laws it recognised, recognition by a second primary norm-applying organ of the power-conferring law conferring power on the first organ would entail recognition by the second of all the laws recognised by the first as well (within that organ's scope of authority): this is the consequence of the genetic relations.

As the quotation above reveals, Raz's model does not work in this way: recognition is not normative. The normative power exercised by primary norm-applying organs is the power to make binding applicative determinations. One norm-applying organ may recognise a norm conferring

101 Above, text to n 19.

102 Raz, *Practical Reason and Norms* (n 2), 136.

103 Raz, *Concept of a Legal System* (n 1), 195.

104 ibid, 196 (emphasis added).

power on another organ, or a norm constituted by a determination of that second organ, but in neither case does this entail recognition of the norms recognised by the second organ in making the determination.

The more fundamental problem with understanding recognition as effecting normative change is that adverted to above: it would entail that the norms recognised stood in a genetic relation to the power-conferring law establishing the organ; the organs would be law-creating, not law-applying, institutions.

Without exploring the point in detail, Raz contemplates legal systems that have multiple primary norm-applying organs, which recognise several sets of laws.[105] Clearly, if one organ is bound to apply laws recognised by another, there is a regulative relation between the power-conferring laws conferring power on each of the organs, and they are part of the same system. Absent an obvious hierarchical relationship of this kind, recognition by one organ of the laws establishing another may, as just noted, be an important factor in determining whether the norms they recognise are part of the same legal system, though it is not conclusive.[106] Raz notes the potential for conflict where recognition of the laws establishing two or more primary norm-applying organs, and recognition of the laws recognised by them, is not mutual.[107] This may not be problematic in practice, as it may simply entail one organ's deference to another, but it signals a need to refer to other considerations in determining whether the unrecognised organ is part of the same system. A second factor is the degree to which the several organs' practices in recognising laws converge: the model holds that courts belong to the same system if they practise the same rules of recognition.[108] A final factor invites recourse to non-autonomous considerations reflecting the social dimension of legal systems: Raz suggests that 'it may make good sense to resort here again to the character of the political system of which that legal system is a part and to distinguish between those courts which are organs of that political system and those which are not'.[109]

IV. CONTINUITY

In Raz's account, the temporal continuity of legal systems—their identity over time—'depends on the identity of the social forms to which they belong'.[110] This relationship of dependency means that the continuity of

[105] ibid, 192.
[106] ibid, 196.
[107] ibid, 197.
[108] ibid, 211.
[109] ibid.
[110] ibid, 189.

the legal system is 'tied' to the continuity of a political system, itself a subset of a more comprehensive social system:[111] there will be discontinuity in a legal system when there is discontinuity in the social form of which it is part, and—it seems—there will be continuity in the legal system so long as there is continuity in that social form. Whereas, for the Kelsenian legal scientist, a social form is wholly constituted by (and is the personification of) a legal system,[112] for Raz, the legal system is (or may be) only *partly* constitutive of the political system, which may include many non-legal norms.[113] Continuity of the legal system may thus be affected by changes to non-legal norms of the political system, as well as by changes to legal norms.[114] Continuity is determined 'not only by jurisprudential or legal considerations but by other considerations as well, considerations belonging to other social sciences'.[115]

Since he does not 'trespass' on the field of those other social sciences,[116] Raz does not purport to offer a fully developed account of continuity but his model holds, 'first, that continuity depends on the interaction of legal and non-legal norms, and the extent and manner of their change; and secondly, that among the legal norms concerned some are more relevant than others'.[117] The first observation restates the central feature of the account—that continuity of the legal system depends on the continuity of the political system—and highlights three relevant factors: first, the extent and manner of change in legal norms; second, the extent and manner of change in non-legal norms; and, third, the interaction of legal and non-legal norms. The second observation adds an important refinement in considering the first of those factors.

This is the extent of the model's express account of continuity, an account that has, after the model's careful exposition of laws and relations between laws, been described as 'an anticlimax'.[118] Anticlimactic it may be, in view of its brevity and consciously limited discussion, but the reason that the model's detailed exposition of laws and relations between laws, and of primary norm-applying institutions and the principle of authoritative recognition, is not (overtly) implicated in the account of continuity is that such an approach would necessarily fail. The difficulty would be that the ultimate

[111] Raz, 'The Identity of Legal Systems' (n 3), 100.

[112] H Kelsen, *General Theory of Law and State* (A Wedberg tr, New York, Harvard University Press, 1945) 20–21, 181–83, 233; H Kelsen, *Pure Theory of Law, Reine Rechtslehre*, first published 1960, 2nd edn (M Knight tr, Berkley, Ca, University of California Press, 1967) 150, 234, 287.

[113] Raz, 'The Identity of Legal Systems' (n 3), 100.

[114] Raz, *Concept of a Legal System* (n 1), 189; Raz, 'The Identity of Legal Systems' (n 3), 100.

[115] Raz, *Concept of a Legal System* (n 1), 189.

[116] ibid.

[117] Raz, 'The Identity of Legal Systems' (n 3), 100.

[118] D Rosenthal, 'The Concept of a Legal System (Book review)' (1971) 88 *South African Law Journal* 142, 143.

rules that govern the duties and powers of primary norm-applying organs are constituted by the practice of those organs[119] and, as Raz and Finnis point out, it is not clear how the diachronic identity of such customary rules should be analysed—it is not clear which changes are consistent with continuity and which compel the conclusion that there is a new rule.[120] The problem is similar to that which arises if, on a Hartian account, the unity of the legal system is a function of an ultimate rule of recognition. In substance, Hart gave little attention to what constituted a legal system over time,[121] apart from suggesting that the factual change wrought by the courts of a recently emancipated colony or post-revolutionary society in practising a new ultimate rule of recognition entails discontinuity (even if many of the criteria applied in recognising valid laws are the same after the change[122]).[123] As Raz observes, Hart did not (purport to) deal with the relationship between the legal system and the political system,[124] which is the substantive issue for continuity in Raz's view, and which explains why the approach in this aspect of the model appears to differ from its approach to taxonomy and to the principle of authoritative recognition. Nonetheless, a role for the model's understanding of laws, relations between laws and recognition is revealed by more detailed analysis of the three factors to which the model's account of continuity draws attention—the extent and manner of change in legal norms, the extent and manner of change in non-legal norms, and the interaction of legal and non-legal norms. Indeed, it is submitted that close attention to other parts of the model reveals that there is much more to the model's account of continuity than the two-and-a-half lines identifying those factors suggest. Without implying that they should be applied separately—the factors themselves, as well as the way in which they are framed in the extract set out above, suggest they cannot be considered as entirely separate requirements—it is convenient to unpack each of the three factors in turn.

A. Legal Changes

Although Raz expresses the first factor in terms of legal *norms*, it is submitted that it is more consistent with the rest of the model to understand the first factor as concerned with *laws*, some of which may, as explained above,

[119] Above, text to n 91.

[120] Raz, 'The Identity of Legal Systems' (n 3), 98; Finnis, 'Revolutions and Continuity of Law' (n 95), 427–28.

[121] PC Oliver, 'The 1982 Patriation of the Canadian Constitution: Reflections on Continuity and Change' (1994) 28 *Revue Juridique Themis* 875, 902.

[122] Hart, 'The Morality of Law (Book Review)' (n 95), 1295.

[123] Hart, *The Concept of Law* (n 95), 120–21.

[124] Raz, 'The Identity of Legal Systems' (n 3), 98.

not be norms.[125] It appears that Raz speaks of legal 'norms' in this sentence in consequence of his observation in the preceding paragraph that the 'legal system is only part of the norms constituting the political system', which may include many non-legal norms.[126] However, Raz reprises the language of 'political laws' in the sentence immediately following this extract.[127] Moreover, since laws that are not norms include laws concerning status and juristic persons,[128] they may figure prominently amongst the legal aspects of the political system. Accordingly, it is submitted that, though Raz's use of the language of 'laws' and 'norms' is careful, the clarification may, in this instance, be advanced without undue hesitation.

In accounting for this first factor, the extent and manner of change in laws, Raz's model refers to the genetic structure of a legal system but ultimately accords pre-eminence to content-based considerations of constitutional or political importance. A legal system's genetic structure arranges laws by reference to the laws conferring power to create them.[129] It is thus similar to a Kelsenian hierarchy of norms, though Raz's model includes laws that are not norms and his genetic structure does not bear the function of sustaining the present validity of laws. Recognition—in particular, recognition of genetic relations—by primary norm-applying organs is central to mapping this genetic structure, which reveals the laws that are or have been part of the system, and the powers and institutions that are able to create laws or have been able to do so in the past.[130] Raz further contends that a genetic structure provides for priority among laws, mechanisms for resolving conflicts between laws, the temporal validity and possible retroactivity of laws, and the degrees of voidability of laws.[131] Accordingly, Raz proposes that the primary basis for the structure—genetic relations between laws—should be refined by reference to other factors, including the date of a law's creation, the function and authority of the body creating it, and laws determining methods of amendment and repeal.[132]

Unlike Kelsen's model, Raz's account does not hold that the existence of an (effective) law that cannot be depicted within the genetic structure of a pre-existing legal system (refined as just explained) establishes discontinuity. Nor does it hold that the existence of genetic relations establishes continuity. Even before taking the other two factors into consideration, the account holds that continuity is only interrupted by a 'constitutional law of great importance', whether or not that law has a genetic relation

[125] Above, section I.A.iv.
[126] Raz, 'The Identity of Legal Systems' (n 3), 100.
[127] ibid.
[128] Above, n 36.
[129] Raz, *Concept of a Legal System* (n 1), 184.
[130] ibid, 184–85.
[131] ibid, 184.
[132] ibid.

with pre-existing laws.[133] The nature and extent of legal change are thus to be considered, as well as its manner. While no metric of 'importance' is expounded, Raz's account suggests that importance is, at least in part, content-based: Raz indicates that changes to constitutional and administrative laws, being political laws, are more relevant than changes to other laws in evaluating the continuity of the political system and therefore of the legal system, which is part of it.[134] The sole example of a constitutional change of great importance that Raz provides is achieving national independence.[135] It may reasonably be inferred that the opposite process—merger rather than separation of political systems—would also be an example. Wholesale change from secular to religious law (or vice versa) appears to operate at a similar level of importance in terms of nature and extent, even though it may be achieved in a genetically related—constitutionally authorised—manner. Less dramatic changes affecting the political system in similarly significant ways might also qualify.

B. Non-legal Political Changes

As noted above, for fear of trespassing into other social sciences, Raz's model does not provide a fully worked-out account of the second factor, the extent and manner of change in the non-legal political norms. The only clear illustration of discontinuity provided in the model, national independence,[136] will ordinarily involve reference to non-legal as well as legal norms, but the example does not develop our understanding very far. Raz's model does, however, indicate in formal terms the kinds of norms involved. The non-legal norms of the political system comprise:

(a) political norms that are neither the ultimate rules practised by primary norm-applying organs, nor laws (addressed to individuals) that those ultimate rules require the organs to apply; and
(b) political norms that the ultimate rules require the primary norm-applying organs to apply that are not recognised as part of the law but are enforced on the ground that part of the law's function is to support other social systems.[137]

Constitutional conventions are an example of non-legal political norms of the first type.[138] The rules of a political party—for example, those governing the selection of a leader—may be an example of adopted norms of the

[133] ibid, 188.
[134] Raz, 'The Identity of Legal Systems' (n 3), 100.
[135] Raz, *Concept of a Legal System* (n 1), 188.
[136] ibid.
[137] Raz, 'The Identity of Legal Systems' (n 3), 101–02.
[138] ibid, 100.

second type. These definitions give some—though perhaps only a little—sense of the content of the non-legal political norms with which this second factor is concerned. It is submitted that further insight may be gained by considering the related work of Honoré and Finnis, and by reference to other parts of Raz's own scholarship.

Honoré's notion of a 'social group' is relevant because it illuminates a functional dimension of the norms of a political system and because it appears, in several respects, to underlie Raz's model. As noted above, Raz's model includes a social parameter: legal systems are always part of political systems, themselves subsystems of broader social systems.[139] The social forms of which the model assumes legal systems are part are 'complex forms of social life, such as religions, states, regimes, tribes, etc'.[140] While the model itself does not expand on the features of these social forms, the necessary assumption that '[a]ll law is the law of a group of individuals or of groups made up of individuals'[141] suggests that the model contemplates, at some level, something in the nature of Honoré's notion of a 'social group'. To distinguish collections of individuals from members of groups, this notion focuses attention on two conditions (each of which is a matter of degree):[142] first, coordination in pursuit of a common purpose or activity (an 'enterprise') known to active members;[143] and, second, the existence of a 'shared understanding' as to the means to be pursued in that enterprise, by which is meant a set of effective prescriptive conventions operating between, or generally known to, members.[144] Importantly, Honoré's notion fits what Raz's model implies, in that questions about the source and normativity of prescriptive conventions are relevant but not determinative in defining the membership of the group:[145] in Raz's terms, the manner of change is relevant but not conclusive in considering continuity (identity) over time. The similarity between Honoré's notion and the unexpressed assumptions about political systems in Raz's model is further revealed elsewhere in Raz's work where, in explaining what it means for individuals to belong to the same political society, he says:[146]

[139] Above, n 3.

[140] Raz, *Concept of a Legal System* (n 1), 188.

[141] AM Honoré, 'Groups, Laws and Obedience' (1973) in *Making Law Bind: Essays Legal and Philosophical* (Oxford, Clarendon Press, 1987) 32, 33.

[142] ibid, 34.

[143] ibid, 34, 38; AM Honoré, 'What is a Group?' (1975) in *Making Law Bind: Essays Legal and Philosophical* (Oxford, Clarendon Press, 1987) 52, 56.

[144] Honoré, 'Groups, Laws and Obedience' (n 141), 35, 38; Honoré, 'What is a Group?' (n 143), 64.

[145] Honoré, 'Groups, Laws and Obedience' (n 141), 37.

[146] J Raz, 'Multiculturalism: A Liberal Perspective' in *Ethics in the Public Domain: Essays in the Morality of Law and Politics*, rev edn (Oxford, Clarendon Press, 1995) 170, 188.

> They will all be educated and placed to enjoy roughly equal access to the sources of political power and to decision-making positions. They will have to acquire a common political language, and common conventions of conduct, to be able to compete effectively for resources and to be able to protect their group as well as individual interests in a shared political arena.

Some of the detail of this explanation is particular to the multicultural Western liberal democracy Raz is discussing, but, abstracted from that context, the features to which Raz adverts accord with Honoré's dual criteria of coordination in pursuit of a common enterprise known to members and the existence of a shared understanding comprising conventions operating between members. Some of Raz's remarks in a related context may appear to diverge from Honoré's account, in relation to the role of sentiment or self-identification in defining a political group. Raz suggests that[147]

> [u]ltimately political unity depends on people's free and willing identification with the political society they belong to: on the fact that they feel German, that their sense of their own identity as German is totally instinctive and unproblematic. And it depends on the fact that they are proud to be German.

Honoré, in contrast, considers that neither benevolent nor hostile sentiments can, by themselves, create or truncate groups, citing the examples of a pure apartheid doctrine, which holds that black people do not belong to the same political group as others, and a pure Irish nationalist doctrine, which holds that residents of Northern Ireland are (despite all practical differences) really part of the same political group as residents of the Irish Republic.[148] This apparent divergence is explained, once again, by Raz's focus, in context, on stable multicultural Western liberal democratic welfare states: the normatively richer criterion of a 'free and willing identification with the political society they belong to' addresses only a particular subset of political systems. Sentimental self-identification should thus not be understood as essential in Raz's model either, though, as will be seen, it is relevant in respect of adjudicating between competing group identities.[149] Accordingly, it is submitted that reference to Honoré's account of groups is helpful in unpacking the unexpressed assumptions of Raz's model, at least in so far as it indicates that, for the purposes of considering identity, the relevant norms of a political system are those that establish the common enterprise of the participants in the system and those that comprise the associated shared understanding. In the case of a political system, many of the norms relating to the common enterprise and to the prescriptive conventions operating between, or generally known to,

[147] J Raz, 'Multiculturalism' (1998) 11 *Ratio Juris* 193, 203.

[148] Honoré, 'What is a Group?' (n 143), 62–63.

[149] Below, text to n 167.

participants will be legal norms, but others may be non-legal, and it is to those that the second factor in Raz's account of continuity directs attention.

It is also relevant to consider Honoré's account of the continuity of groups.[150] This depends on two conditions: first, the continued existence of shared understandings, though, importantly, any or all of the understandings may cease without disrupting the continuity of the group, as long they are replaced by others; and, second, the broad effectiveness of the prescriptive conventions to which the shared understandings relate.[151] As these are necessary conditions for the continuity of the group, the loss of either entails discontinuity. The second condition relates, in substance, to the continued existence of a group at all: the effectiveness of prescriptive conventions is the criterion that distinguishes a group from a mere collection of individuals who happen to have coincidentally concordant purposes but whose actions are not mutually coordinated. The first condition relates, in substance, to the continued existence *of the same group*: what define this particular group (given its existence) are its shared understandings. However, as noted above, it is the shared understandings *at any given moment* that define a group; in Honoré's account, the process by which these understandings were acquired at any given moment is a relevant but not a conclusive consideration. Accordingly, the shared understandings may change over time: as long as *some* understandings are shared between the members of the group, it is the same group. A group of freedom fighters may become a group of political prisoners or a government-in-exile: in each case, many and perhaps all of the prescriptive conventions operating between the members will be changed but the group retains its identity.

Despite the striking underlying similarities and consistencies between Honoré's account of social groups and Raz's model of legal systems, only the second of Honoré's conditions for the continuity of a social group can readily inform what Raz's model contemplates in terms of the extent and manner of change in the non-legal norms of a political system. The difficulty is that, because content-based considerations of constitutional or political importance apply in relation to the extent of change in the laws of the political system,[152] it would be inconsistent for the model to contemplate, as Honoré's account of group continuity appears to do, continuity as long as there is *some* content of the non-legal norms of the political system. In other words, while the existence of shared understandings may

[150] It may be noted in passing that Honoré's account also ties the (continuing) existence of a legal system to that of the group, rather than to any legal criterion, albeit for different reasons: Honoré, 'What is a Group?' (n 143), 68.

[151] Honoré, 'Groups, Laws and Obedience' (n 141), 38.

[152] Raz flags this expressly in the second observation set out above, text to n 117. While he does not there make a parallel observation regarding changes in non-legal political norms, it is submitted that that is because Raz refrains from analysing these in general and because his focus, in context, is the relationship between law and the state.

suffice for continuity of a group *in general*, some measure of continuity in the content of at least the more 'important' prescriptive conventions operating between, or generally known to, members must, for consistency, be necessary for continuity *of a political system*, as a particular kind of social group. A cohort of individuals may comprise the same *social group* when they exist as a personal (non-territorial) totalitarian theocracy and when they exist as a territorial liberal democracy (assuming a seamless substitution of one set of shared understandings for the other), but the *political system* that is, in the contemplation of Raz's model, a subsystem of that social group is surely not continuous. This observation recalls, and draws support from, the reference to values in the model's account of rights and other legal phenomena.[153] That account acknowledged that reference to substantive considerations of value and interests was necessary to provide a more complete description of phenomena such as rights than the description provided by reference to configurations of laws and internal relations alone. Just as the model recognises commonality of value, independent of internal relations, as a necessary dimension of an account of rights as legal phenomena, so, too, it is submitted, must Raz's model be understood to accord weight to commonality—and continuity—of substantive considerations of value in the non-legal norms of the political system. Once again, it is submitted that the nature, as well as the manner and the extent, of change in non-legal political norms is implicated in Raz's account.

The second condition for continuity of a social group in Honoré's account—broad effectiveness of the prescriptions to which the shared understandings relate—already finds a place in Raz's model in so far as it deals with the *existence* of institutionalised normative systems. As noted above, the primary criterion of existence is general conformity to the norms of the system by norm subjects, and endorsement and enforcement of the norms by norm-applying institutions.[154] It will be necessary to return to relationship between the model's account of existence and its account of continuity.[155]

Reference to Finnis's work provides more focused consideration of the subject matter of the non-legal political norms to which the second factor in Raz's model directs attention. Like Raz, Finnis concludes that the continuity of a legal system 'is a function of the continuity and identity of the society in whose ordered existence in time the legal system participates'.[156] His approach considers that the non-legal considerations

153 Above, section I.C.
154 Above, 172.
155 Below, 189–91.
156 Finnis, 'Revolutions and Continuity of Law' (n 95), 428.

of other social sciences to which Raz's second factor adverts are the history of a society and the ethical obligations it has or may have.[157] The consideration of history is present in Raz's model through its account of the genetic structure of a legal system. There is, however, no direct equivalent to the consideration of ethics in Finnis's terms: while Raz's model expressly alludes to commonality or continuity in value in relation to rights and, as contended above, in relation to the non-legal norms of the political system,[158] Finnis's consideration is one of full-blooded normative ethics and political and legal theory, not merely commonality of value as a matter of positive morality.[159] Finnis notes the difficulties in establishing the social entity whose history or identity is in issue, but he suggests it may be less problematic to establish the social entity to which an individual owes allegiance and in whose collective debts that individual is concerned.[160] Although expressly only sketching relevant considerations, he suggests that both historical and ethical enquiries will generally point towards continuity unless, in terms of history, a society becomes unwilling to recognise past decisions or actions as a standard for action in the present, and, in terms of ethics, considerations of legal coherence and respect for acquired rights are outweighed and it would be unreasonable to maintain allegiance to a new political order as the continuation of the old.[161] Like Kelsen and Raz, Finnis uses the revolutionary establishment of a new national society as an example of discontinuity, suggesting that the view of Rhodesian judges that a new legal system had arisen was inevitable once they had accepted that Rhodesia was a distinct society with its own accepted power structure and intelligible commonweal.[162] Finnis's work helpfully expands on the kinds of substantive questions in issue when considering the nature, manner and extent of changes to the non-legal norms of a political system, but ultimately, like Raz's account, consciously avoids propounding a specific test.[163]

C. Interaction Between Laws and Non-legal Norms

Raz does not elaborate on what the third factor, the interaction between laws and non-legal norms of the political system, entails. 'Interaction',

[157] ibid, 431.

[158] Above, 186.

[159] cp Raz's remarks on the relationship between the 'analytical' and 'critical' parts of legal philosophy: Raz, *Concept of a Legal System* (n 1), 209. See also Raz, *Practical Reason and Norms* (n 2), 11.

[160] Finnis, 'Revolutions and Continuity of Law' (n 95), 431–32.

[161] ibid, 434.

[162] ibid, 429.

[163] C Arnold, 'Institutional Aspects of Law' (1979) 42 *MLR* 667, 679–80.

however, invites attention to the impact of (changes to) laws on non-legal norms and that of (changes to) non-legal norms on laws. Interaction essentially (though perhaps not exclusively) occurs where the laws and non-legal political norms overlap in some respect—where, for example, they concern the same subject matter or actors. In areas of overlap, laws and non-legal political norms may be (or changes to one or both may render them) compatible or incompatible with one another. It is convenient to deal with the case of incompatibility first.

Though, as noted, the model is silent on the point, whether the interaction between incompatible laws and non-legal political norms entails continuity or discontinuity should—by analogy, and for consistency, with the first two factors—be understood as a matter of degree, turning upon the nature, manner and extent of the incompatibility. Consider, for example, a law, according to which the Queen may withhold assent from a Bill, whether or not she is advised to assent to it, and a non-legal political norm in the form of a constitutional convention, according to which the Queen may not withhold assent from a Bill to which she is advised to assent. The law and the convention are (partly) incompatible: the latter (partly) contradicts the former. However, the emergence of the convention should not be understood as entailing discontinuity in the political system or the legal system that is part of it. Assuming the convention prevails in the case of overlap, the change is, ex hypothesi, consistent with many other laws and non-legal political norms; the convention arose out of the sustained and consensual practice of all actors; and, though important in principle and potentially far-reaching in its consequences, it represents an adaptation within the legal and political systems rather than a persistent and insurmountable conflict. Similarly, if the law prevails in a case of overlap rather than the convention, there may be serious political ramifications—including the modification or termination of the convention itself—but not, it is submitted, ramifications of an order that would entail discontinuity in the legal and political systems; there would, again, be adaptation rather than persistent and insurmountable conflict.

What is in issue, fundamentally, is a conflict between (institutionalised) normative systems. Such conflicts are addressed in that part of Raz's model concerned with questions of 'existence'. Allusion has already been made to the model's general account of existence by reference to general conformity to norms by norm-subjects, and to the endorsement and enforcement of norms by norm-applying institutions.[164] That criterion addresses the question of existence in the abstract: whether, given a complete description of a legal system, that legal system exists in a particular

[164] Above, 172.

society.[165] However, Raz's model also addresses the question of existence in competition: whether, given that a particular society is governed by a legal system, it is governed by a *given* legal system.[166] In addressing this question, the model applies a test of 'exclusion':[167]

> This test assigns special importance to people's attitude and actions towards the state, the regime, or the other form of social organization of which the legal system concerned is an integral part. Does the population defy or disregard part of one of the legal systems concerned because of its allegiance to one regime rather than another? It is here that people's intentions in violating certain duties, in exercising or abstaining from the exercise of legal powers, become relevant … Other factors which are assigned special importance by the test of exclusion are the efficacy of major constitutional laws, i.e. the operations of the important law-applying and law-creating organs, and the efficacy of other laws that possess a political character.

This test invites attention to the critical reaction to laws of members of a social group (and, in particular, but by no means exclusively, the reaction of individuals acting as members of primary organs in institutionalised normative systems), on the basis of the prevailing facts and non-legal norms: in other words, it operates precisely at the intersection between laws and non-legal norms of the underlying social form of which the legal system is part. Strikingly, the test adverts to a similar range of matters to that which the first two factors presented for consideration, which tends to confirm the amplification of the account suggested above. The reference to 'allegiance' as a factor in individuals' critical reactions is further emphasised by Finnis:[168]

> The distinction between nationals and aliens is an indispensable framework for articulating, expressing, ratifying, and demanding [the willingness to share that is necessary for a political society], such awareness of being part owner of a shared inheritance and future, such integration in and assimilation to *this* nation-state rather than some other.

The test of exclusion is relative: whichever of the competing normative systems comes out better is the existing one; where competing systems may have roughly equal claims, 'the case must be judged unsettled'.[169] Raz acknowledges that an account of continuity and discontinuity might have to explain both 'a short and intense period of fundamental change' and 'a slow and gradual transformation of one system into another'.[170]

[165] Raz, *Concept of a Legal System* (n 1), 203, 205–06.

[166] ibid, 206.

[167] ibid, 207.

[168] JM Finnis, 'Nationality and Alienage' (2007) in *Human Rights and Common Good—Collected Essays: Volume III* (Oxford, OUP, 2011) 133, 148 (footnotes omitted).

[169] Raz, *Concept of a Legal System* (n 1), 208. In a similar vein, see Hart, *The Concept of Law* (n 95), 118.

[170] Raz, 'The Identity of Legal Systems' (n 3), 100, fn 39.

In the latter case, it is likely that there will be a period in which the case is unsettled.

Although expressed in empirical terms, the test appears equally capable of hypothetical application, especially in light of the option to regard a case as unsettled. Accordingly, it is submitted that, in relation to this third factor, the model envisages a similar (and, where relevant, hypothetical) approach to the test of exclusion: weighing the critical reactions of individuals and primary organs to the (changes to the) laws and non-legal norms of the political system—in light of the nature, manner and extent of the incompatibility that characterises the 'interaction' between them—may reveal continuity or discontinuity, or it may be inconclusive. Accordingly, the test of exclusion could be used to evaluate whether legislation applying to the Commonwealth of Australia enacted by the Westminster Parliament in 1980 but without the request and consent of the Commonwealth *would have been upheld* in Australian courts in the face of an inconsistent convention requiring request and consent. The fact that no such test cases arose does not preclude a confident prediction based on the hypothetical.[171]

It is submitted that the analysis just described in relation to incompatible or competing normative systems applies equally to areas of overlap where the laws and non-legal political norms concerned are compatible. It is initially tempting to suggest that compatibility simply implies continuity: after all, there will be no observable difference in behaviour. However, that conclusion would permit an epistemic consideration to obscure an underlying difference in principle. For example, performance of an action required both by law and by political convention may be more (or less) legitimate than performance of an action required by only one normative system: the reasons and motivations matter, as Raz points out in referring to 'people's intentions in violating certain duties, in exercising or abstaining from the exercise of legal powers'.[172] Where laws and non-legal political norms are compatible, the test of exclusion must operate hypothetically, on the counterfactual premise that there *was* conflict, in order to evaluate which of the competing institutionalised normative systems would prevail (or to reach the conclusion that the case would be unsettled). For example, while both by (Imperial as well as Australian) law and by non-legal political norm, the Westminster Parliament has had no authority to legislate with respect to Australia since 1986, the interaction between laws and non-legal norms can be evaluated by assuming a counterfactual incompatible change—such as the reassertion of legislative competence by the Westminster Parliament in 1990—in order to evaluate

[171] Below, text to ch 6, n 93, and 217.
[172] Raz, *Concept of a Legal System* (n 1), 207.

which of the normative systems would prevail. Since it is reasonable to conclude that the normative system that would prevail in the hypothetical is also the normative system that is effective in producing the compatible result (in the example, the non-legal political norms of national independence), the test of exclusion can usefully identify the character of the interaction between laws and non-legal political norms even where they are consistent. The answer so arrived at may then be factored into the analysis of continuity or discontinuity.

D. The Reconstruction Summarised and Compared

As stressed at the outset, the three factors by reference to which Raz's model accounts for the continuity and discontinuity of legal systems may be explained separately, but they ought not to be dissociated too far. Certainly, no conclusion in the application of any one factor is presented as a necessary condition for either continuity or discontinuity. However, it is probable that, in certain circumstances, a conclusion of discontinuity in relation to any one of the three factors would be a sufficient condition for systemic discontinuity.[173] In terms of the nature, manner and extent of change in laws, a large number of changes to fundamental constitutional laws brought about by an unauthorised process—for example, where an alien legal system is imposed in the aftermath of a violent conquest—would justify a conclusion of discontinuity. In terms of the nature, manner and extent of change in non-legal political norms, fundamental changes to the power structures and ultimate ends of a political system brought about by popular consent—as, for example, when a particular group or region asserts independence and disregards old allegiances in favour of a discrete commonweal—would justify a conclusion of discontinuity. Illustrating the frequent interconnection of the factors in substance, both of the scenarios just mentioned also depict competition between laws and non-legal political norms of such a nature, manner and extent as to justify a conclusion of discontinuity, in a way that, in contrast, the conflict between the convention regarding royal assent to Bills and the prerogative discretion to withhold assent does not.

At this point, it is convenient to compare the reconstruction of Raz's account of continuity and discontinuity advanced here with the way in which Oliver contends that the account applies. Oliver himself offers a new and different account of constitutional independence—a phenomenon

[173] See the parallel discussion in relation to the identity of the state in NW Barber, *The Constitutional State* (Oxford, OUP, 2010) 141–42.

closely related, but arguably not identical, to the continuity or discontinuity of legal systems—grounded in the application of a self-embracing conception of the sovereignty of the Westminster Parliament.[174] However, in considering Canada, a parallel example to Australia, Oliver proposes a range of considerations that, in his view, are implicated in Raz's account by reference to continuity of the underlying political system. Oliver's suggested considerations include: national political independence; lack of reliance on the exercise of Imperial powers and controls, despite their continuing legal availability; a presumption in favour of connection between a constitution and its subjects, especially in a system of representative government and democratic accountability; the ideal that a constitution should be legitimate as well as legal; the relevance of the larger historical context of constitutional development to the interpretation of fundamental rules; and the independence of courts, as primary norm-applying organs, from foreign control or supervision.[175] He especially stresses the last consideration—judicial independence and the allegiance of the judges—as a result of the model's focus on primary norm-applying organs.[176]

It is submitted that the considerations Oliver mentions helpfully flesh out the kinds of substantive questions in issue. Moreover, each of the considerations can be understood in terms of the reconstruction of Raz's account advanced here. National political independence is an example of a consideration to which the second and third factors—change in non-legal political norms, and the interaction between laws and non-legal political norms—advert, as it involves a shift in non-legal political norms of allegiance and commonweal and the (potential) competition between institutionalised normative systems. The lack of reliance on available Imperial legal mechanisms may be similarly characterised, though this factor alone would probably not be sufficient, as the circumstances to which it draws attention are arguably at the 'adaptation' rather than the 'insurmountable conflict' end of the spectrum. The presumption in favour of a connection between the constitution and its subjects may best be understood as directing attention to the shared understandings or prescriptive conventions that are considered in applying the second factor—change in non-legal political norms. The ideal that a constitution should possess legitimacy as well as legal force is a matter that would fall for consideration under the third factor—the interaction between laws and non-legal political norms—in terms of the critical reactions to which the

[174] PC Oliver, *The Constitution of Independence: the Development of Constitutional Theory in Australia, Canada, and New Zealand* (Oxford, OUP, 2005) 348–49. See also above, ch 1, n 12.
[175] ibid, 24, 321; Oliver (n 121), 912.
[176] Oliver, *The Constitution of Independence* (n 174), 299–300, 313.

test of exclusion refers. Reference to the larger historical context of constitutional development in interpreting fundamental rules is, again, a consideration to which an application of all three factors adverts. The second and third factors also encompass judicial independence from outside influence, and the particular significance of this consideration in Oliver's treatment is referable to the 'special importance' that the test of exclusion assigns to 'the operations of the important law-applying and law-creating organs'.[177] However, while Oliver arguably concentrates exclusively on evaluating the critical reaction of officials (in particular, courts), the application of the third factor in Raz's model as reconstructed here also assigns 'special importance' to popular (non-official) reactions.[178] Accordingly, it is submitted that the reconstruction advanced here, grounded in Raz's work and closely related scholarship, derives support from the fact that it is able to accommodate, as well as classify and generalise, the particular substantive considerations raised by Oliver in his application of Raz's account.

V. CONCLUSIONS

This chapter reconstructed Raz's taxonomy of laws and internal relations, rendering express the underlying structure of normative function and normative connection, and deducing two additional kinds of internal relation implied but not named in the account. It elucidated what is entailed in the central doctrine of authoritative recognition, especially in relation to recognising internal relations as well as laws. The chapter then proceeded to unpack—and, where necessary, fill in—what Raz's account signifies when it holds that the continuity and discontinuity of legal systems is a function of the continuity and discontinuity of their underlying social form, and that continuity and discontinuity depends on the nature, manner and extent of the changes in, and the interactions between, laws and non-legal political norms. Allied insights in the work of Honoré and Finnis were used to amplify Raz's account of changes in non-legal political norms, exposing, in particular, the account's unexpressed assumptions about social groups and the considerations that are relevant to analysing the nature, manner and extent of changes in political norms. Analysis of interactions between laws and non-legal political norms was explained in terms of conflicting normative systems, and resolved by reference to the nature, manner and extent of incompatibility and by the application of Raz's (hypothetical) test of exclusion. This test, integrated from Raz's model of the existence of legal systems in competition, drew on the critical

[177] Raz, *Concept of a Legal System* (n 1), 207.
[178] ibid.

reactions of participants on the basis of considerations similar to those implicated in the amplified account of changes to laws and to non-legal political norms. The chapter concluded by demonstrating consistency between the account as reconstructed and amplified and the framework adopted in the only other substantive consideration of Raz's model in the context of a concrete legal system that was identified, in anticipation of the systematic application to Australia between 1788 and 2001 that is undertaken in the next chapter.

6

Application of Raz's Account

THIS CHAPTER APPLIES Raz's account of continuity and discontinuity of legal systems, as reconstructed and amplified in chapter five, to the specific instance of Australia between 1788 and 2001. Section I addresses the period from settlement to Federation, examining the effect of the legal and non-legal political changes connected with the movement from autocratic penal Colony to representative and responsible government, with particular attention to the changing roles played by Imperial institutions. Section II continues this analysis in relation to the period following Federation, grappling with continuity and discontinuity in the Colonies-turned-States, the Commonwealth, the Territories and in the Imperial system considered as a whole, in light of key constitutional landmarks such as the Statute of Westminster 1931 (Imp) and the *Australia Acts*, but also the myriad other developments uncovered in chapter two. The application of Raz's account shows how far it avoids problems highlighted in applying Kelsen's account, but it also reveals weaknesses of its own. The effect of some of the gaps or inadequacies of the account identified in chapter five is noted, but the sophistication of the varied and detailed analysis it permits is also brought to light.

I. CONTINUITY: SETTLEMENT TO FEDERATION

A. Settlement

From settlement, the law in New South Wales reflected all of the types of laws and relations between laws that Raz's model holds are required in any legal system. Duty-imposing laws addressed to ordinary individuals are evident in the criminal and civil law, whether received common law or local gubernatorial legislation.[1] Power-conferring laws are present in both regulative and legislative forms in, for example, Phillip's Commission and Instructions.[2] Examples of laws that are not norms are those parts of the

[1] Above, 12–13.

[2] A regulative power-conferring law is that empowering the Governor to 'execute martial law': Commission (02.04.1787) in FM Bladen (ed), *Historical Records of New South Wales*, vol I, pt 2 (Sydney, Government Printer, 1892) 64. A legislative power-conferring law is that empowering the Governor to make regulations relating to convicts: Instructions (25.04.1787), ibid, 87.

Instructions declaring Phillip Captain-General and Commander-in-Chief, and defining the geographical limits of the Colony.[3] Genetic relations exist between the legislative power-conferring laws empowering the Governor to make regulations relating to convicts and the regulations so made. To the extent that those regulations also imposed duties on convicts, there also exist regulative relations between those duty-imposing laws and the legislative power-conferring law empowering the Governor to make them. Applicative relations exist between the non-normative laws defining the limits of the Colony and all of the powers conferred on the Governor within it.

Beyond these taxonomical points, the core elements of Raz's model of law as a particular kind of institutionalised normative system are also present from 1788. The criminal and civil courts established by the King and the magistrates appointed by the Governors[4] are archetypal primary norm-applying organs. The distinctive claims of legal systems to comprehensiveness, supremacy and openness can be discerned in the breadth of matters regulated or permitted by the received common law (including, with respect to openness, the recognition and enforcement of, for example, contracts and wills) and—notwithstanding the limited local legislative authority of the Governors—the unlimited legislative competence of the Parliament at Westminster.[5]

The presence of laws and relations between laws of the kinds predicted by Raz's model does not entail that there was a discrete legal system in New South Wales: in other words, from the perspective of continuity, the establishment of the Colony did not of itself entail the creation of a New South Wales legal system discontinuous with the Imperial legal system.[6] Raz's account of continuity, by reference to continuity of the underlying social form, may be applied by considering the three factors identified above,[7] though it should be reiterated that they are treated separately only for expository convenience, since the three are inherently interconnected. So far as the nature, manner and extent of changes to laws is concerned, the picture that emerges at settlement is that of an outpost of Imperial law adapted to govern, and regulate the institutional governance of, a contingent of convicts, accompanied by small group of free settlers, initially comprising only officials, soldiers and their families. The governing laws were Imperial in origin. Executive government was autocratic, military

[3] Instructions (n 2), 85.

[4] Above, 14.

[5] See, eg, W Blackstone, *Commentaries on the Laws of England*, 16th edn (London, Butterworths, 1825) [160]–[161]; AV Dicey, *Introduction to the Study of the Law of the Constitution*, 1st edn 1885, 10th edn (London, Macmillan, 1959) 39–40.

[6] Recall the connection between propositions of discontinuity and propositions that a discrete legal system exists: above, 1.

[7] Above, ch 5.IV.

and vested in a serviceman bound to obey his Imperial military superiors as well as the Instructions of the Secretary of State in London. There were autochthonous primary norm-applying organs in the Governor and courts. However, the extensive provisions of the 1787 Act with respect to courts are explained, first, by the fact that, like executive power, judicial power had to be exercised locally and, second, by the fact that the enforcement of the law, in combination with the discipline and organisation of military rule, was a principal means of ensuring order and survival. As to legislative power, none was conferred on local organs in general terms, but there were, as noted, specific powers in relation to regulating convicts. As to the wider legislative powers assumed by the early Governors, in Raz's model, any illegality of their general orders[8]—which would lack genetic relations to laws recognised by the primary norm-applying organs—would not entail discontinuity with the Imperial legal system unless they amounted to constitutional laws of great importance.[9] Since the law-making powers assumed by the Governors were essentially confined to matters of regulation where the laws of England were insufficient for the administration of the Colony—there was no hint, for example, of any claim to reform or constitute new organs of government—this criterion is not satisfied and, accordingly, no basis for discontinuity appears from consideration of the first factor in the model's account of continuity.

Consideration of the second factor—the nature, manner and extent of change in non-legal norms of the political system—similarly discloses no grounds for discerning discontinuity upon settlement. The establishment of a colony *could* be considered a common enterprise of the settlers, and there is some evidence consistent with a discrete political identity from the start in, for example, the New South Wales great seal.[10] However, it is impossible to discern any sense that the norms of the broader Imperial political system ceased to operate as standards for action or decision, or to discern any change in allegiance or any discrete commonweal. The Empire provided the officers and soldiers, settlers, convicts and equipment: in other words, its officials, population, finance and defence. The Colony was in every sense a 'dependency' of the UK. It should readily be admitted that the colonists formed a group of people with distinct needs living in a distinct territory—with, doubtless, some distinct political conventions operating between them, especially as regards the office of Governor. However, their purpose in New South Wales was Imperial and their institutions—including their primary norm-applying organs—were part of the machinery of Imperial government. The convicts and free settlers alike regarded themselves as British, and by law they owed

[8] Above, 13.
[9] Above, text to ch 5, n 134.
[10] Above, 47–48.

allegiance to the sovereign of the UK.[11] There was, moreover, no scope for independent popular participation in government by an Imperial autocrat (whose officers even staffed the courts).[12] Accordingly, application of the second factor to which Raz's account directs attention indicates that settlement of New South Wales did not entail discontinuity in the underlying political system, which remained that of the Empire.

It was argued above that the third factor—the interaction between laws and non-legal political norms—concerns the nature, manner and extent of competition between institutionalised normative systems, with particular reference to the test of exclusion. As the consideration of the first two factors revealed, there is no basis to discern competition between legal and non-legal political norms at (or immediately after) settlement: both the laws and the non-legal political norms are unequivocally those of an Imperial system (which included New South Wales). To the extent that a competing normative system could be postulated on the basis of distinct local New South Wales political conventions (and perhaps locally applied but technically unconstitutional gubernatorial general orders), application of the test of exclusion suggests that the critical reactions of both ordinary individuals and primary norm-applying organs would result in the Imperial system's being preferred. Accordingly, no ground for discontinuity is discerned in the application of the third factor, and no discontinuity in the Imperial political (and therefore legal) system is to be discerned upon settlement.

B. Settlement to Responsible Government

The creation of a local Legislative Council and a Supreme Court in 1823, followed by the revision of constitutional arrangements in 1828, effected important changes to the government of New South Wales: '[I]n effect, [they] made New South Wales a colony with a civil, as distinct from a military, government. It was no longer merely a penal settlement'.[13] However, in terms of Raz's first factor—the nature, manner and extent of changes to laws—it is submitted that they did not amount to constitutional laws of sufficient importance to bring about, in themselves, discontinuity in the underlying political system. Attention to the detail of the system set out above is critical.[14] The Colony was no longer a military autocracy, but it remained a tightly-controlled British settlement. The Governors' wide

[11] As reflected in Phillip's oath of abjuration: above, ch 2.III.C.

[12] Above, 14.

[13] WJV Windeyer, *Lectures on Legal History* (Sydney, LBC, 1938) 258. See also J Quick and RR Garran, *The Annotated Constitution of the Australian Commonwealth* (Sydney, Angus & Robertson, 1901) 36.

[14] Above, ch 2.I.A.i.

powers remained, but were tempered by the creation of Legislative and Executive Councils. Local legislative authority now existed on a clear footing, but was confined within strict limits and subject to control from London, as is evident in the provisions dealing with reservation and disallowance by the Imperial Government and certification by the Chief Justice that proposed laws were not repugnant to English law, as well as the significant subject-matter limitations in both the empowering Act and the Governor's Instructions.[15] The reconstituted courts were more closely modelled on their English counterparts, but their composition and procedure were still minutely regulated and they were now subject to an express statutory direction to apply English law as at the date of the 1828 Act, so far as possible in the circumstances of the Colony. They were, moreover, subject to supervision and correction by the Privy Council, just as the Governor was still subject to instruction and direction by the Secretary of State. With reference to a law that is not a norm, the boundaries of New South Wales were in this period redefined so as to exclude Van Diemen's Land, South Australia and New Zealand, though the first had always been administered with a degree of independence from Sydney, the second had been surveyed but not settled and the last had never been more than nominally part of the Australian Colony.[16] All of these changes were effected by Imperial legislation and served to regularise the government of a semi-autonomous (redefined) geographical division of the Empire, rather than to bring about legal changes of the nature or extent, or in the manner, contemplated by the first factor in Raz's account.

As to the non-legal norms of the political system, the Colony still depended on the Empire for its laws and officials, for its population (transportation continued until 1840),[17] for its economy[18] and for its defence.[19] The government and people of New South Wales flew the Union flag, not distinguished by the badge of the Colony until 1869.[20] That New South Wales as a body politic was subject, in all respects, to the Imperial political system, of which it was part, is similarly demonstrated in terms of norms of membership (as reflected in the legal norms of nationality): when denization was provided for in 1828, it applied only within the Colony and required the consent of the Secretary of State.[21]

It is submitted that the interaction between laws and non-legal political norms may be analysed in the same fashion as at settlement: there is little

[15] Above, ch 2.I.A.ii.

[16] Above, ch 2.II.A.

[17] Above, ch 2, n 72.

[18] Though the Colony became self-supporting by around 1828 (above, ch 2, n 48), it did not acquire control over wastelands, Colonial revenues or mining royalties until 1855: above, text to ch 2, n 83.

[19] Above, text to ch 2, n 377.

[20] Above, 51.

[21] Above, ch 2, n 504.

basis to discern competing institutionalised normative systems and, in so far as one is hypothesised, the test of exclusion can reliably be understood to show preference for the (legal and non-legal) norms of the Imperial political system. Accordingly, New South Wales in the period from settlement to self-government enjoyed greater autonomy, but was no more independent, legally or socially, from the UK than might be expected as a result of its distance and isolation. There was no change in the underlying social form and no discontinuity in the Imperial political (and therefore legal) system.

C. Responsible Government to Federation

The sum of the constitutional changes between 1842 and 1855 refashioned New South Wales into a self-governing, representative and responsible political community.[22] By 1855, Imperial law had conferred on the Colony legislative institutions representing its inhabitants and executive institutions responsible to those representatives. The control of all local norm-creating and norm-applying institutions was vested in institutions within New South Wales, along with the power of constitutional amendment, though subject to reservation for royal assent (on the advice of the Imperial Government) in some instances, and still formally subject to disallowance, though the use of this procedure was rare. As observed above, the mechanisms of Imperial administration combined local self-government in a wide range of matters with central oversight and control—exercised in the interests of the Empire as a whole, but including New South Wales—in others.

How should the nature, manner and extent of these legal changes be evaluated in applying Raz's model? The nature and extent of the reforms were such as to confer a very significant degree of autonomy but not legal independence. Of course, it must be stressed that, while it is the only case cited in the model, independence need not be the sole example of a 'constitutional law of great importance'.[23] The manner of effecting the changes was by Imperial legislation, such that a structure of genetic relations continued to tie New South Wales law to Imperial law. Again, that fact alone is not determinative of the continuity or discontinuity of the social form in Raz's model.[24] Importantly, a depiction of that genetic structure, further developed by reference to some of the additional detail that

[22] Above, ch 2.I.A.iii.

[23] J Raz, *The Concept of a Legal System: An Introduction to the Theory of Legal System*, 2nd edn (Oxford, Clarendon Press, 1980) 188.

[24] Above, 181.

Raz sketches,[25] indicates that, after 1855, Imperial law was still accorded priority over local law in the case of conflict, as the Colonial Laws Validity Act 1865 (Imp) amply demonstrates (notwithstanding its intention to reduce the range of possible conflicts). The territorial scope of New South Wales law was further redefined in this period with, most significantly, the separation of Victoria in 1851 and Queensland in 1859.[26] Each separation involved an alteration in terms of population and territory, but it is submitted that none implies discontinuity. There was no quantitative change so far as the Imperial political system was concerned, only an internal reorganisation. It might be argued that the separations represent constitutional laws of great importance, entailing a species of 'independence', for putative Victorian and Queensland legal systems. However, the constitutional arrangements erected in those Colonies simply put them on a more equal footing with New South Wales, as units within the Empire, so the better conclusion is that the continuity or discontinuity of their political systems is to be analysed in the same terms as that of New South Wales, with reference to the broader Imperial political system. Accordingly, an application of the first, content-based, factor in Raz's account provides some basis for discerning discontinuity but is perhaps best understood as rendering, of itself, an 'unsettled' result.

A range of material canvassed in chapter two is implicated in an application of the second factor to New South Wales in the second half of the nineteenth century. Significant changes to non-legal political norms of the community paralleled the constitutional and legal changes of the period, and point to increasing self-reliance and independence. Though only partly a matter of convention, the increasing political independence of New South Wales is evident in the negotiations between the Imperial Secretary of State and the local legislature that ultimately led to the constitutional reforms of 1855 (themselves essentially authored by the Legislative Council).[27] Responsible and representative government saw the substitution of the Queen for the Governor in the enacting formula of legislation, a constitutional convention that similarly denoted maturity and increasingly distinct political identity,[28] as did the adoption of a New South Wales flag for government use.[29] The cessation of transportation was swiftly followed by an end to the practice of assigning convicts for private or domestic labour and, together with contemporary equal enfranchisement of freemen and emancipists, led to—distinctively local—changes in social stratification.[30] Local military and naval forces were formed, but naval

[25] Above, text to ch 5, n 131.
[26] Above, ch 2.II.A.
[27] Above, 19–20.
[28] Above, text to ch 2, n 266.
[29] Above, text to ch 2, n 346.
[30] Above, 18–19.

defence, though financed by Colonial contributions, was still essentially in the hands of the Imperial Navy.[31]

Norms related to membership, reflected in nationality legislation of this period, show both an increasing separation from the UK, with naturalisation becoming a matter for Colonial regulation, and also an increasing alignment with the other Australian Colonies, through the naturalisation legislation of the Federal Council of Australasia.[32] Although New South Wales did not join this body, which had virtually no legal powers of its own,[33] New Zealand, Victoria, Tasmania and South Australia did participate in this forum, which reflects another development in non-legal political norms embodying a reorientation away from the UK and towards Australia. So far as naturalisation is concerned, however, it is important to stress that, in this period, the underlying concept was still that of allegiance, common across the Empire, albeit with recognition of discrete communities in particular geo-political subdivisions. This Imperial-Colonial relationship was reflected in oaths of allegiance to 'Her Majesty Queen Victoria as lawful Sovereign of the United Kingdom of Great Britain and Ireland and of this Colony of New South Wales *dependent on and belonging to* the said United Kingdom'.[34] The other relevant reflection of community membership outlined in chapter two for this period is the franchise. When representative government was introduced, it was circumscribed by limitations of allegiance, age, sex, conviction for infamous offences and property, but this was relaxed by degrees such that, by Federation, all adult male subjects of the Queen resident for one year could vote, subject to certain disqualifications.[35]

What the sum of these changes reveals is an increasing consciousness of an emerging identity—based on geography, distinctive colonial history, self-government and an associated identification of distinct needs—but an identity that was self-consciously that of a group within the Empire rather than that of a discrete political society. The changes were encouraged and facilitated by the Imperial institutions at Westminster; while the principal institutions of government for the people of New South Wales were increasingly local, they were those of a dependency: the framework was Imperial, and factors from defence to allegiance show that the political commonweal in which those people participated was intelligible only as part of an Imperial whole. Accordingly, it is submitted that while the manner, nature and extent of changes to non-legal political norms in this period do provide some evidence in support of discontinuity, the better

[31] Above, text to ch 2, n 385.
[32] Above, text to ch 2, n 511.
[33] Above, ch 4, n 63.
[34] *Naturalization Act 1853* (NSW), s 2 (emphasis added).
[35] Above, ch 2.III.B.i.

conclusion is that they import continuity of the underlying social form—and therefore the legal system—rather than discontinuity.

Consideration of the third factor in Raz's model, the interaction between laws and non-legal political norms is instructive in an analysis of continuity that cannot be as clear-cut as in the preceding periods. It was suggested above that, in the legislative and judicial—though not necessarily the executive—spheres, Imperial laws and institutions can be understood to have had an overlapping or amphibious character.[36] That is to say that persuasive support was presented above for the view that institutions and laws that appear to be Imperial might, with increasing cogency, be understood to exist across multiple legal systems and, in so far as they concerned the exercise of functions in New South Wales, be considered institutions and laws of a putative New South Wales legal system rather than of the Imperial legal system. As reconstructed here, Raz's model relies on the application—if necessary, the hypothetical application—of the test of exclusion to adjudicate between notionally competing institutionalised normative systems.[37] Accordingly, the (predicted) critical reactions of individuals and primary organs to the interactions between laws and non-legal norms of the political system must be weighed in light of the nature, manner and extent of the (hypothetical) incompatibility that characterises those interactions. In the case of New South Wales, there is no need to rely on predicted critical reactions to a hypothetical change: at the end of this period, the constitutional structure and the political system that, ex hypothesi, would constitute its political system separate from that of the Empire underwent fundamental change that, because it encompassed all of the Australian Colonies, could only have been effected by laws and institutions that were truly Imperial (rather than Imperial only in form but substantively those of New South Wales). Federation was, as outlined above,[38] substantially home-grown, but the critical attitudes of both officials and the voting population at the time can only be understood as consistent with the reorganisation of a complex and differentiated but undivided *Imperial* political system. Accordingly, despite the not insignificant evidence that might support an argument of discontinuity during the period between responsible government and Federation, the application of the three factors provided in Raz's model leads to the conclusion of continuity of the Imperial political (and therefore legal) system.

In applying Raz's model to New South Wales between settlement and Federation, and characterising New South Wales as a legal and administrative unit within an Imperial whole, a significant inadequacy is revealed in the account: the lack of theoretical tools with which to describe and

[36] Above, 21–23.
[37] Above, 189–91.
[38] Above, ch 2.I.B.i.

analyse a complex social form such as a political system incorporating one or more subsystems. Albeit underdeveloped, an account of partial and total systems was present in Kelsen's model,[39] but no corresponding sophistication is present in Raz's treatment of social forms in general or political systems in particular. Of course, it should be reiterated that Raz's model as a whole is consciously only an 'introduction',[40] and his treatment of continuity in particular does not purport to trespass on the subject matter of social sciences other than law.[41] Accordingly, the possibility of systems and subsystems is by no means excluded. However, application of the account remains potentially uncertain, because it is not clear whether the relevant underlying social form is that of the (total) political system or the (partial) political subsystem. Nonetheless, given the wide range of possible structures and different bases for division and differentiation, it seems that the most defensible course is to regard Raz's model as accounting for continuity with reference to the political system as a (complex) whole, and this was the approach taken above. To do otherwise would entail artificiality of a kind similar to that discerned above when applying a strict criterion of unauthorised constitutional change to the unconstitutional gubernatorial orders before 1823:[42] to make sense of changes at the New South Wales level (or lower) as a discrete legal system, a whole range of laws and non-legal norms of the Imperial political system as a whole that continued to be in force would have to be considered duplicated in that putative New South Wales political system. Such an analysis is strained and unrealistic, and should be rejected. By way of contrast, it should be noted that the similar problem that arose in the context of multiple sufficient basic norms in the application of Kelsen's model[43] is avoided in Raz's account as reconstructed here, in view of the test of exclusion that is integrated into consideration of the third factor. This, relative to Kelsen's account, is a clear strength of Raz's model.

II. FEDERATION AND DISCONTINUITY

A. Federation

Federation was arguably the single most important change to occur in Australia after settlement, from both legal and political perspectives. The six Australian Colonies became States, the federal Commonwealth was brought into existence, and a new and complex phase in the relationships

39 Above, ch 3.III.B.
40 Raz, *Concept of a Legal System* (n 23), 1–2, 208.
41 Above, ch 5, n 116.
42 Above, 127.
43 Above, ch 4.II.B.

between these seven entities, and between the Imperial and Australian authorities and communities, commenced. The question in applying Raz's model to these changes is whether they entailed discontinuity between the *Imperial* political system of which the Australian Colonies were part and any putative emergent Australian legal system(s). In answering that question, it is useful, first, to interrogate the effect of Federation on the political systems of the Colonies-turned-States—not because discontinuity in subsystems would necessarily entail discontinuity in the Imperial political (and therefore legal) system, but because the analysis of those changes at the level of the subsystems is part of the analysis of their effect on the system as a whole.

i. Continuity in the Colonial-turned-State Legal Systems

As set out above,[44] despite their fundamental character, the constitutional and legal changes wrought by the Commonwealth of Australia Constitution Act 1900 (Imp) for the New South Wales political system were only those that were absolutely necessary to effect the federal project and create a new level of government between the New South Wales and Imperial governments. A new High Court was created, but Privy Council appeals continued; new limitations were imposed on New South Wales legislative, executive and judicial power, but, aside from these diminutions in responsibility (the practical effect of which took some time to manifest), the constitutions and laws were substantively 'continue[d]'.[45] The replacement, consequent on Federation, of New South Wales's 1855 constitution by the *Constitution Act 1902* (NSW), together with the further amendments made in 1907,[46] was scarcely more than an exercise in consolidation: the local constitution now acknowledged New South Wales as a State in the Federation and repealed most (but not all) of the Imperial reservation provisions, but it left in place the provisions with respect to disallowance and repugnancy. In terms of the first factor in Raz's account of continuity, while the nature of the legal changes associated with Federation certainly merits their characterisation as constitutional laws of great importance, the manner of those changes (Imperial enactment—but see below in relation to popular participation by referenda approving Federation) does not imply discontinuity between pre- and post-Federation political subsystems in the States, and their extent (as just described) is best considered unsettled at this time.

In terms of changes to non-legal political norms, New South Wales's status as an integer of the Federation was reflected in the new Commonwealth

[44] Above, ch 2.I.A.iv.
[45] *Commonwealth Constitution*, ss 106–108.
[46] Above, text to ch 2, n 120.

flag in 1903[47] and the second set of Commonwealth arms in 1912.[48] Naturalisation and citizenship became a Commonwealth responsibility; though the underlying concept remained that of allegiance (blind to Imperial subdivisions) and nationality was still 'British', an emergent sense of membership of a discrete community was apparent shortly after Federation.[49] After Federation, oaths of allegiance, in the New South Wales, Commonwealth and also the UK contexts, became somewhat opaque, referring simply to allegiance to Her Majesty Queen Victoria, her heirs and successors according to law.[50] The significant changes to the franchise were its extension to women in 1902 and its recognition of residence in the Commonwealth as a qualifying criterion in 1912.[51] The nature, manner and extent of these changes was such as to recognise New South Wales and its community as a part of the political community of the new Australian Commonwealth, but not to deny the fact that both the New South Wales and the Commonwealth political communities were parts of the broader Imperial political system. It is submitted that they point to continuity rather than discontinuity between the pre- and post-Federation political subsystems of the States: the actions of the political community before Federation continued to function as standards for action afterwards, and no new commonweal or distinct political order is revealed.

The central aspect of the material to be considered in evaluating the interaction between the legal and non-legal changes is arguably the fact of popular participation in effecting the changes associated with Federation. As set out above, Federation was ultimately and legally the product of legislation enacted by the Imperial Parliament.[52] However, the changes were the result of over a decade of debate and drafting in Australia, for the most part through collaboration between Colonial officials, many of whom were elected rather than appointed by their governments. The changes were, in addition, the subject of widespread popular discussion through federation leagues and people's conventions; and the substance of the changes was approved (albeit without direct legal effect, with only a limited franchise and with vocal opposition) by referenda in each Colony. The distinctive political consciousness to which these features attest is important, but what is decisive is its organisation largely along the lines of the Colonial polities that became the States. In other words, the interaction between the non-legal political norms that identify the people of New South Wales as a subsystem of the Imperial political subsystem, on the one hand, and the laws that effected Federation and the establishment

[47] Above, text to ch 2, n 350.
[48] Above, text to ch 2, n 342.
[49] Above, text to ch 2, n 520.
[50] Above, text to ch 2, n 625.
[51] Above, 80.
[52] Above, ch 2.I.B.i.

of the State of New South Wales, on the other, point to continuity between the political community of the Colony and the political community of the State. There was, moreover, no conflict between competing institutionalised normative systems in New South Wales before and after Federation.

ii. Continuity in the Imperial Legal System

The last section considered whether the changes associated with Federation revealed any discontinuity between the political communities of the pre-Federation Colonies (as subsystems of the Imperial political system) and those of the post-Federation States, and concluded that they did not. It remains to be evaluated whether the creation of the Commonwealth of Australia nonetheless entailed discontinuity in the Imperial political system—and therefore its legal system—as a whole, so far as Australia is concerned.[53] From the Imperial perspective, the Commonwealth was a new colonial subdivision, and its creation entailed the reorganisation of six existing Colonies into one federal Colony. The nature of the legal changes effected by the Commonwealth of Australia Constitution Act 1900 (Imp) was not novel: Colonies—and even a federal Colony, in Canada—had been created before, with significant powers of self-government. As noted above, the Commonwealth was (at Federation) subject to the standard kinds of Imperial limitations with respect to repugnancy, extra-territorial legislation, disallowance, reservation and lack of international legal personality.[54] The Commonwealth acquired responsibility for defence, and took over the Colonial units existing at Federation, but defence remained in substance an Imperial concern, as the renewed Anglo-Australian Naval Agreement, in particular, illustrates.[55] Accordingly, the application of the first factor in Raz's account of continuity is analytically reminiscent of settlement in 1788. In particular, given that self-government had already been granted—without, as argued above, any consequential discontinuity—it is submitted that the nature, manner, and extent of the legal changes associated with Federation was not such as to entail discontinuity in the Imperial political (and therefore legal) system as a whole.

The application of the second factor is arguably less clear-cut. If six independent political systems merged into a federal system, it is likely that, however this were achieved, an analysis of the change in non-legal political norms would, of itself, suffice to establish discontinuity in the underlying political systems and the emergence of a new social form.

[53] There is no suggestion here that the 'rump' of the Imperial political system would be discontinuous with the system that existed before any change in Australia.

[54] Above, 33.

[55] Above, 56.

This is, as suggested above, a counterpart to the only express example of discontinuity indicated by Raz, that of national independence.[56] However, the creation of a new political subsystem within the Imperial political system—a creation that operated upon, but did not extinguish, pre-existing political subsystems—is a more subtle phenomenon. Insignia of government—flags, arms and a great seal—accompanied the creation of the Commonwealth but did not, for example, displace the continuing pre-eminence of the Union flag,[57] and the choice of enacting words for Commonwealth legislation consciously imitated the forms used at Westminster.[58] The royal style acknowledged the Commonwealth as a Dominion,[59] though oaths of allegiance referred, on their face, to an undifferentiated monarch.[60] Nationality and allegiance, as noted in relation to the States,[61] remained British and transcended subdivisions of the Empire, though locally effective laws on naturalisation and immigration—which restricted the rights of non-Australian British subjects as well as non-British subjects—helped to engender a sense of membership of a discrete Australian community. Further, the franchise was initially the same as that prescribed for the States, with amendments soon after Federation that produced a similar result, save in respect of 'coloured races'.[62] A new level of political organisation in Australia necessarily entailed the creation of a range of new non-legal political norms, as well as consequential alterations to existing norms, both at the level of the States and also in relation to the interactions between the Commonwealth and Imperial authorities. While this brief recapitulation of the survey undertaken in chapter two reveals several respects in which an intelligible Australian commonweal can be discerned, it is submitted that, on balance, Federation itself did not establish a political community sufficiently distinct or autonomous to be considered anything except a part of the Imperial political system. Imperial norms (and laws) continued to function as standards for action and decision, allegiance and international relations still operated (and were conceived of) in Imperial terms, and the power structure and commonweal of the Commonwealth were still bound up at every level with the broader Imperial frame of government and Empire-wide commonweal.

The relevance of popular participation in the Federation process was considered in the last section in terms of the interactions between laws and non-legal political norms so far as continuity between the Colonies and the States as subordinate political systems within the Imperial political

[56] Above, ch 5, n 136.
[57] Above, text to ch 2, n 353.
[58] Above, text to ch 2, nn 280, 285.
[59] Above, text to ch 2, n 321.
[60] Above, 85–86.
[61] Above, text to n 49.
[62] Above, text to ch 2, n 598.

system was concerned. There, the conclusion was that participation, though Australia-wide, was in important respects focused on each Colony, in such a way that it supported continuity not discontinuity. In relation to continuity of the Imperial political system as a whole, it was noted above that some judges and commentators have suggested that popular participation in achieving the federal project might be understood as an exercise of constituent power, either concurrently with, or as an alternative to, the legal constituent power of the Imperial Parliament to effect Federation.[63] Though not necessarily advocating the position, Oliver suggests it would at least have been coherent for Australian judges between 1901 and 1986 to regard Federation as the product of a concurrence of popular sovereignty and Imperial legal sovereignty.[64] Of course, no test case arose and, despite the occasional suggestion from individual judges, no such position has ever been adopted by any primary norm-applying organ in Australia. The more likely counterfactual analysis is that, had a question arisen shortly after Federation, any conflict between Imperial law and post-Federation non-legal political norms would have been resolved in accordance with Imperial law, in such a way that no persistent or insurmountable conflict would have arisen—an analysis, that is, suggesting continuity. The strong influence of Imperial law and of Imperial political norms summarised in the last two paragraphs leaves little room to doubt that these hypothetical critical reactions would reveal the application of Imperial law to the exclusion—or, rather, the consequential adaptation—of local political norms. In any event, a hypothetical is probably not required, because there was a point of difference between the proposals endorsed by popular referendum and the provisions ultimately enacted by the Imperial Parliament: the Imperial Government and Parliament were unhappy with the draft Bill's wide exclusion of Privy Council appeals on matters involving the interpretation of the *Commonwealth Constitution*, and a compromise was reached that resulted in what became the text of section 74.[65] The acquiescence of the Australian people and courts, both at the moment of Federation and thereafter,[66] in relation to section 74 illustrates that the Imperial political and legal system was preferred in the event of any conflicting local legal and political norms, and that this preference led to

[63] Above, 39–40.

[64] PC Oliver, *The Constitution of Independence: the Development of Constitutional Theory in Australia, Canada, and New Zealand* (Oxford, OUP, 2005) 330.

[65] Above, 32–33. Australian opposition to Privy Council appeals arose out of the awareness, in light of prior Canadian experience, of the potential for unsatisfactory decisions, and out of a desire for a final and self-sufficient appellate court in Australia: *Baxter v Commissioners of Taxation (NSW)* (1907) 4 CLR 1087 (HCA), 1111–18 (Griffith CJ, Barton and O'Connor JJ).

[66] Notwithstanding this acquiescence, the High Court soon decided it was not bound by the advice of the Privy Council (above, ch 2, n 108) and granted only one certificate under s 74: above, text to ch 2, n 136.

adaptation of the local norms without sustained conflict. Accordingly, it is submitted that the nature, manner and extent of interactions between laws and non-legal political norms indicates that Federation did not entail discontinuity in the underlying Imperial political system.

B. Federation to the Statute of Westminster

In the period between Federation and the Statute of Westminster 1931 (Imp), the most significant constitutional and legal changes identified above concerned the transfer of State debts to the Commonwealth and the abandonment of the reserved powers doctrine of constitutional interpretation,[67] each of which constitute legal reflections of the 'growing realization that Australians were now one people and Australia one country and that national laws might meet national needs'.[68] Australia as a territorial entity also expanded in this period: the Crown Colony of British New Guinea, having been administered by the Governor of Queensland and underwritten by Queensland, New South Wales and Victoria since 1888 by agreement with the Imperial authorities, became the first external Territory of the Commonwealth.[69] Norfolk Island was similarly placed by the King under the authority of, and accepted by, the Commonwealth in 1914, and Nauru and New Guinea were accepted under League of Nations Mandates,[70] the former to be administered jointly with the UK and New Zealand (but in effect by Australia) and the latter in the name of 'His Britannic Majesty for and on behalf of the Government of the Commonwealth of Australia'.[71] These changes were undoubtedly significant but, in terms of the content-based considerations upon which the first factor in Raz's account of continuity turns, the nature, manner and extent of these changes in laws was not such as to entail discontinuity in the Imperial political system or, therefore, in the legal system.

More can be said with respect to changes to non-legal political norms. As detailed above, the early twentieth century saw a range of constitutional conventions emerge that fundamentally altered the status of the Dominions, including the Commonwealth. The equality of status with the UK proclaimed in the Balfour Declaration, the power to enter international treaties, the convention that the Westminster Parliament would not legislate for a Dominion without its prior request and consent, and

[67] Above, 34.
[68] *Victoria v The Commonwealth* (1971) 122 CLR 353 (HCA), 396 (Windeyer J).
[69] Above, ch 2, n 422.
[70] Above, ch 2, n 425.
[71] *Mandate for the German Possessions in the Pacific Ocean Situated South of the Equator, other than German Samoa and Nauru* (1921) 2 *League of Nations Official Journal* 85 (entered into force: generally and for Australia 17.12.1920), art 1.

the requirement that the King act on the advice of local, national—rather than Imperial—ministers were all non-legal political norms that emerged during the period between Federation and the Statute of Westminster that reshaped the relationship between the Commonwealth (if not necessarily the States) and the Imperial authorities.[72] The Imperial Parliament's side-stepping of Western Australia's petition to secede from the Commonwealth, on the ground that legislation on Australian matters required the consent of the Commonwealth,[73] vividly illustrates both the increasing separateness and autonomy of the Australian political system *and* the shift in the role of Imperial institutions. The legal powers of the latter were undoubted, but the conventional limitations on their exercise were transformative and—again, at least so far as the Commonwealth was concerned—support a characterisation of them as agents of, or within, the Commonwealth legal and political systems: amphibious or trans-systemic institutions with multiple, overlapping roles, as described above.[74] This character also touched the King, who, as noted above,[75] was obliged by the convention that he act on the advice of his Dominion ministers to acquiesce in his Australian Prime Minister's nominee for the post of Governor-General, despite his own misgivings. The same limitations on Imperial power were only partially true in respect of the States: while a convention did emerge that the Imperial Parliament would only legislate with effect in a State at the request and consent of the State, and while the Imperial Government had abandoned its power to issue Instructions to State Governors by the time of the Balfour Declaration, other Imperial links remained and, in particular, the King still acted on Imperial ministerial advice in relation to State matters.[76]

Other non-legal political norms in this period similarly point to an increasingly distinct Australian political community. As flagged above, an Australian military identity—one capable of reconciling both Imperial and Australian aspects—was forged during the Great War, in particular at Gallipoli.[77] The people of Australia were recognised separately in King George VI's coronation oath.[78] The position in relation to norms of community membership, as reflected in nationality and citizenship legislation, is more complex. As explained above,[79] the 'common code' preserved the concept of British nationality across the Empire, but, significantly, the statutory scheme expressly preserved the right of Dominions to enact their

[72] Above, ch 2.I.B.i.
[73] Above, 37–38.
[74] Above, 21–23.
[75] Above, 36.
[76] Above, text to ch 2, n 131.
[77] Above, 56.
[78] Above, ch 2, n 544.
[79] Above, ch 2.III.A.ii.

own nationality laws, and, indeed, the scheme of Imperial naturalisation had to be adopted by a Dominion to come into force there. The consequence of these developments, concurrent with the emergent enhanced status of Dominions, was that the status of a British subject became essentially meaningless: nationality was formally uniform across the Empire but substantively a matter of local regulation. As the Imperial Conferences in 1929 and 1930 concluded, common allegiance and the common status could be preserved while allowing each of the Members of the Commonwealth of Nations to determine whom it would recognise as its own nationals, and by 1937 it was clear that 'membership' of a political community in a part of the Commonwealth of Nations had become entirely separated from the concept of British nationality. It is submitted that the nature, manner and extent of these diverse but consistent changes in non-legal political norms in the period between Federation and the Statute of Westminster 1931 (Imp) was such as to indicate discontinuity in the Imperial political system. While the past norms of the Imperial political system were far from extinct, and still provided a basis for evaluating actions and decisions, they no longer did so across the same breadth of areas, nor with the same force as had previously been the case. Clearer still is the identification of an essentially (though not entirely) autonomous political order that was associated and coordinate with, rather than dependent on and subordinate to, the Imperial political system. Accordingly, while application of Raz's first factor points towards continuity, the second, it is submitted, points towards discontinuity.

It is the third factor to which Raz's account of continuity draws attention that resolves the divergent conclusions reached in applying the first and second factors: the nature, manner and extent of the interactions between laws and the non-legal political norms just described, considered with particular attention to the test of exclusion. It is submitted that the kind of incompatibilities between law and, in particular, constitutional convention in this period were what were described above as adaptations and do not present persistent or insurmountable conflicts.[80] Moreover, if the test of exclusion were applied to a hypothetically insurmountable conflict, it seems reasonable to judge that, notwithstanding the strength and direction of the changed landscape of political convention, the critical reactions of the courts, as well as of ordinary citizens, would have been in favour of Imperial law and convention, not local law and convention—and, again, in a way that would have produced adaptation rather than persistent or insurmountable conflict and open breach. In short, the application of the test to that hypothesis suggests continuity. Accordingly, considering the three factors in the round, and, in particular the critical third factor, it is

[80] Above, 188.

submitted that there was, on Raz's model, no discontinuity in the Imperial political system between Federation and the Statute of Westminster 1931 (Imp), and thus no discontinuity in the legal system associated with it.

C. After the Statute of Westminster

i. Statute of Westminster to the Australia Acts

Imperial law codified constitutional convention in the Statute of Westminster 1931 (Imp), which was adopted by the Commonwealth in 1942, with effect retrospective to the outbreak of war in 1939.[81] This legal change freed the Commonwealth from its colonial status and removed virtually all of the associated Imperial constraints. Further important subsequent constitutional changes brought social welfare within the Commonwealth's sphere of competence, removed the restrictions on the Commonwealth's legislating for Aboriginal people and on their being counted in determining population, permitted representation of the Territories in the Parliament and accorded dominant fiscal power to the Commonwealth over the States, by means of de facto (though not de jure) control over income taxation and the de jure power to make grants to the States on conditions that were legally binding, regardless of the constitutional allocation of legislative powers between the Commonwealth and the States.[82] Privy Council appeals were abolished in federal jurisdiction, with the consequence that the High Court considered itself no longer bound by the Imperial tribunal's decisions, whenever made.[83] The further consequence was the inauguration of a period during which, in the State judicial hierarchy, there were two ultimate appellate courts, neither subject to the other; this afforded the occasion to the New South Wales courts, for example, to choose where their loyalty lay, which they did by holding that it was no longer appropriate for them to grant leave to appeal to the Privy Council.[84] Though in large part simply embodying in law the non-legal political norms that had developed between Federation and the Statute of Westminster, the constitutional and legal changes effected by the Statute and in its aftermath were, it is submitted, legal changes of such a nature, manner and extent as to signify discontinuity. The decision of the courts as primary norm-applying organs no longer to recognise aspects of Imperial law, such as advice of the Privy Council, as standards for action and decision—a change stressed by Oliver[85]—is a central feature to be observed in applying this first factor and also, as will be seen, the third.

[81] Above, ch 2, n 203.
[82] Above, 38–39.
[83] Above, 27.
[84] Above, ch 2, n 141.
[85] Above, ch 5, n 176.

In terms of changes to non-legal political norms, legal reflections of a political community separate from the Imperial whole of which it was originally part are discernible in the conventions established and codified in the preamble to the Statute of Westminster 1931 (Imp) relating to Dominion assent to alterations to the royal style and titles, and in the recasting of those titles themselves, with a distinctly Australian version enacted in 1953 (and promulgated under the great seal of Australia).[86] Also proximate in time to the accession of Queen Elizabeth II was the adoption of distinctive Australian national flags—albeit not displacing the Union flag in popular use for some decades afterwards.[87] Australian ensigns for the armed forces were also in place by the 1970s,[88] when norms of national political independence and consciousness also gained legal recognition through the establishment of the Australian honours system and the adoption of *Advance Australia Fair* as the national anthem, in preference to the British *God Save the Queen*.[89] Legislation first provided for an exclusive title of Australian citizenship in 1949, with associated oaths.[90] Significantly, the concept of allegiance became, by statute, the consequence not the cause of nationality; accordingly, Australians became subjects of the Queen of Australia, while subjects of Her Majesty in right of her other realms came to be aliens from the perspective of the Australian political and legal system. Further changes to norms of community membership are reflected in the abolition of racial exclusions to the Commonwealth franchise, and the substitution of Australian citizenship for the status of British subject as the qualifying nationality criterion for the vote.[91] As noted above, some judges went so far as to suggest that the common understanding of membership of the Australian community as entailing universal adult suffrage was a fact upon which their interpretation of the *Commonwealth Constitution* should operate.[92] It is submitted that the changes to non-legal political norms summarised here, especially considered in light of those of the period between Federation and the Statute of Westminster 1931 (Imp), are of such a nature, manner and extent as unequivocally to point to discontinuity rather than continuity in the Imperial political system. The power structures and commonweal of the political community in Australia were, in other words, no longer those of a component part of an Imperial social form.

Unsurprisingly, it is submitted that the third factor, concerning the interactions between laws and non-legal political norms, similarly indicates

[86] Above, text to ch 2, n 331.
[87] Above, 52.
[88] Above, 53.
[89] Above, ch 2.I.E.iii.
[90] Above, ch 2.III.A.iii.
[91] Above, 82. With the exception of the special case of Norfolk Island, discussed above, ch 2.III.B.iii.
[92] Above, text to ch 2, n 609.

discontinuity rather than continuity. Notwithstanding the Imperial legal roots depicted in the genetic structure of Australian laws, it is suggested that any (hypothetical) conflict between, say, an Act of the Westminster Parliament applying to Australia but enacted without the request and consent of the relevant integer(s) of the Federation would have been held ineffective by Australian courts,[93] and, accordingly, that Raz's test of exclusion identifies critical reactions in favour of the norms of an Australian political and legal system over the (hypothetical) competing Imperial institutionalised normative system. That preference would not have been of the kind described above as adaptation: the conflict would involve preferring not merely an Australian political convention but an Australian statute over an Imperial statute that would, in earlier times, have been regarded as effective by paramount force. Accordingly, it is submitted that a distinct Australian political system, a social form separate from that of the Imperial political system, emerges in this period. This system was no longer a component subsystem of a (total) Imperial political system: while it retained links—important links—with the political system of the UK, the relationship had, before the Statute of Westminster 1931 (Imp), ceased to be characterised by subordination. Critically, after the Statute of Westminster, it is possible to assert—in a way in which, it was submitted above, it was not possible to assert before the Statute—that the interaction between laws and non-legal political norms was such as, in Raz's model, to sustain a conclusion of discontinuity.

ii. The States and the Australia Acts

It might be protested that the analysis above is inconsistent in not discerning discontinuity before the Statute of Westminster 1931 (Imp) effected legal changes that embodied the non-legal norms of political independence of the Commonwealth that preceded the Statute, and then identifying such discontinuity after the Statute of Westminster but before the *Australia Acts* effected parallel legal codification of similar conventional changes in relation to the States. In other words, the fact that the Statute of Westminster applied to the Commonwealth but not to the States might be understood to have left the States as political subsystems subordinate to the Imperial political system. This challenge identifies an important point about the laws and the non-legal political norms that constituted and defined the relationship between the States, the Commonwealth and the Empire, but it is submitted that it does not affect the discontinuity analysis

[93] RD Lumb, 'Fundamental Law and the Processes of Constitutional Change in Australia' (1978) 9 *Federal Law Review* 148, 157–58; A Twomey, *The Australia Acts 1986: Australia's Statutes of Independence* (Leichhardt, NSW, Federation Press, 2010) 375.

propounded above: both the position of the States and the application of Raz's model are more sophisticated than this challenge implies.

Federation altered the relationship between the Empire and the States. That direct links were, quite deliberately, retained is not disputed, though it is salient to note that the links seem not to have been properly understood by Commonwealth or State governments in the 1970s.[94] However, whatever their *legal* features (notably that the Queen acted on the advice of Imperial ministers in relation to State matters), the Imperial response to the Western Australian secession crisis illustrates that, as a matter of—the then Imperial—*social and political form*, Federation had transformed the States from direct political subsystems of the Imperial political system to (more or less) direct political subsystems of the Commonwealth political system, and therefore only indirectly subsystems of the Imperial political system. The legal links between the States and the Imperial authorities that were left untouched by the Statute of Westminster 1931 (Imp) were aspects of the constitutional and legal position assessed in terms of the first factor in Raz's account of continuity above—as, too, were the residual links between the Commonwealth and the Imperial authorities, such as the legislative competence of the Westminster Parliament at the request and consent of the Commonwealth. Raz's account of continuity and discontinuity is not so mechanical as to require complete legal independence—itself not a mechanical or univocal term—in order to conclude that there is discontinuity. The application of the model, with reference to the three factors (dissociated, it is stressed again, only for expository convenience), is sufficiently sophisticated to take account of the complexities presented by the legal and political dimensions of the relationship between the States, the Commonwealth and the Empire. It was submitted above that, before the Statute of Westminster, the application of the factors in the round, and, in particular, the examination of the interactions between laws and non-legal political norms, was not such as to tip the balance in favour of discontinuity. After the Statute of Westminster, it was suggested that, notwithstanding the continuing legal subordination of the States, in certain respects, to Imperial authorities and concerns, the balance of legal and non-legal changes and, again, the assessment of the critical factor of the interaction between them, provided sufficient grounds to discern discontinuity within the terms of Raz's model.

For the sake of completeness, the three factors in Raz's account may be applied to the remaining period, from the *Australia Acts* to the centenary of Federation. The constitutional and legal effects of the *Australia Acts* were outlined above:[95] in summary, residual Imperial links were terminated,

[94] A Twomey, 'Responsible Government and the Divisibility of the Crown' [2008] *PL* 742, 754–55.

[95] Above, ch 2.I.A.v, I.B.iii.

for both the States and the Commonwealth (and consequential changes removing the vestiges of Imperial authority in relation to State Governors were enacted in New South Wales). In this period, the High Court—the sole ultimate appellate court, with the abolition of all appeals to the Privy Council (save for the notional but unreal possibility of a certificate under section 74 of the *Commonwealth Constitution*)[96]—developed the notion of the single common law of Australia.[97] It is submitted that, on the analysis advanced above, pursuant to which a discrete Australian legal system came into existence before the *Australia Acts*, there are significant constitutional and legal changes, but not such, in terms of nature, manner or extent, as to imply discontinuity in that Australian legal system.

Concordant with these legal changes were changes in non-legal political norms that similarly reflect further separation from the Imperial political past, including the simplification of enacting formulae to exclude references to the Queen as a component of both New South Wales and Commonwealth legislatures.[98] Again, these changes build on those of the period after the Statute of Westminster 1931 (Imp) and do not import, in their nature, manner or extent, discontinuity in the Australian legal system.

Finally, it is submitted that the interactions between laws and non-legal political norms in the post-*Australia Acts* period would fall to be analysed in the same terms, and with the same result, as is suggested above in relation to the period between the Statute of Westminster 1931 (Imp) and the *Australia Acts*. One interesting dimension to the application of this factor concerns the debate, recounted above,[99] about which element in the legislative scheme of the *Australia Acts* is the operative one from the perspective of Australian law. This debate encapsulates precisely the kind of interactions between laws and non-legal political norms with which Raz's third factor is concerned. That the courts—primary norm-applying organs—should subsequently have pointed to the exclusive legal sufficiency of the Commonwealth Parliament's legislation on the basis of the non-legal political norms of independence, thus ignoring the genetic relations that also implicate the Westminster Parliament's legislation in the Australian legal system, further supports the conclusion advanced above in relation to the application of the model's test of exclusion. Accordingly, neither the changes in laws and non-legal political norms, nor the interaction between them in the period between the *Australia Acts* and the centenary of Federation, suggests any break in the continuity of the Australian legal system in terms of Raz's model.

[96] Above, 27.
[97] Above, text to ch 2, n 238.
[98] Above, 44, 47.
[99] Above, 29–30.

iii. Discontinuity in the Territories

The survey undertaken in chapter two noted the acquisition (and loss) of Territories in the period following Federation. The circumstances of each differ, and no detailed exploration was presented in relation, in particular, to the non-legal political norms in those Territories before and after acquisition or loss by the Commonwealth. However, some observations may be indicated so far as the constitutional and legal changes the subject of Raz's first factor are concerned. The separation out of territory within the Empire (for example, Van Diemen's Land, South Australia, North Australia [twice], Norfolk Island and Queensland) would likely fall to be evaluated in a similar fashion to the legal changes effecting settlement or—more closely, since it involved no net territorial acquisition—those effecting Federation. These subdivisions and reorganisations, which generally entailed continuity of the laws in force in the territories,[100] were certainly significant, but they were not of such a nature, manner or extent as to imply discontinuity in the Imperial political (and therefore legal) system.

The same observation may be advanced in relation to direct mergers of one territory into another (for example, New Zealand, Norfolk Island, Torres Strait Islands and North Australia), where, again, laws were generally continued subject to inconsistent laws of the incorporating territory.[101] The same observation also applies in relation to the analytically similar cases[102] of acquisition of territory by the Commonwealth by surrender from the States (for example, Federal Capital Territory and Northern Territory) or by placement of territory by the Queen (for example, Ashmore and Cartier Islands, Cocos (Keeling) Islands, Christmas Island and Coral Sea Islands). As noted above, however, Norfolk Island provides an interesting exception, since the continuation of laws on transfer from New South Wales to the Commonwealth was preceded by the wholesale repeal and substitution (albeit in large part re-enactment) of existing law.[103] Whether the legal changes in this instance might have been of such a nature, manner and extent as to suggest discontinuity would require further detailed consideration.

Further consideration might also be necessary in relation to: the repeal of German laws and the reception of Imperial, Commonwealth, Queensland, Papuan and English laws in New Guinea on its acquisition by the Commonwealth;[104] the annexation—meaning the wholesale application of laws without territorial integration—of the Jervis Bay Territory to the

[100] Above, 63.
[101] Above, 63–64.
[102] Above, 64–65.
[103] Above, text to ch 2, n 46.
[104] Above, 65.

Federal Capital Territory;[105] the termination of existing laws in the Territory of Heard Island and McDonald Islands;[106] and the subsequent wholesale application of the laws of Western Australia to Christmas Island and the Cocos (Keeling) Islands.[107] The final, related, curiosity is the position of the three territories administered by an Australian polity but not incorporated into it: British New Guinea (between 1888 and 1906, when it became the Territory of Papua), Norfolk Island (when administered by New South Wales after separation from Tasmania and before acceptance by the Commonwealth) and Nauru.[108] It may tentatively be suggested that only the instances of (German) New Guinea and Nauru are likely, upon closer investigation, to reveal legal changes of such a nature, manner and extent as to point to discontinuity. That discontinuity would be between the pre-existing German (or New Guinean) and Nauruan legal systems and the Imperial legal system that displaced them. The other situations all arose within the Empire (suggesting an analogy to internal reorganisation of the kind seen in continental Australia at Federation), and it is suggested that the substantive legal changes may, in any event, have been less extensive than might initially appear from the bare statutory provisions. Finally, it is submitted that the grant of independence to territories administered by the Commonwealth (for example, Nauru and Papua and New Guinea) did not entail changes in law or in non-legal political norms of such a nature, manner or extent as to entail discontinuity in the 'rump' of the Australian legal system—though, of course, independence does, in Raz's model, entail discontinuity from the point of view of the legal systems subsequently identifiable in Nauru and in Papua New Guinea. So far as the rest of the Australian political and legal system is concerned, these changes were, in several senses, peripheral, and only a minor alteration in the power structures and commonweal of the Australian system was associated with their departures.

III. CONCLUSIONS

This chapter has applied Raz's account of continuity and discontinuity, as reconstructed and amplified in chapter five, to the case of Australia between 1788 and 2001. In the period between settlement and Federation, that application was relatively straightforward to undertake using the tools provided. However, problems were encountered in characterising the self-governing Colony of New South Wales, since total legal and

[105] Above, text to ch 2, n 465.
[106] Above, text to ch 2, n 466.
[107] Above, 65.
[108] Above, ch 2.II.D.

political independence of a nation-state is the model's only example of the emergence of a discontinuous underlying social form. Since a unit within the Imperial whole does not constitute an entirely discrete political society, the case was, in certain respects, adjudged unsettled. While the option of judging a situation unsettled is a realistic and mature feature of Raz's model, the lack of attention in the account to the nature and properties of subsystems of legal systems proved to be a significant weakness. While the paucity of detailed exemplification in Raz's account was again a limiting feature in its application to the period following Federation, this chapter demonstrated that it was possible to develop and apply the several factors and considerations implicated in the model and draw conclusions accordingly. However, the merger of subordinate units was again not clear-cut, since their situation is rather different from the merger of independent national political systems.

The analysis undertaken of the period between Federation and the Statute of Westminster 1931 (Imp) traversed a range of material changes to laws and non-legal political norms. Preliminary findings of continuity as to laws and discontinuity as to non-legal political norms were reconciled in favour of continuity through the test of exclusion that was applied to the interaction between them. After the Statute, all three factors pointed towards discontinuity. It was argued that, notwithstanding the lack of detailed examples, the political form factors that are disclosed in the model, when applied—in particular in relation to Western Australia's attempted secession—necessitated a sophisticated analysis of a kind that was facilitated by Raz's model. It was further contended that discontinuity could be apprehended in a situation involving something less than total legal and political independence of a nation-state. The test of exclusion, in particular, proved essential to the examination of the legal materials and the legal reflections of non-legal political norms: in many instances, no conclusive analysis would have been possible without resort to this device, notwithstanding the general terms in which it is set out in Raz's account.

In terms of the principal objectives of this book, it is submitted that the overall conclusions to be drawn from this analysis are similar to those proposed in light of the application of Kelsen's model. First, Raz's model of continuity and discontinuity was exposed to require elaboration and amplification in important respects, but, so refined, it was also shown to achieve general success in accounting for relevant phenomena in a fashion that accorded with both contemporary and subsequent intuitions. Moving from theory to practice, the process of application afforded the occasion to subject both legal changes and non-legal political developments to scrutiny that challenged those intuitions, although ultimately not requiring their modification in substantive respects.

7

Evaluation

THE PRIMARY OBJECTIVE of this book comprised three elements: critical exposition and reconstruction of Kelsen's and Raz's models; development and enrichment of the accounts where appropriate; and evaluation of the accounts, individually and in comparison. Save for the final dimension, of comparative evaluation, detailed conclusions of the analysis in respect of all three elements—relative to their fit with the facts of the concrete instance of Australia—are set out at the end of chapters three, four, five and six, and those conclusions are not recapitulated here. What remains is to draw together the threads of argument connected to the comparative evaluation of Kelsen's and Raz's accounts. The first objective thus concluded, it will be germane to offer some concluding reflections on the ways in which the fine-grained application of the accounts has enhanced an understanding of Australian legal systems between 1788 and 2001.

I. CONTINUITY IN THEORY: FIT AND EXPLANATORY POWER

As noted in chapter one, factors that influence the degree of fit between a theoretical model and the facts for which it purports to offer an account include consistency, accuracy, efficiency and concordance with intuitive judgements made by contemporary or subsequent participants, observers or commentators.[1] Articulation of some new insight into, or understanding of, the facts was suggested as a further factor distinguishing an account that achieves a good fit, relative to other accounts.

In terms of consistency, close analysis and critical reconstruction of Kelsen's account demonstrated the need to appreciate subtleties concerning the different principles governing—and the different operation of the exceptions to the account in relation to—the continuity of partial legal systems, as well as the relationship between total and partial legal systems, national legal systems and historically first constitutions. Moreover, at the theoretical level, some amplification of the account—in particular, the addition of a principle of ultimacy—proved necessary in order to justify

[1] Above, 2.

some of the exceptions. Some measure of consistency in the operation of the criterion of authorised constitutional change thus had to be sacrificed to avoid ad hoc solutions that produced an acceptable fit in practice but appeared arbitrary in principle. The theoretical and practical—applied—analysis of Raz's account revealed little in the way of inconsistencies in the model, but it did expose significant shortcomings, both in terms of insufficiently detailed explication of the operation of the conceptual tools it provided and in terms also of largely under-theorised phenomena such as subsystems or partial legal systems. Important dimensions of the account—in particular, the mode of analysing changes in non-legal political norms and their interactions with changes to laws—required amplification, although pursuing the indications within the account and within selected aspects of Raz's broader scholarship proved fruitful in filling in many of these gaps. There is, accordingly, little to separate the accounts in terms of internal coherence or consistency in their application to the facts.

Differentiation is possible, however, in relation to accuracy in characterising the facts in all their complexity. It was necessary to suggest modifications to Kelsen's account to overcome a counter-intuitive and unreal result on the hypothesis that early gubernatorial legislation was unconstitutional but tolerated and effective over a period of some 30 years. Further, Kelsen's model of federal systems required adjustment to remove an unwarranted equation between central and total legal systems, which distorted the characterisation of the Australian Federation. In contrast, the relatively open texture of the concepts employed in Raz's model, and its reference to a wide range of considerations from neighbouring disciplines, meant that the account could be applied with marked sophistication, flexibility and sensitivity to the facts. Accordingly, Raz's account achieves a better fit from the perspective of accuracy in characterising the relevant materials.

The third measure of fit, efficiency of application, is perhaps insignificant relative to other factors but highlights a distinction in evaluating Kelsen's and Raz's accounts. The only major problem in applying Kelsen's account concerned the identification of the basic norm when inference from the relevant legal materials was consistent with presupposing multiple sufficient basic norms. Since the basic norm is central to the model, the significance of that problem is not to be underestimated. On the other hand, because it adopts a criterion that operates as a bright-line test, because it requires reference—only—to legal materials of standard kinds, and because it includes detailed provision for total and partial legal systems and a developed set of principles and exceptions, the model otherwise proved straightforward to apply. In contrast, Raz's account is encapsulated at a higher level of abstraction, and calls for more subtle judgements about the relevance and weight of (legal reflections of) changes in the non-legal norms of the underlying political society, according to criteria that are not susceptible of detailed elaboration in advance or of mechanical application. In terms of accuracy, the realism this approach affords is a mark of sophistication—and the possibility of judging a case unsettled, expressly granted in the account, was characterised above as a mark of maturity—but it also signifies at least the potential for difficulty in application. Accordingly, Kelsen's model emerges as the more successful from the perspective of efficiency, even if that be a relatively unimportant measure.

With one exception, both models (including both versions of Kelsen's model) ultimately proved serviceable in their practical application to the facts and—perhaps contrary to expectations—reached a similar conclusion in identifying the emergence of a discrete Australian legal system, discontinuous with the Imperial legal system, in the margins of the Statute of Westminster 1931 (Imp) and its adoption in Australia. This conclusion—and the conclusions that there was otherwise continuity within the Imperial legal system before the Statute of Westminster and within the Australian legal system thereafter—accords with contemporary judgements expressed by participants within the system, and also with subsequent appraisals by participants, observers and commentators. The exception is the unreal result generated by the application of Kelsen's model in an unmodified form to the arguably unconstitutional general orders of early Governors. In light of this unacceptable discordance and the fact that the test of exclusion in Raz's model directly incorporates critical reactions of contemporary participants, Raz's account is, on balance, to be preferred, according to the measure of concordance with intuitive judgements made about the diachronic identity of legal systems.

The final general measure of the degree of fit recognises value in an account that articulates some new or original insight. This is a difficult measure to apply. On the one hand, Raz's model, in virtue of its reference to neighbouring disciplines, necessarily invites and facilitates a wider range of insights. On the other hand, there is great depth and complexity in Kelsen's account, within the carefully and deliberately drawn analytical parameters he imposes. To take a particular example, the test of exclusion in Raz's account capitalises on the insight that legal systems represent only one dimension of political and social systems, while Kelsen's treatment of continuity by reference to international law and his characterisation of total and partial legal systems teases out more subtle insights arising from a legal system's relationship to other legal systems. On balance, given that the reconstructed and amplified renditions of the accounts presented in this book reveal a greater degree of convergence between the models than has generally been supposed, Raz's model is to be preferred on this measure because it *expressly* directs attention to the kinds of matters that ultimately enter into both accounts, whereas Kelsen's strictures preclude his grappling explicitly with some of the considerations that drive his conclusions—especially in relation to national independence.

This comparative evaluation of Kelsen's and Raz's accounts—and, in particular, the demonstration of their convergence in practice—perhaps hints at the possibility of a hybrid approach, combining strengths and insights from each account. Such a hybrid approach might, for example, deploy Raz's insights about the interaction between legal and non-legal norms of a political system to explain and regularise resort to principles of legitimacy and ultimacy as exceptions to Kelsen's principle of authorised constitutional change. It might also draw on Kelsen's conceptualisation of total and partial legal systems to articulate largely unexpressed assumptions about social groups in Raz's model, providing a means to begin to express and classify the sophistications that that more abstract, flexible account offers. In many ways, the outlines of such an approach are already present in Raz's account, which recognises the 'importance of those autonomous considerations which do contribute to a doctrine of identity'[2] but seeks to supplement intra-systemic criteria of continuity or discontinuity with reference to extra-systemic indicia of community. As indicated at the end of the last paragraph, it is for this reason that Raz's account ultimately possesses greater explanatory power.

II. CONTINUITY IN PRACTICE: AUSTRALIA 1788–2001

The central explanatory focus for the theoretical accounts applied in this book were the phenomena reflected in the legal materials concerning continuity and discontinuity. In terms of that primary enquiry, the application of the theoretical accounts has been shown to offer new means of understanding the evolution of Australian legal systems between 1788 and 2001. For example, the light of theory—whether implicating intra-systemic hierarchical relationships between norms, or invoking economic and political conventions constituting non-legal norms of social identity—prompted reflection on the character of the relationship between the Imperial (total) and New South Wales (partial) legal systems over time. In particular, it revealed a case for reconceptualising as amphibious, or overlapping, the role of Imperial laws, such as the New South Wales Constitution Act 1855 (Imp), and institutions, including the Privy Council, during the late nineteenth and early twentieth centuries. Theoretical modelling provided criteria by which to apprehend relevant legal hierarchies as well as connections in political society, community and commonweal, and by which to understand the relationship between those connections and norms of legal control and autonomy. Appreciating the relevant materials in terms of these criteria and applying theoretical devices such as Raz's

[2] J Raz, *The Concept of a Legal System: An Introduction to the Theory of Legal System*, 2nd edn (Oxford, Clarendon Press, 1980) 212.

test of exclusion or Kelsen's notion of historically first constitutions helped clarify the interrelationship between Colonial, State, Commonwealth and Imperial legal systems, both before and after Federation. Where that application encountered difficulties, the modifications of theory explored in consequence—such as historically sufficient constitutions and quasi-transcendental-logical historically first constitutions—facilitated yet more sophisticated engagement with the rich detail of Australian law and history. Subject always to the soundness of the theories and their underlying assumptions, an understanding informed by theory thus assisted in evaluating claims about the nature of Australian legal systems and the time at which they became distinct or independent.

Beyond their application to phenomena of continuity, Kelsen's and Raz's theoretical accounts also provided a conceptual framework within which other particular historical and doctrinal controversies could be classified, and their significance explained. For example, applying a theoretical understanding of total and partial legal systems, and a model for weighing legal and non-legal indicia of community, provided modes of conceptualising the establishment of a dependency that blurred doctrinal categories, in being at once a settled colony, a crown colony and a military penitentiary.[3] Those understandings similarly assisted in comprehending that legal system's place as a self-governing but legally subordinate political community within an undifferentiated Imperial scheme of government and, ultimately, its integration into a federal structure that came to embody a distinct underlying social form. The theoretical accounts similarly revealed means by which we might grasp apparently anomalous doctrinal features, such as the States' residual pre-*Australia Acts* Imperial links—features that Western Australia's attempted secession and 1970s confusion about the role of UK ministers suggest may have been misunderstood by contemporary participants.

Even where the potential for practical problems was plainly appreciated by participants in the legal system—as in the cases, for example, of invalid gubernatorial orders and of multiple coordinate ultimate courts of appeal—the nature and scope of those problems was elucidated, and the solutions adopted were explained (and perhaps in some measure legitimated), by consideration from a theoretical perspective that highlighted the possible systemic consequences of effective but unconstitutional rule-making and of divergent reason-giving by primary norm-applying organs. At a still more finely grained level of analysis, the systematic application of criteria implicated in the theoretical models uncovered the reason for early colonial laws' focus on denization rather than naturalisation, and exposed the broader significance of formal—and perhaps largely unnoticed—practices in the use of enacting formulae by Australian

[3] Above, ch 2, n 27.

legislatures after 1824. In sum, the exercise of mutual reflection and adaptation involved in applying theoretical accounts to the concrete historical instance of Australia served to refine our understanding of Australian law, as well as our understanding of the accounts, at both macroscopic and microscopic levels.

***

Kelsen's and Raz's models are only two accounts of continuity. Their overall successes and failures, as revealed in this book, together with the demonstration that Australia between 1788 and 2001 is an especially challenging, interesting and fruitful example, point the way for future enquiries relating to other accounts of the temporal continuity and discontinuity of legal systems. It may be that criteria other than authorised constitutional change and underlying social form, or a combination of those criteria, would prove more successful in unifying a sequence of momentary legal systems as a project in time—or that the sequence-of-sets analysis should be abandoned in favour of more diachronic notions such as tradition or melody. Further, it may be that testing accounts by reference to additional, more richly normative criteria connected with justice and with desirable forms of social life would illuminate different strengths and weaknesses from those identified by evaluating their factual fit and explanatory power. In any event, it is submitted that, by combining a critical conceptual analysis of Kelsen's and Raz's accounts with the insights gained by applying them to the particular historical instance of Australia between 1788 and 2001, this book has advanced—if only by a step or two—our understanding of a persistent and fascinating aspect of theorising about legal systems.

Bibliography

Anon, 'ANZAC Legend' in *The Oxford Companion to Australian Military History*, 2nd edn (Melbourne, OUP, 2008) 37

—— 'Colonial Naval Defence Act' in *The Oxford Companion to Australian Military History*, 2nd edn (Melbourne, OUP, 2008) 147

—— 'Judicial Evidence taken by Mr Commissioner Bigge' (1819) in Watson, F (ed), *Historical Records of Australia*, vol 1, Series IV (Sydney, Library Committee of the Commonwealth Parliament, 1922) 755

Adler, MD and Himma, KE, 'Introduction' in Adler, MD and Himma, KE (eds), *The Rule of Recognition and the US Constitution* (Oxford, OUP, 2009) xiii

Arnold, C, 'Institutional Aspects of Law' (1979) 42 *MLR* 667

Aroney, N, 'A Public Choice? Federalism and the Prospects of a Republican Preamble' (1999) 20 *University of Queensland Law Journal* 262

Barber, NW, *The Constitutional State* (Oxford, OUP, 2010)

Bell, J, 'Legal Revolutions and the Continuity of Public Law' in Attwooll, E (ed), *Shaping Revolution* (Aberdeen, Aberdeen University Press, 1991) 119

Bennion, FAR, *Bennion on Statutory Interpretation*, 5th edn (London, LexisNexis, 2008)

Bent, E, 'Deputy Judge-Advocate Bent to Earl Bathurst' (1814) in Watson, F (ed), *Historical Records of Australia*, vol 1, Series IV (Sydney, Library Committee of the Commonwealth Parliament, 1922) 100

—— 'Deputy Judge-Advocate Bent to Earl Bathurst' (1815) in Watson, F (ed), *Historical Records of Australia*, vol 1, Series IV (Sydney, Library Committee of the Commonwealth Parliament, 1922) 122

Bentham, J, *A Plea for the Constitution* (London, Mawman, Poultry and Hatchard, 1803)

Besant, CW, 'Two Nations, Two Destinies: A Reflection on the Significance of the Western Australian Secession Movement to Australia, Canada and the British Empire' (1990) 20 *University of Western Australia Law Review* 209

Blackstone, W, *Commentaries on the Laws of England*, 16th edn (London, Butterworths, 1825)

Brazil, P, 'Australian Nationality and Immigration' in Ryan, KW (ed), *International Law in Australia*, 2nd edn (North Ryde, NSW, LBC, 1984) 210

Campbell, E, 'Prerogative Rule in New South Wales, 1788–1823' (1964) 50 *Royal Australian Historical Society Journal* 161

Campbell, J, *The Lives of the Lord Chancellors and Keepers of the Great Seal of England*, vol 1 (London, John Murray, 1845)

Campbell, WB, 'A Note on Jeremy Bentham's "A Plea for the Constitution of New South Wales"' (1951) 25 *Australian Law Journal* 59

Carney, G, *The Constitutional Systems of the Australian States and Territories* (Cambridge, CUP, 2006)

Castles, AC, *An Australian Legal History* (Sydney, LBC, 1982)

—— *An Introduction to Australian Legal History* (Sydney, LBC, 1971)
Cicero, *De Legibus*, original c. 46–43 BC (Keyes, CW tr, Cambridge, Mass, Harvard University Press, 1928)
Clive, E, 'Law-Making in Scotland: From APS to ASP' (1999) 3 *Edinburgh Law Review* 131
Commonwealth of Australia, Parliamentary Library, *Parliamentary Handbook of the Commonwealth of Australia*, 31st edn (Canberra, 2008)
Craven, GJ, 'A Few Fragments of State Constitutional Law' (1990) 20 *University of Western Australia Law Review* 353
de Garis, BK, 'The Colonial Office and the Commonwealth Constitution Bill' in Martin, AW (ed), *Essays in Australian Federation* (Melbourne, Melbourne University Press, 1969) 94
Deakin, A, 'The Federal Council of Australasia' (1895) 6 *Review of Reviews for Australasia* 154
Dicey, AV, *Introduction to the Study of the Law of the Constitution*, 1st edn 1885, 10th edn (London, Macmillan, 1959)
Dillon, A, 'A Turtle by Any Other Name: The Legal Basis of the Australian Constitution' (2001) 29 *Federal Law Review* 241
Duxbury, N, 'Kelsen's Endgame' (2008) 67 *CLJ* 51
Dworkin, RM, *Justice in Robes* (Cambridge, Mass, Harvard University Press, 2006)
—— 'Comments on the Unity of Law (A Response)' in Kiefer, HE and Munitz, MK (eds), *Ethics and Social Justice* (Albany, NY, State University of New York Press, 1970) 200
Else-Mitchell, R, 'The Foundation of New South Wales and the Inheritance of the Common Law' (1963) 49 *Royal Australian Historical Society Journal* 1
Evatt, HV, 'The Legal Foundations of New South Wales' (1938) 11 *Australian Law Journal* 409
Field, B, 'Legal opinion on validity of duties imposed in the colony' (1818) in Watson, F (ed), *Historical Records of Australia*, vol 9, Series I (Sydney, Library Committee of the Commonwealth Parliament, 1917) 774
Finnis, JM, 'Revolutions and Continuity of Law' (1971) in *Philosophy of Law—Collected Essays: Volume IV* (Oxford, OUP, 2011) 407
—— 'Nationality and Alienage' (2007) in *Human Rights and Common Good—Collected Essays: Volume III* (Oxford, OUP, 2011) 133
—— 'Common Law Constraints: Whose Common Good Counts?' (2008) *University of Oxford Faculty of Law Legal Studies Research Paper Series Working Paper No 10/2008*, available at <http://papers.ssrn.com/sol3/papers.cfm?abstract_id=1100628>
—— 'The Responsibilities of the United Kingdom Parliament and Government under the Australian Constitution' (1983) 9 *Adelaide Law Review* 91
Finnis, JM and Carnegie, AR, 'Constitutional Law' [1969] *Annual Survey of Commonwealth Law* 1
Foley, K, 'The Australian Constitution's Influence on the Common Law' (2003) 31 *Federal Law Review* 131
Frame, T, 'Royal Australian Navy' in Dennis, P and others (eds), *The Oxford Companion to Australian Military History*, 2nd edn (Melbourne, OUP, 2008) 466
Glenn, HP, 'Doin' the Transsystemic: Legal Systems and Legal Traditions' (2005) 50 *McGill Law Journal* 863

Golding, MP, 'Kelsen and the Concept of "Legal System"' in Summers, RS (ed), *More Essays in Legal Philosophy: General Assessments of Legal Philosophies* (Oxford, Blackwell, 1971) 69

Goldring, JL, 'The Australia Act 1986 and the Formal Independence of Australia' [1986] *PL* 192

Green, MS, 'Legal Revolutions: Six Mistakes about Discontinuity in the Legal Order' (2005) 83 *North Carolina Law Review* 331

—— 'Hans Kelsen and the Logic of Legal Systems' (2003) 54 *Alabama Law Review* 365

Greenawalt, K, 'The Rule of Recognition and the Constitution' (1987) in Adler, MD and Himma, KE (eds), *The Rule of Recognition and the US Constitution* (Oxford, OUP, 2009) 1

Grey, J, *The Australian Army: A History* (Melbourne, OUP, 2001)

Harris, JW, 'The Basic Norm and the Basic Law' (1994) 24 *Hong Kong Law Journal* 207

—— 'Kelsen, Revolutions and Normativity' in Attwooll, E (ed), *Shaping Revolution* (Aberdeen, Aberdeen University Press, 1991) 1

—— 'When and Why Does the Grundnorm Change?' (1971) 29 *CLJ* 103

Hart, HLA, *The Concept of Law*, 2nd edn (Oxford, OUP, 1994)

—— 'Kelsen's Doctrine of the Unity of Law' (1970) in *Essays in Jurisprudence and Philosophy* (Oxford, OUP, 1983) 309

—— 'The Morality of Law (Book Review)' (1965) 78 *Harvard Law Review* 1281

Hartney, M, 'Introduction: The Final Form of The Pure Theory of Law' in Kelsen, H, *General Theory of Norms* (Hartney, M tr, Oxford, Clarendon Press, 1991) ix

Holdsworth, W, *A History of English Law*, vol 2, 4th edn(London, Methuen, 1936)

Honoré, AM, 'What is a Group?' (1975) in *Making Law Bind: Essays Legal and Philosophical* (Oxford, Clarendon Press, 1987) 52

—— 'Groups, Laws and Obedience' (1973) in *Making Law Bind: Essays Legal and Philosophical* (Oxford, Clarendon Press, 1987) 32

—— 'Reflections on Revolutions' (1967) 2 *Irish Jurist* 268

Hubbard, FP, '"One Man's Theory ...": A Metatheoretical Analysis of HLA Hart's Model of Law' (1976) 36 *Maryland Law Review* 39

Irving, H (ed), *The Centenary Companion to Australian Federation* (Cambridge, CUP, 1999)

Jackson, BS, 'Who Enacts Statutes?' (1997) 18 *Statute Law Review* 177

Jakab, A, 'Problems of the *Stufenbaulehre*: Kelsen's Failure to Derive the Validity of a Norm from Another Norm' (2007) 20 *Canadian Journal of Law and Jurisprudence* 35

Jenks, E, *A History of the Australasian Colonies* (Cambridge, CUP, 1896)

Kelsen, H, *General Theory of Norms, Allgemeine Theorie der Normen*, first published 1979 (Hartney, M tr, Oxford, Clarendon Press, 1991)

—— 'The Function of a Constitution' in Tur, RHS and Twining, W (eds), *Essays on Kelsen*, 'Die Funktion der Verfassung', first published 1964 (Stewart, I tr, Oxford, Clarendon Press, 1986) 111

—— *Pure Theory of Law, Reine Rechtslehre*, first published 1960, 2nd edn (Knight, M tr, Berkley, Ca, University of California Press, 1967)

—— 'On the Pure Theory of Law' (1966) 1 *Israel Law Review* 1

—— 'Professor Stone and the Pure Theory of Law' (1965) 17 *Stanford Law Review* 1128

—— 'Sovereignty and International Law' (1960) 48 *Georgetown Law Journal* 627

—— 'Law, State, and Justice in the Pure Theory of Law' (1948) in *What is Justice? Justice, Law, and Politics in the Mirror of Science* (Berkeley, Ca, University of California Press, 1957) 288

—— *General Theory of Law and State* (Wedberg, A tr, New York, Harvard University Press, 1945

—— 'The Pure Theory of Law and Analytical Jurisprudence' (1941) 55 *Harvard Law Review* 44

Kerr, A, *A Federation in These Seas* (Canberra, Attorney General's Department, 2009)

King, PG, 'Memorandum on the legality of government and general orders' (1806) in Watson, F (ed), *Historical Records of Australia*, vol 1, Series IV (Sydney, Library Committee of the Commonwealth Parliament, 1922) 43

Kingston, B, *A History of New South Wales* (Port Melbourne, CUP, 2006)

Kwan, E, 'National Parliament, National Symbols: From British to Australian Identity' (Senate Occasional Lecture Series, Canberra, 04.05.2007)

—— 'Celebrating Australia: A History of Australia Day' (2007), available at <http://www.australiaday.org.au/australia-day/history/>

La Nauze, JA, *The Making of the Australian Constitution* (Melbourne, Melbourne University Press, 1972)

Latham, RTE, *The Law and the Commonwealth* (London, OUP, 1949)

Lindell, G, 'Further Reflections on the Date of the Acquisition of Australia's Independence' in French, R, Lindell, G and Saunders, C (eds), *Reflections on the Australian Constitution* (Annandale, NSW, Federation Press, 2003) 51

—— 'Why is Australia's Constitution Binding?—The Reasons in 1900 and Now, and the Effect of Independence' (1986) 16 *Federal Law Review* 29

Lumb, RD, 'Fundamental Law and the Processes of Constitutional Change in Australia' (1978) 9 *Federal Law Review* 148

MacCormack, G, '"Law" and "Legal System"' (1979) 42 *MLR* 285

MacCormick, DN, 'Does the United Kingdom Have a Constitution? Reflections on MacCormick v Lord Advocate' (1978) 29 *Northern Ireland Legal Quarterly* 1

—— 'Constitutional and Administrative Law (Book Review)' [1972] *PL* 174

Maher, G, 'Custom and Constitutions' (1981) 1 *OJLS* 167

—— 'Analytical Jurisprudence and Revolution' in Curiel, JL (ed), *Memoria del X Congreso Mundial Ordinario de Filosofía del Derecho y Filosofía Social*, vol V (Mexico City, Universidad Nacional Autónoma de México, 1981) 343

—— 'The Identity of the Scottish Legal System' [1977] *Juridical Review* 21

Maitland, FW, *The Constitutional History of England* (Cambridge, CUP, 1908)

—— 'The Crown as Corporation' (1901) 17 *LQR* 131

Martin, WL, 'The British Constitution' (1904) 12 *American Lawyer* 179

McPherson, BH, *The Reception of English Law Abroad* (Brisbane, Supreme Court of Queensland Library, 2007)

Menzies, RG, *Afternoon Light* (London, Cassell, 1967)

Moore, WH, 'The Australian Commonwealth Constitution, 1901–2' (1903) 5 *Journal of the Society of Comparative Legislation* 115

Mordike, J, *An Army for a Nation* (Sydney, Allen & Unwin, 1992)

Moshinsky, M, 'Re-Enacting the Constitution in an Australian Act' (1989) 18 *Federal Law Review* 134

Navarro, PE and Moreso, JJ, 'Applicability and Effectiveness of Legal Norms' (1997) 16 *Law and Philosophy* 201

Nicolson, H, *King George the Fifth: His Life and Reign* (London, Constable & Co, 1952)

O'Brien, B, 'The Australia Acts' in Ellinghaus, MP, Bradbrook, AJ and Duggan, AJ (eds), *The Emergence of Australian Law* (Sydney, Butterworths, 1989) 337

Oliver, PC, *The Constitution of Independence: the Development of Constitutional Theory in Australia, Canada, and New Zealand* (Oxford, OUP, 2005)

—— 'The 1982 Patriation of the Canadian Constitution: Reflections on Continuity and Change' (1994) 28 *Revue Juridique Themis* 875

Parry, C, *Nationality and Citizenship Laws of the Commonwealth and of the Republic of Ireland* (London, Stevens & Sons, 1957)

Paulson, SL, 'Arriving at a Defensible Periodization of Hans Kelsen's Legal Theory' (1999) 19 *Oxford Journal of Legal Studies* 351

—— 'Introduction' in Paulson, SL and Paulson, BL (eds), *Normativity and Norms: Critical Perspectives on Kelsenian Themes* (Oxford, OUP, 1998) xxiii

—— 'Four Phases in Hans Kelsen's Legal Theory? Reflections on a Periodization' (1998) 18 *OJLS* 153

—— 'Kelsen's Legal Theory: the Final Round' (1992) 12 *OJLS* 265

Pickert, P, 'The Concept of a Legal System (Book review)' (1975) 20 *American Journal of Jurisprudence* 154

Pierce, JO, 'Constitutional Phases of English History in the Seventeenth Century' (1903) 37 *American Law Review* 26

Plutarch, 'Theseus' in *Plutarch's Lives*, vol I, original 1st century AD (Perrin B, tr, London, Heinemann, 1914) 1

Postema, GJ, 'Melody and Law's Mindfulness of Time' (2004) 17 *Ratio Juris* 203

Premier's Department of New South Wales, *Emblem Book of the State of New South Wales* (Sydney, New South Wales, Premier's Department, 2002)

Quick, J and Garran, RR, *The Annotated Constitution of the Australian Commonwealth* (Sydney, Angus & Robertson, 1901)

Rawls, J, *A Theory of Justice*, revised edn (Oxford, OUP, 1999)

Raz, J, 'The Institutional Nature of Law' (1975) in *The Authority of Law*, 2nd edn (Oxford, OUP, 2009) 103

—— 'Incorporation by Law' (2003) in *Between Authority and Interpretation: On the Theory of Law and Practical Reason* (Oxford, OUP, 2009) 182

—— 'The Identity of Legal Systems' (1971) in *The Authority of Law*, 2nd edn (Oxford, OUP, 2009) 78

—— 'The Functions of Law' (1973) in *The Authority of Law*, 2nd edn (Oxford, OUP, 2009) 163

—— 'Multiculturalism' (1998) 11 *Ratio Juris* 193

—— 'Multiculturalism: A Liberal Perspective' in *Ethics in the Public Domain: Essays in the Morality of Law and Politics*, rev edn (Oxford, Clarendon Press, 1995) 170

—— 'Legal Rights' in *Ethics in the Public Domain: Essays in the Morality of Law and Politics*, rev edn (Oxford, Clarendon Press, 1995) 254

—— *Practical Reason and Norms*, 2nd edn (Oxford, OUP, 1990)

—— 'The Nature of Rights' in *The Morality of Freedom* (Oxford, OUP, 1988) 165
—— *The Concept of a Legal System: An Introduction to the Theory of Legal System*, 2nd edn (Oxford, Clarendon Press, 1980)
—— 'On the Functions of Law' in Simpson, AWB (ed), *Oxford Essays in Jurisprudence (Second Series)* (Oxford, Clarendon Press, 1973) 278
Roberts-Wray, K, *Commonwealth and Colonial Law* (London, Stevens & Sons, 1966)
Roos, NHM, 'The Identity of Legal Systems in the Light of some Paradoxes of Constitutional Law' in Attwooll, E (ed), *Shaping Revolution* (Aberdeen, Aberdeen University Press, 1991) 56
Rosenthal, D, 'The Concept of a Legal System (Book review)' (1971) 88 *South African Law Journal* 142
Ross, A, 'On Self-Reference and a Puzzle in Constitutional Law' (1969) 78 *Mind* 1
Selway, BM, 'The Constitutional Role of the Queen of Australia' (2003) 32 *Commonwealth Law World Review* 248
Shepherd, S and Gifford, R, 'Opinion re illegality of taxes imposed by governors in NSW' (1819) in Watson, F (ed), *Historical Records of Australia*, vol 1, Series IV (Sydney, Library Committee of the Commonwealth Parliament, 1922) 330
Stephen, J, 'Opinion re prosecution under port regulations' (1823) in Watson, F (ed), *Historical Records of Australia*, vol 1, Series IV (Sydney, Library Committee of the Commonwealth Parliament, 1922) 486
—— 'Opinion re validity of statute 20 George II c xix' (1822) in Watson, F (ed), *Historical Records of Australia*, vol 1, Series IV (Sydney, Library Committee of the Commonwealth Parliament, 1922) 412
Stone, J, *Legal System and Lawyers' Reasonings* (London, Stevens & Sons, 1964)
Stubbs, W, *The Constitutional History of England*, vol 3, first published Clarendon Press 1897, 5th edn (New York, Barnes & Noble, 1967)
Sutherland, JG, *Statutes and Statutory Construction*, vol I, 2nd edn (Lewis, J ed, Chicago, Ill, Callaghan & Co, 1904)
Swinfen, DB, 'The Legal Status of Royal Instructions to Colonial Governors' [1968] *Juridical Review* 21
Tayyab, M, 'Jurisprudence of Successful Treason: Coup d'Etat & Common Law' (1994) 27 *Cornell International Law Journal* 49
Teles, MG, 'Revolution, *Lex Posterior* and *Lex Nova*' in Attwooll, E (ed), *Shaping Revolution* (Aberdeen, Aberdeen University Press, 1991) 69
Thomson, JA, 'Altering the Constitution: Some Aspects of Section 128' (1983) 13 *Federal Law Review* 323
Twomey, A, *The Australia Acts 1986: Australia's Statutes of Independence* (Leichhardt, NSW, Federation Press, 2010)
—— 'The States, the Commonwealth and the Crown—the Battle for Sovereignty' in Walsh, K (ed), *Papers on Parliament No 48: The Senate and Accountability* (Canberra, Department of the Senate, 2008) 21
—— 'Responsible Government and the Divisibility of the Crown' [2008] *PL* 742
—— 'The Making of the *Australia Acts* 1986' in Winterton, G (ed), *State Constitutional Landmarks* (Sydney, Federation Press, 2006) 167
—— *The Constitution of New South Wales* (Annandale, NSW, Federation Press, 2004)
—— 'International Law and the Executive' in Opeskin, BR and Rothwell, DR (eds), *International Law and Australian Federalism* (Melbourne, Melbourne University Press, 1997) 69

Watson, F, 'Editorial Note' in Watson, F (ed), *Historical Records of Australia*, vol 1, Series IV (Sydney, Library Committee of the Commonwealth Parliament, 1922) v
—— 'Introduction' in Watson, F (ed), *Historical Records of Australia*, vol 1, Series IV (Sydney, Library Committee of the Commonwealth Parliament, 1922) vii
Wentworth, WC, *A Statistical, Historical, and Political Description of The Colony of New South Wales, and its dependent Settlements in Van Diemen's Land*, 2nd edn (London, G and WB Whittaker, 1820)
Western Australia, Parliament, *The Case of the People of Western Australia* (Perth, Government Printer, 1934)
Wheare, KC, *Federal Government*, 4th edn (London, OUP, 1963)
Wight, M, *The Development of the Legislative Council 1606–1945* (London, Faber & Faber, 1946)
Wilcox, C, 'Colonial Military Forces' in Dennis, P and others (eds), *The Oxford Companion to Australian Military History*, 2nd edn (Melbourne, OUP, 2008) 143
Williams, JM, *The Australian Constitution: A Documentary History* (Melbourne, Melbourne University Press, 2005)
Windeyer, WJV, '"A Birthright and Inheritance": The Establishment of the Rule of Law in Australia' (1962) 1 *Tasmanian University Law Review* 635
—— *Lectures on Legal History* (Sydney, LBC, 1938)
Winterton, GG, 'The Acquisition of Independence' in French, R, Lindell, G and Saunders, C (eds), *Reflections on the Australian Constitution* (Annandale, NSW, Federation Press, 2003) 31
—— 'Popular Sovereignty and Constitutional Continuity' (1998) 26 *Federal Law Review* 1
—— 'Extra-Constitutional Notions in Australian Constitutional Law' (1986) 16 *Federal Law Review* 223
—— 'Can the Commonwealth Parliament Enact "Manner and Form" Legislation?' (1980) 11 *Federal Law Review* 167
Wishart, DA, 'Allegiance and Citizenship as Concepts in Constitutional Law' (1986) 15 *Melbourne University Law Review* 662
Zines, L, *The High Court and the Constitution*, 5th edn (Sydney, Federation Press, 2008)
—— *Constitutional change in the Commonwealth* (Cambridge, CUP, 1991)

Reports and Command Papers

Australian Law Reform Commission, *The Recognition of Aboriginal Customary Laws* (Rep No 31, 1986)
Conference of the Prime Ministers and Representatives of the United Kingdom, the Dominions, and India, *Summary of Proceedings and Documents* (Cmd 1474, 1921)
Correspondence relating to the Inspection of the Military Forces of the Australasian Colonies by Major-General J Bevan Edwards CB (C 6188, 1890)
Home Office, *The Title of the Sovereign* (Cmd 8748, 1953)

Imperial Conference, 1911, 'Memorandum of Conferences between the British Admiralty and Representatives of the Dominion of Canada and the Commonwealth of Australia' in Imperial Conference, 1911, *Papers laid before the Imperial Conference: Naval and Military Defence* (Cd 5746-II, 1911) 1

Imperial Conference, 1911, *Minutes of Proceedings of the Imperial Conference, 1911* (Cd 5745, 1911)

Imperial Conference, 1923, *Summary of Proceedings* (Cmd 1987, 1923)

Imperial Conference, 1926, *Summary of Proceedings* (Cmd 2768, 1926)

Imperial Conference, 1930, *Summary of Proceedings* (Cmd 3717, 1930)

Imperial Conference, 1937, *Summary of proceedings* (Cmd 5482, 1937)

Imperial War Conference, 1917, *Extracts from Minutes of Proceedings and Papers Laid before the Conference* (Cd 8566, 1917)

Joint Committee appointed to consider the petition of the State of Western Australia, *Report* (HL 52 and 75; HC 88, 1935)

Secretary of State for Dominion Affairs, *Report of the Conference on the Operation of Dominion Legislation and Merchant Shipping Legislation, 1929* (Cmd 3479, 1930)

Select Committee on Transportation, *Report* (HC 669, 1838)

Thomas, JH, *The Constitutional Position in New South Wales* (CAB 24/222; former reference CP 177 (31), 1931)

Parliamentary Debates (Hansard)

Commonwealth of Australia, *Parliamentary Debates* (House of Representatives, 11.06.1901)

Commonwealth of Australia, *Parliamentary Debates* (House of Representatives, 12.06.1901)

Commonwealth of Australia, *Parliamentary Debates* (House of Representatives, 13.06.1901)

Commonwealth of Australia, *Parliamentary Debates* (House of Representatives, 14.06.1901)

Commonwealth of Australia, *Parliamentary Debates* (House of Representatives, 21.06.1901)

Commonwealth of Australia, *Parliamentary Debates* (House of Representatives, 30.09.1948)

Commonwealth of Australia, *Parliamentary Debates* (House of Representatives, 18.11.1948)

Commonwealth of Australia, *Parliamentary Debates* (House of Representatives, 29.11.1951)

Commonwealth of Australia, *Parliamentary Debates* (House of Representatives, 29.05.1969)

Commonwealth of Australia, *Parliamentary Debates* (House of Representatives, 25.02.1976)

Commonwealth of Australia, *Parliamentary Debates* (House of Representatives, 07.11.1990)

Commonwealth of Australia, *Parliamentary Debates* (Senate, 19.06.1901)

Commonwealth of Australia, *Parliamentary Debates* (Senate, 09.10.1901)

Commonwealth of Australia, *Parliamentary Debates* (Senate, 15.11.1990)
Commonwealth of Australia, *Parliamentary Debates* (Senate, 09.09.1992)
New South Wales, *Parliamentary Debates* (Legislative Council, 10.11.1987)
United Kingdom, *Parliamentary Debates (Fourth Series)*, vol 83 (HC, 14.05.1900)
United Kingdom, *Parliamentary Debates (Fifth Series)*, vol 193 (HC, 15.03.1926)
United Kingdom, *Parliamentary Debates (Fifth Series)*, vol 246 (HC, 16.12.1930)

Other

Constitution Alteration (Establishment of Republic) Bill 1999 (Cth)
National Film and Sound Archive, 'Menzies Speech: Declaration of War' (*NFSA title number 188388*, 03.09.1939), available at <https://aso.gov.au/titles/radio/menzies-speech-declaration-war>

Index

www.ingramcontent.com/pod-product-compliance
Lightning Source LLC
LaVergne TN
LVHW052302200926
848481LV00002B/442

* 9 7 8 1 5 0 9 9 2 0 0 6 8 *